THE AUTHORITY

RELENTLESS

WARREN ELLIS
writer

BRYAN HITCH
penciler

PAUL NEARY
inker

LAURA DEPUY
colorist

David Baron - Chris Garcia - Michael Garcia - Eric Guerrero
color assists

Bill O'Neil - Ali Fuchs - Robbie Robbins
letterers

Cover Illustration and Gallery Art by
Bryan Hitch, Paul Neary and Laura DePuy

Collected Edition Design by
Darren Nylec

The Authority Created by
Warren Ellis and Bryan Hitch

THE AUTHORITY: RELENTLESS Published by WildStorm Productions. SECOND PRINTING. ISBN 1-56389-661-3
THE AUTHORITY is ™ WildStorm Productions, an imprint of DC Comics.
Cover, design pages, and compilation © 2000 WildStorm Productions. All Rights Reserved. Originally
published in single magazine form as THE AUTHORITY #1-8. Copyright © 1999 WildStorm Productions.
Editorial offices: 7910 Ivanhoe St., #438, La Jolla, CA 92037. Any similarities to persons living or dead are purely coincidental.
PRINTED IN CANADA
DC Comics, a division of Warner Bros. — A Time Warner Entertainment Company

THE AUTHORITY is the first great superhero team book of the 21st century. Beside it everything else seems pale and stale and repetitive. Be honest.

These words are like thoughts which ran through my mind when I read THE AUTHORITY number one back in early 1999: Warren peaking on pure intravenous Warren, self-generating. Hitch and Neary downloading and reprocessing epic DVDs to reimagine the way superheroes might look one more time for the hell of it, reaching higher again. Laura DePuy with God's own Paintshop splashing beauty across these pages. How could it fail to define the way everything felt? Warren knows what he's playing around with, and it's your head. Don't forget that. He harbors many a grudge, and a number of those are political.

Because traditional superhero teams always put the flag back on top of the White House, don't they? They always dust down the statues and repair the highways and everything ends up just the way it was before...

But what "IF"? What if the superheroes really decided to make a few changes according to a "higher moral authority"? What if they started to act the way WE might act faced with impossible problems? What if every problem was a solution in disguise? What if WE began to think like superhumans, on a scale we never imagined before?

THE AUTHORITY dares to imagine a world beyond the post-modern ironic hopelessness of endless recycled TV quotes and retro-nostalgic feedback. Welcome to a superteam with an agenda, on a scale beyond the billion dollar budgets. A superteam whose headquarters looks like a dog's nose and still kicks ass.

At a stroke THE AUTHORITY has endowed the tired superhero archetypes with vigorous new meaning, pumping the volume until noses bleed and bass patterns register deep on the Richter scale in Norway.

Welcome to the first volume of continuing mind-battering adventures in a landmark series, ye lucky bastards....

Tell your jealous brats: the storm broke here...

       -Grant Morrison
       LA 2000

"THE CIRCLE"

They think there's
no one left to
save the world.

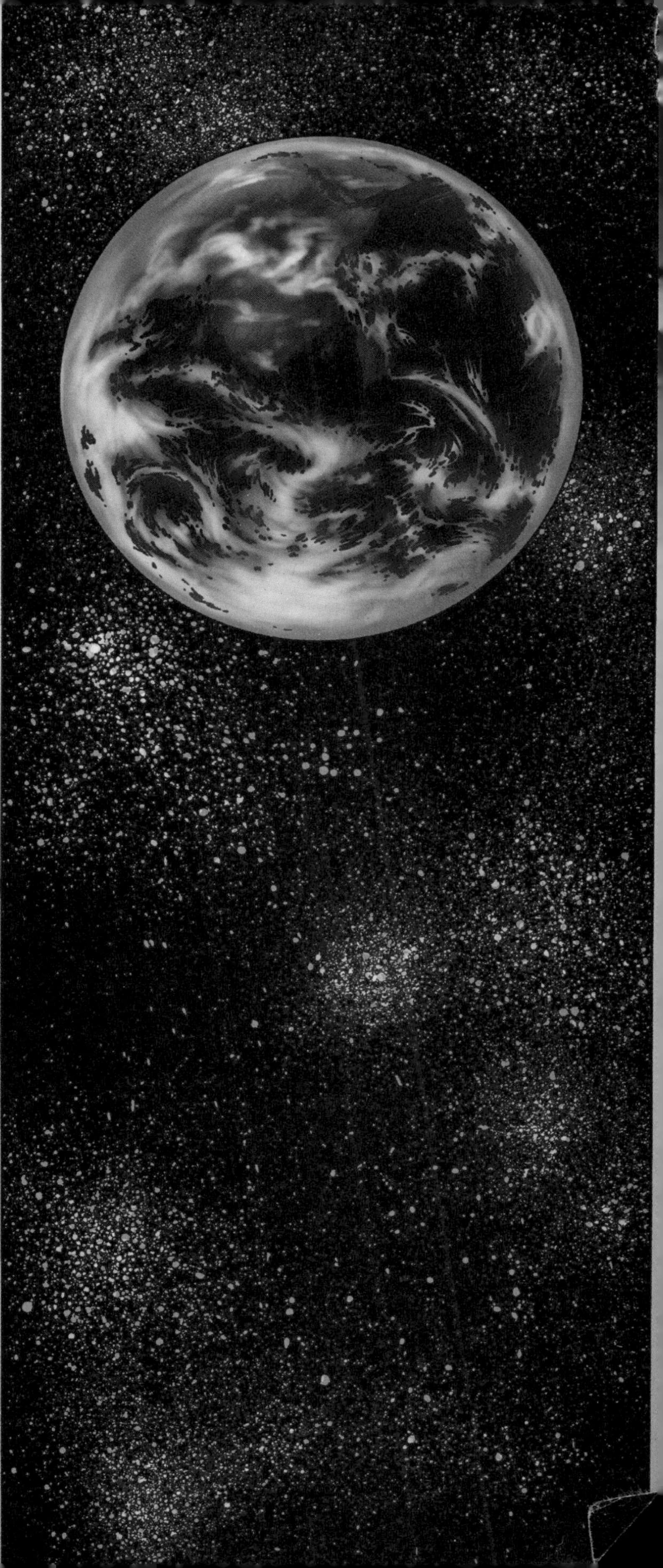

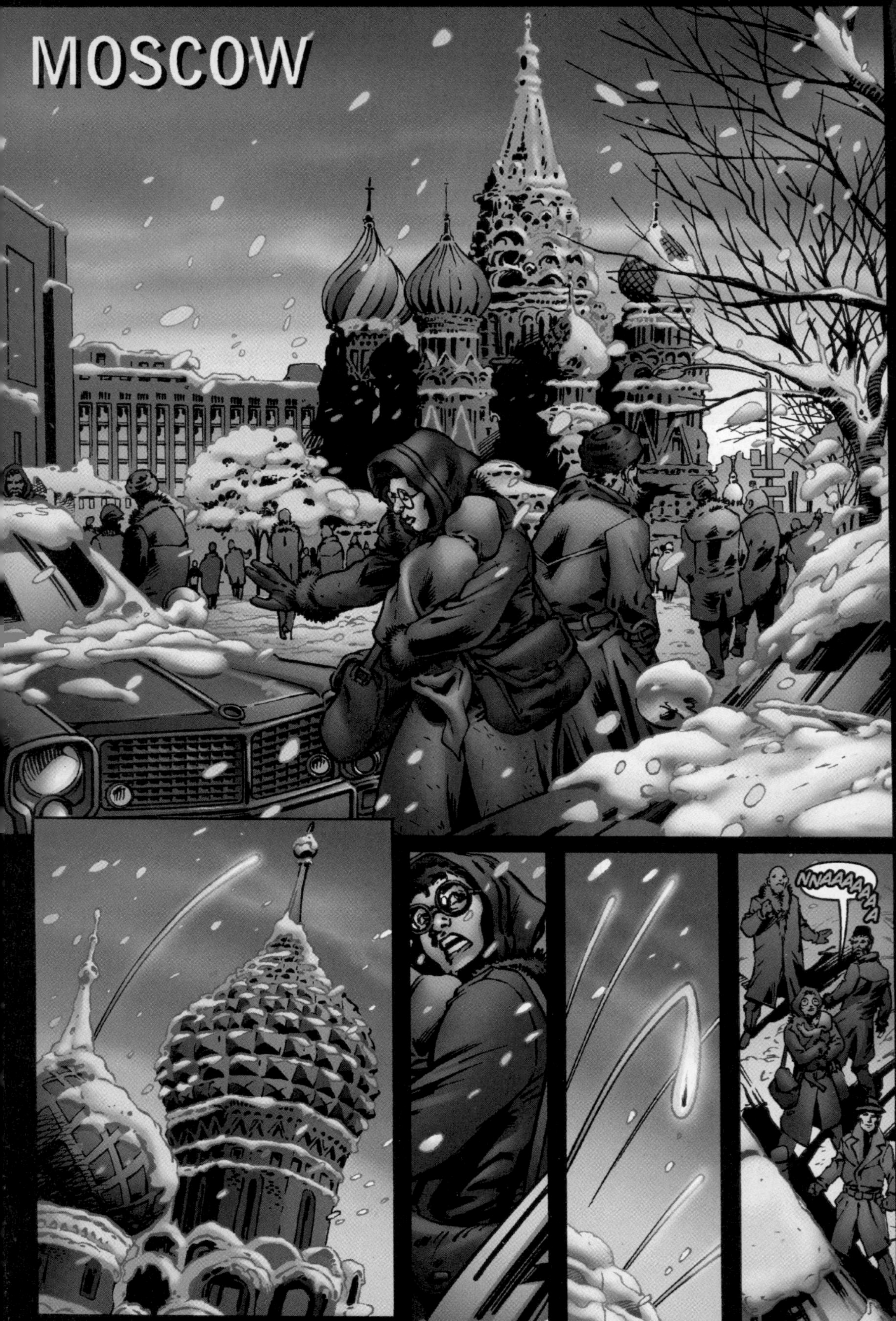
MOSCOW
NNAAAAAAAA

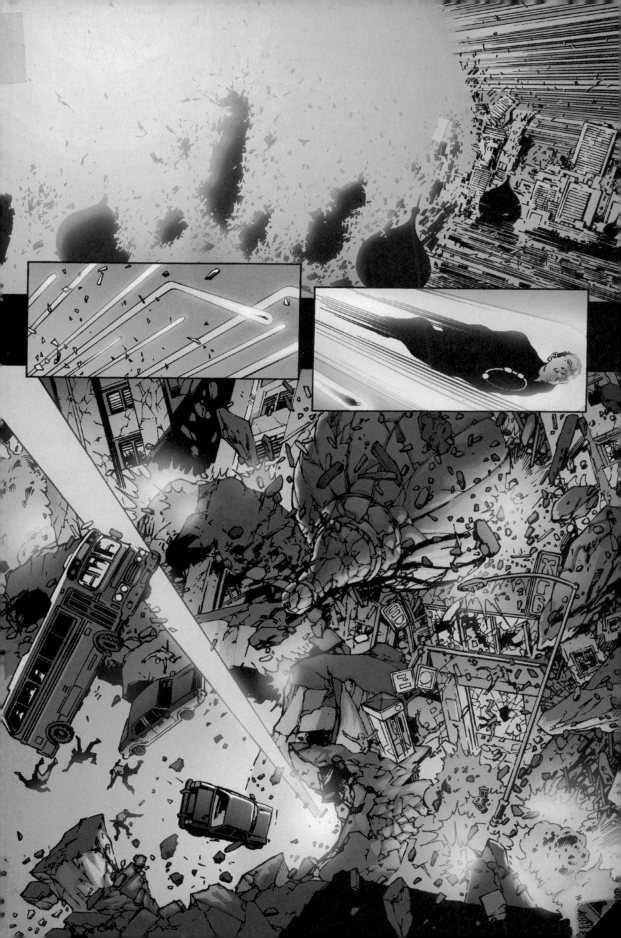

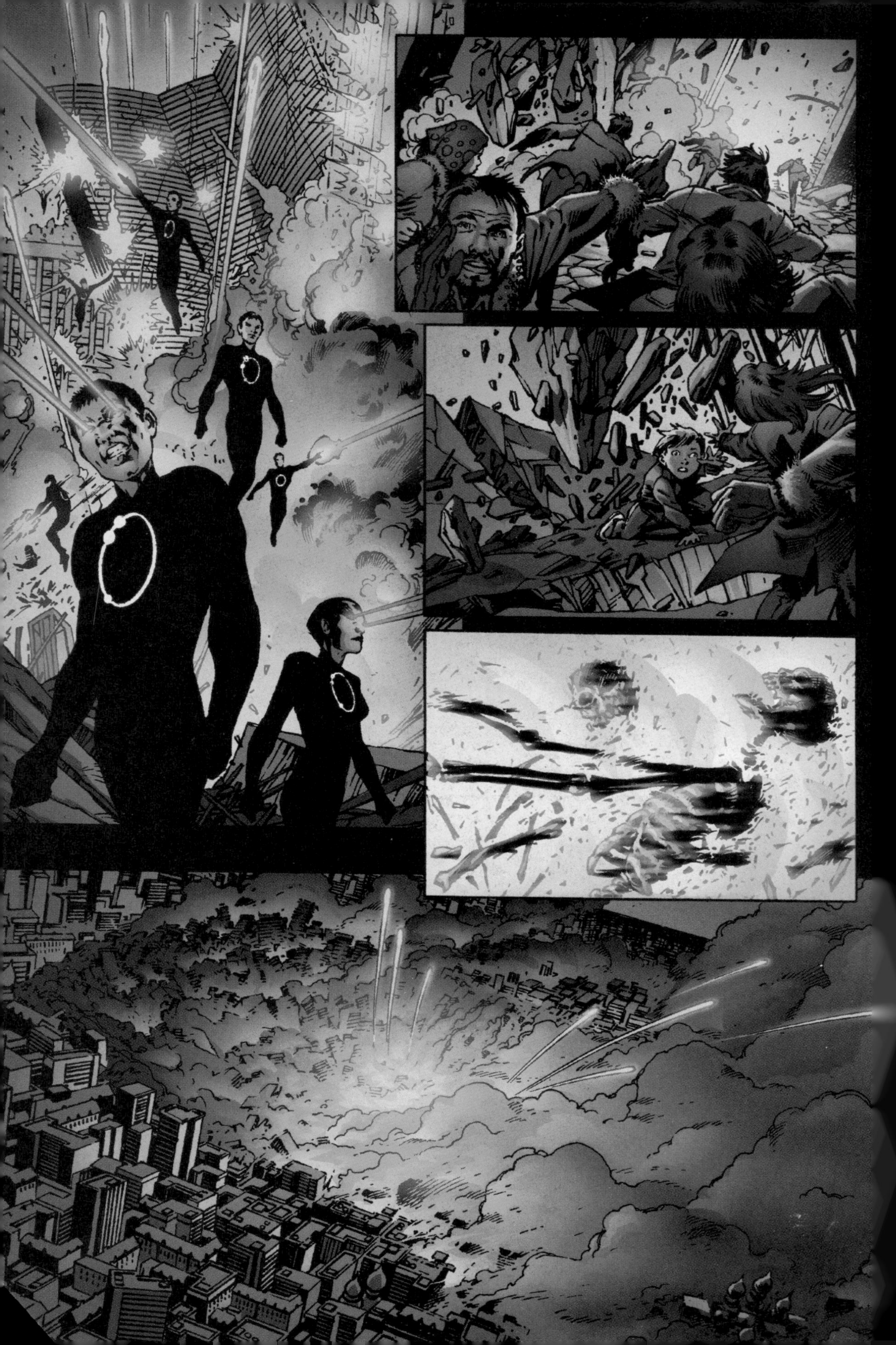

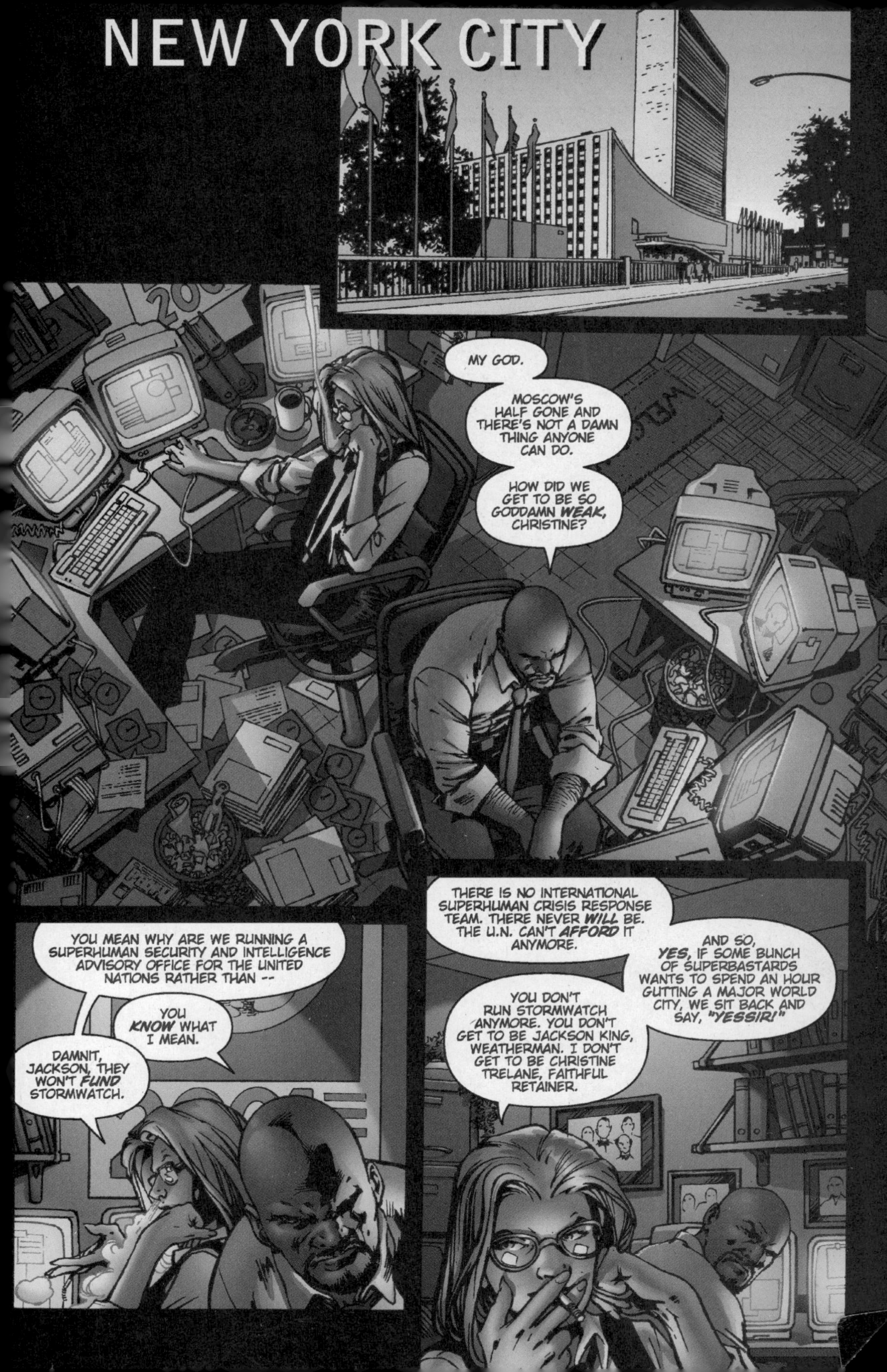
NEW YORK CITY
MY GOD.
MOSCOW'S HALF GONE AND THERE'S NOT A DAMN THING ANYONE CAN DO.
HOW DID WE GET TO BE SO GODDAMN WEAK, CHRISTINE?
YOU MEAN WHY ARE WE RUNNING A SUPERHUMAN SECURITY AND INTELLIGENCE ADVISORY OFFICE FOR THE UNITED NATIONS RATHER THAN --
YOU KNOW WHAT I MEAN.
DAMNIT, JACKSON, THEY WON'T FUND STORMWATCH.
THERE IS NO INTERNATIONAL SUPERHUMAN CRISIS RESPONSE TEAM. THERE NEVER WILL BE. THE U.N. CAN'T AFFORD IT ANYMORE.
AND SO, YES, IF SOME BUNCH OF SUPERBASTARDS WANTS TO SPEND AN HOUR GUTTING A MAJOR WORLD CITY, WE SIT BACK AND SAY, "YESSIR!"
YOU DON'T RUN STORMWATCH ANYMORE. YOU DON'T GET TO BE JACKSON KING, WEATHERMAN. I DON'T GET TO BE CHRISTINE TRELANE, FAITHFUL RETAINER.

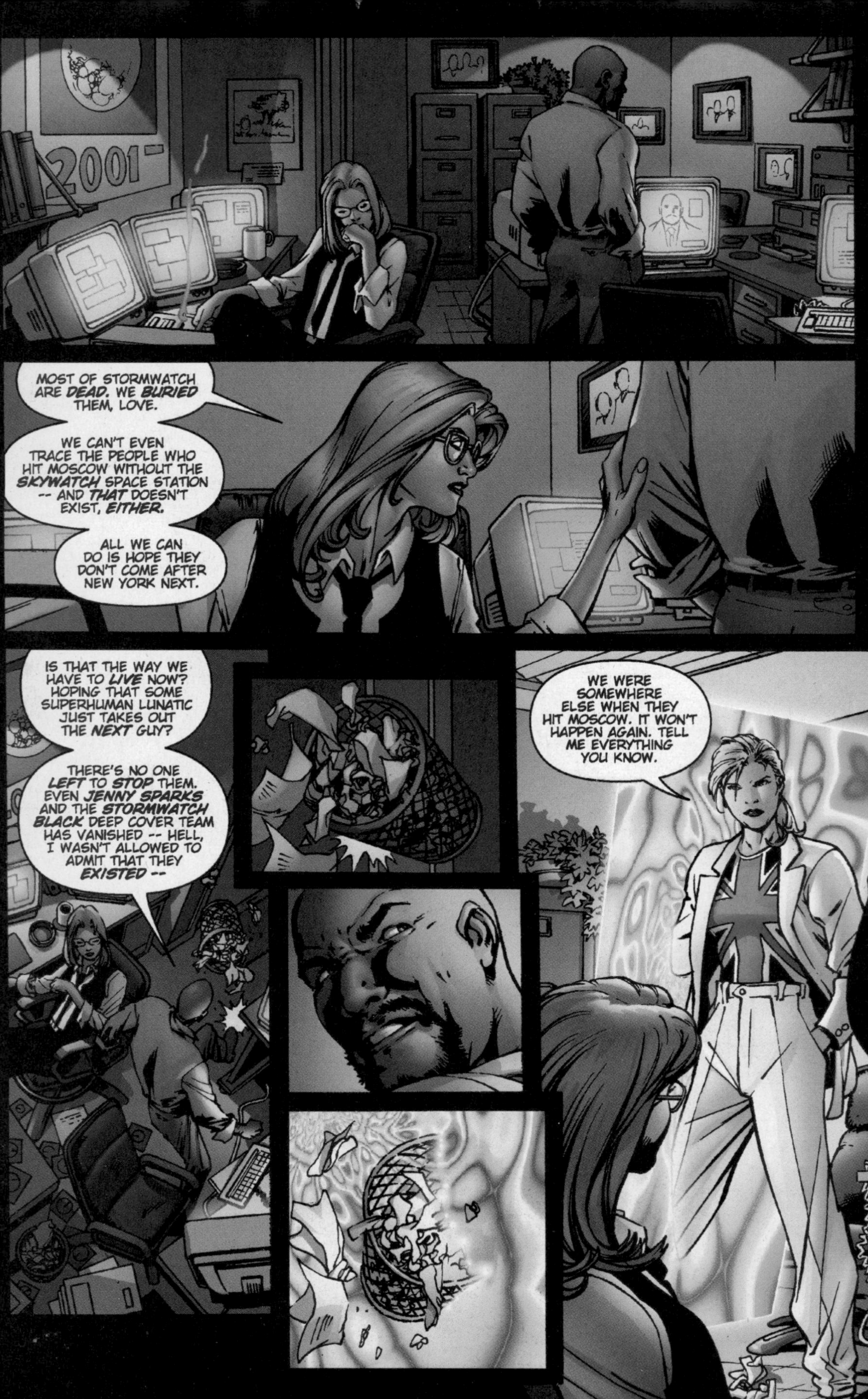
MOST OF STORMWATCH ARE DEAD. WE BURIED THEM, LOVE.
WE CAN'T EVEN TRACE THE PEOPLE WHO HIT MOSCOW WITHOUT THE SKYWATCH SPACE STATION -- AND THAT DOESN'T EXIST, EITHER.
ALL WE CAN DO IS HOPE THEY DON'T COME AFTER NEW YORK NEXT.
IS THAT THE WAY WE HAVE TO LIVE NOW? HOPING THAT SOME SUPERHUMAN LUNATIC JUST TAKES OUT THE NEXT GUY?
THERE'S NO ONE LEFT TO STOP THEM. EVEN JENNY SPARKS AND THE STORMWATCH BLACK DEEP COVER TEAM HAS VANISHED -- HELL, I WASN'T ALLOWED TO ADMIT THAT THEY EXISTED --
WE WERE SOMEWHERE ELSE WHEN THEY HIT MOSCOW. IT WON'T HAPPEN AGAIN. TELL ME EVERYTHING YOU KNOW.

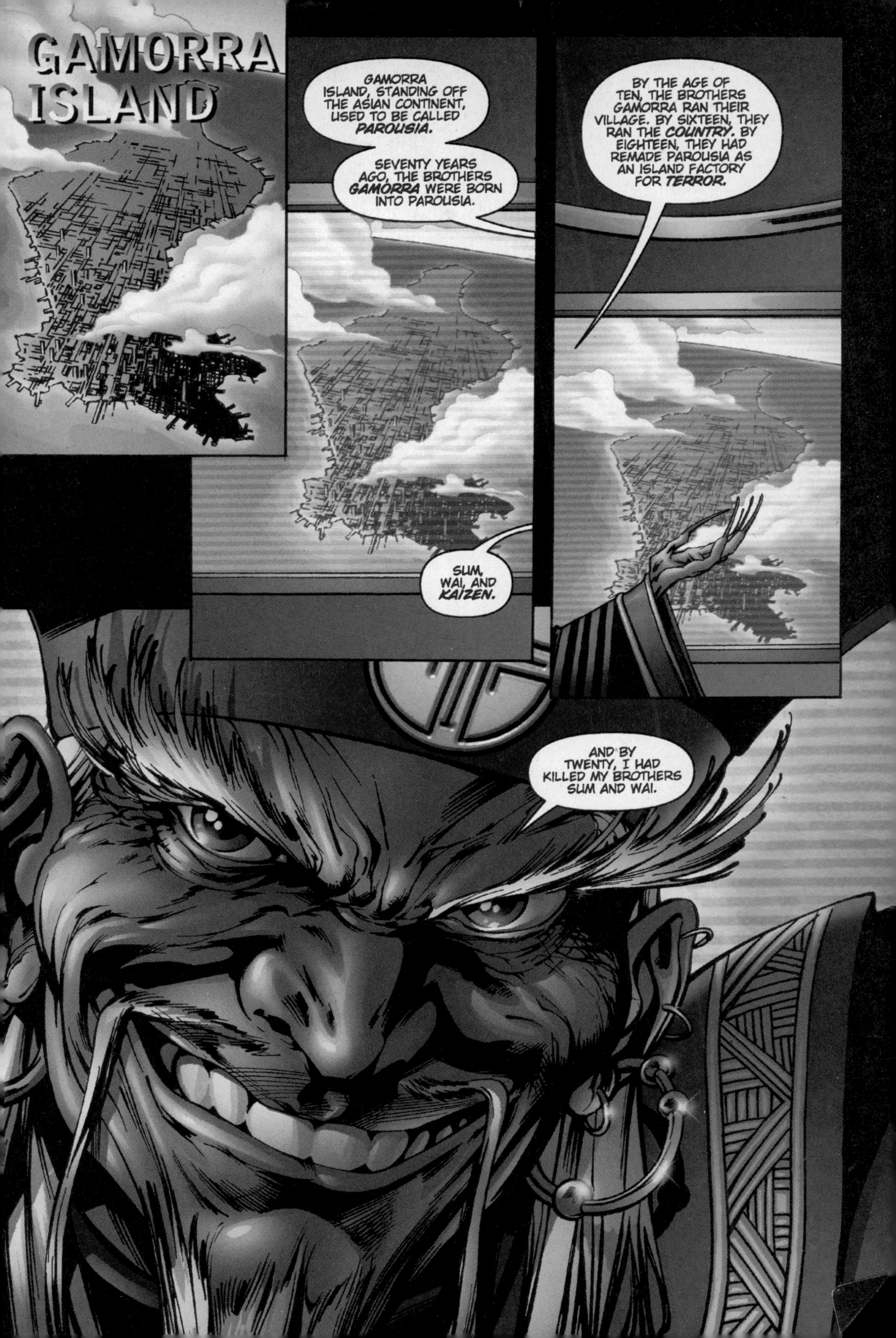
GAMORRA ISLAND
GAMORRA ISLAND, STANDING OFF THE ASIAN CONTINENT, USED TO BE CALLED PAROUSIA.
SEVENTY YEARS AGO, THE BROTHERS GAMORRA WERE BORN INTO PAROUSIA.
SUM, WAI, AND KAIZEN.
BY THE AGE OF TEN, THE BROTHERS GAMORRA RAN THEIR VILLAGE. BY SIXTEEN, THEY RAN THE COUNTRY. BY EIGHTEEN, THEY HAD REMADE PAROUSIA AS AN ISLAND FACTORY FOR TERROR.
AND BY TWENTY, I HAD KILLED MY BROTHERS SUM AND WAI.

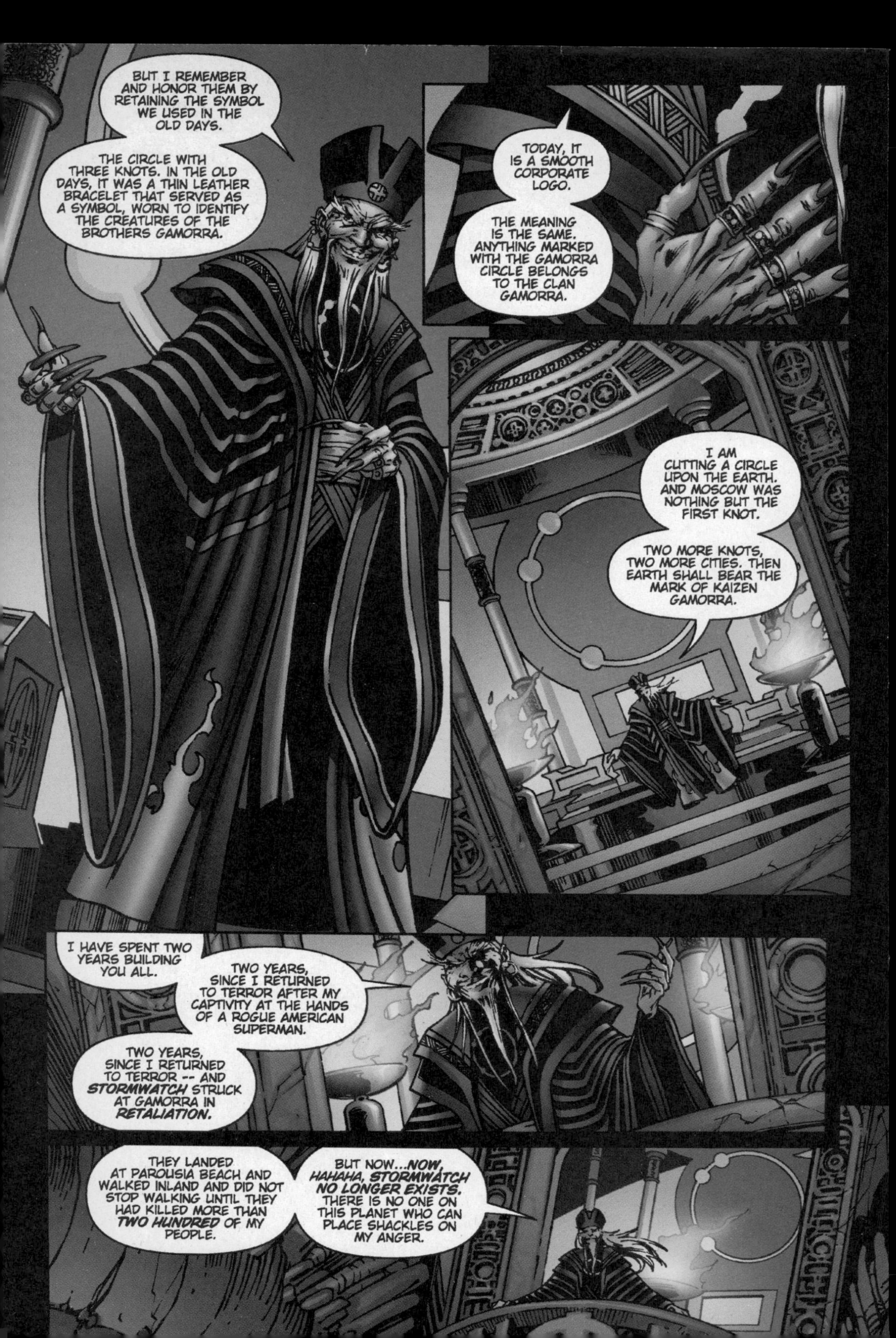
BUT I REMEMBER AND HONOR THEM BY RETAINING THE SYMBOL WE USED IN THE OLD DAYS.
THE CIRCLE WITH THREE KNOTS. IN THE OLD DAYS, IT WAS A THIN LEATHER BRACELET THAT SERVED AS A SYMBOL, WORN TO IDENTIFY THE CREATURES OF THE BROTHERS GAMORRA.
TODAY, IT IS A SMOOTH CORPORATE LOGO.
THE MEANING IS THE SAME. ANYTHING MARKED WITH THE GAMORRA CIRCLE BELONGS TO THE CLAN GAMORRA.
I AM CUTTING A CIRCLE UPON THE EARTH. AND MOSCOW WAS NOTHING BUT THE FIRST KNOT.
TWO MORE KNOTS, TWO MORE CITIES. THEN EARTH SHALL BEAR THE MARK OF KAIZEN GAMORRA.
I HAVE SPENT TWO YEARS BUILDING YOU ALL.
TWO YEARS, SINCE I RETURNED TO TERROR AFTER MY CAPTIVITY AT THE HANDS OF A ROGUE AMERICAN SUPERMAN.
TWO YEARS, SINCE I RETURNED TO TERROR -- AND STORMWATCH STRUCK AT GAMORRA IN RETALIATION.
THEY LANDED AT PAROUSIA BEACH AND WALKED INLAND AND DID NOT STOP WALKING UNTIL THEY HAD KILLED MORE THAN TWO HUNDRED OF MY PEOPLE.
BUT NOW...NOW, HAHAHA, STORMWATCH NO LONGER EXISTS. THERE IS NO ONE ON THIS PLANET WHO CAN PLACE SHACKLES ON MY ANGER.

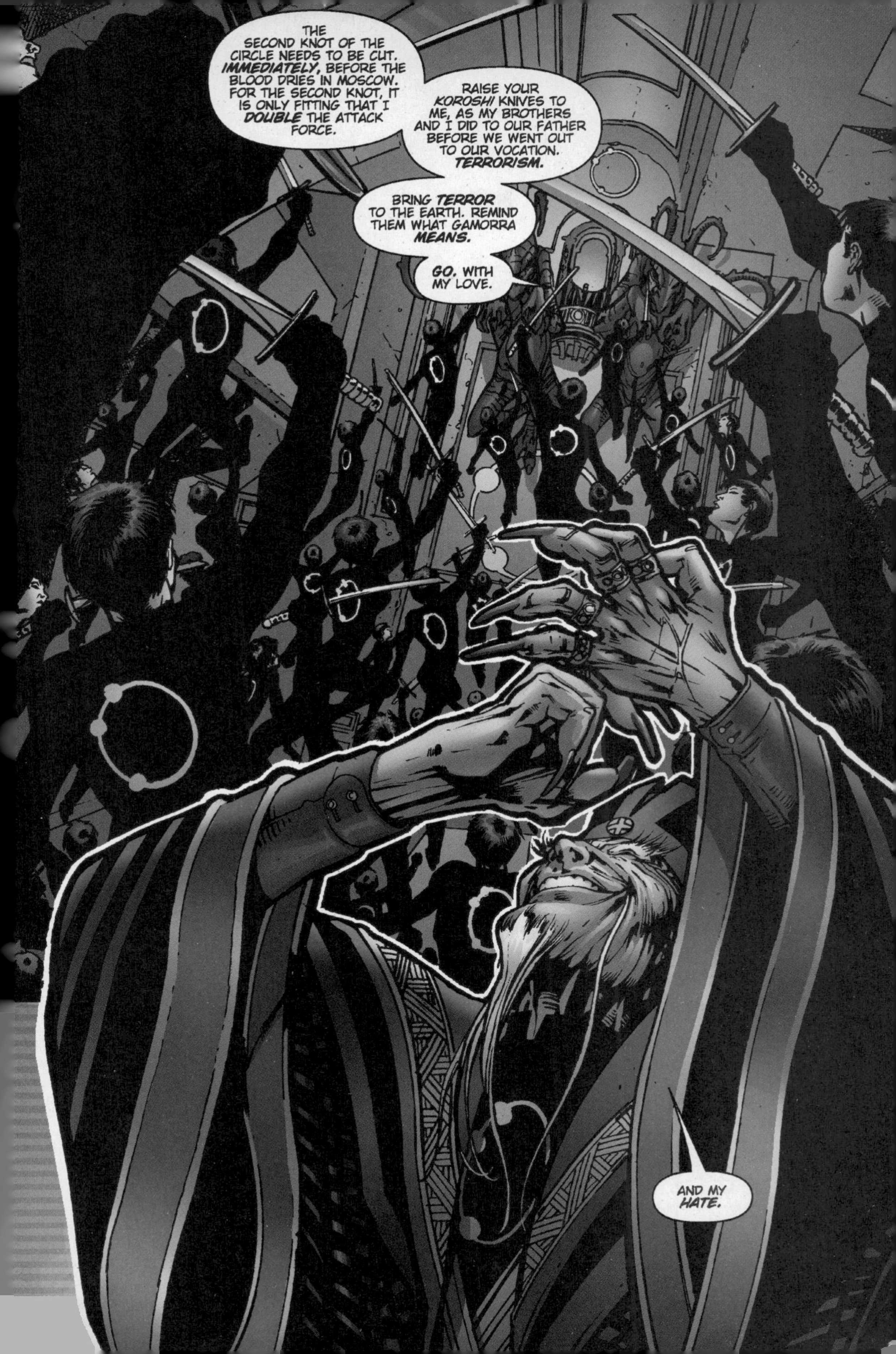
THE SECOND KNOT OF THE CIRCLE NEEDS TO BE CUT. IMMEDIATELY, BEFORE THE BLOOD DRIES IN MOSCOW. FOR THE SECOND KNOT, IT IS ONLY FITTING THAT I DOUBLE THE ATTACK FORCE.
RAISE YOUR KOROSHI KNIVES TO ME, AS MY BROTHERS AND I DID TO OUR FATHER BEFORE WE WENT OUT TO OUR VOCATION. TERRORISM.
BRING TERROR TO THE EARTH. REMIND THEM WHAT GAMORRA MEANS.
GO. WITH MY LOVE.
AND MY HATE.

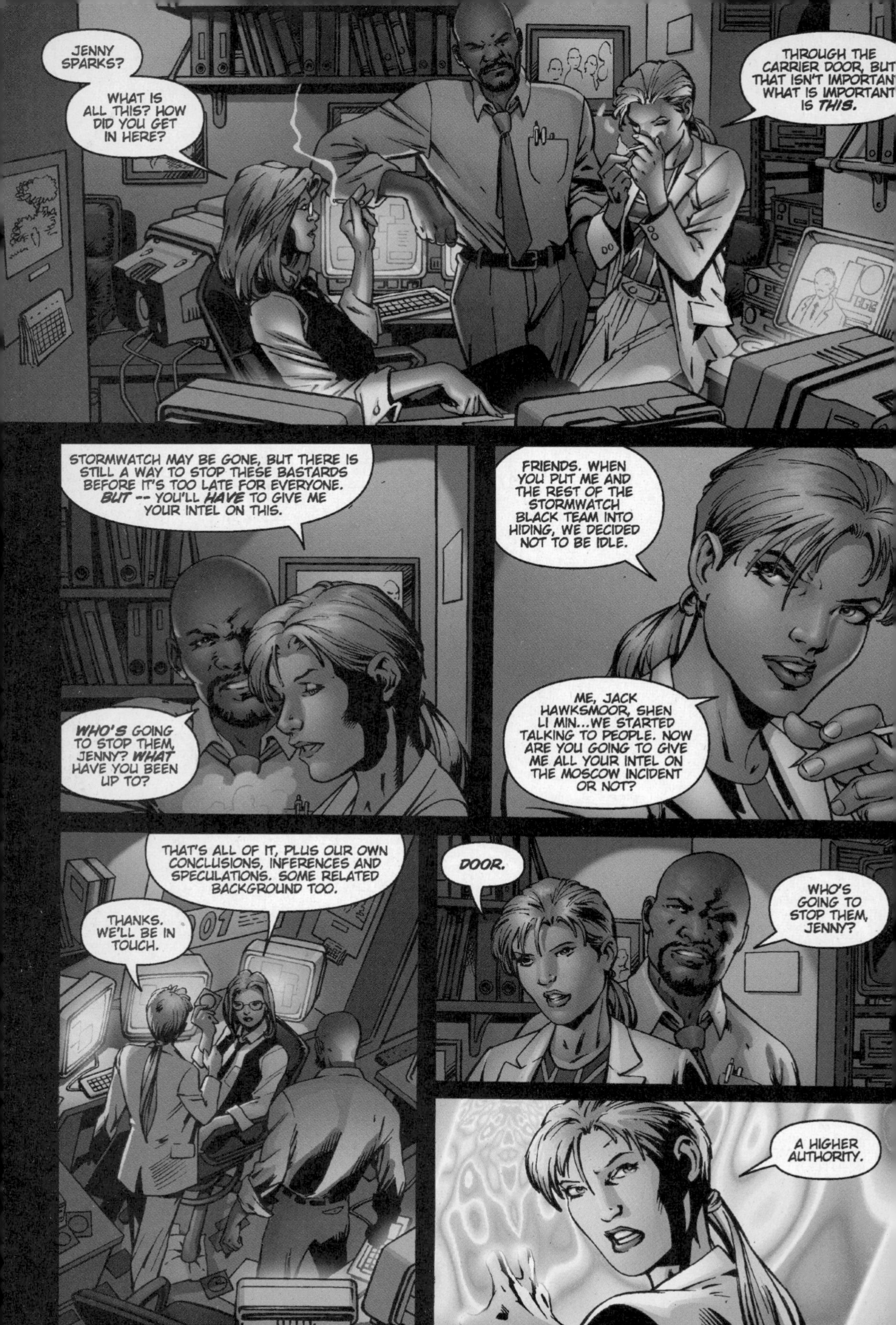
JENNY SPARKS?
WHAT IS ALL THIS? HOW DID YOU GET IN HERE?
THROUGH THE CARRIER DOOR, BUT THAT ISN'T IMPORTANT. WHAT IS IMPORTANT IS THIS.
STORMWATCH MAY BE GONE, BUT THERE IS STILL A WAY TO STOP THESE BASTARDS BEFORE IT'S TOO LATE FOR EVERYONE. BUT -- YOU'LL HAVE TO GIVE ME YOUR INTEL ON THIS.
WHO'S GOING TO STOP THEM, JENNY? WHAT HAVE YOU BEEN UP TO?
FRIENDS. WHEN YOU PUT ME AND THE REST OF THE STORMWATCH BLACK TEAM INTO HIDING, WE DECIDED NOT TO BE IDLE.
ME, JACK HAWKSMOOR, SHEN LI MIN...WE STARTED TALKING TO PEOPLE. NOW ARE YOU GOING TO GIVE ME ALL YOUR INTEL ON THE MOSCOW INCIDENT OR NOT?
THAT'S ALL OF IT, PLUS OUR OWN CONCLUSIONS, INFERENCES AND SPECULATIONS. SOME RELATED BACKGROUND TOO.
THANKS. WE'LL BE IN TOUCH.
DOOR.
WHO'S GOING TO STOP THEM, JENNY?
A HIGHER AUTHORITY.

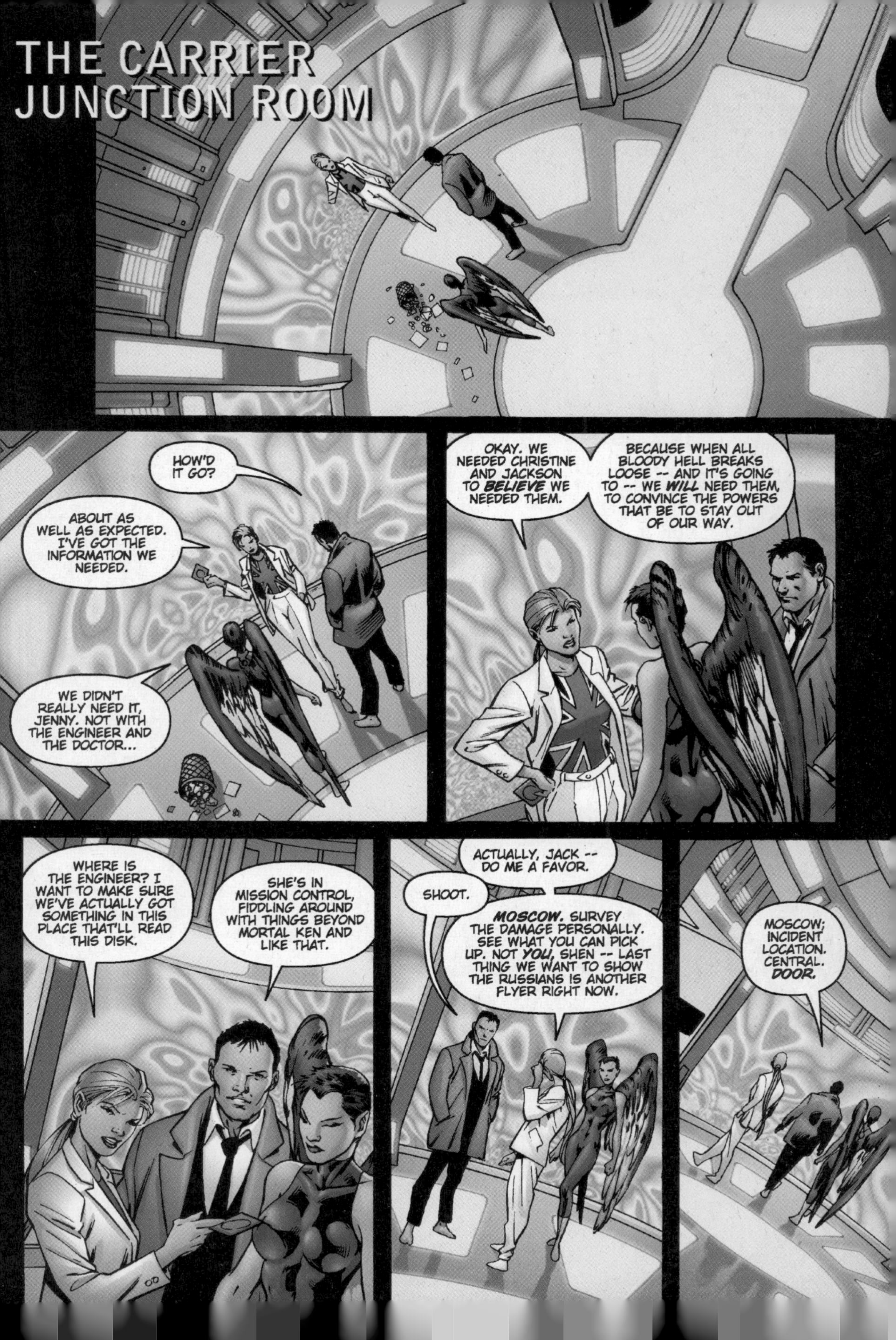
THE CARRIER
JUNCTION ROOM
HOW'D IT GO?
ABOUT AS WELL AS EXPECTED. I'VE GOT THE INFORMATION WE NEEDED.
WE DIDN'T REALLY NEED IT, JENNY. NOT WITH THE ENGINEER AND THE DOCTOR...
OKAY. WE NEEDED CHRISTINE AND JACKSON TO BELIEVE WE NEEDED THEM.
BECAUSE WHEN ALL BLOODY HELL BREAKS LOOSE -- AND IT'S GOING TO -- WE WILL NEED THEM, TO CONVINCE THE POWERS THAT BE TO STAY OUT OF OUR WAY.
WHERE IS THE ENGINEER? I WANT TO MAKE SURE WE'VE ACTUALLY GOT SOMETHING IN THIS PLACE THAT'LL READ THIS DISK.
SHE'S IN MISSION CONTROL, FIDDLING AROUND WITH THINGS BEYOND MORTAL KEN AND LIKE THAT.
ACTUALLY, JACK -- DO ME A FAVOR.
SHOOT.
MOSCOW. SURVEY THE DAMAGE PERSONALLY. SEE WHAT YOU CAN PICK UP. NOT YOU, SHEN -- LAST THING WE WANT TO SHOW THE RUSSIANS IS ANOTHER FLYER RIGHT NOW.
MOSCOW; INCIDENT LOCATION. CENTRAL. DOOR.

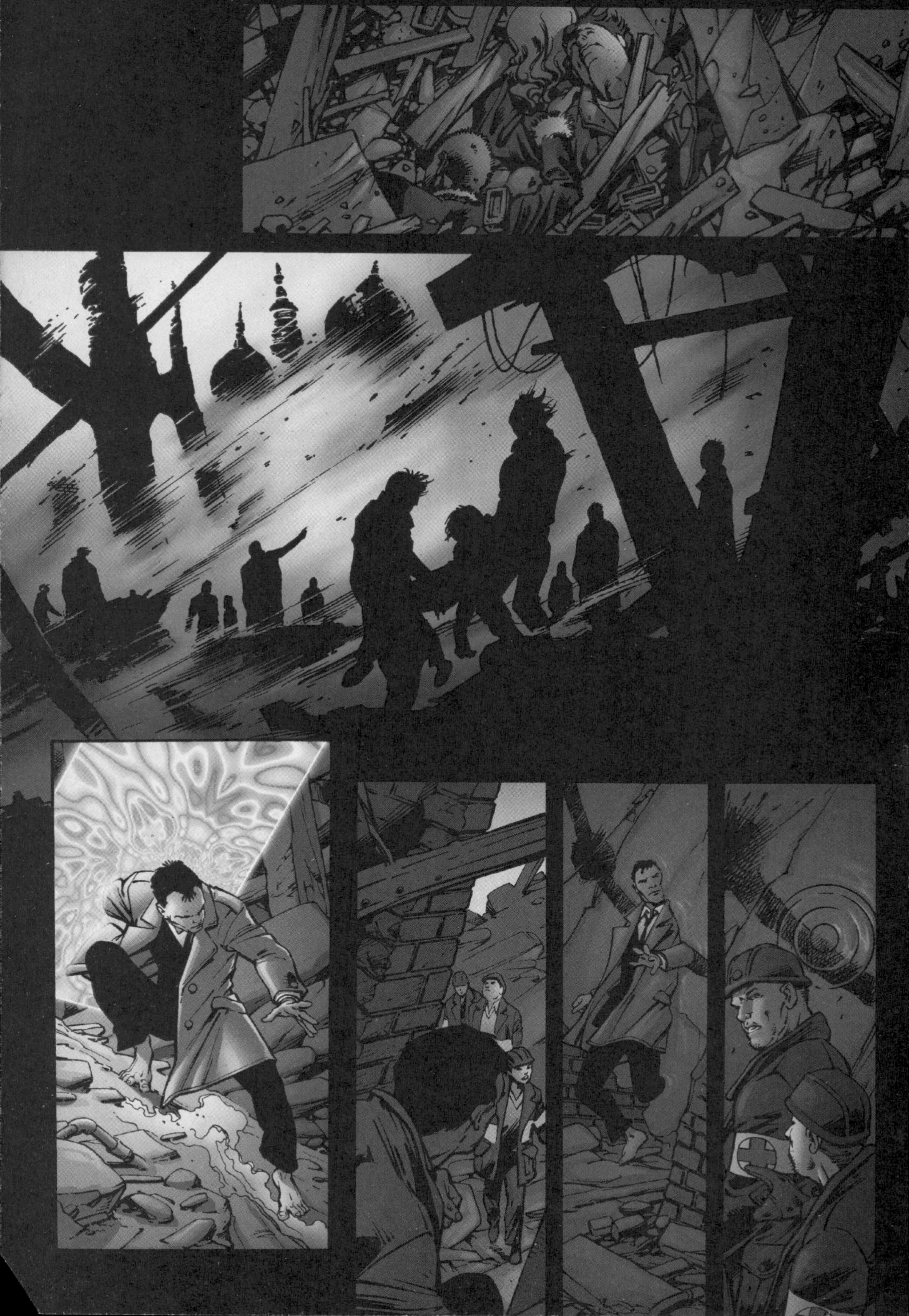

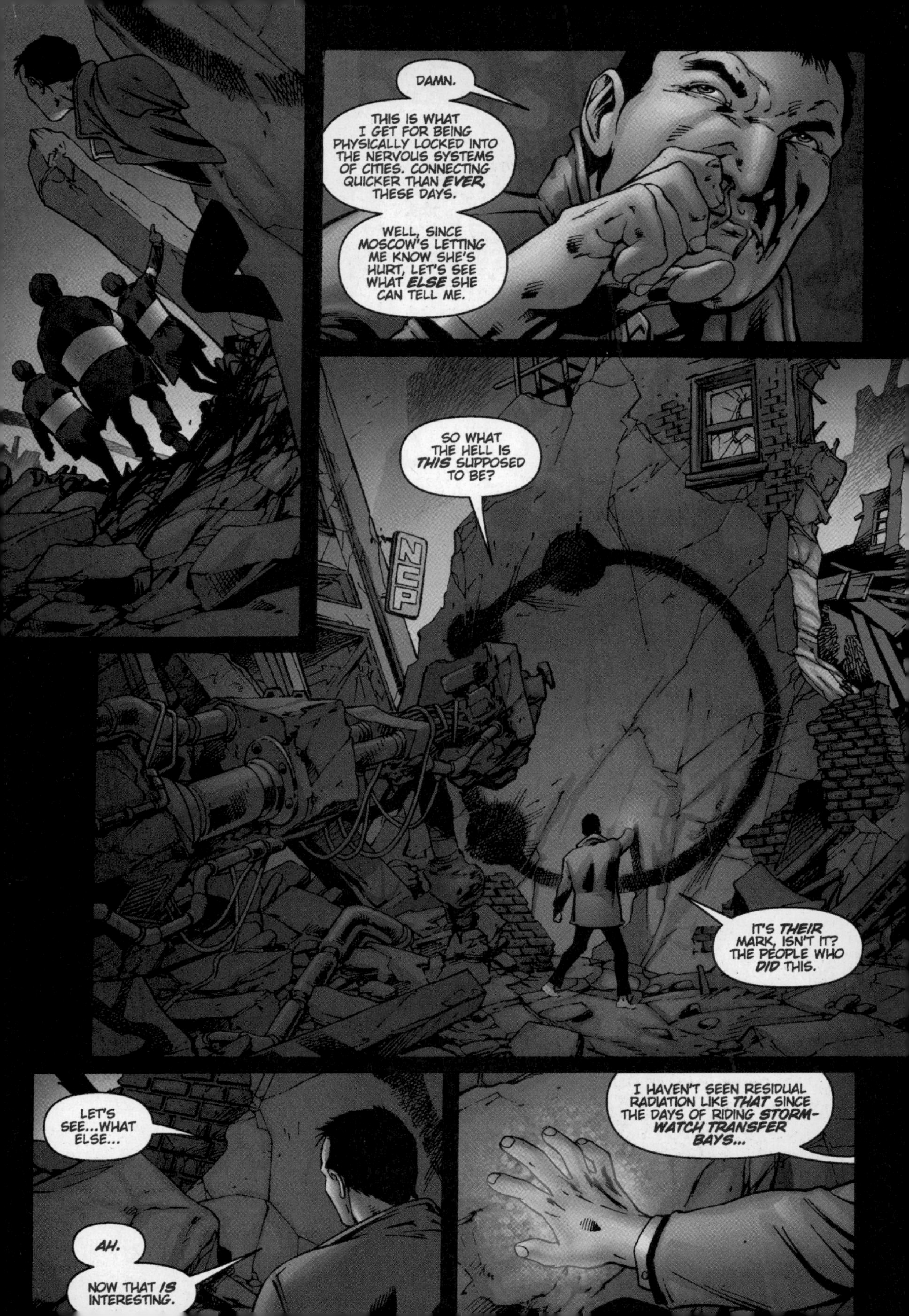
DAMN.
THIS IS WHAT I GET FOR BEING PHYSICALLY LOCKED INTO THE NERVOUS SYSTEMS OF CITIES. CONNECTING QUICKER THAN EVER, THESE DAYS.
WELL, SINCE MOSCOW'S LETTING ME KNOW SHE'S HURT, LET'S SEE WHAT ELSE SHE CAN TELL ME.
SO WHAT THE HELL IS THIS SUPPOSED TO BE?
NCP
IT'S THEIR MARK, ISN'T IT? THE PEOPLE WHO DID THIS.
LET'S SEE...WHAT ELSE...
AH.
NOW THAT IS INTERESTING.
I HAVEN'T SEEN RESIDUAL RADIATION LIKE THAT SINCE THE DAYS OF RIDING STORM-WATCH TRANSFER BAYS...

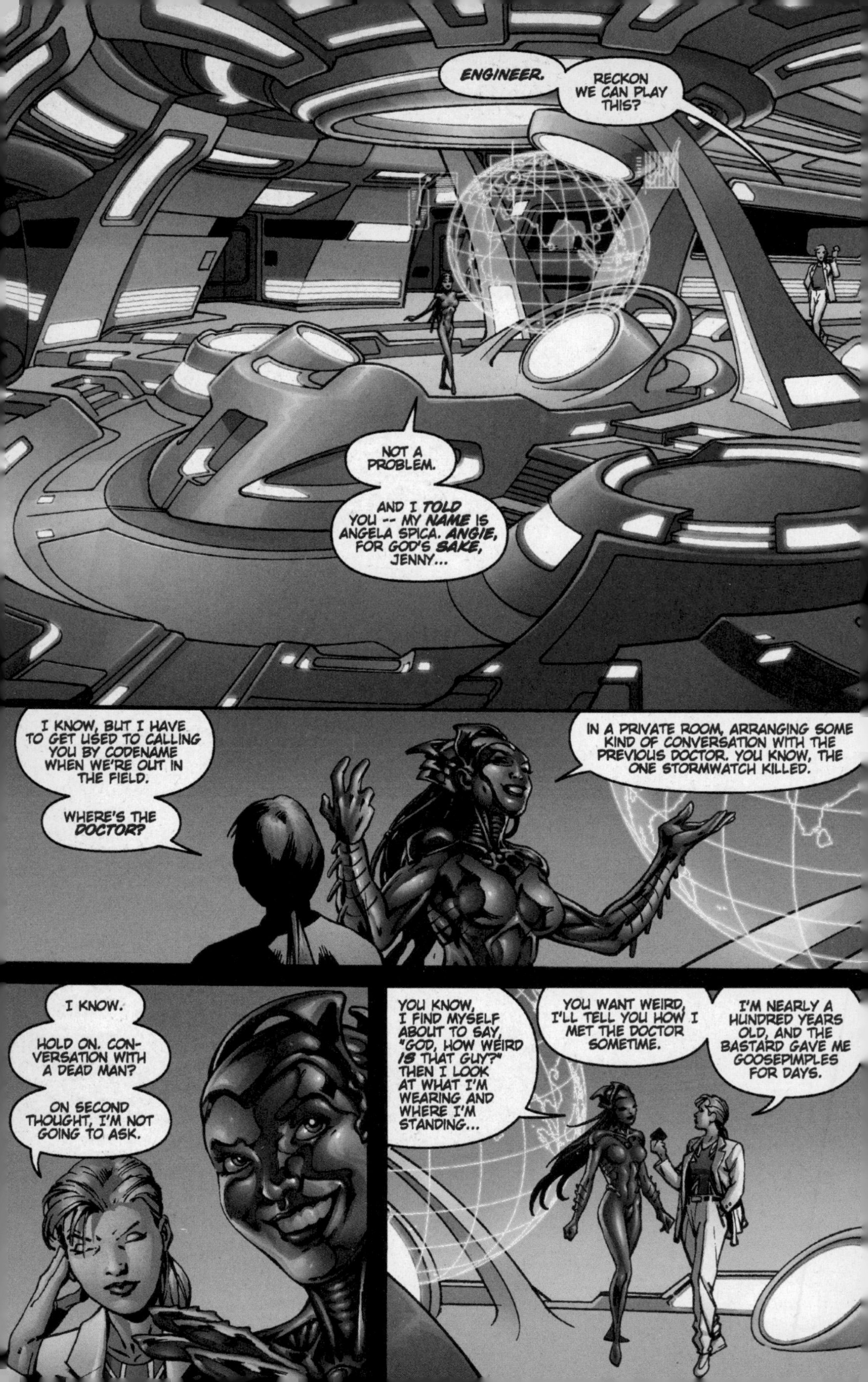
ENGINEER.
RECKON WE CAN PLAY THIS?
NOT A PROBLEM.
AND I TOLD YOU -- MY NAME IS ANGELA SPICA. ANGIE, FOR GOD'S SAKE, JENNY...
I KNOW, BUT I HAVE TO GET USED TO CALLING YOU BY CODENAME WHEN WE'RE OUT IN THE FIELD.
WHERE'S THE DOCTOR?
IN A PRIVATE ROOM, ARRANGING SOME KIND OF CONVERSATION WITH THE PREVIOUS DOCTOR. YOU KNOW, THE ONE STORMWATCH KILLED.
I KNOW.
HOLD ON. CONVERSATION WITH A DEAD MAN?
ON SECOND THOUGHT, I'M NOT GOING TO ASK.
YOU KNOW, I FIND MYSELF ABOUT TO SAY, "GOD, HOW WEIRD IS THAT GUY?" THEN I LOOK AT WHAT I'M WEARING AND WHERE I'M STANDING...
YOU WANT WEIRD, I'LL TELL YOU HOW I MET THE DOCTOR SOMETIME.
I'M NEARLY A HUNDRED YEARS OLD, AND THE BASTARD GAVE ME GOOSEPIMPLES FOR DAYS.

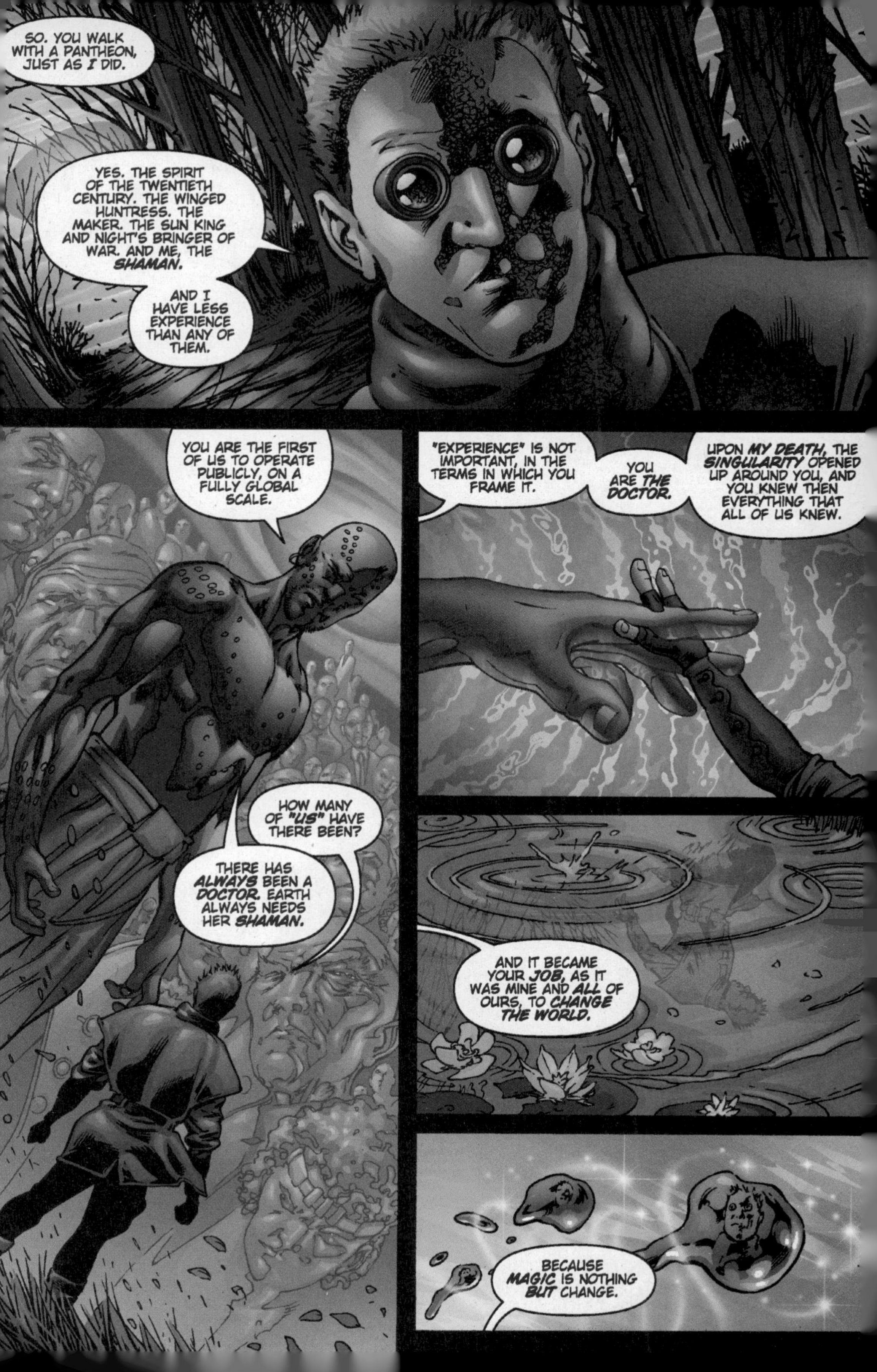
SO. YOU WALK WITH A PANTHEON, JUST AS *I* DID.
YES. THE SPIRIT OF THE TWENTIETH CENTURY. THE WINGED HUNTRESS. THE MAKER. THE SUN KING AND NIGHT'S BRINGER OF WAR. AND ME, THE *SHAMAN.*
AND I HAVE LESS EXPERIENCE THAN ANY OF THEM.
YOU ARE THE FIRST OF US TO OPERATE PUBLICLY, ON A FULLY GLOBAL SCALE.
HOW MANY OF *"US"* HAVE THERE BEEN?
THERE HAS *ALWAYS* BEEN A *DOCTOR.* EARTH ALWAYS NEEDS HER *SHAMAN.*
"EXPERIENCE" IS NOT IMPORTANT, IN THE TERMS IN WHICH YOU FRAME IT.
YOU ARE *THE DOCTOR.*
UPON *MY DEATH*, THE *SINGULARITY* OPENED UP AROUND YOU, AND YOU KNEW THEN EVERYTHING THAT ALL OF US KNEW.
AND IT BECAME YOUR *JOB*, AS IT WAS MINE AND *ALL* OF OURS, TO *CHANGE THE WORLD.*
BECAUSE *MAGIC* IS NOTHING *BUT* CHANGE.

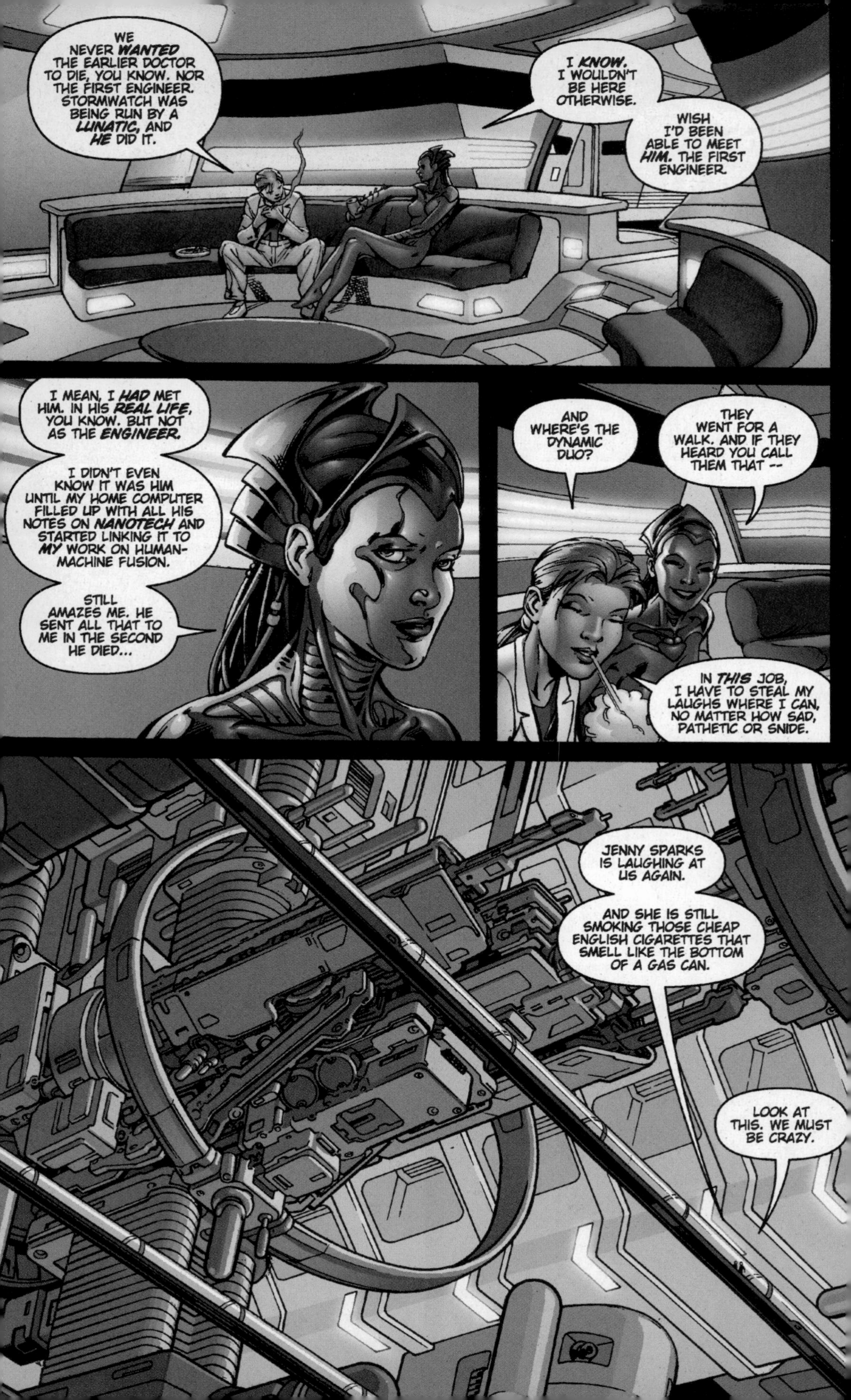
WE NEVER WANTED THE EARLIER DOCTOR TO DIE, YOU KNOW. NOR THE FIRST ENGINEER. STORMWATCH WAS BEING RUN BY A LUNATIC, AND HE DID IT.
I KNOW. I WOULDN'T BE HERE OTHERWISE.
WISH I'D BEEN ABLE TO MEET HIM. THE FIRST ENGINEER.
I MEAN, I HAD MET HIM. IN HIS REAL LIFE, YOU KNOW. BUT NOT AS THE ENGINEER.
I DIDN'T EVEN KNOW IT WAS HIM UNTIL MY HOME COMPUTER FILLED UP WITH ALL HIS NOTES ON NANOTECH AND STARTED LINKING IT TO MY WORK ON HUMAN-MACHINE FUSION.
STILL AMAZES ME. HE SENT ALL THAT TO ME IN THE SECOND HE DIED...
AND WHERE'S THE DYNAMIC DUO?
THEY WENT FOR A WALK. AND IF THEY HEARD YOU CALL THEM THAT --
IN THIS JOB, I HAVE TO STEAL MY LAUGHS WHERE I CAN, NO MATTER HOW SAD, PATHETIC OR SNIDE.
JENNY SPARKS IS LAUGHING AT US AGAIN.
AND SHE IS STILL SMOKING THOSE CHEAP ENGLISH CIGARETTES THAT SMELL LIKE THE BOTTOM OF A GAS CAN.
LOOK AT THIS. WE MUST BE CRAZY.

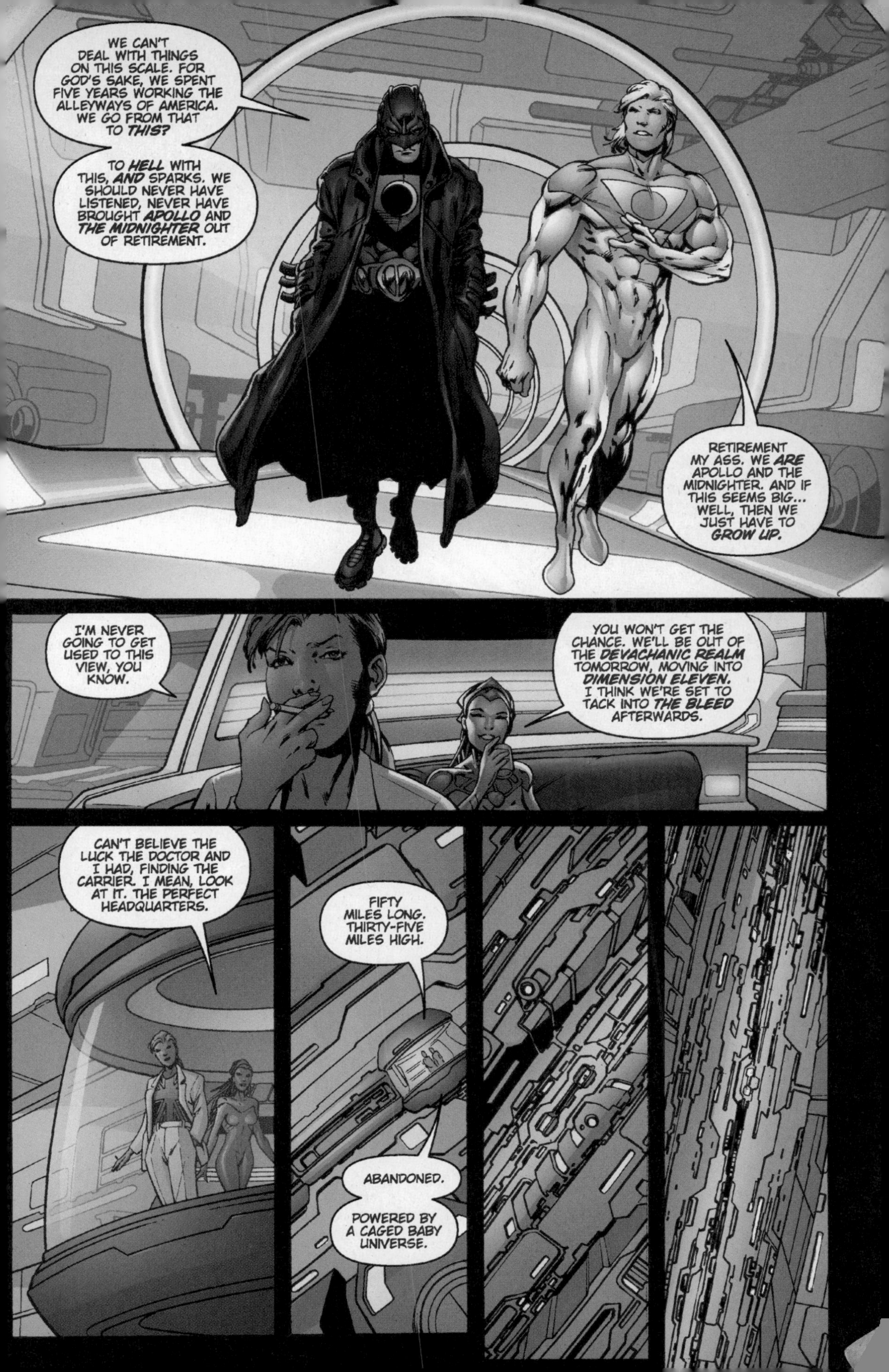
WE CAN'T DEAL WITH THINGS ON THIS SCALE. FOR GOD'S SAKE, WE SPENT FIVE YEARS WORKING THE ALLEYWAYS OF AMERICA. WE GO FROM THAT TO *THIS?*
TO *HELL* WITH THIS, *AND* SPARKS. WE SHOULD NEVER HAVE LISTENED, NEVER HAVE BROUGHT *APOLLO* AND *THE MIDNIGHTER* OUT OF RETIREMENT.
RETIREMENT MY ASS. WE *ARE* APOLLO AND THE MIDNIGHTER. AND IF THIS SEEMS BIG... WELL, THEN WE JUST HAVE TO *GROW UP.*
I'M NEVER GOING TO GET USED TO THIS VIEW, YOU KNOW.
YOU WON'T GET THE CHANCE. WE'LL BE OUT OF THE *DEVACHANIC REALM* TOMORROW, MOVING INTO *DIMENSION ELEVEN.* I THINK WE'RE SET TO TACK INTO *THE BLEED* AFTERWARDS.
CAN'T BELIEVE THE LUCK THE DOCTOR AND I HAD, FINDING THE CARRIER. I MEAN, LOOK AT IT. THE PERFECT HEADQUARTERS.
FIFTY MILES LONG. THIRTY-FIVE MILES HIGH.
ABANDONED.
POWERED BY A CAGED BABY UNIVERSE.

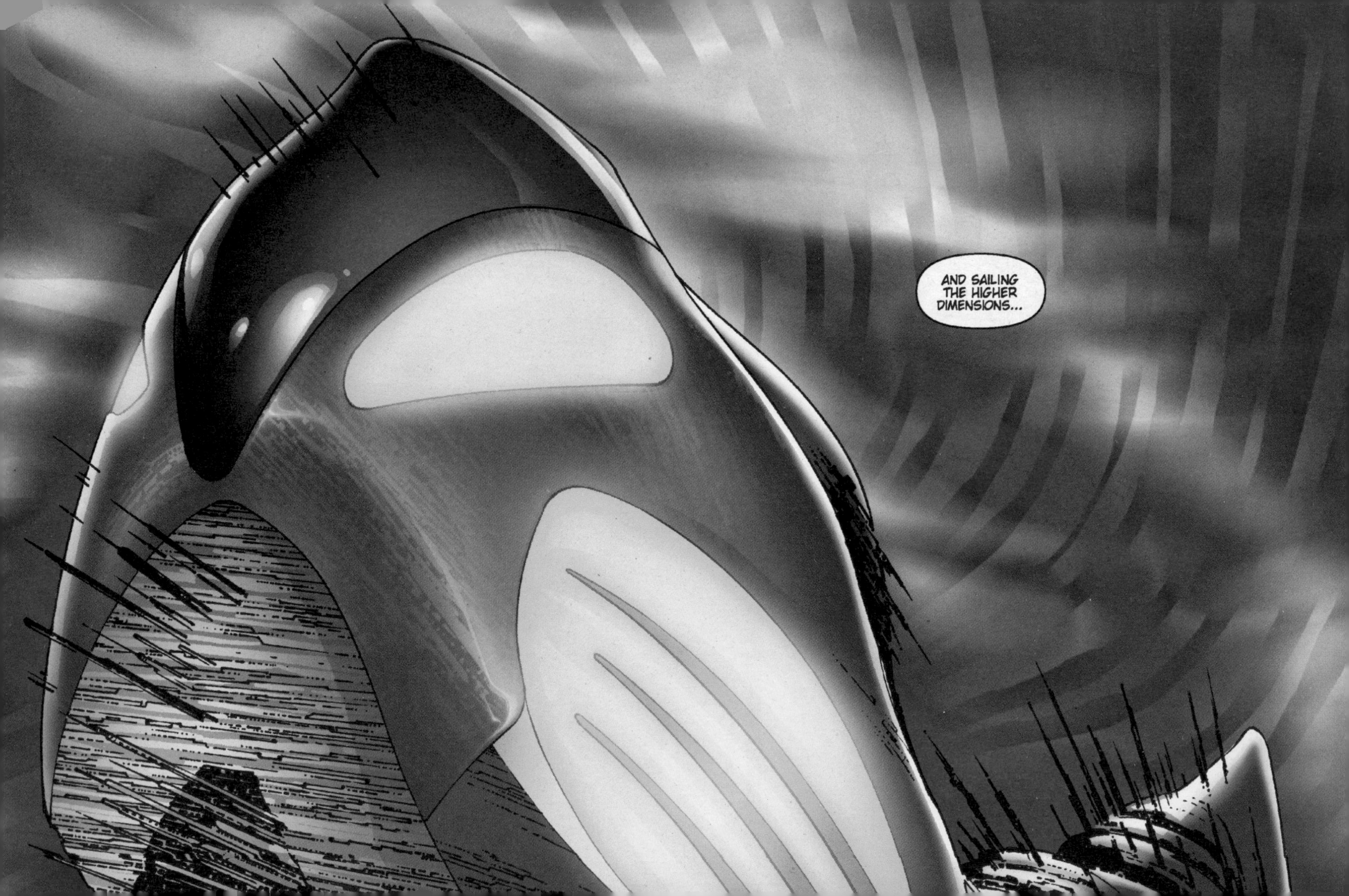
AND SAILING THE HIGHER DIMENSIONS...

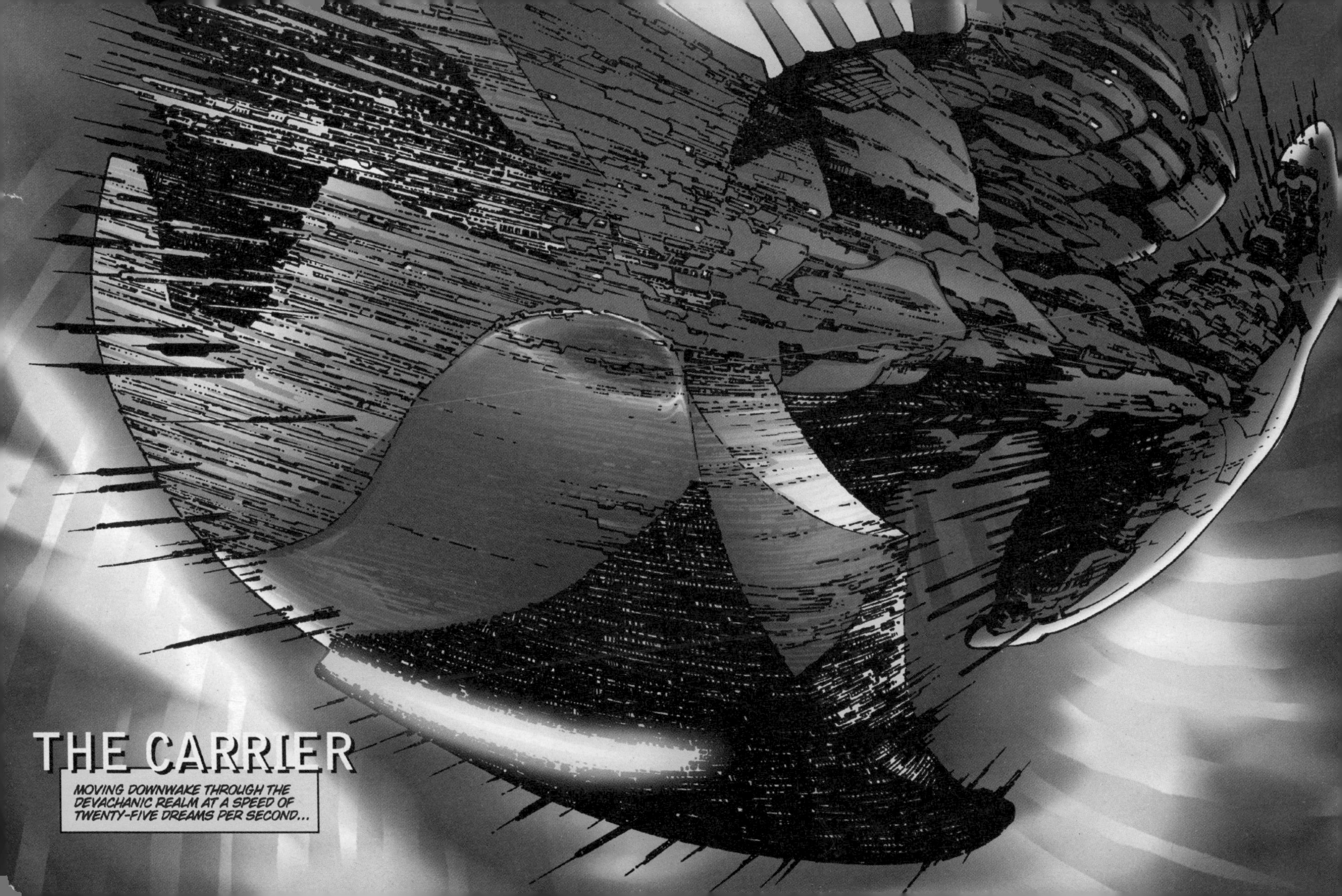
THE CARRIER
MOVING DOWNWAKE THROUGH THE DEVACHANIC REALM AT A SPEED OF TWENTY-FIVE DREAMS PER SECOND...

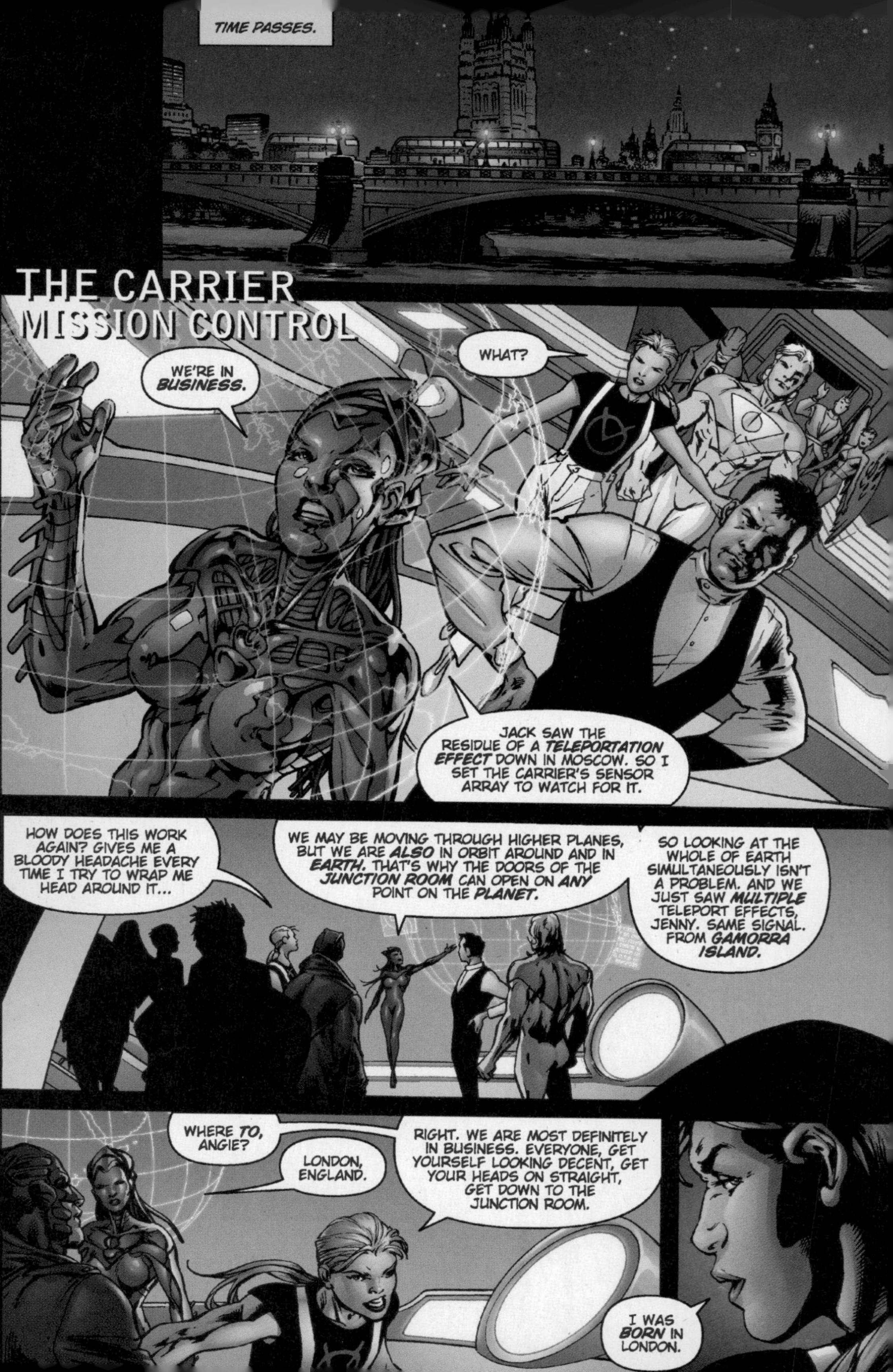
TIME PASSES.
THE CARRIER MISSION CONTROL
WE'RE IN BUSINESS.
WHAT?
JACK SAW THE RESIDUE OF A TELEPORTATION EFFECT DOWN IN MOSCOW. SO I SET THE CARRIER'S SENSOR ARRAY TO WATCH FOR IT.
HOW DOES THIS WORK AGAIN? GIVES ME A BLOODY HEADACHE EVERY TIME I TRY TO WRAP ME HEAD AROUND IT...
WE MAY BE MOVING THROUGH HIGHER PLANES, BUT WE ARE ALSO IN ORBIT AROUND AND IN EARTH. THAT'S WHY THE DOORS OF THE JUNCTION ROOM CAN OPEN ON ANY POINT ON THE PLANET.
SO LOOKING AT THE WHOLE OF EARTH SIMULTANEOUSLY ISN'T A PROBLEM. AND WE JUST SAW MULTIPLE TELEPORT EFFECTS, JENNY. SAME SIGNAL. FROM GAMORRA ISLAND.
WHERE TO, ANGIE?
LONDON, ENGLAND.
RIGHT. WE ARE MOST DEFINITELY IN BUSINESS. EVERYONE, GET YOURSELF LOOKING DECENT, GET YOUR HEADS ON STRAIGHT, GET DOWN TO THE JUNCTION ROOM.
I WAS BORN IN LONDON.

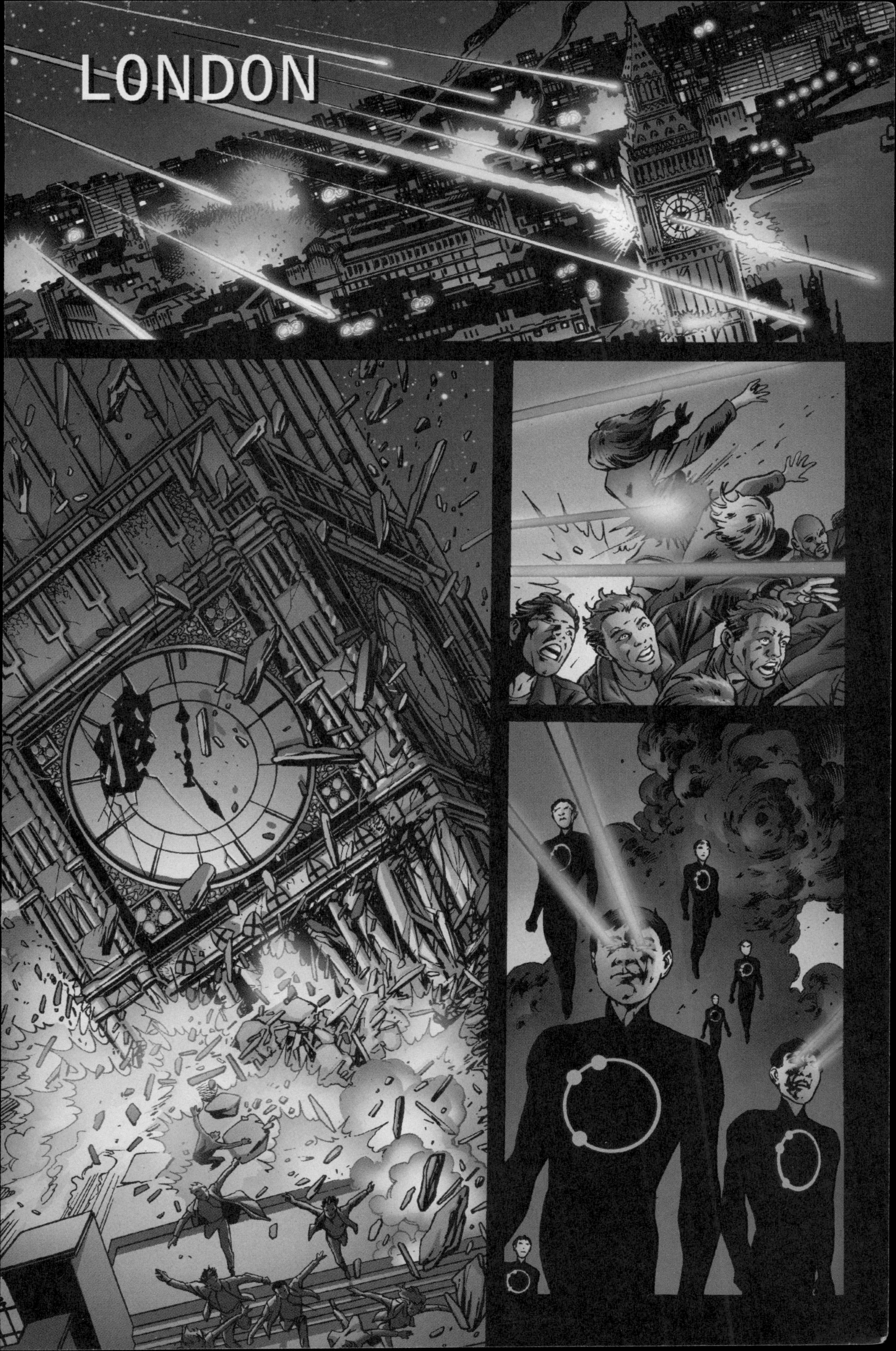
LONDON

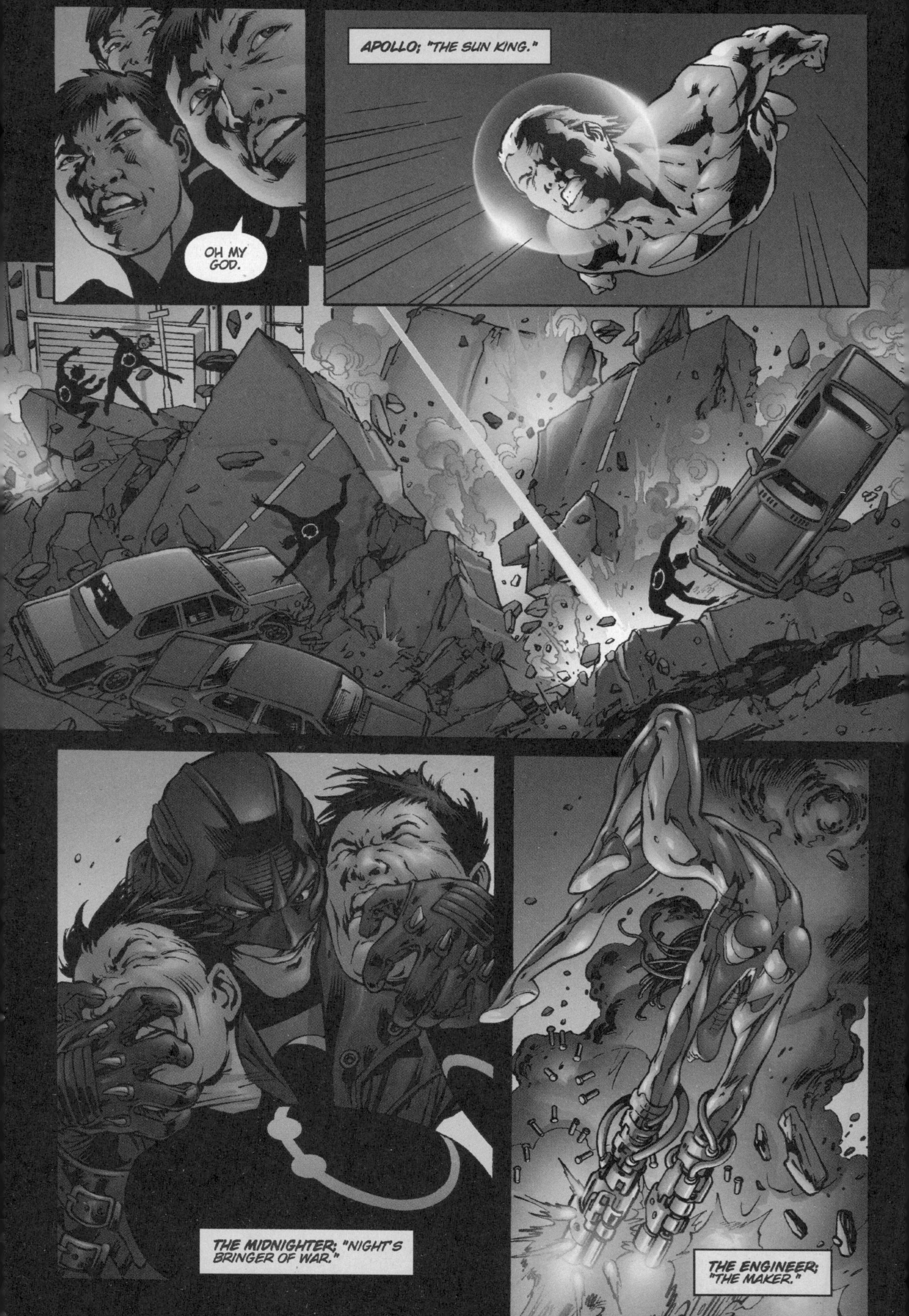
OH MY GOD.
APOLLO; "THE SUN KING."
THE MIDNIGHTER; "NIGHT'S BRINGER OF WAR."
THE ENGINEER; "THE MAKER."

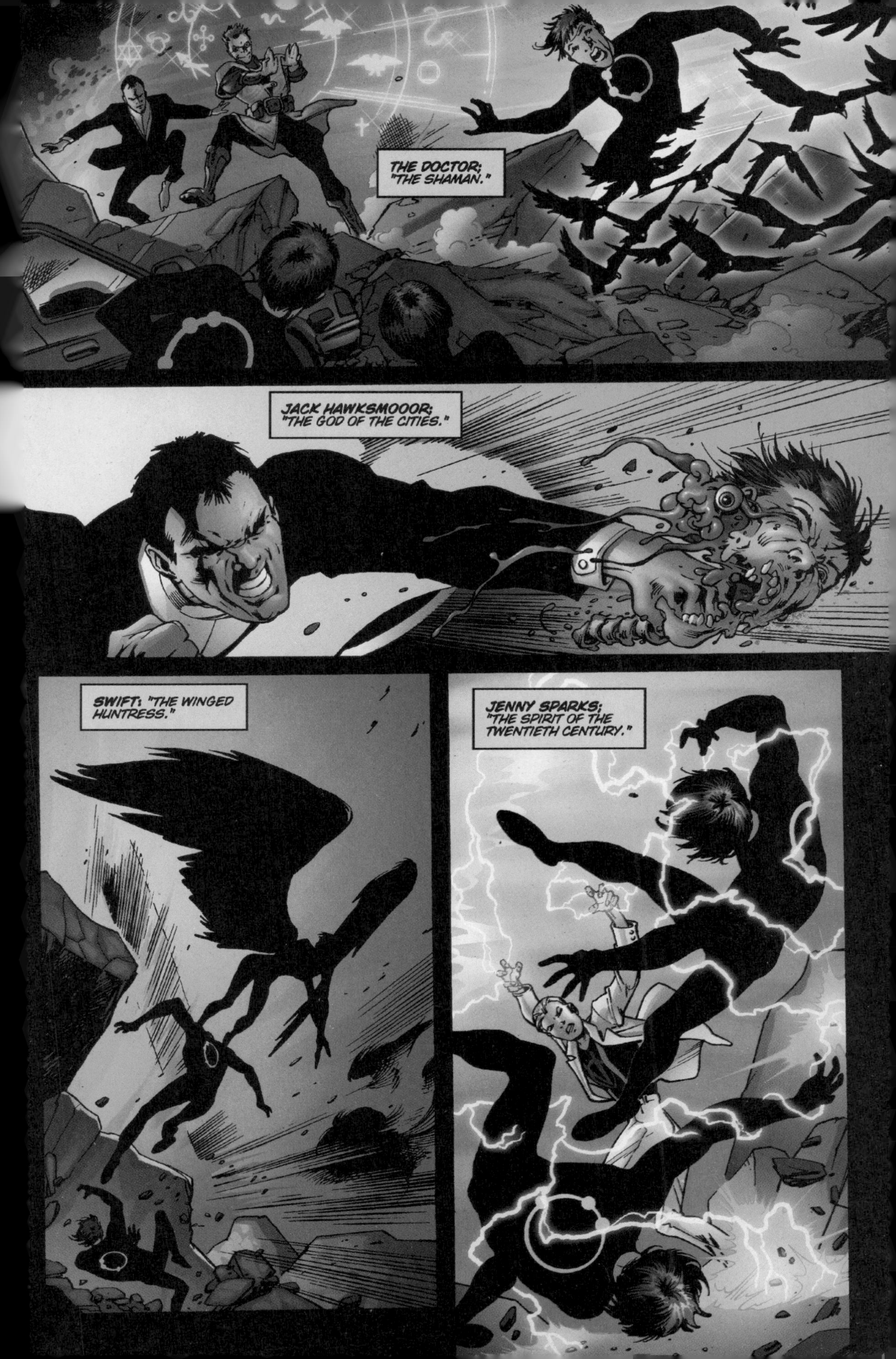

THE DOCTOR; "THE SHAMAN."
JACK HAWKSMOOOR; "THE GOD OF THE CITIES."
SWIFT: "THE WINGED HUNTRESS."
JENNY SPARKS; "THE SPIRIT OF THE TWENTIETH CENTURY."

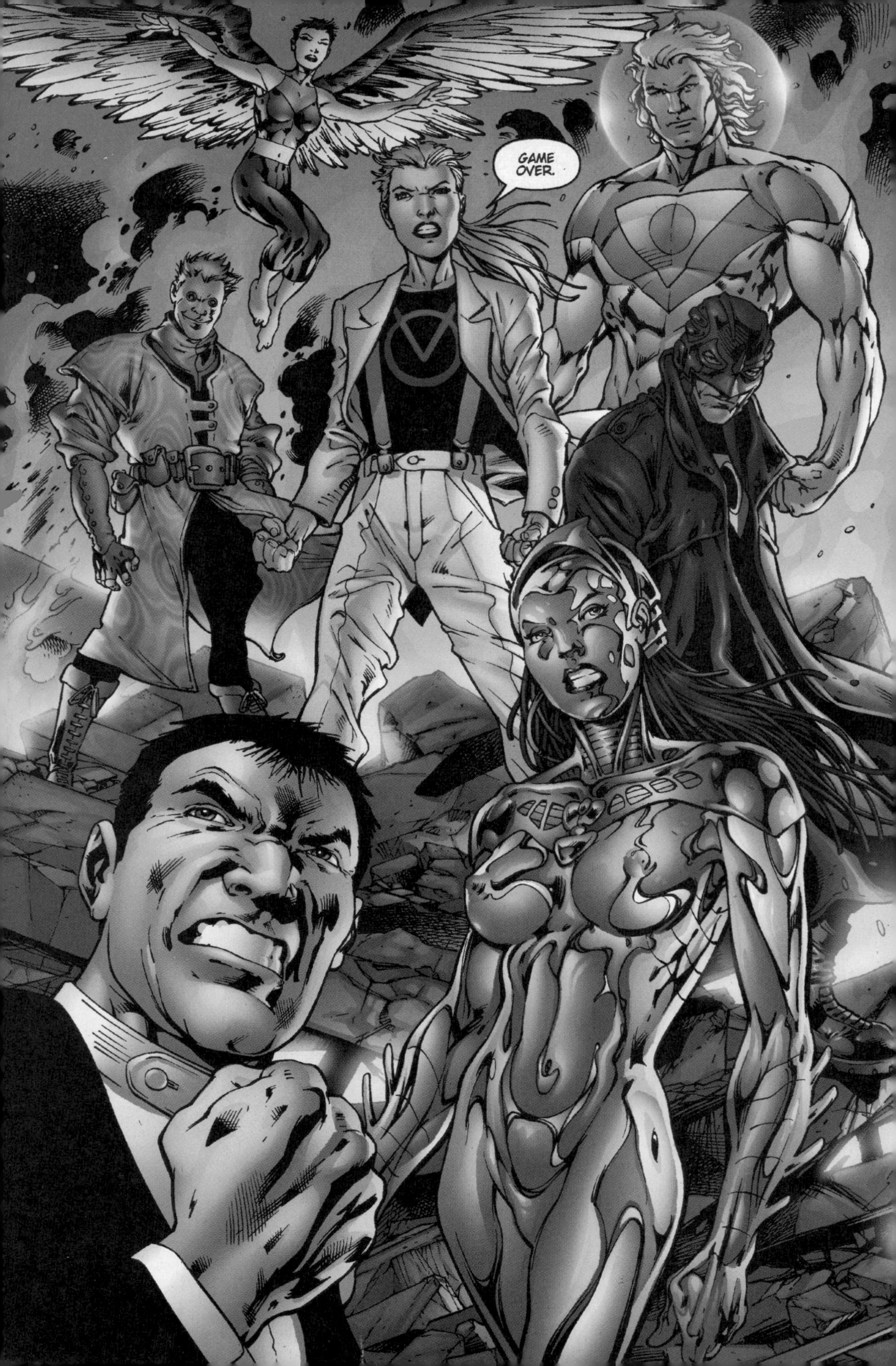
GAME OVER.

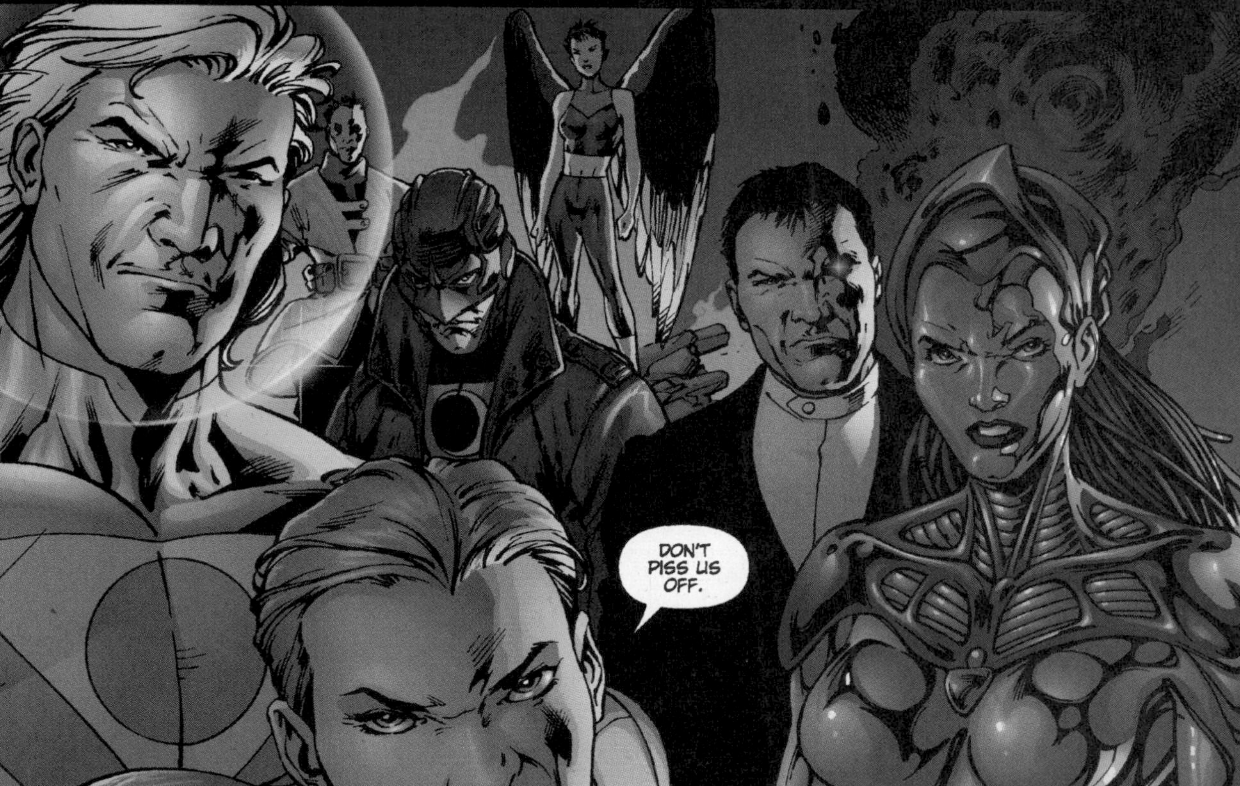
DON'T PISS US OFF.

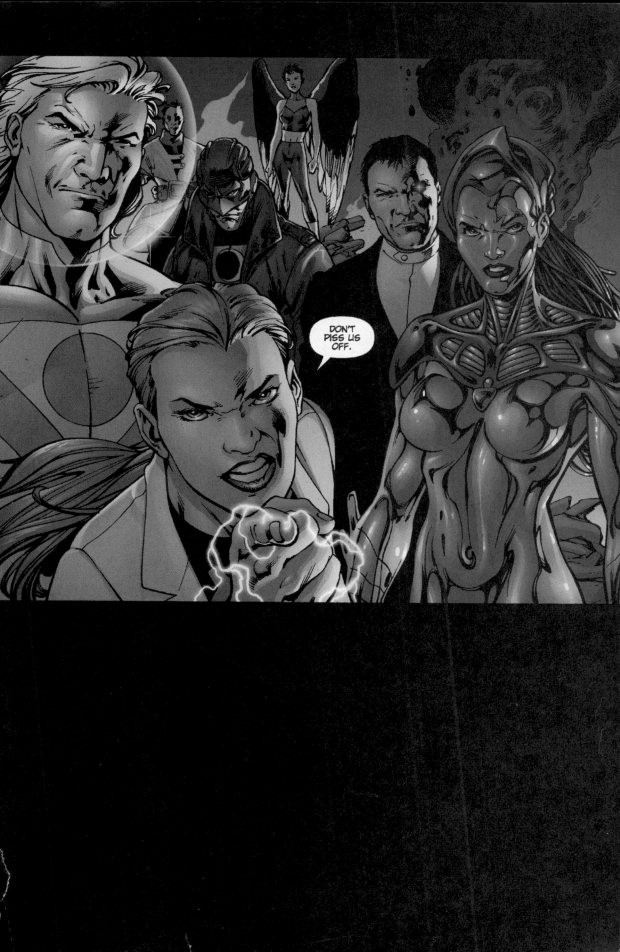

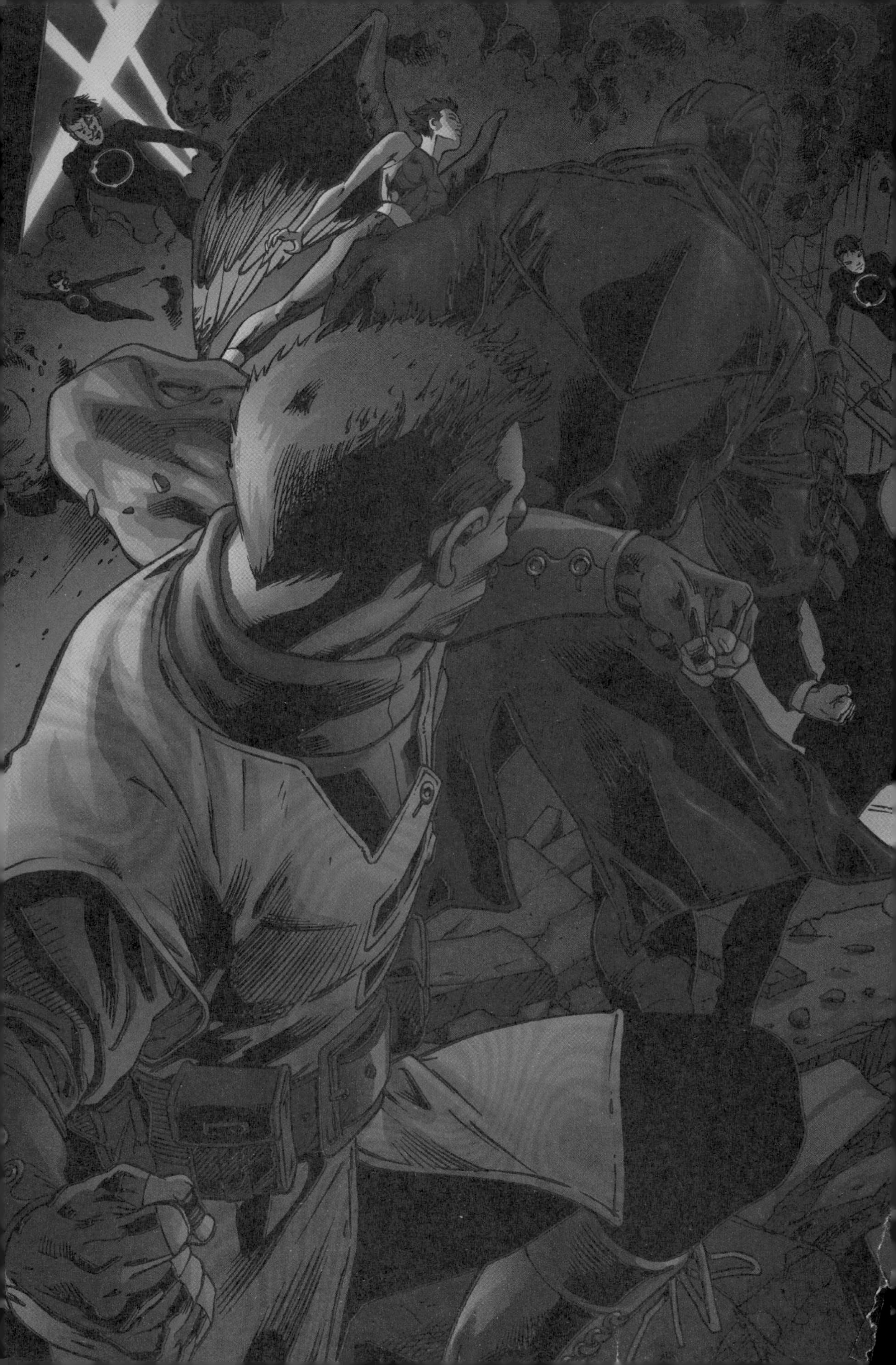

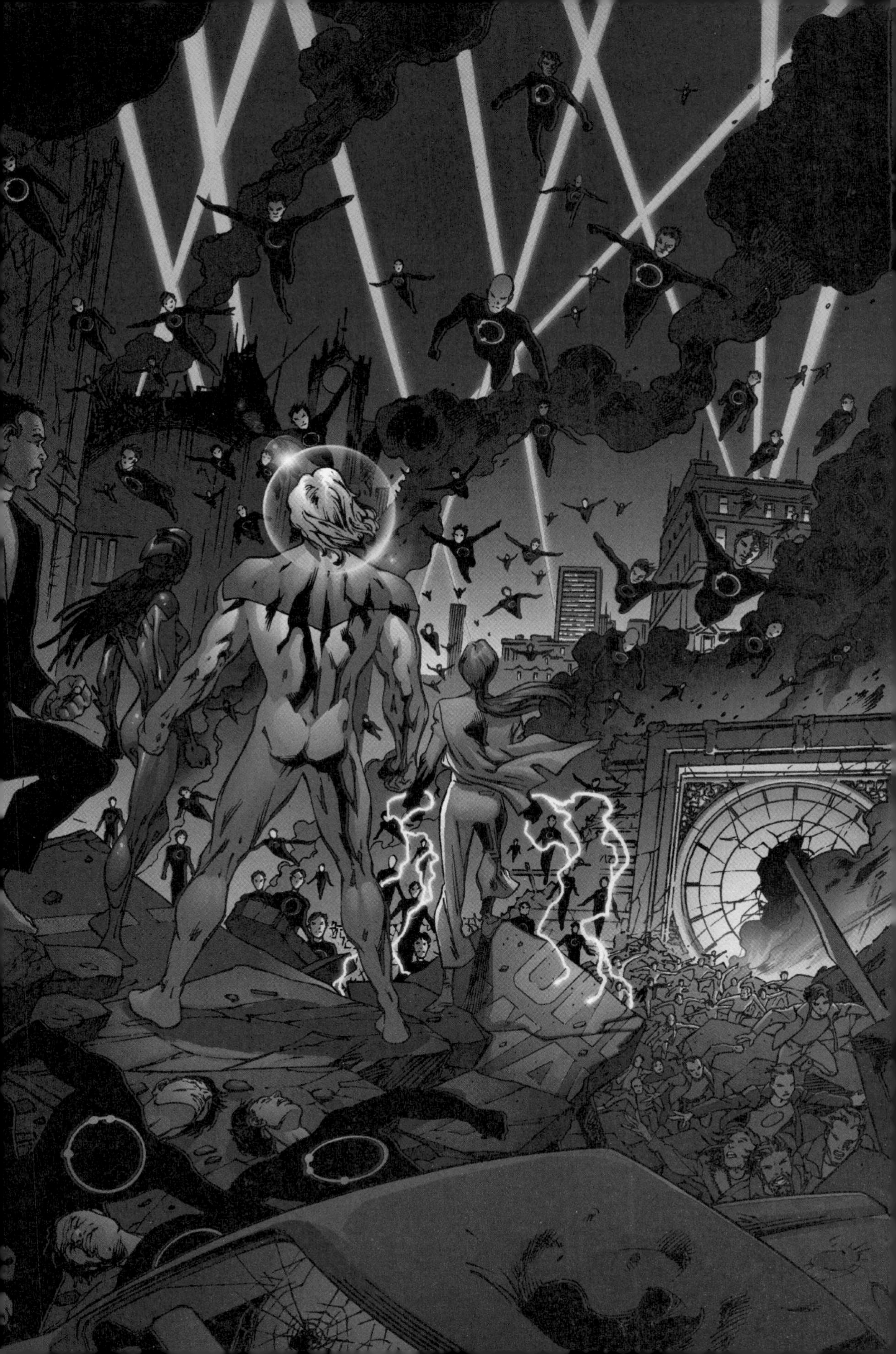

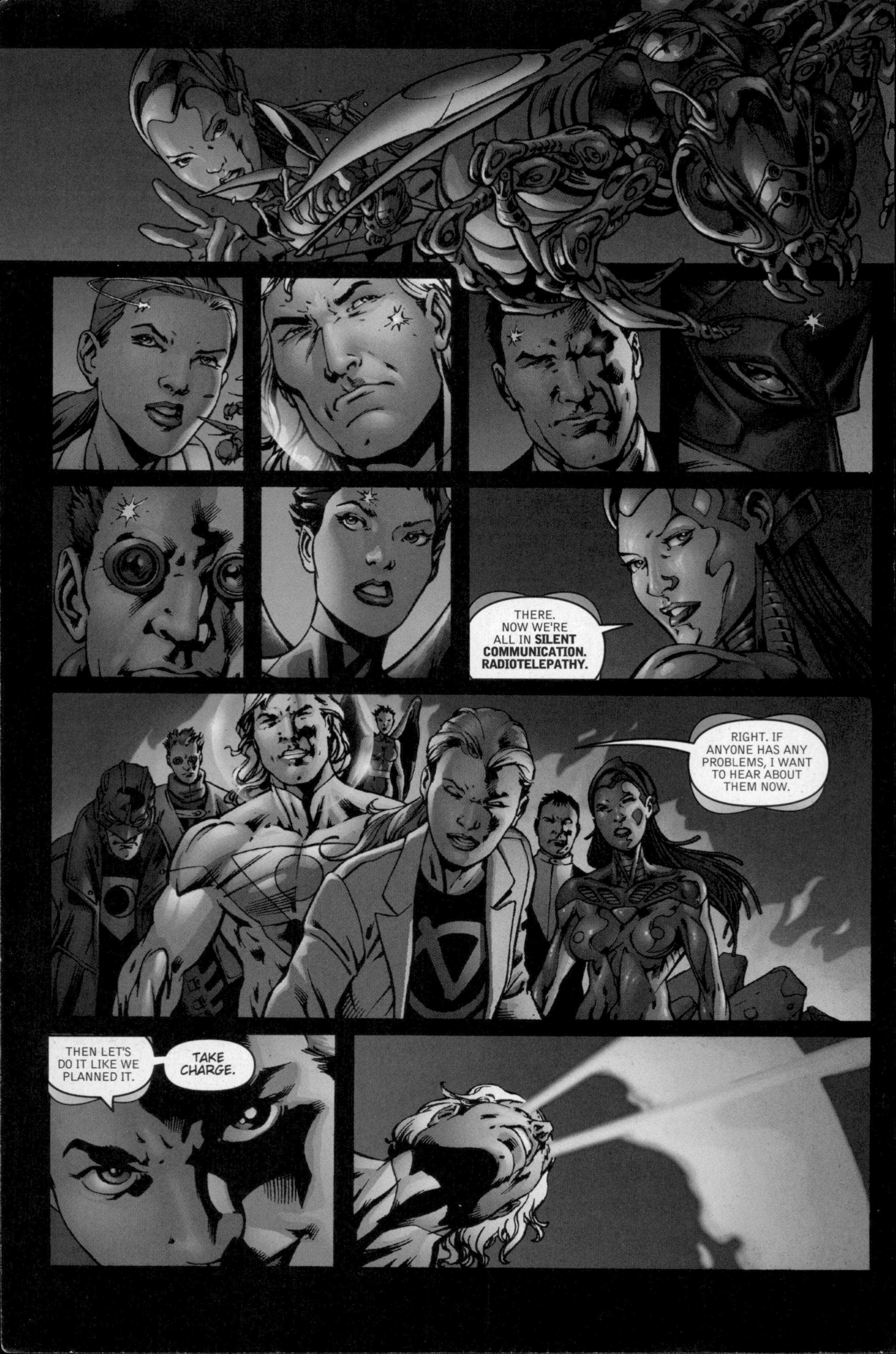
THERE. NOW WE'RE ALL IN SILENT COMMUNICATION. RADIOTELEPATHY.
RIGHT. IF ANYONE HAS ANY PROBLEMS, I WANT TO HEAR ABOUT THEM NOW.
THEN LET'S DO IT LIKE WE PLANNED IT.
TAKE CHARGE.

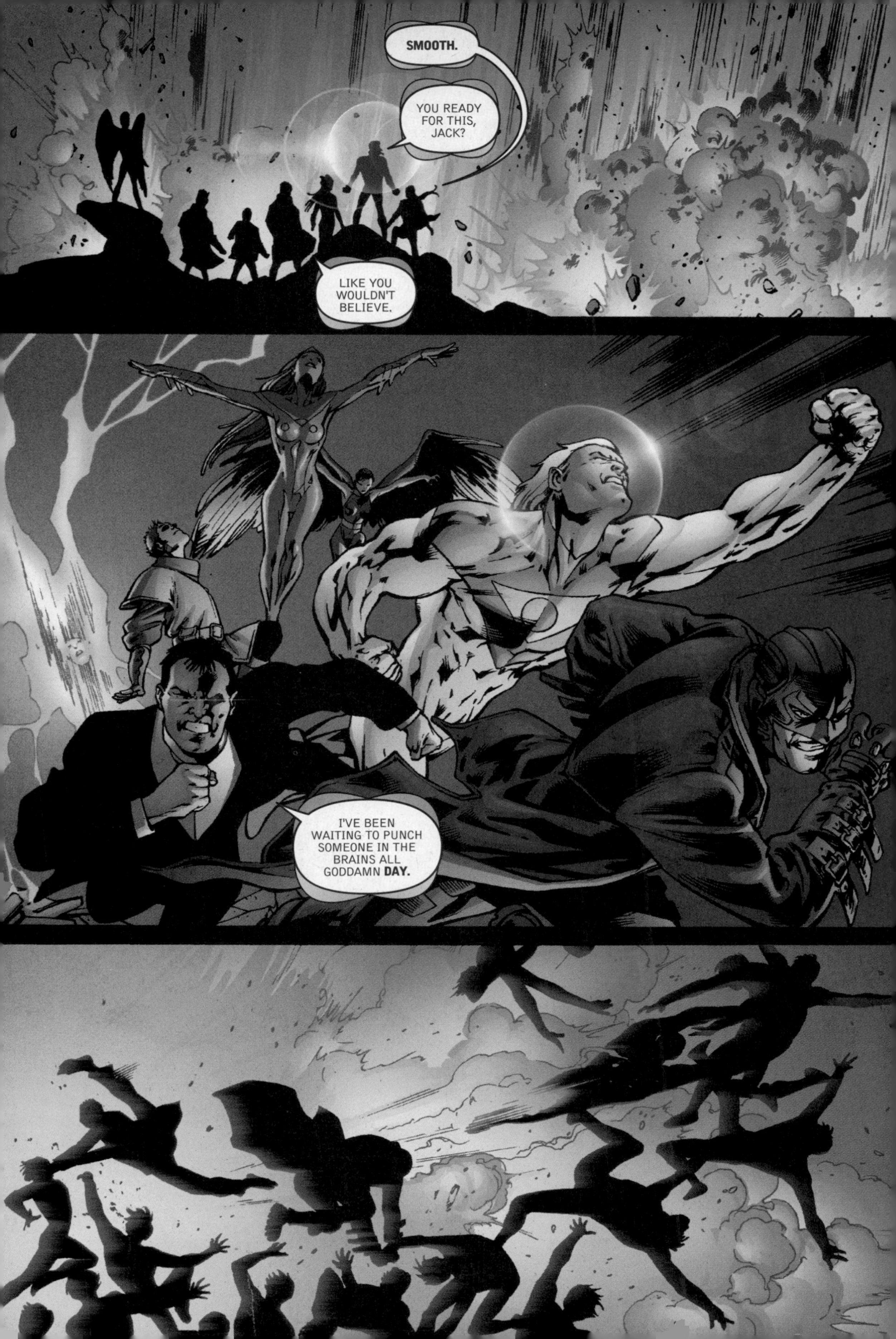
SMOOTH.
YOU READY FOR THIS, JACK?
LIKE YOU WOULDN'T BELIEVE.
I'VE BEEN WAITING TO PUNCH SOMEONE IN THE BRAINS ALL GODDAMN DAY.

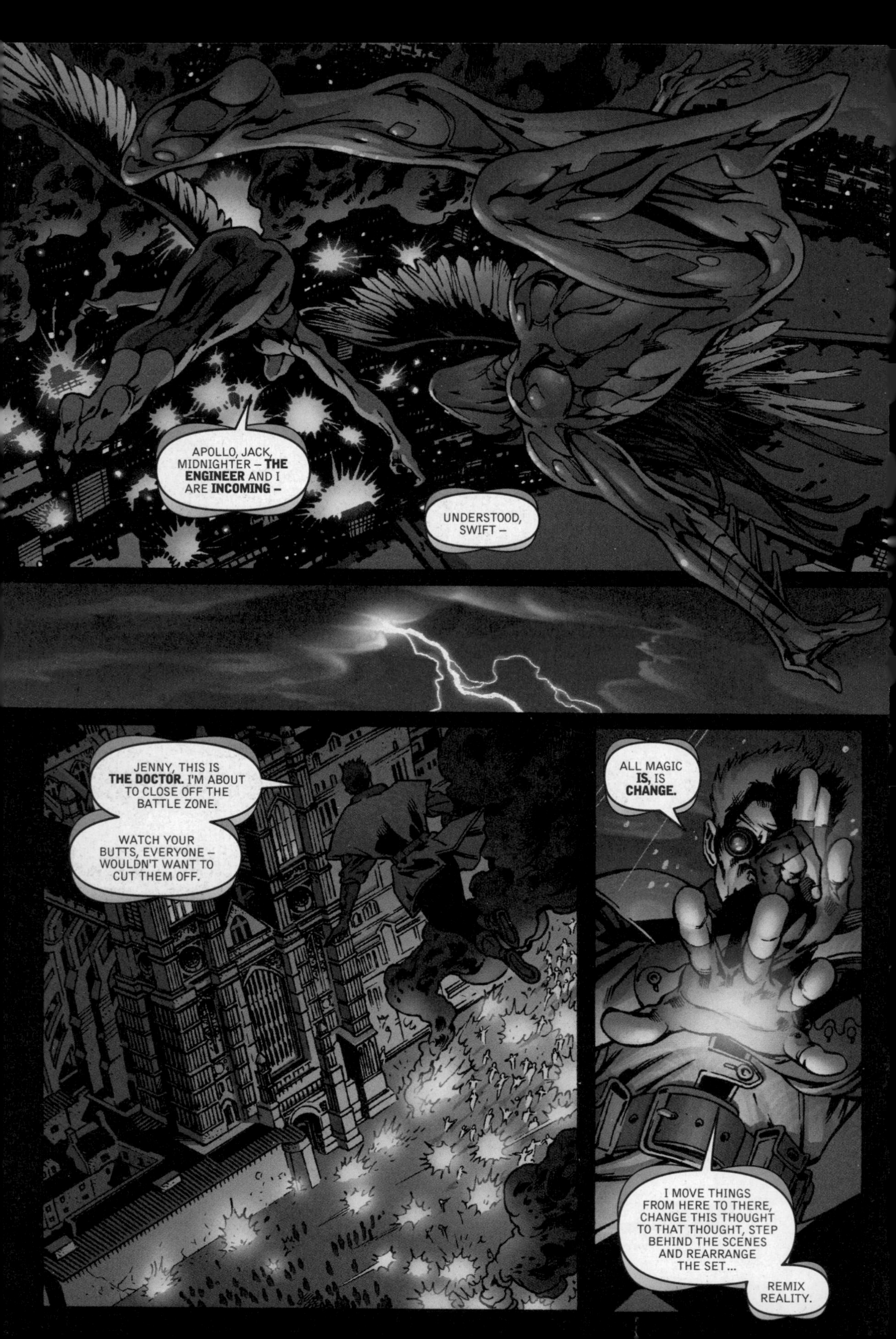
APOLLO, JACK, MIDNIGHTER – THE ENGINEER AND I ARE INCOMING –
UNDERSTOOD, SWIFT –
JENNY, THIS IS THE DOCTOR. I'M ABOUT TO CLOSE OFF THE BATTLE ZONE.
WATCH YOUR BUTTS, EVERYONE – WOULDN'T WANT TO CUT THEM OFF.
ALL MAGIC IS, IS CHANGE.
I MOVE THINGS FROM HERE TO THERE, CHANGE THIS THOUGHT TO THAT THOUGHT, STEP BEHIND THE SCENES AND REARRANGE THE SET...
REMIX REALITY.

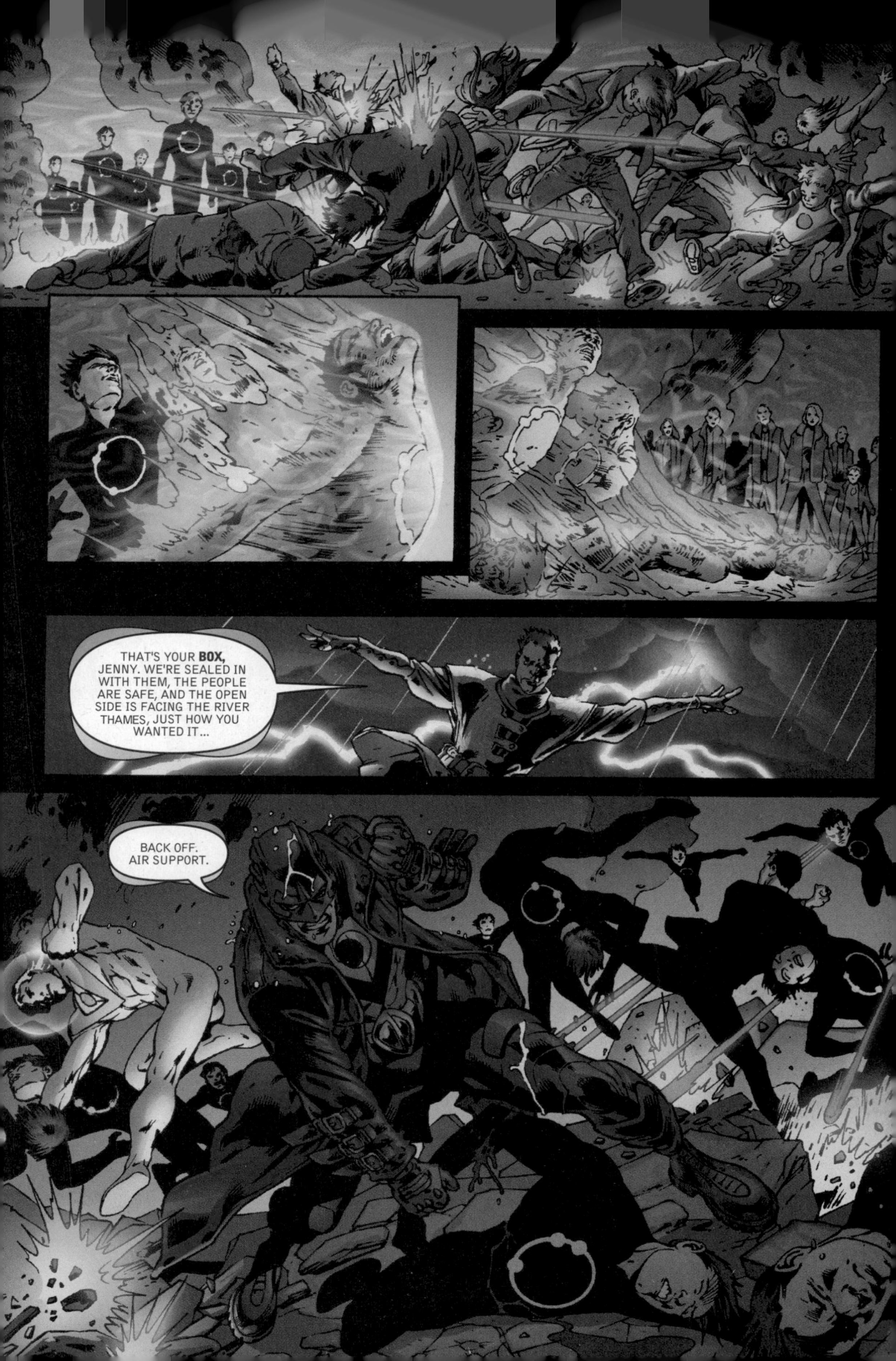
THAT'S YOUR **BOX,** JENNY. WE'RE SEALED IN WITH THEM, THE PEOPLE ARE SAFE, AND THE OPEN SIDE IS FACING THE RIVER THAMES, JUST HOW YOU WANTED IT...
BACK OFF. AIR SUPPORT.

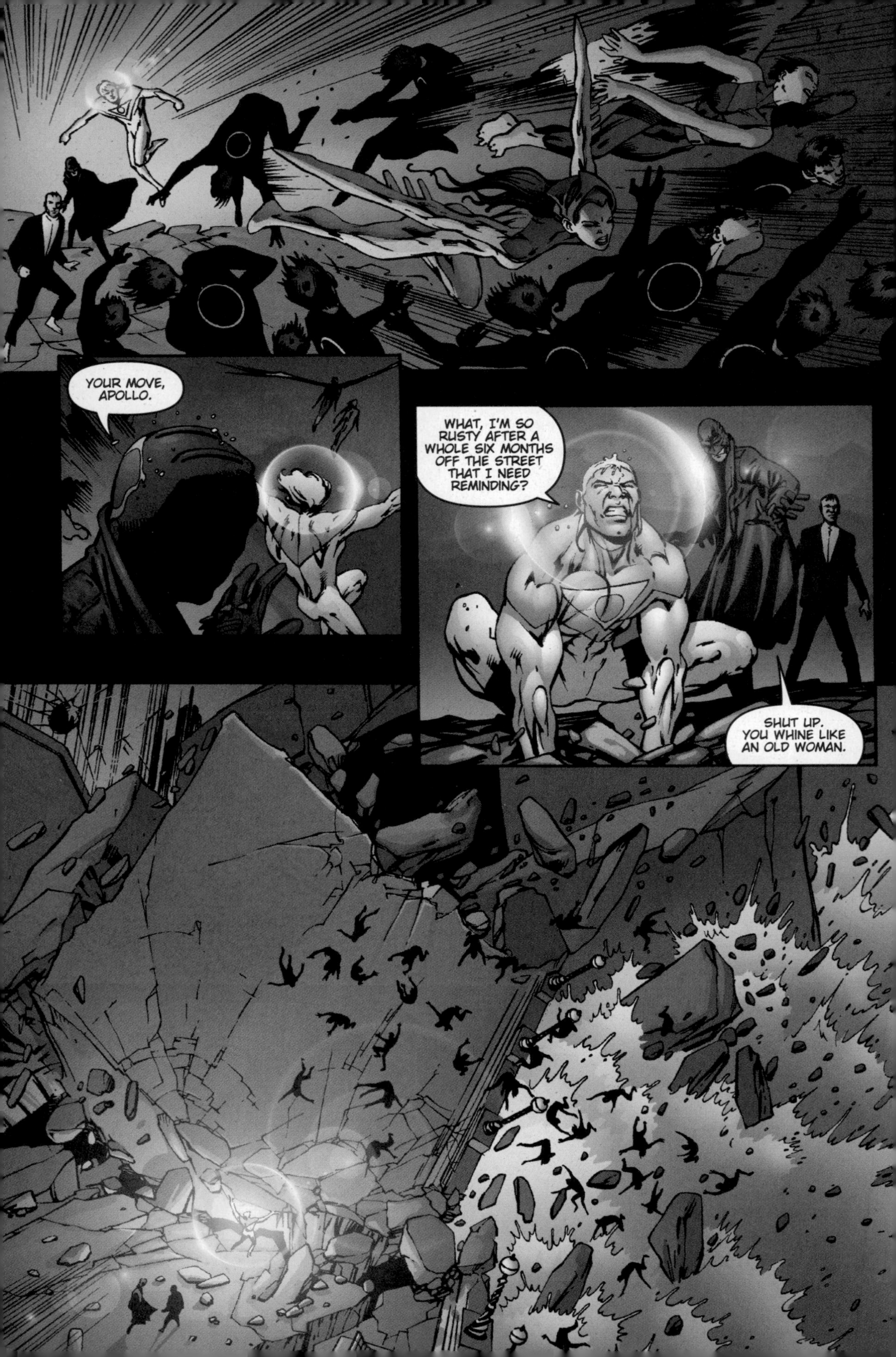
YOUR MOVE, APOLLO.
WHAT, I'M SO RUSTY AFTER A WHOLE SIX MONTHS OFF THE STREET THAT I NEED REMINDING?
SHUT UP. YOU WHINE LIKE AN OLD WOMAN.

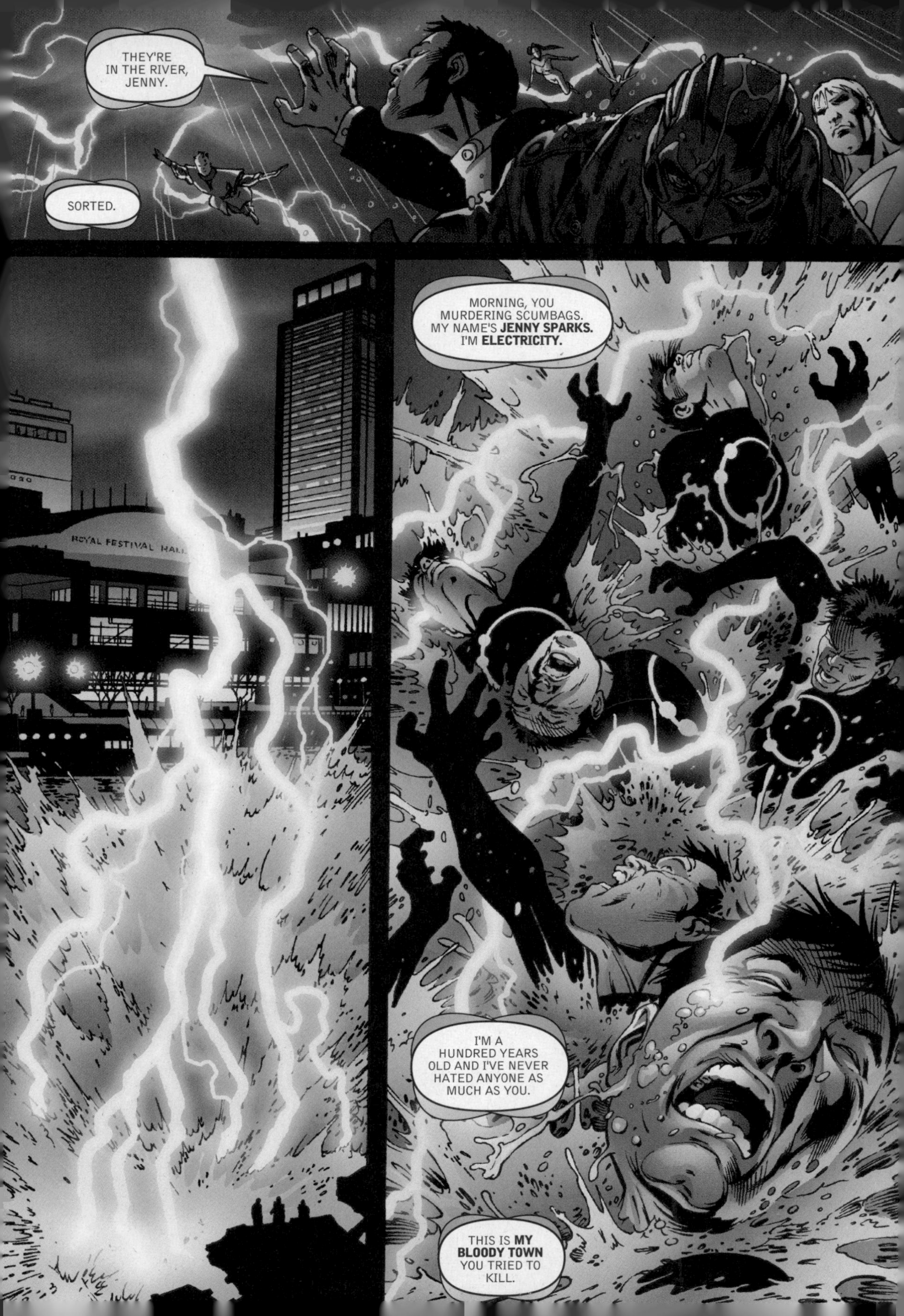

THEY'RE IN THE RIVER, JENNY.
SORTED.
ROYAL FESTIVAL HALL
MORNING, YOU MURDERING SCUMBAGS. MY NAME'S **JENNY SPARKS.** I'M **ELECTRICITY.**
I'M A HUNDRED YEARS OLD AND I'VE NEVER HATED ANYONE AS MUCH AS YOU.
THIS IS **MY BLOODY TOWN** YOU TRIED TO KILL.

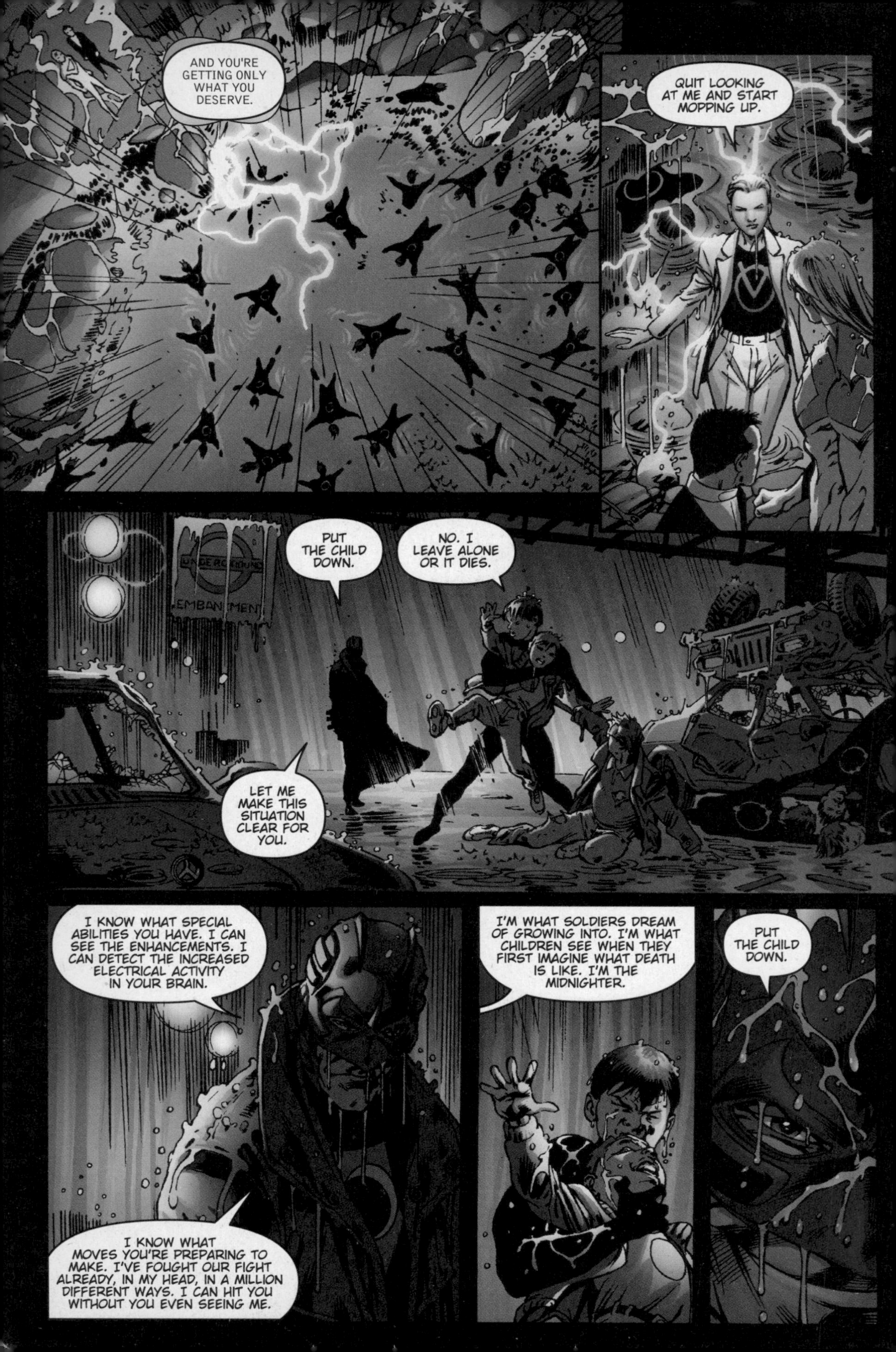

AND YOU'RE GETTING ONLY WHAT YOU DESERVE.
QUIT LOOKING AT ME AND START MOPPING UP.
PUT THE CHILD DOWN.
NO. I LEAVE ALONE OR IT DIES.
LET ME MAKE THIS SITUATION CLEAR FOR YOU.
I KNOW WHAT SPECIAL ABILITIES YOU HAVE. I CAN SEE THE ENHANCEMENTS. I CAN DETECT THE INCREASED ELECTRICAL ACTIVITY IN YOUR BRAIN.
I KNOW WHAT MOVES YOU'RE PREPARING TO MAKE. I'VE FOUGHT OUR FIGHT ALREADY, IN MY HEAD, IN A MILLION DIFFERENT WAYS. I CAN HIT YOU WITHOUT YOU EVEN SEEING ME.
I'M WHAT SOLDIERS DREAM OF GROWING INTO. I'M WHAT CHILDREN SEE WHEN THEY FIRST IMAGINE WHAT DEATH IS LIKE. I'M THE MIDNIGHTER.
PUT THE CHILD DOWN.

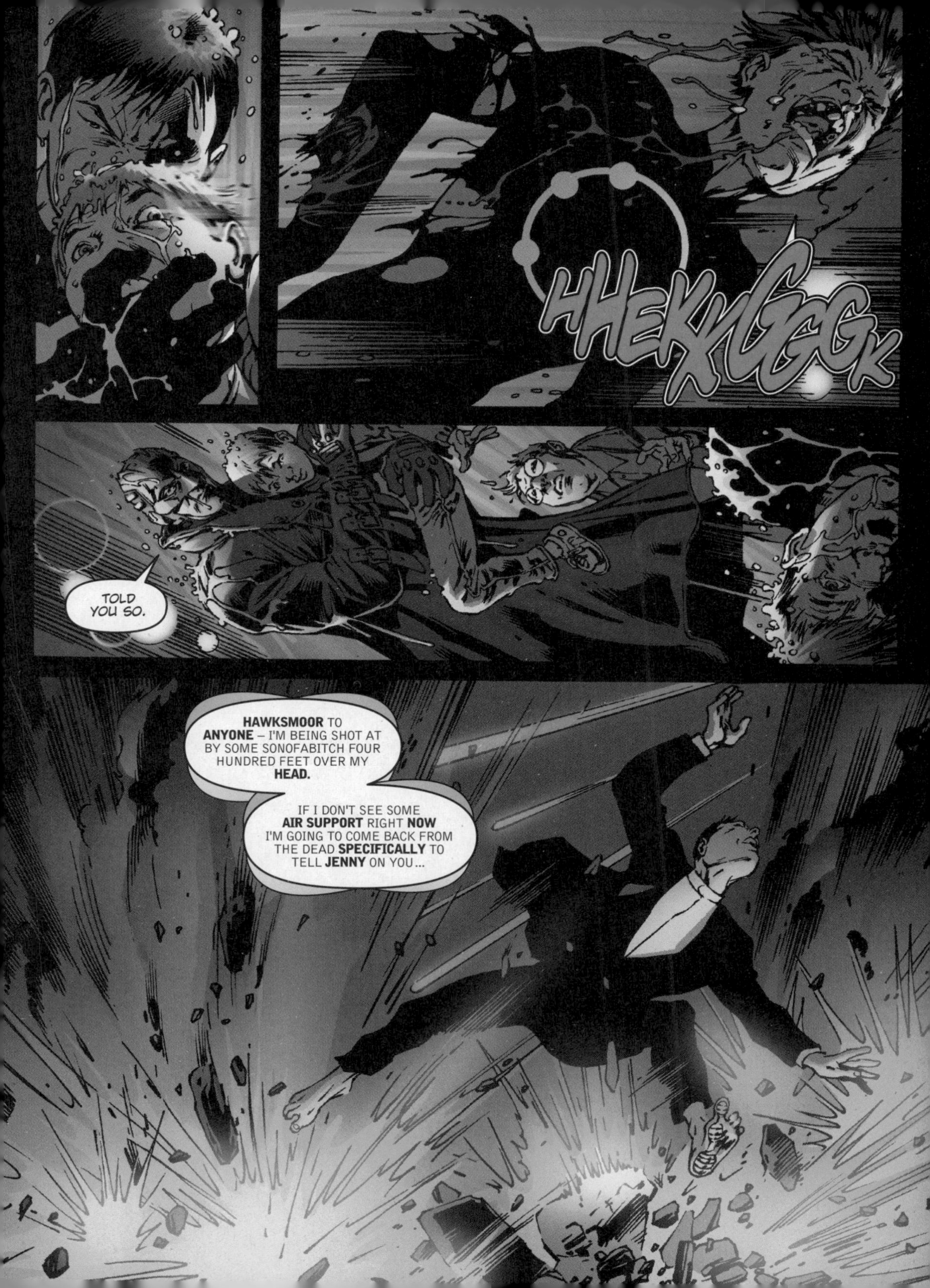
HHEKKGGGk
TOLD YOU SO.
HAWKSMOOR TO ANYONE – I'M BEING SHOT AT BY SOME SONOFABITCH FOUR HUNDRED FEET OVER MY HEAD.
IF I DON'T SEE SOME AIR SUPPORT RIGHT NOW I'M GOING TO COME BACK FROM THE DEAD SPECIFICALLY TO TELL JENNY ON YOU...

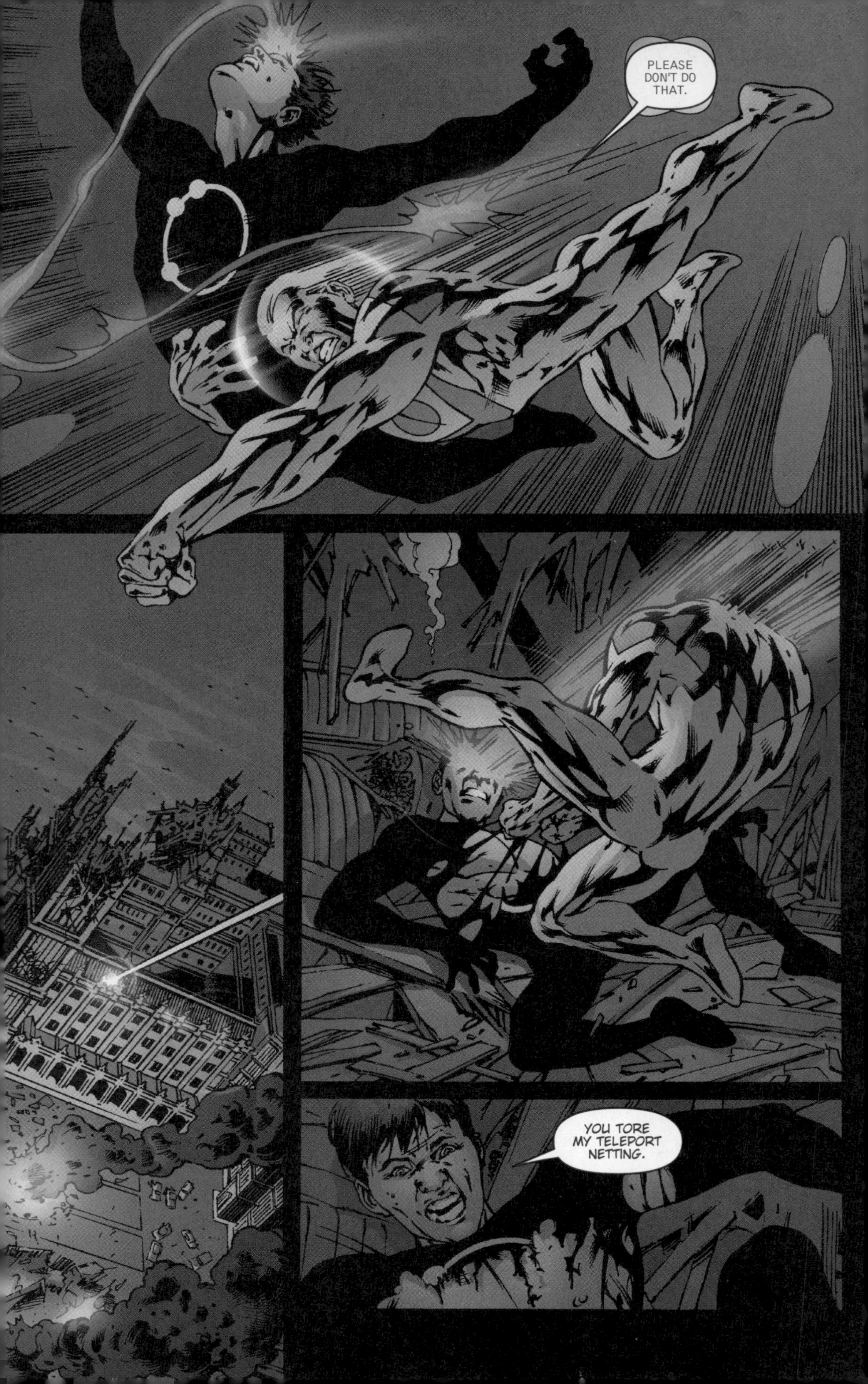
PLEASE DON'T DO THAT.
YOU TORE MY TELEPORT NETTING.

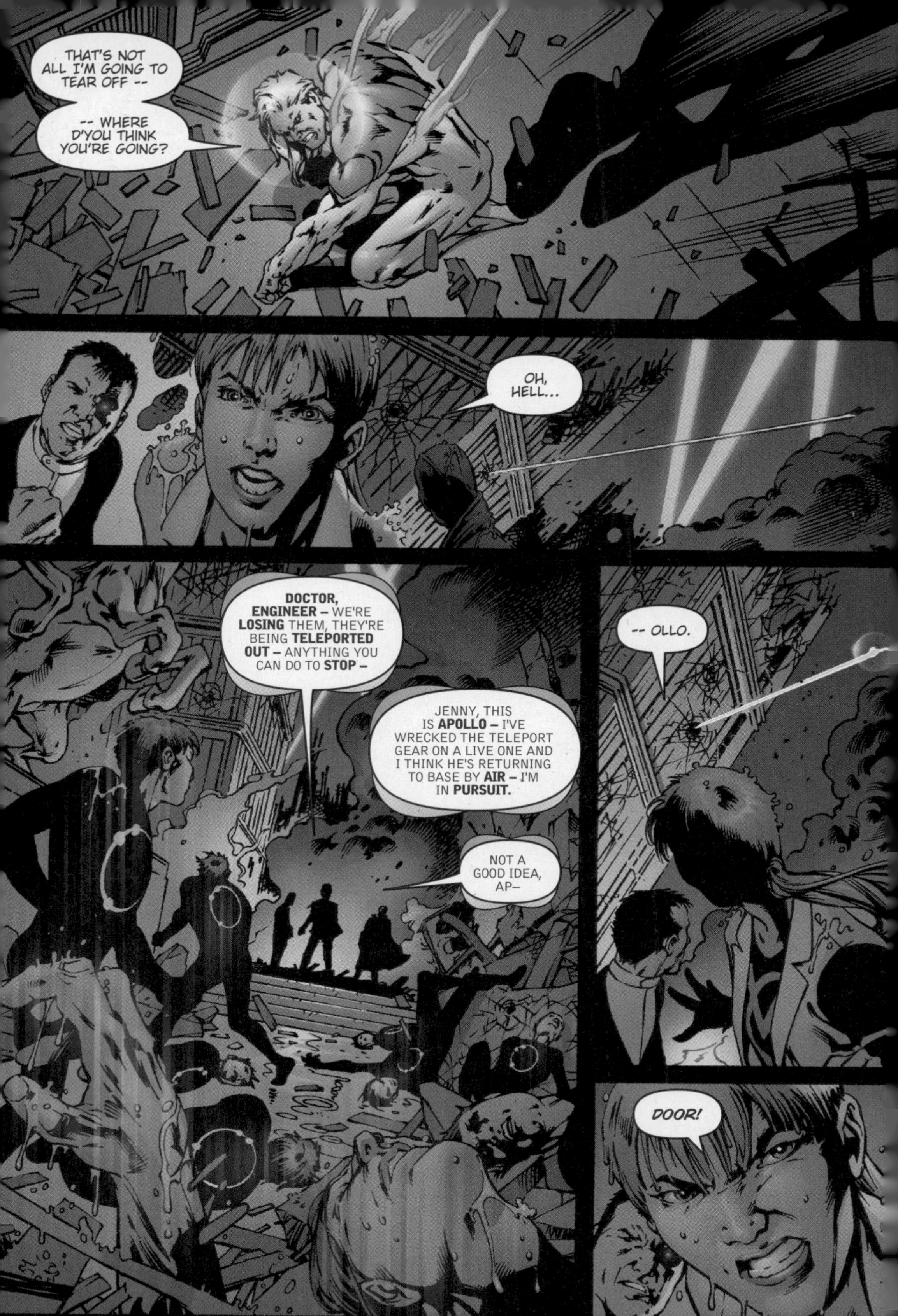
THAT'S NOT ALL I'M GOING TO TEAR OFF --
-- WHERE D'YOU THINK YOU'RE GOING?
OH, HELL...
DOCTOR, ENGINEER – WE'RE LOSING THEM, THEY'RE BEING TELEPORTED OUT – ANYTHING YOU CAN DO TO STOP –
JENNY, THIS IS APOLLO – I'VE WRECKED THE TELEPORT GEAR ON A LIVE ONE AND I THINK HE'S RETURNING TO BASE BY AIR – I'M IN PURSUIT.
NOT A GOOD IDEA, AP–
-- OLLO.
DOOR!

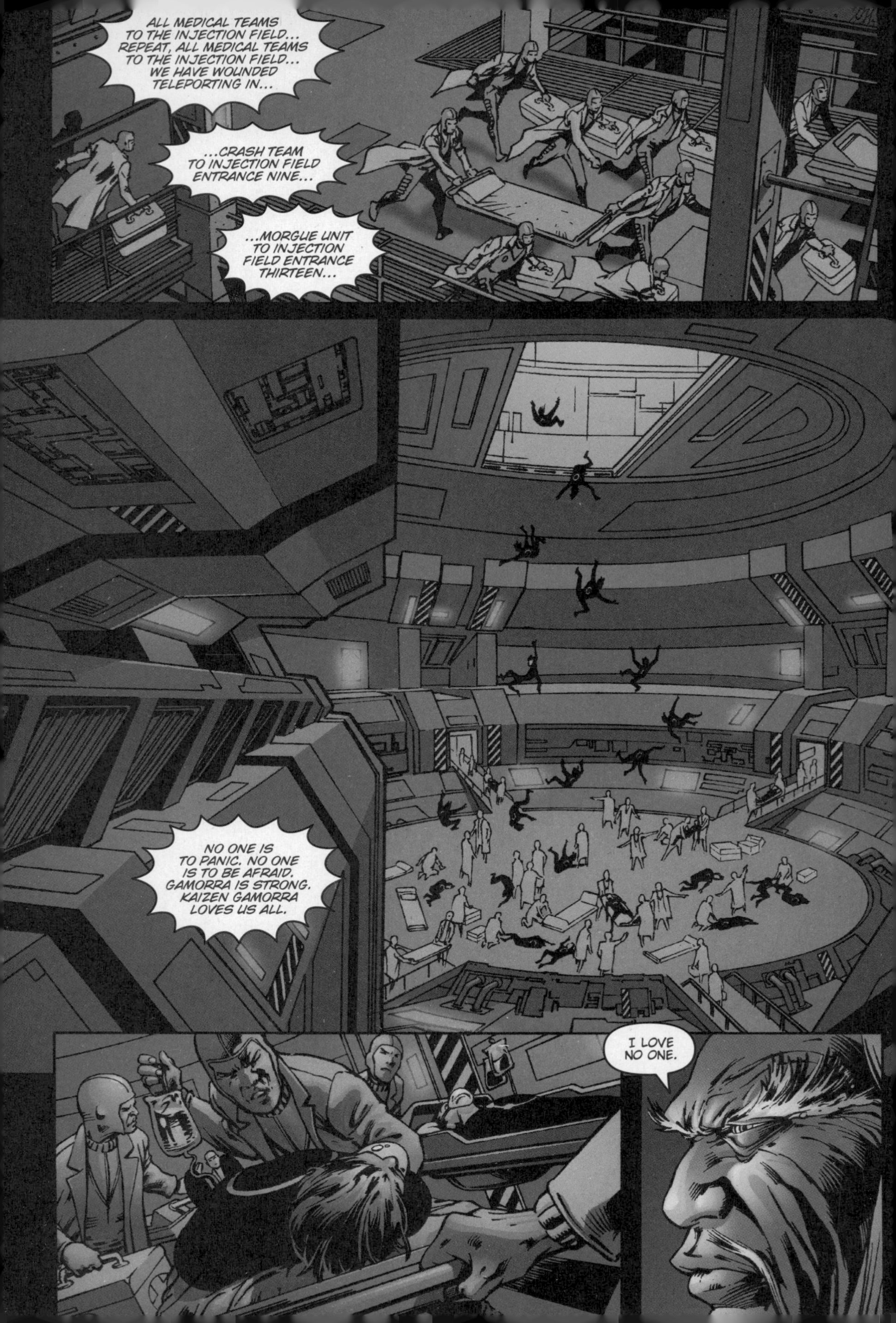
ALL MEDICAL TEAMS TO THE INJECTION FIELD... REPEAT, ALL MEDICAL TEAMS TO THE INJECTION FIELD... WE HAVE WOUNDED TELEPORTING IN...
...CRASH TEAM TO INJECTION FIELD ENTRANCE NINE...
...MORGUE UNIT TO INJECTION FIELD ENTRANCE THIRTEEN...
NO ONE IS TO PANIC. NO ONE IS TO BE AFRAID. GAMORRA IS STRONG. KAIZEN GAMORRA LOVES US ALL.
I LOVE NO ONE.

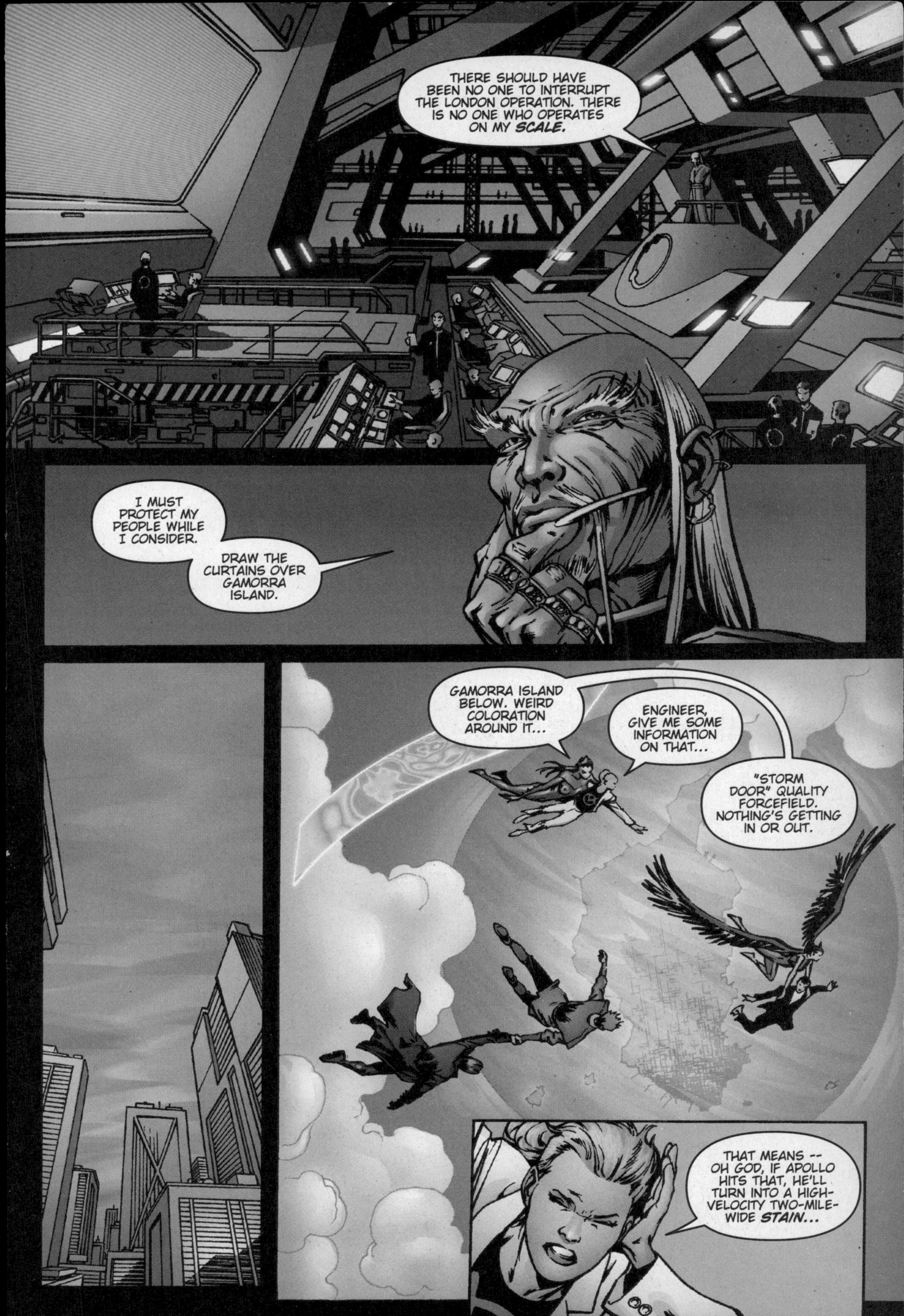

THERE SHOULD HAVE BEEN NO ONE TO INTERRUPT THE LONDON OPERATION. THERE IS NO ONE WHO OPERATES ON MY SCALE.
I MUST PROTECT MY PEOPLE WHILE I CONSIDER.
DRAW THE CURTAINS OVER GAMORRA ISLAND.
GAMORRA ISLAND BELOW. WEIRD COLORATION AROUND IT...
ENGINEER, GIVE ME SOME INFORMATION ON THAT...
"STORM DOOR" QUALITY FORCEFIELD. NOTHING'S GETTING IN OR OUT.
THAT MEANS -- OH GOD, IF APOLLO HITS THAT, HE'LL TURN INTO A HIGH-VELOCITY TWO-MILE-WIDE STAIN...

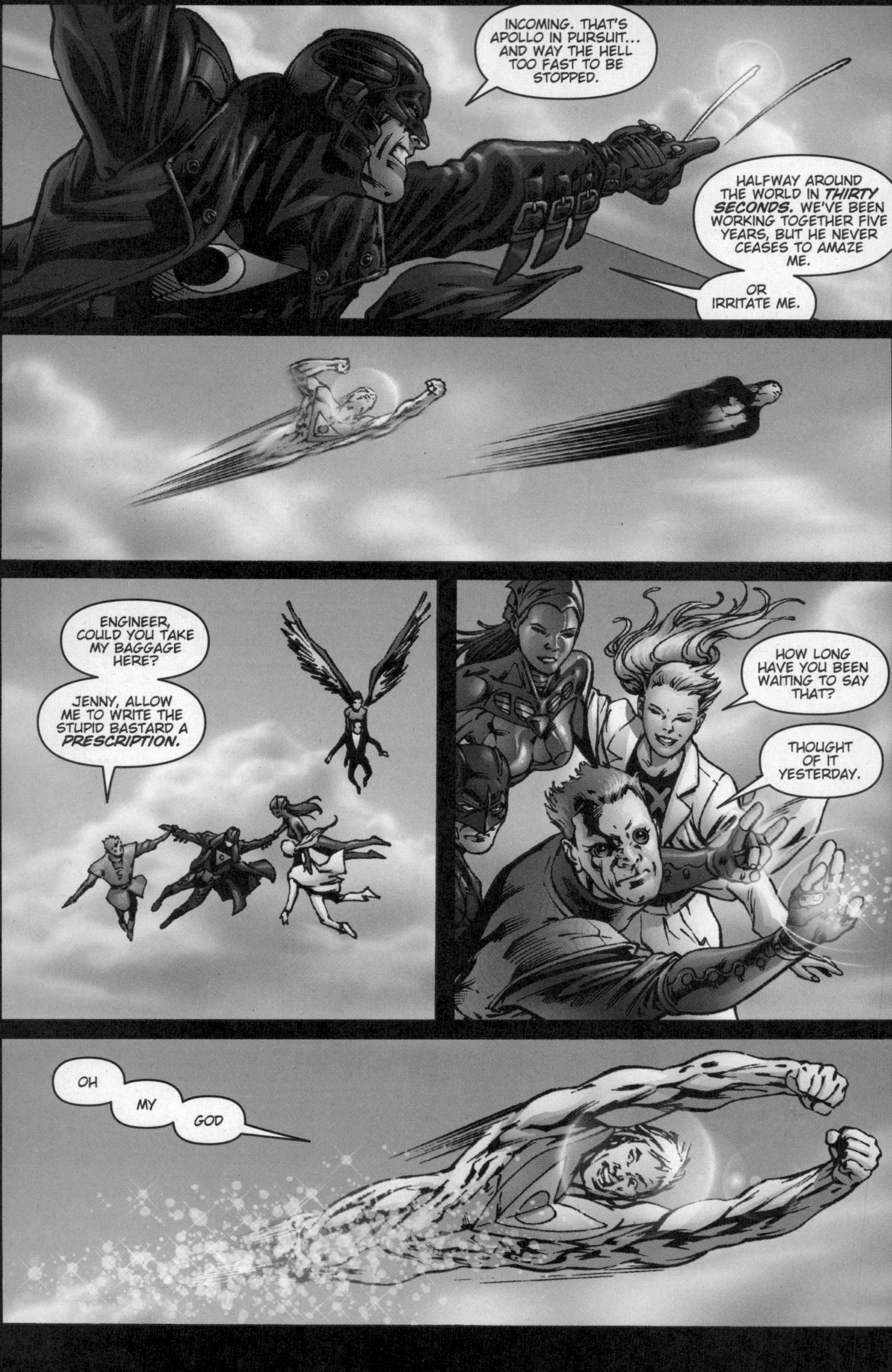
INCOMING. THAT'S APOLLO IN PURSUIT... AND WAY THE HELL TOO FAST TO BE STOPPED.
HALFWAY AROUND THE WORLD IN *THIRTY SECONDS.* WE'VE BEEN WORKING TOGETHER FIVE YEARS, BUT HE NEVER CEASES TO AMAZE ME.
OR IRRITATE ME.
ENGINEER, COULD YOU TAKE MY BAGGAGE HERE?
JENNY, ALLOW ME TO WRITE THE STUPID BASTARD A *PRESCRIPTION.*
HOW LONG HAVE YOU BEEN WAITING TO SAY THAT?
THOUGHT OF IT YESTERDAY.
OH
MY
GOD

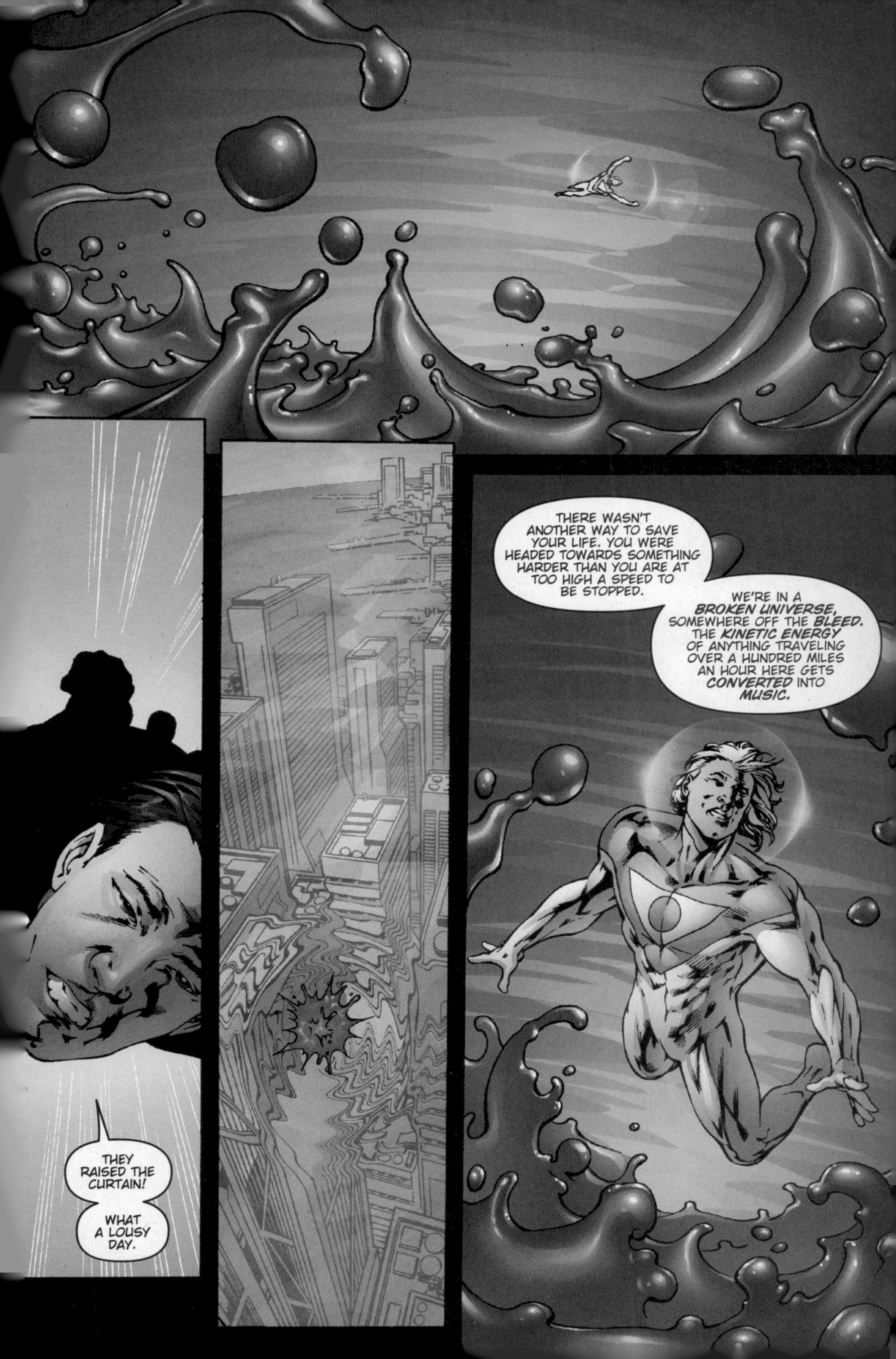
THEY RAISED THE CURTAIN!
WHAT A LOUSY DAY.
THERE WASN'T ANOTHER WAY TO SAVE YOUR LIFE. YOU WERE HEADED TOWARDS SOMETHING HARDER THAN YOU ARE AT TOO HIGH A SPEED TO BE STOPPED.
WE'RE IN A BROKEN UNIVERSE, SOMEWHERE OFF THE BLEED. THE KINETIC ENERGY OF ANYTHING TRAVELING OVER A HUNDRED MILES AN HOUR HERE GETS CONVERTED INTO MUSIC.

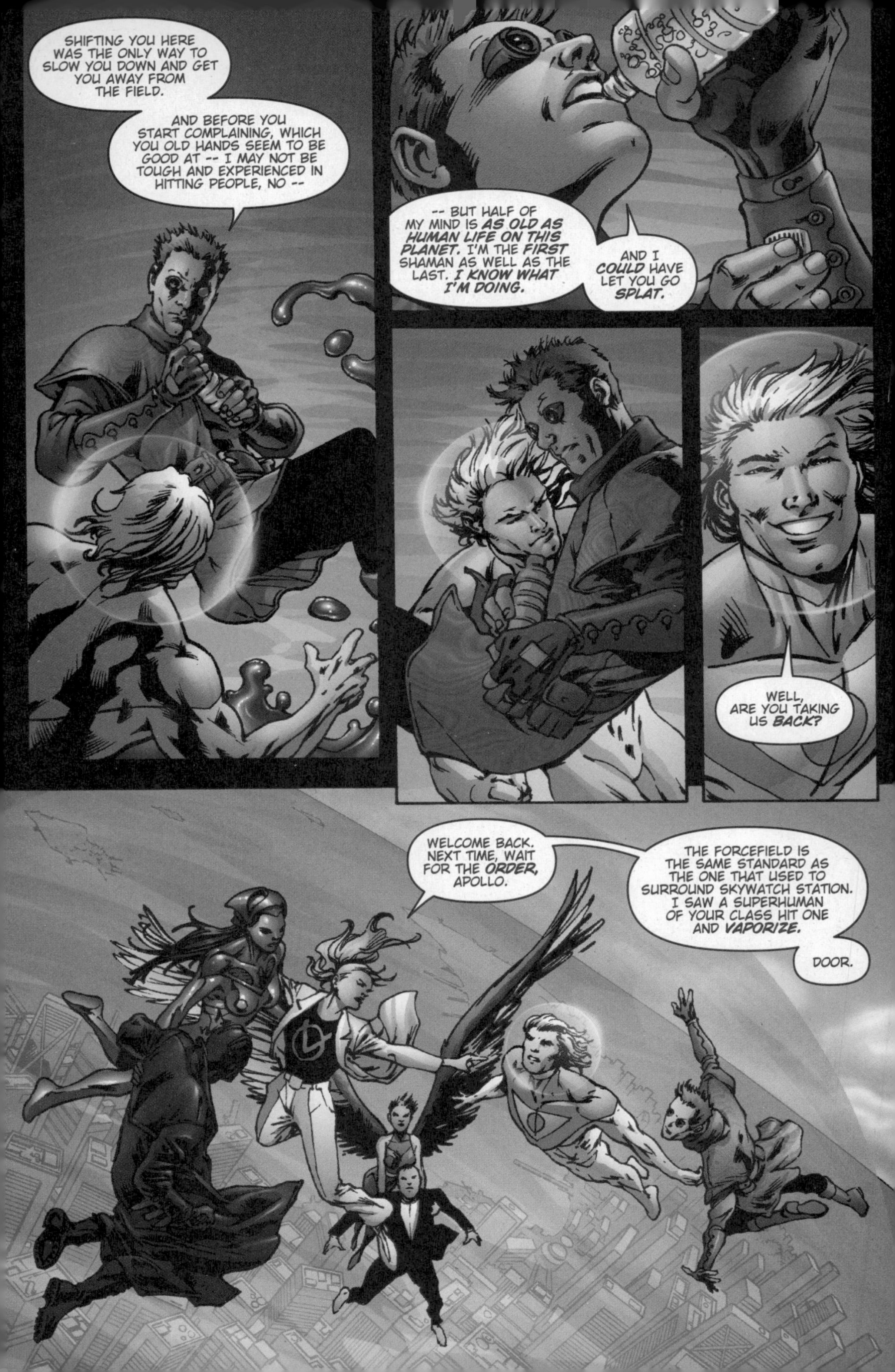
SHIFTING YOU HERE WAS THE ONLY WAY TO SLOW YOU DOWN AND GET YOU AWAY FROM THE FIELD.
AND BEFORE YOU START COMPLAINING, WHICH YOU OLD HANDS SEEM TO BE GOOD AT -- I MAY NOT BE TOUGH AND EXPERIENCED IN HITTING PEOPLE, NO --
-- BUT HALF OF MY MIND IS AS OLD AS HUMAN LIFE ON THIS PLANET. I'M THE FIRST SHAMAN AS WELL AS THE LAST. I KNOW WHAT I'M DOING.
AND I COULD HAVE LET YOU GO SPLAT.
WELL, ARE YOU TAKING US BACK?
WELCOME BACK. NEXT TIME, WAIT FOR THE ORDER, APOLLO.
THE FORCEFIELD IS THE SAME STANDARD AS THE ONE THAT USED TO SURROUND SKYWATCH STATION. I SAW A SUPERHUMAN OF YOUR CLASS HIT ONE AND VAPORIZE.
DOOR.

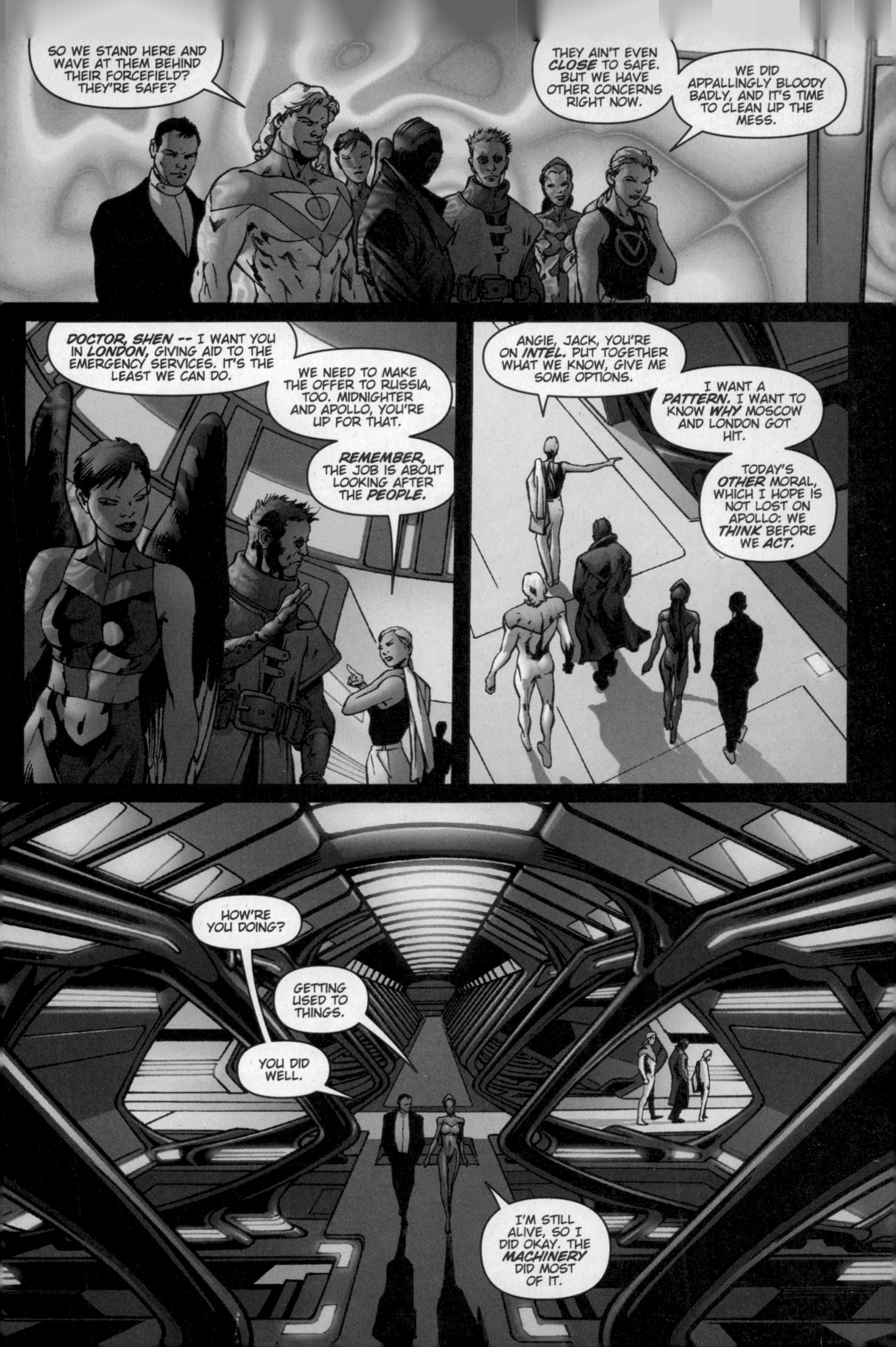
SO WE STAND HERE AND WAVE AT THEM BEHIND THEIR FORCEFIELD? THEY'RE SAFE?
THEY AIN'T EVEN CLOSE TO SAFE. BUT WE HAVE OTHER CONCERNS RIGHT NOW.
WE DID APPALLINGLY BLOODY BADLY, AND IT'S TIME TO CLEAN UP THE MESS.
DOCTOR, SHEN -- I WANT YOU IN LONDON, GIVING AID TO THE EMERGENCY SERVICES. IT'S THE LEAST WE CAN DO.
WE NEED TO MAKE THE OFFER TO RUSSIA, TOO. MIDNIGHTER AND APOLLO, YOU'RE UP FOR THAT.
REMEMBER, THE JOB IS ABOUT LOOKING AFTER THE PEOPLE.
ANGIE, JACK, YOU'RE ON INTEL. PUT TOGETHER WHAT WE KNOW, GIVE ME SOME OPTIONS.
I WANT A PATTERN. I WANT TO KNOW WHY MOSCOW AND LONDON GOT HIT.
TODAY'S OTHER MORAL, WHICH I HOPE IS NOT LOST ON APOLLO: WE THINK BEFORE WE ACT.
HOW'RE YOU DOING?
GETTING USED TO THINGS.
YOU DID WELL.
I'M STILL ALIVE, SO I DID OKAY. THE MACHINERY DID MOST OF IT.

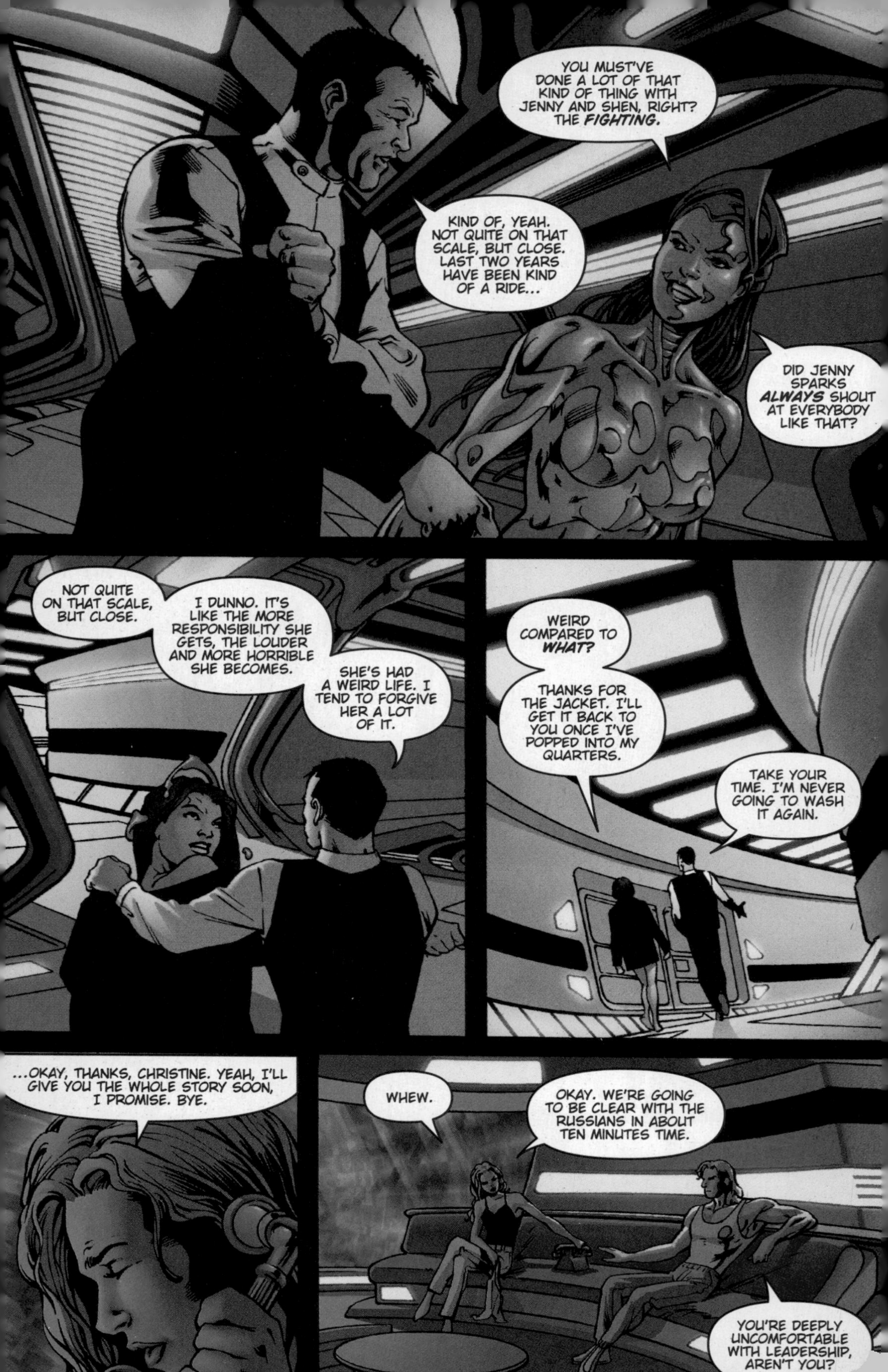
YOU MUST'VE DONE A LOT OF THAT KIND OF THING WITH JENNY AND SHEN, RIGHT? THE FIGHTING.
KIND OF, YEAH. NOT QUITE ON THAT SCALE, BUT CLOSE. LAST TWO YEARS HAVE BEEN KIND OF A RIDE...
DID JENNY SPARKS ALWAYS SHOUT AT EVERYBODY LIKE THAT?
NOT QUITE ON THAT SCALE, BUT CLOSE.
I DUNNO. IT'S LIKE THE MORE RESPONSIBILITY SHE GETS, THE LOUDER AND MORE HORRIBLE SHE BECOMES.
SHE'S HAD A WEIRD LIFE. I TEND TO FORGIVE HER A LOT OF IT.
WEIRD COMPARED TO WHAT?
THANKS FOR THE JACKET. I'LL GET IT BACK TO YOU ONCE I'VE POPPED INTO MY QUARTERS.
TAKE YOUR TIME. I'M NEVER GOING TO WASH IT AGAIN.
...OKAY, THANKS, CHRISTINE. YEAH, I'LL GIVE YOU THE WHOLE STORY SOON, I PROMISE. BYE.
WHEW.
OKAY. WE'RE GOING TO BE CLEAR WITH THE RUSSIANS IN ABOUT TEN MINUTES TIME.
YOU'RE DEEPLY UNCOMFORTABLE WITH LEADERSHIP, AREN'T YOU?

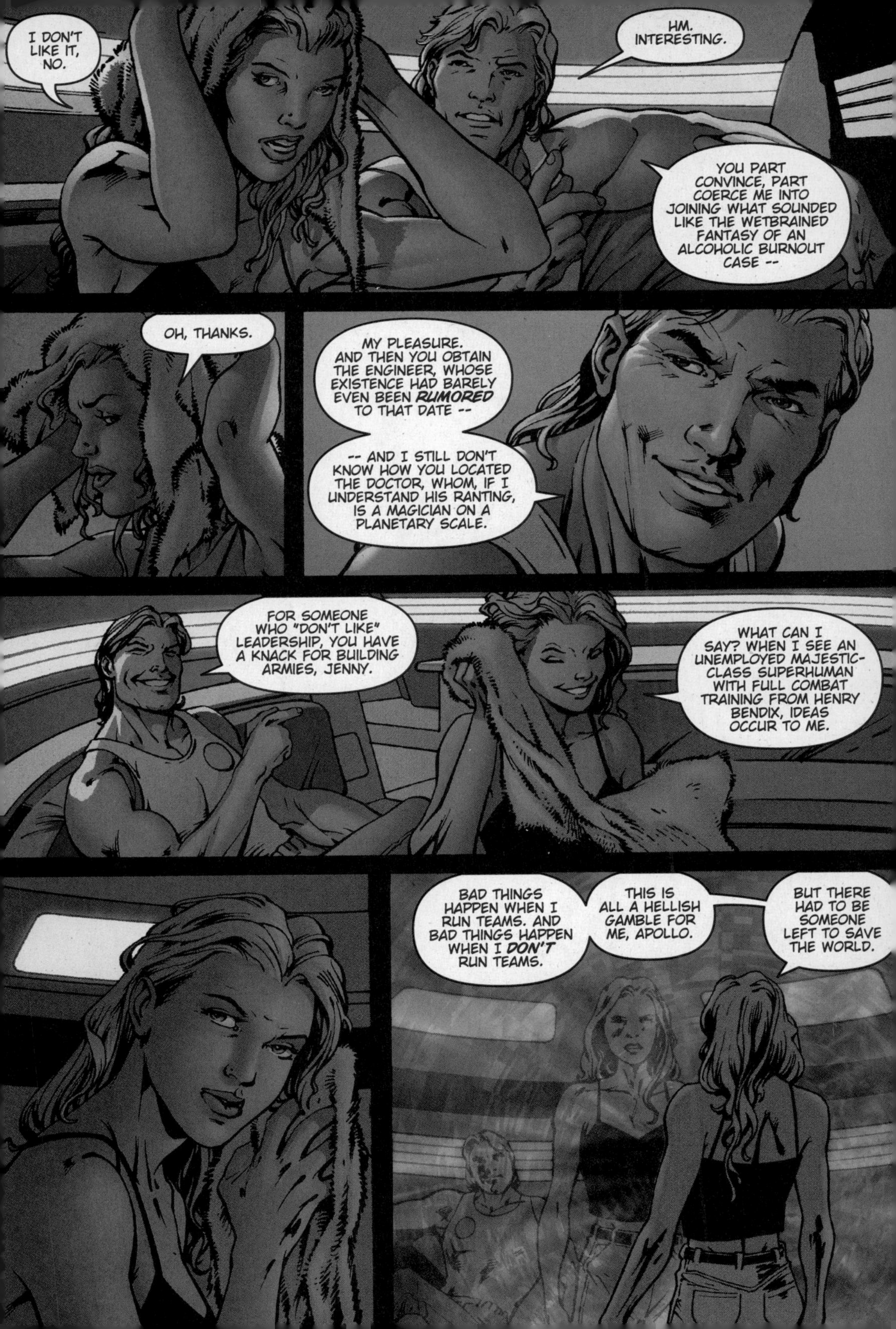
I DON'T LIKE IT, NO.
HM. INTERESTING.
YOU PART CONVINCE, PART COERCE ME INTO JOINING WHAT SOUNDED LIKE THE WETBRAINED FANTASY OF AN ALCOHOLIC BURNOUT CASE --
OH, THANKS.
MY PLEASURE. AND THEN YOU OBTAIN THE ENGINEER, WHOSE EXISTENCE HAD BARELY EVEN BEEN RUMORED TO THAT DATE --
-- AND I STILL DON'T KNOW HOW YOU LOCATED THE DOCTOR, WHOM, IF I UNDERSTAND HIS RANTING, IS A MAGICIAN ON A PLANETARY SCALE.
FOR SOMEONE WHO "DON'T LIKE" LEADERSHIP, YOU HAVE A KNACK FOR BUILDING ARMIES, JENNY.
WHAT CAN I SAY? WHEN I SEE AN UNEMPLOYED MAJESTIC-CLASS SUPERHUMAN WITH FULL COMBAT TRAINING FROM HENRY BENDIX, IDEAS OCCUR TO ME.
BAD THINGS HAPPEN WHEN I RUN TEAMS. AND BAD THINGS HAPPEN WHEN I DON'T RUN TEAMS.
THIS IS ALL A HELLISH GAMBLE FOR ME, APOLLO.
BUT THERE HAD TO BE SOMEONE LEFT TO SAVE THE WORLD.

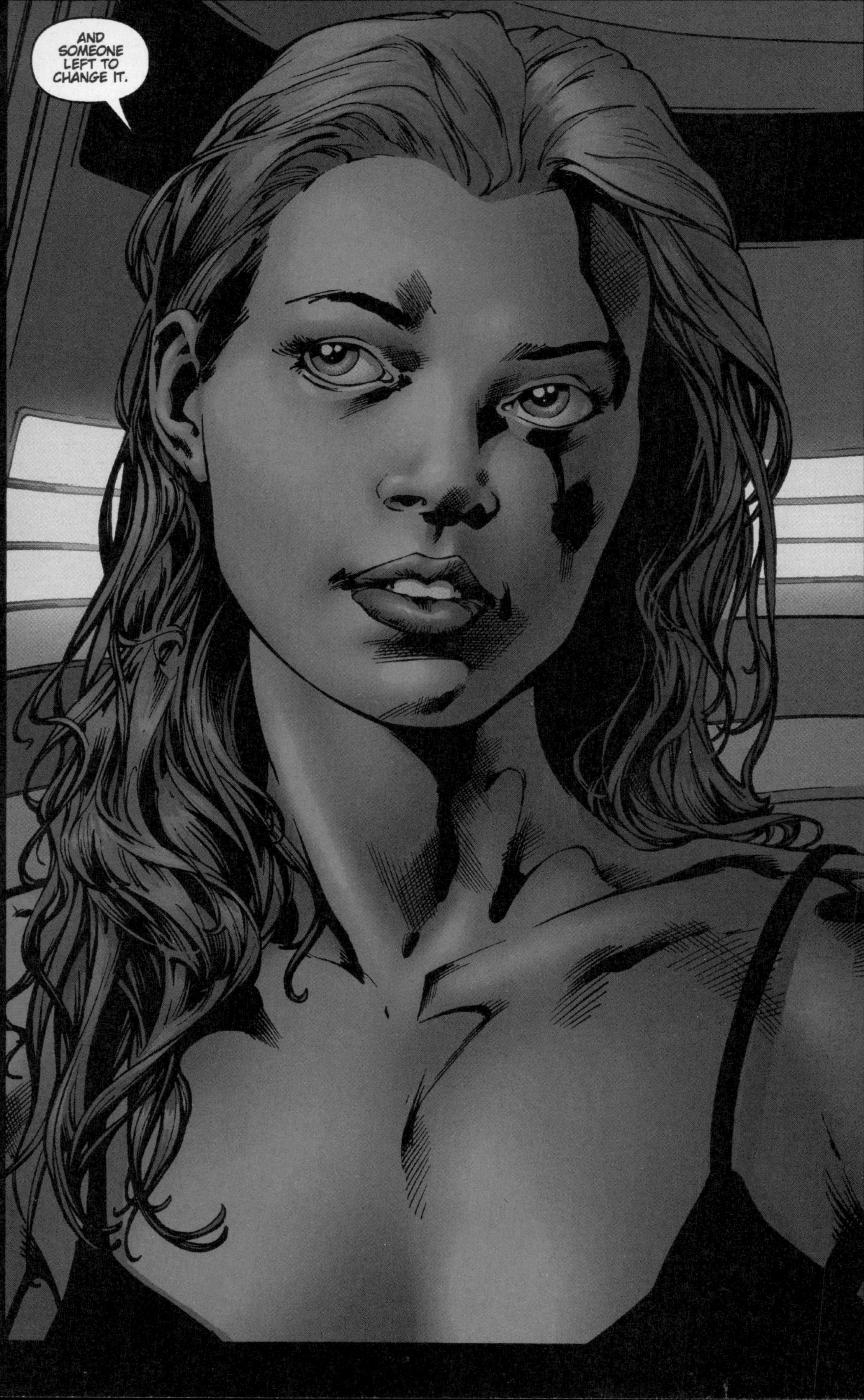
AND SOMEONE LEFT TO CHANGE IT.

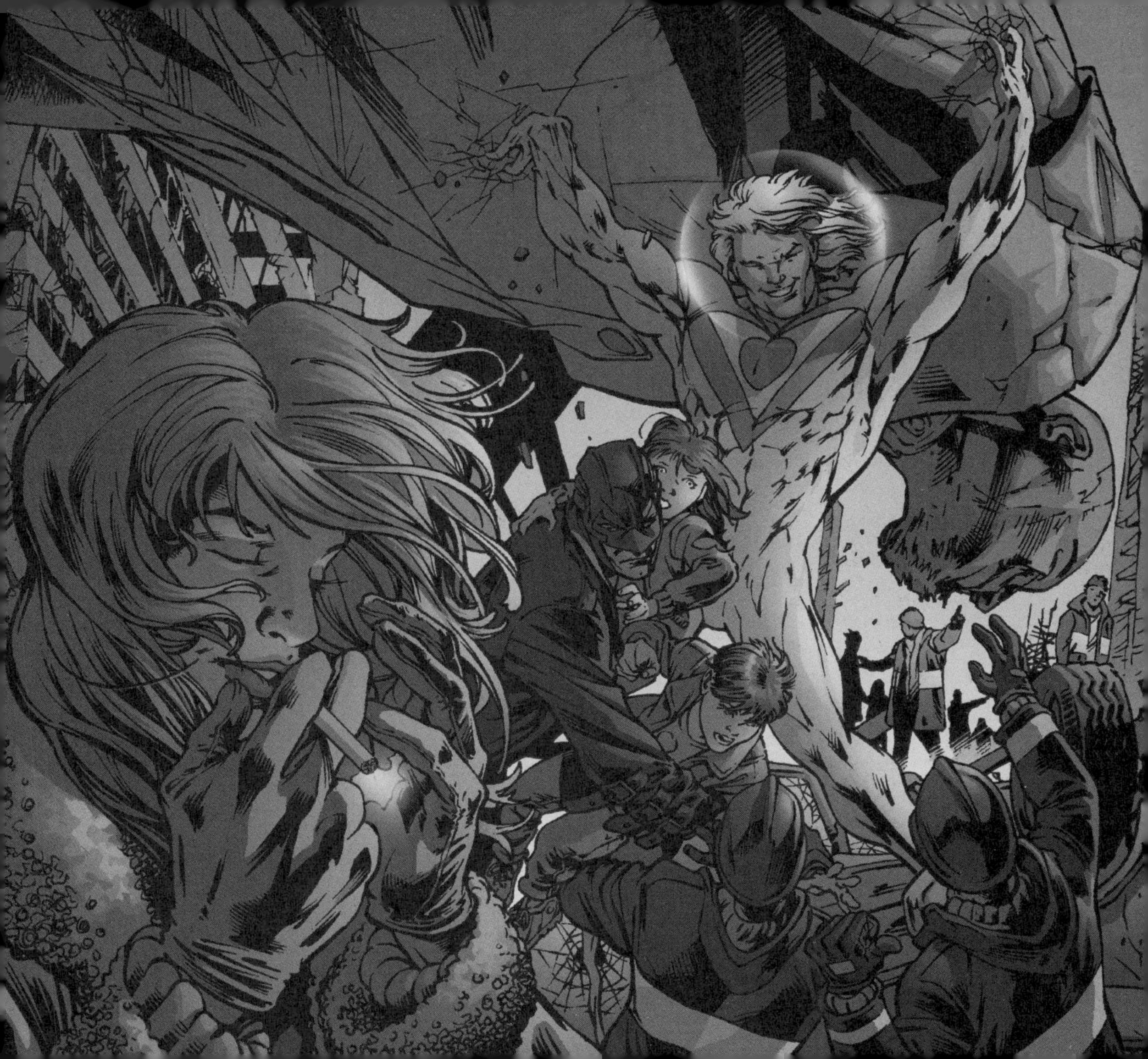

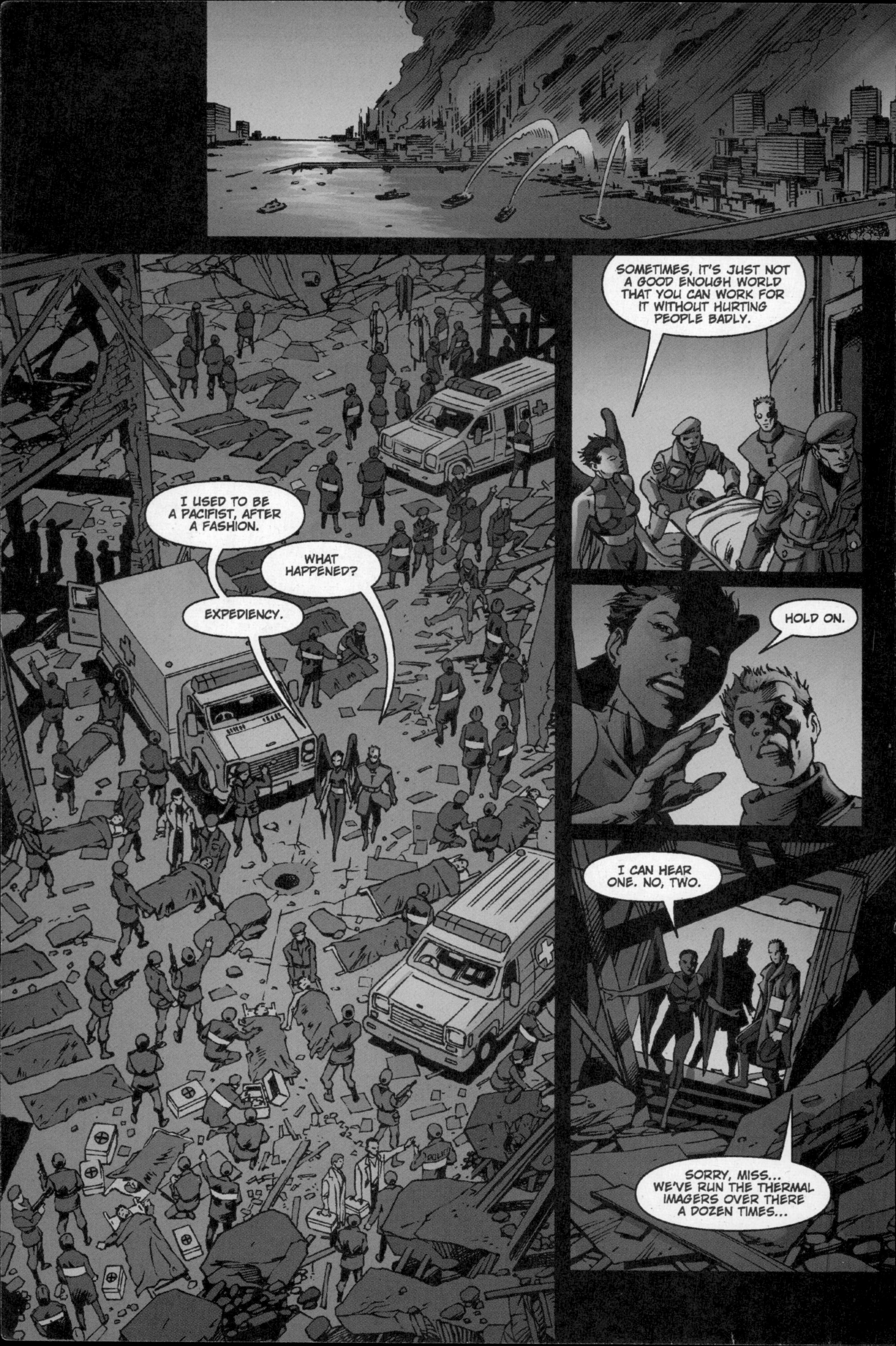
I USED TO BE A PACIFIST, AFTER A FASHION.
WHAT HAPPENED?
EXPEDIENCY.
SOMETIMES, IT'S JUST NOT A GOOD ENOUGH WORLD THAT YOU CAN WORK FOR IT WITHOUT HURTING PEOPLE BADLY.
HOLD ON.
I CAN HEAR ONE. NO, TWO.
SORRY, MISS... WE'VE RUN THE THERMAL IMAGERS OVER THERE A DOZEN TIMES...

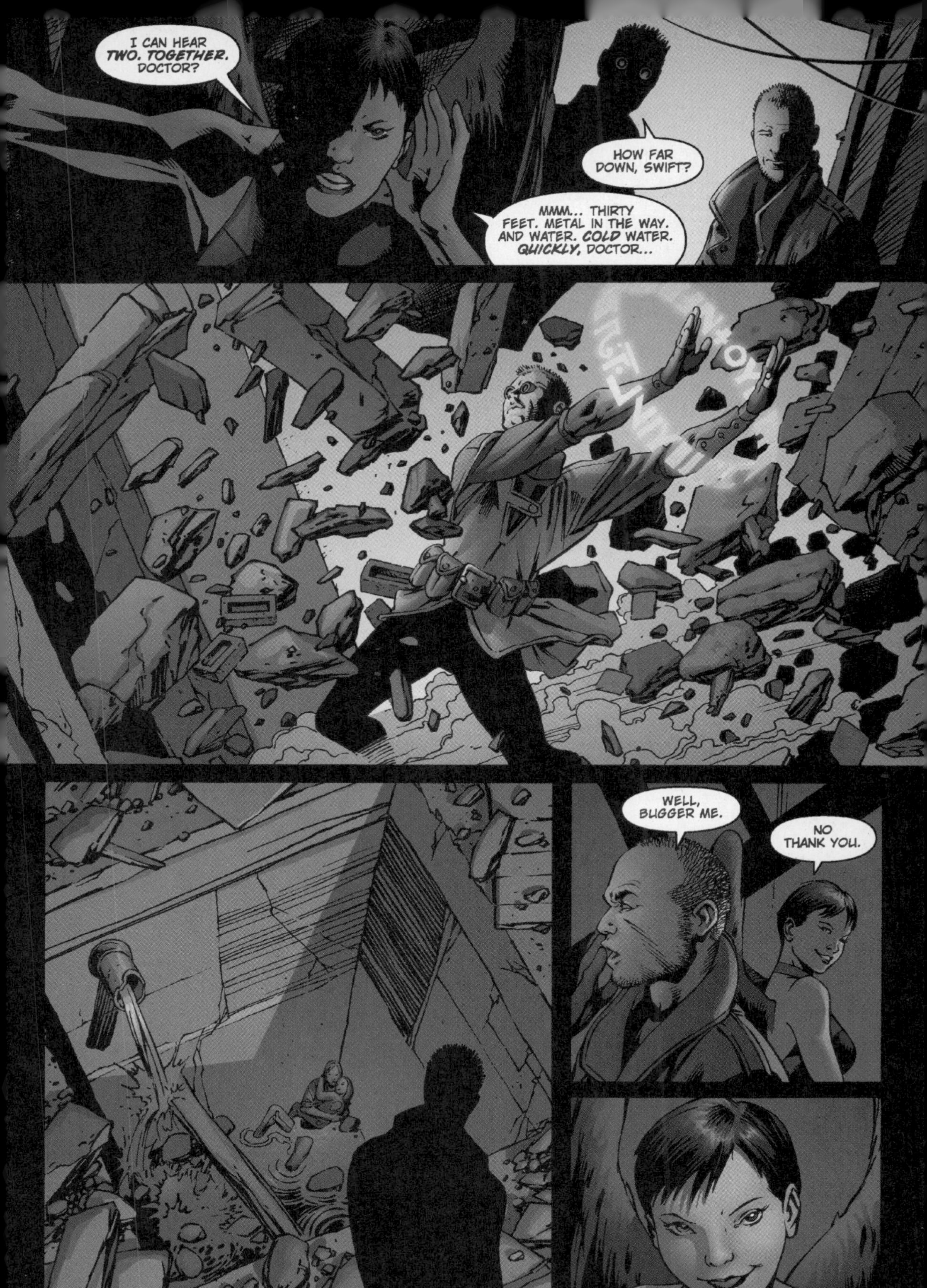
I CAN HEAR *TWO. TOGETHER.* DOCTOR?
HOW FAR DOWN, SWIFT?
MMM... THIRTY FEET. METAL IN THE WAY. AND WATER. *COLD* WATER. *QUICKLY*, DOCTOR...
WELL, BUGGER ME.
NO THANK YOU.

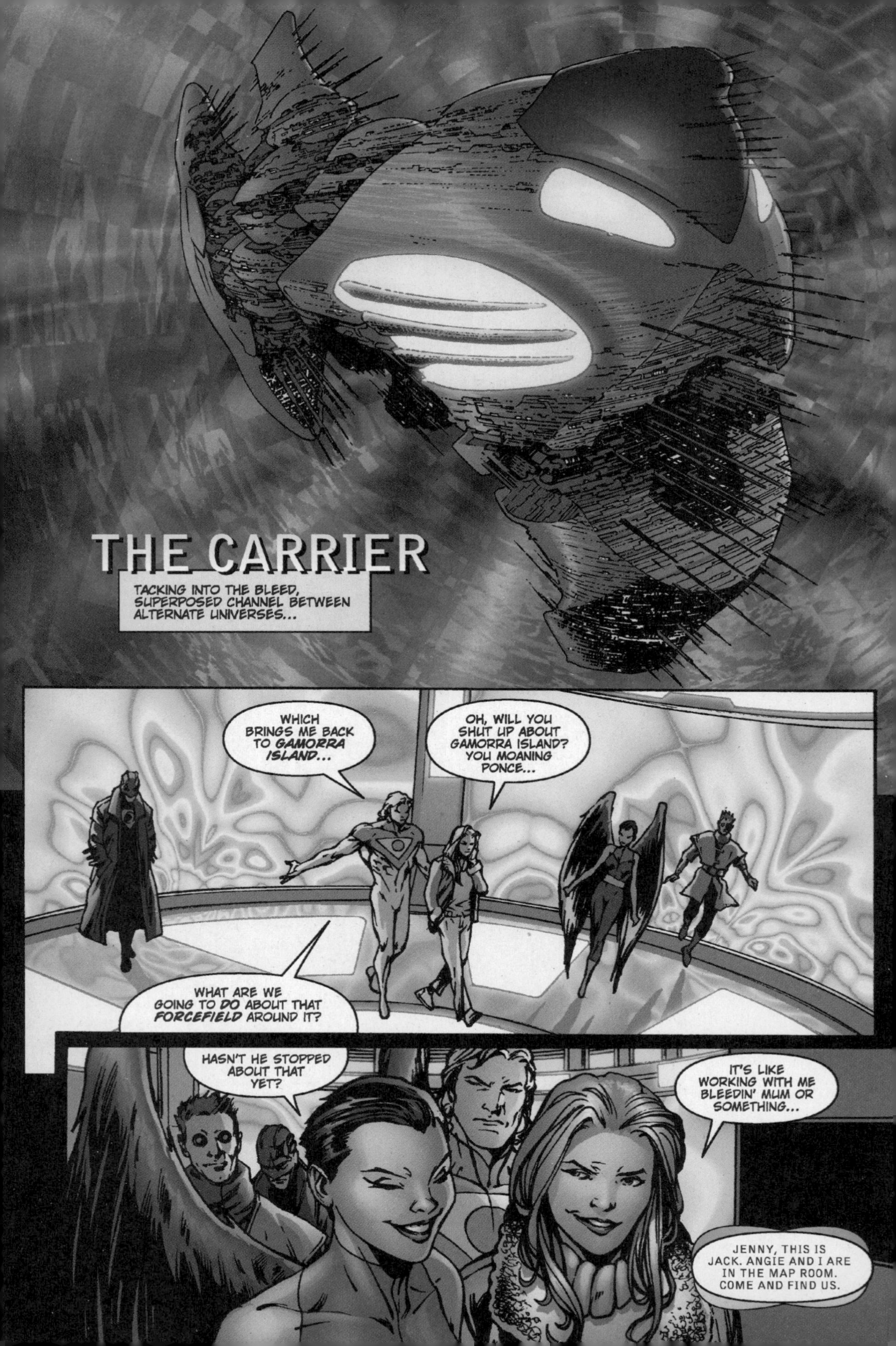
THE CARRIER
TACKING INTO THE BLEED, SUPERPOSED CHANNEL BETWEEN ALTERNATE UNIVERSES...
WHICH BRINGS ME BACK TO GAMORRA ISLAND...
OH, WILL YOU SHUT UP ABOUT GAMORRA ISLAND? YOU MOANING PONCE...
WHAT ARE WE GOING TO DO ABOUT THAT FORCEFIELD AROUND IT?
HASN'T HE STOPPED ABOUT THAT YET?
IT'S LIKE WORKING WITH ME BLEEDIN' MUM OR SOMETHING...
JENNY, THIS IS JACK. ANGIE AND I ARE IN THE MAP ROOM. COME AND FIND US.

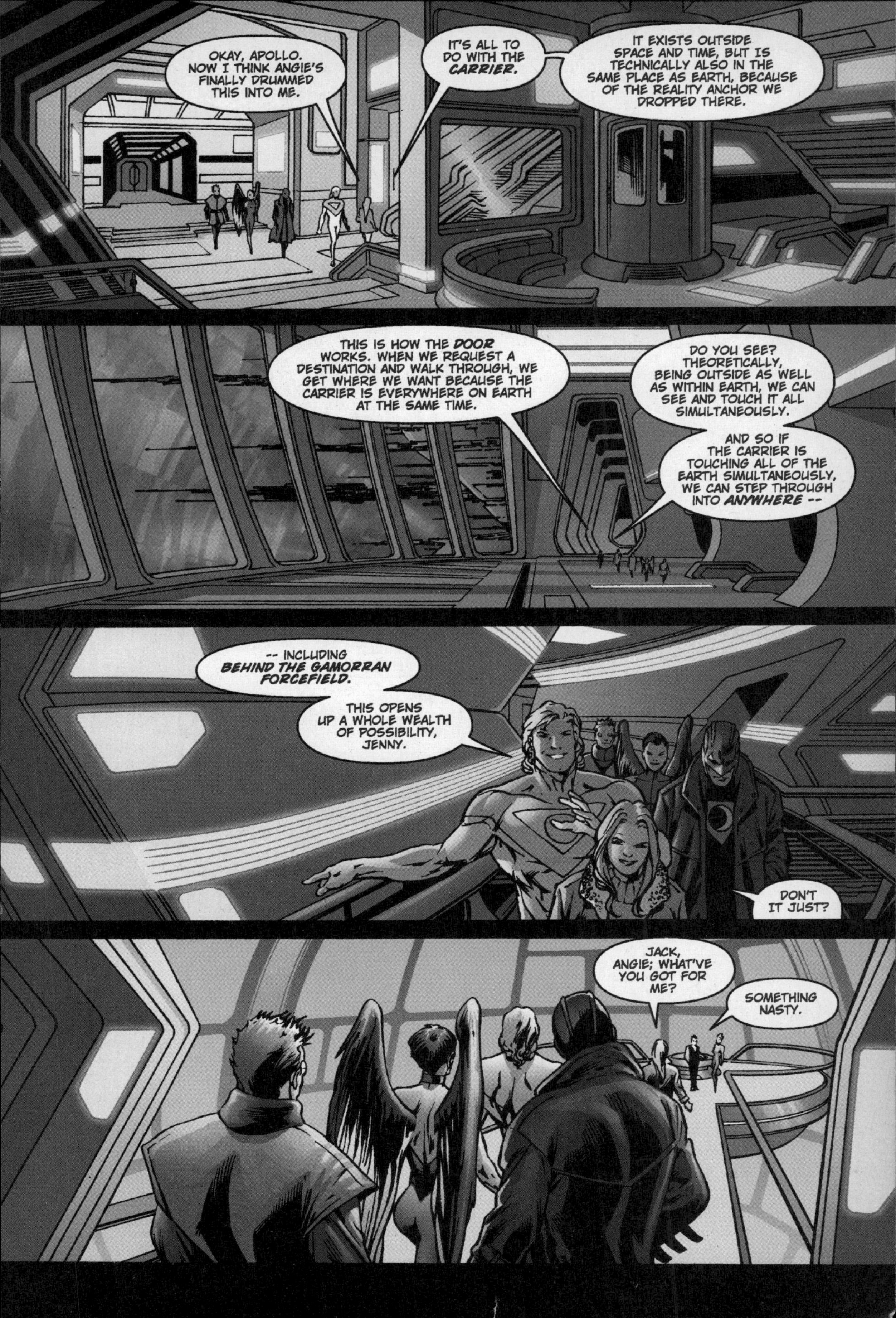
OKAY, APOLLO. NOW I THINK ANGIE'S FINALLY DRUMMED THIS INTO ME.
IT'S ALL TO DO WITH THE *CARRIER.*
IT EXISTS OUTSIDE SPACE AND TIME, BUT IS TECHNICALLY ALSO IN THE SAME PLACE AS EARTH, BECAUSE OF THE REALITY ANCHOR WE DROPPED THERE.
THIS IS HOW THE *DOOR* WORKS. WHEN WE REQUEST A DESTINATION AND WALK THROUGH, WE GET WHERE WE WANT BECAUSE THE CARRIER IS EVERYWHERE ON EARTH AT THE SAME TIME.
DO YOU SEE? THEORETICALLY, BEING OUTSIDE AS WELL AS WITHIN EARTH, WE CAN SEE AND TOUCH IT ALL SIMULTANEOUSLY.
AND SO IF THE CARRIER IS TOUCHING ALL OF THE EARTH SIMULTANEOUSLY, WE CAN STEP THROUGH INTO ***ANYWHERE*** --
-- INCLUDING ***BEHIND THE GAMORRAN FORCEFIELD.***
THIS OPENS UP A WHOLE WEALTH OF POSSIBILITY, JENNY.
DON'T IT JUST?
JACK, ANGIE; WHAT'VE YOU GOT FOR ME?
SOMETHING NASTY.

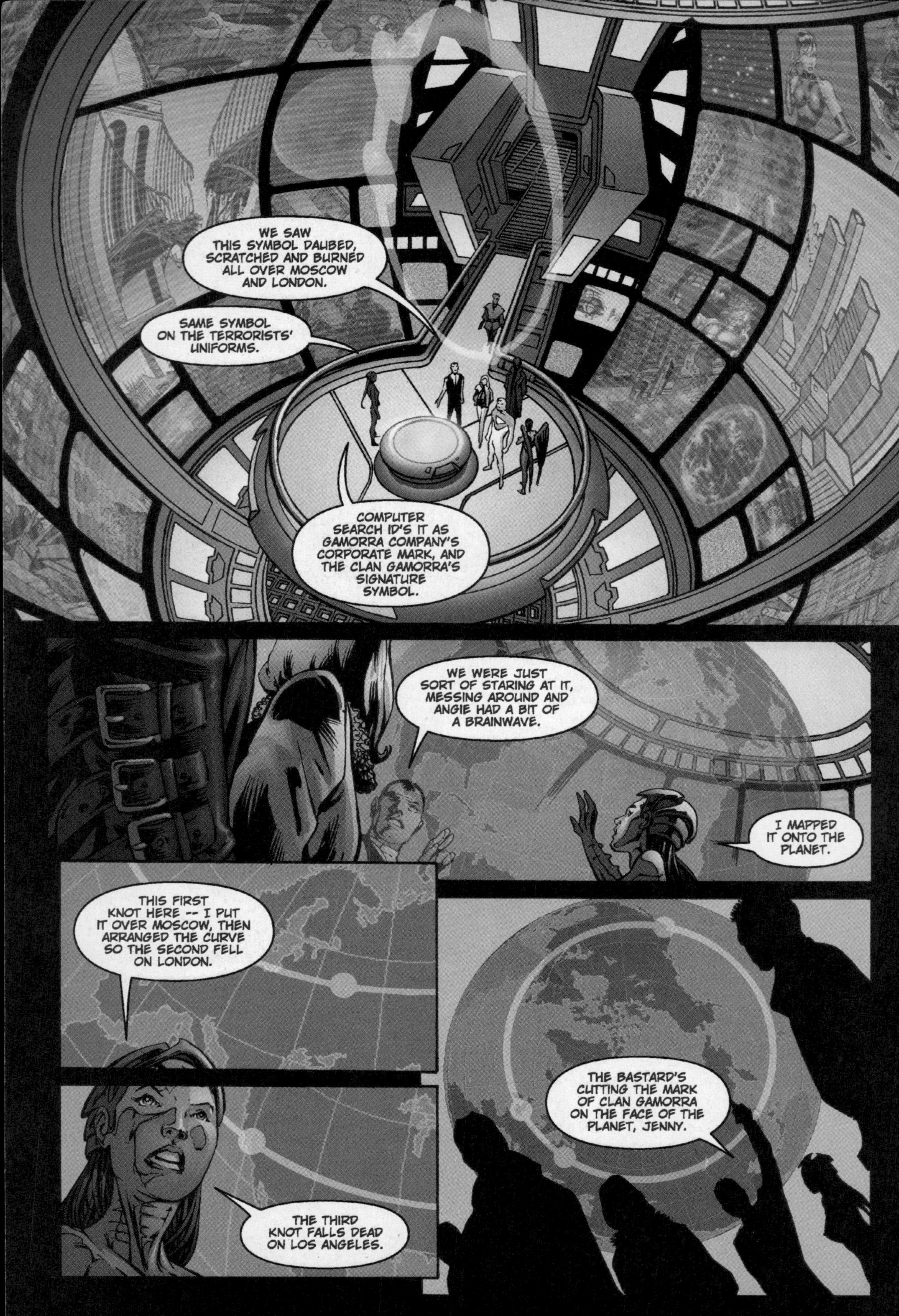
WE SAW THIS SYMBOL DAUBED, SCRATCHED AND BURNED ALL OVER MOSCOW AND LONDON.
SAME SYMBOL ON THE TERRORISTS' UNIFORMS.
COMPUTER SEARCH ID'S IT AS GAMORRA COMPANY'S CORPORATE MARK, AND THE CLAN GAMORRA'S SIGNATURE SYMBOL.
WE WERE JUST SORT OF STARING AT IT, MESSING AROUND AND ANGIE HAD A BIT OF A BRAINWAVE.
I MAPPED IT ONTO THE PLANET.
THIS FIRST KNOT HERE -- I PUT IT OVER MOSCOW, THEN ARRANGED THE CURVE SO THE SECOND FELL ON LONDON.
THE THIRD KNOT FALLS DEAD ON LOS ANGELES.
THE BASTARD'S CUTTING THE MARK OF CLAN GAMORRA ON THE FACE OF THE PLANET, JENNY.

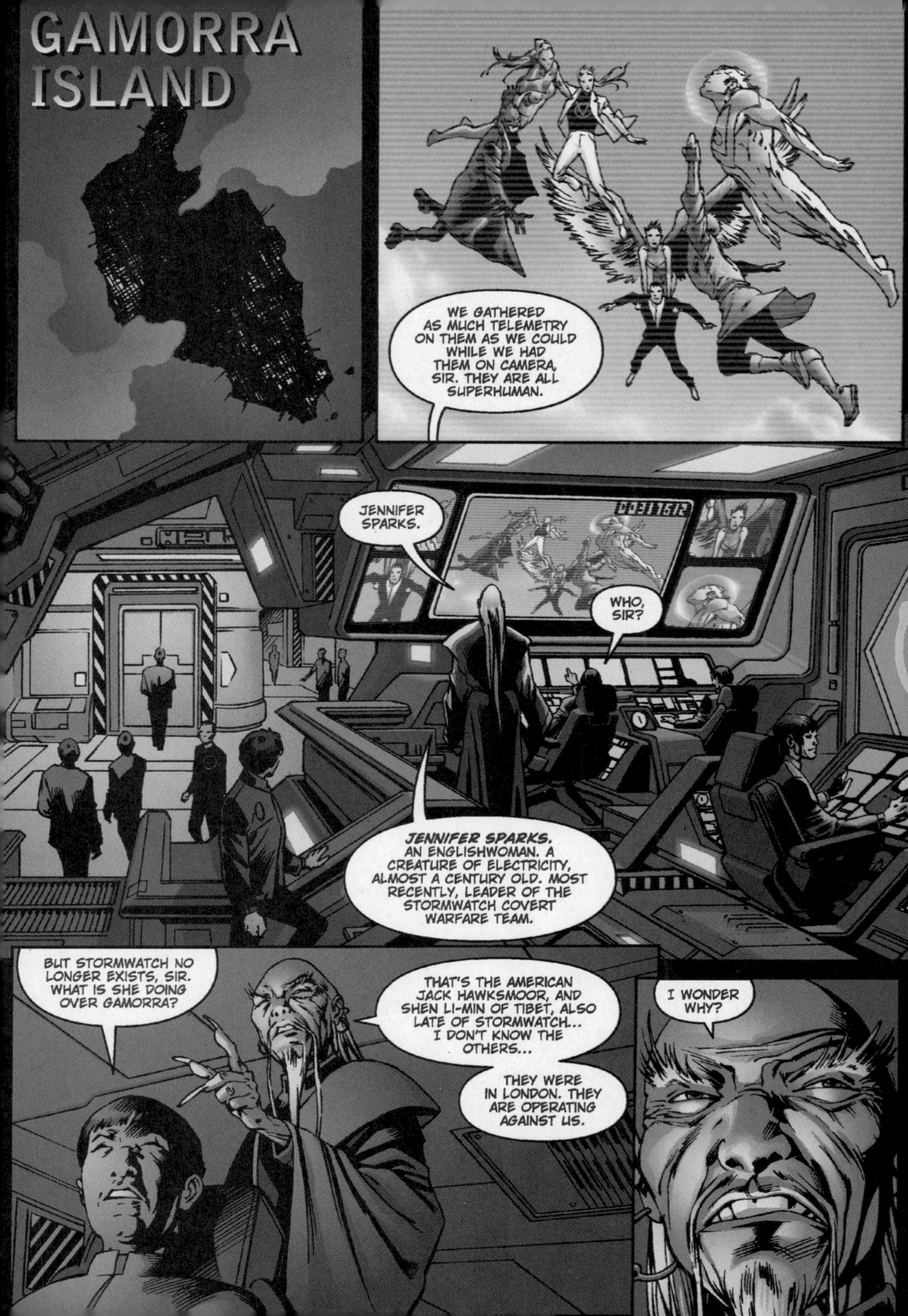
GAMORRA ISLAND
WE GATHERED AS MUCH TELEMETRY ON THEM AS WE COULD WHILE WE HAD THEM ON CAMERA, SIR. THEY ARE ALL SUPERHUMAN.
JENNIFER SPARKS.
WHO, SIR?
JENNIFER SPARKS. AN ENGLISHWOMAN. A CREATURE OF ELECTRICITY, ALMOST A CENTURY OLD. MOST RECENTLY, LEADER OF THE STORMWATCH COVERT WARFARE TEAM.
BUT STORMWATCH NO LONGER EXISTS, SIR. WHAT IS SHE DOING OVER GAMORRA?
THAT'S THE AMERICAN JACK HAWKSMOOR, AND SHEN LI-MIN OF TIBET, ALSO LATE OF STORMWATCH... I DON'T KNOW THE OTHERS...
THEY WERE IN LONDON. THEY ARE OPERATING AGAINST US.
I WONDER WHY?

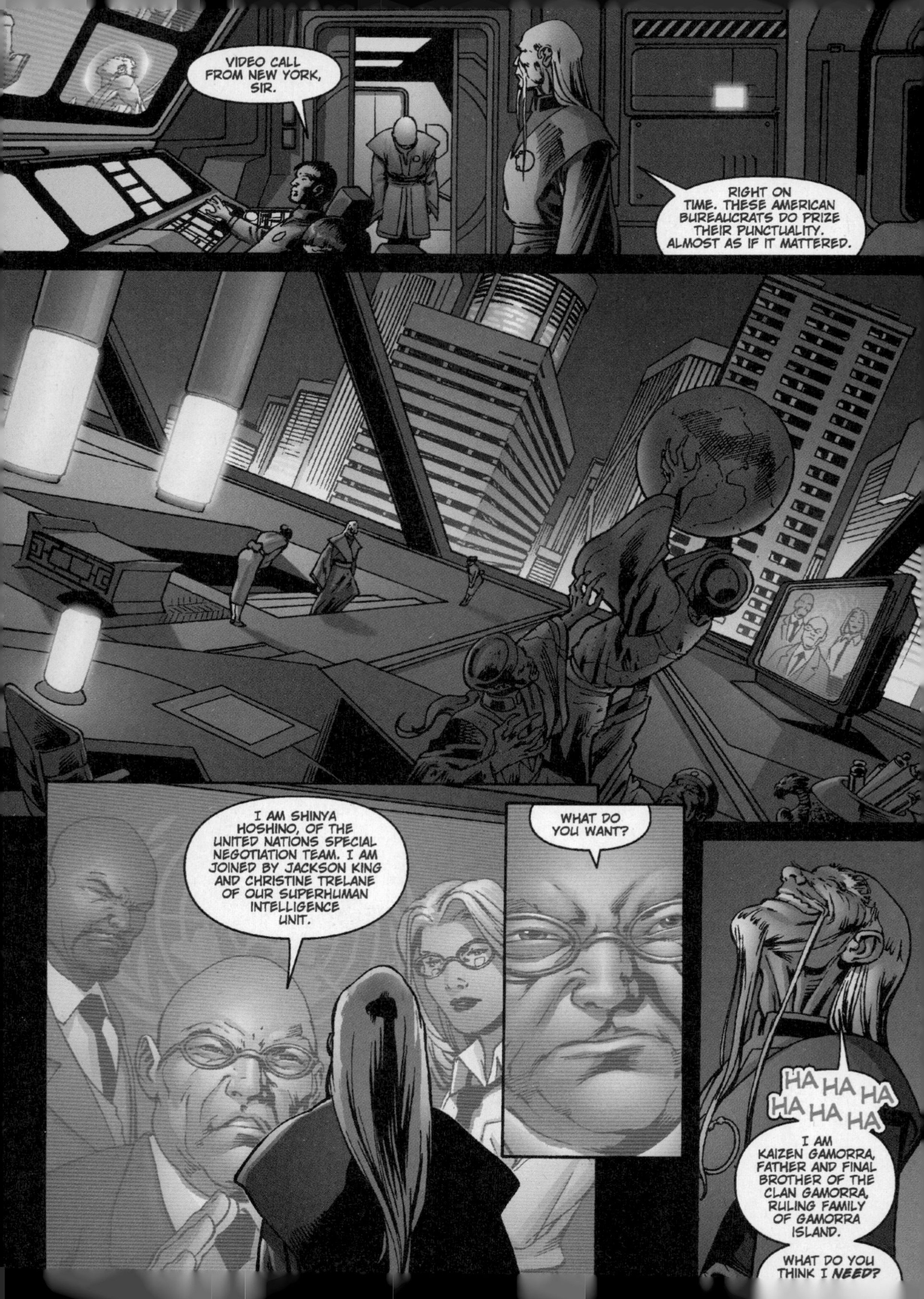
VIDEO CALL FROM NEW YORK, SIR.
RIGHT ON TIME. THESE AMERICAN BUREAUCRATS DO PRIZE THEIR PUNCTUALITY. ALMOST AS IF IT MATTERED.
I AM SHINYA HOSHINO, OF THE UNITED NATIONS SPECIAL NEGOTIATION TEAM. I AM JOINED BY JACKSON KING AND CHRISTINE TRELANE OF OUR SUPERHUMAN INTELLIGENCE UNIT.
WHAT DO YOU WANT?
HA HA HA HA HA HA
I AM KAIZEN GAMORRA, FATHER AND FINAL BROTHER OF THE CLAN GAMORRA, RULING FAMILY OF GAMORRA ISLAND.
WHAT DO YOU THINK I NEED?

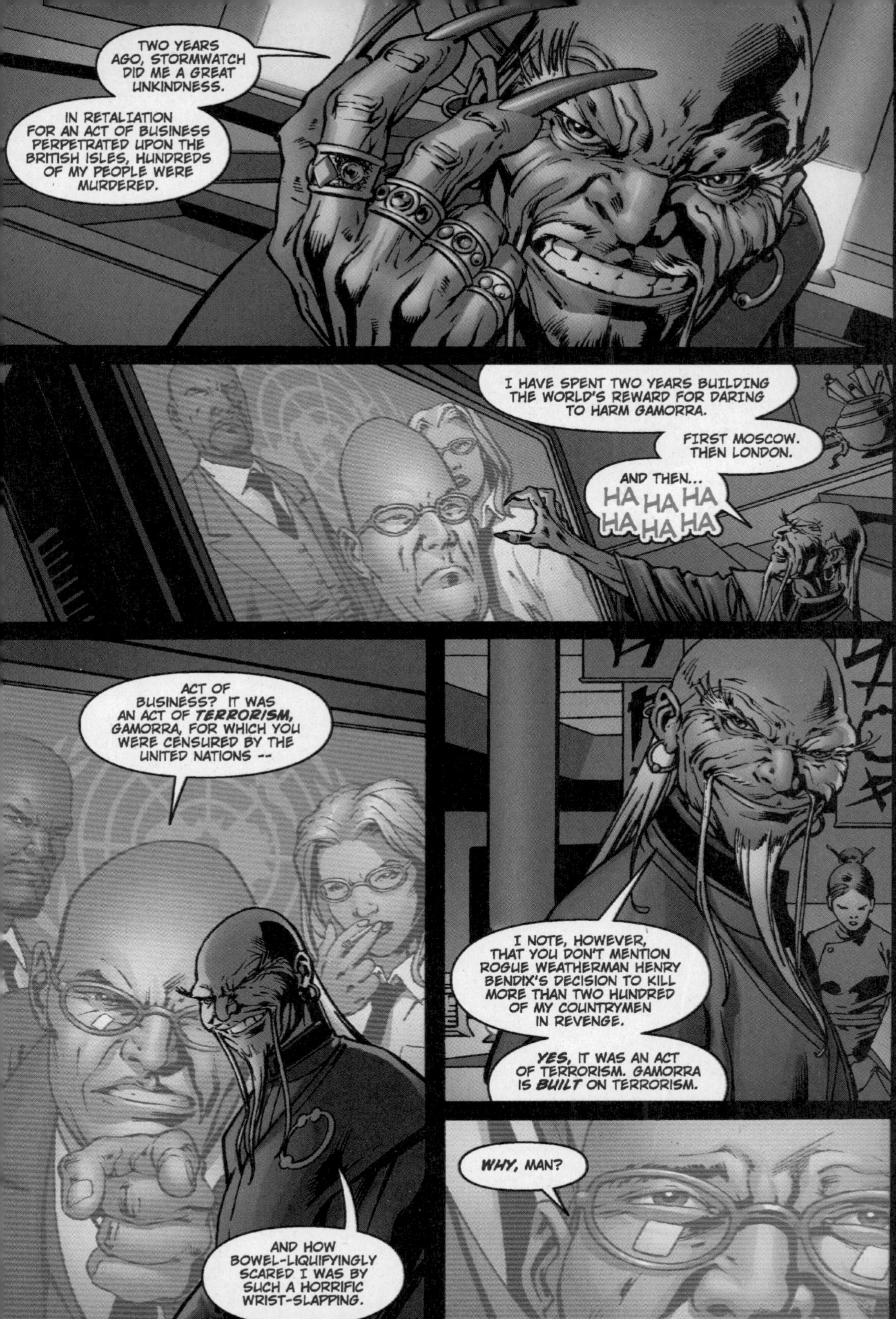

TWO YEARS AGO, STORMWATCH DID ME A GREAT UNKINDNESS.
IN RETALIATION FOR AN ACT OF BUSINESS PERPETRATED UPON THE BRITISH ISLES, HUNDREDS OF MY PEOPLE WERE MURDERED.
I HAVE SPENT TWO YEARS BUILDING THE WORLD'S REWARD FOR DARING TO HARM GAMORRA.
FIRST MOSCOW. THEN LONDON.
AND THEN... HA HA HA HA HA HA
ACT OF BUSINESS? IT WAS AN ACT OF TERRORISM, GAMORRA, FOR WHICH YOU WERE CENSURED BY THE UNITED NATIONS --
AND HOW BOWEL-LIQUIFYINGLY SCARED I WAS BY SUCH A HORRIFIC WRIST-SLAPPING.
I NOTE, HOWEVER, THAT YOU DON'T MENTION ROGUE WEATHERMAN HENRY BENDIX'S DECISION TO KILL MORE THAN TWO HUNDRED OF MY COUNTRYMEN IN REVENGE.
YES, IT WAS AN ACT OF TERRORISM. GAMORRA IS BUILT ON TERRORISM.
WHY, MAN?

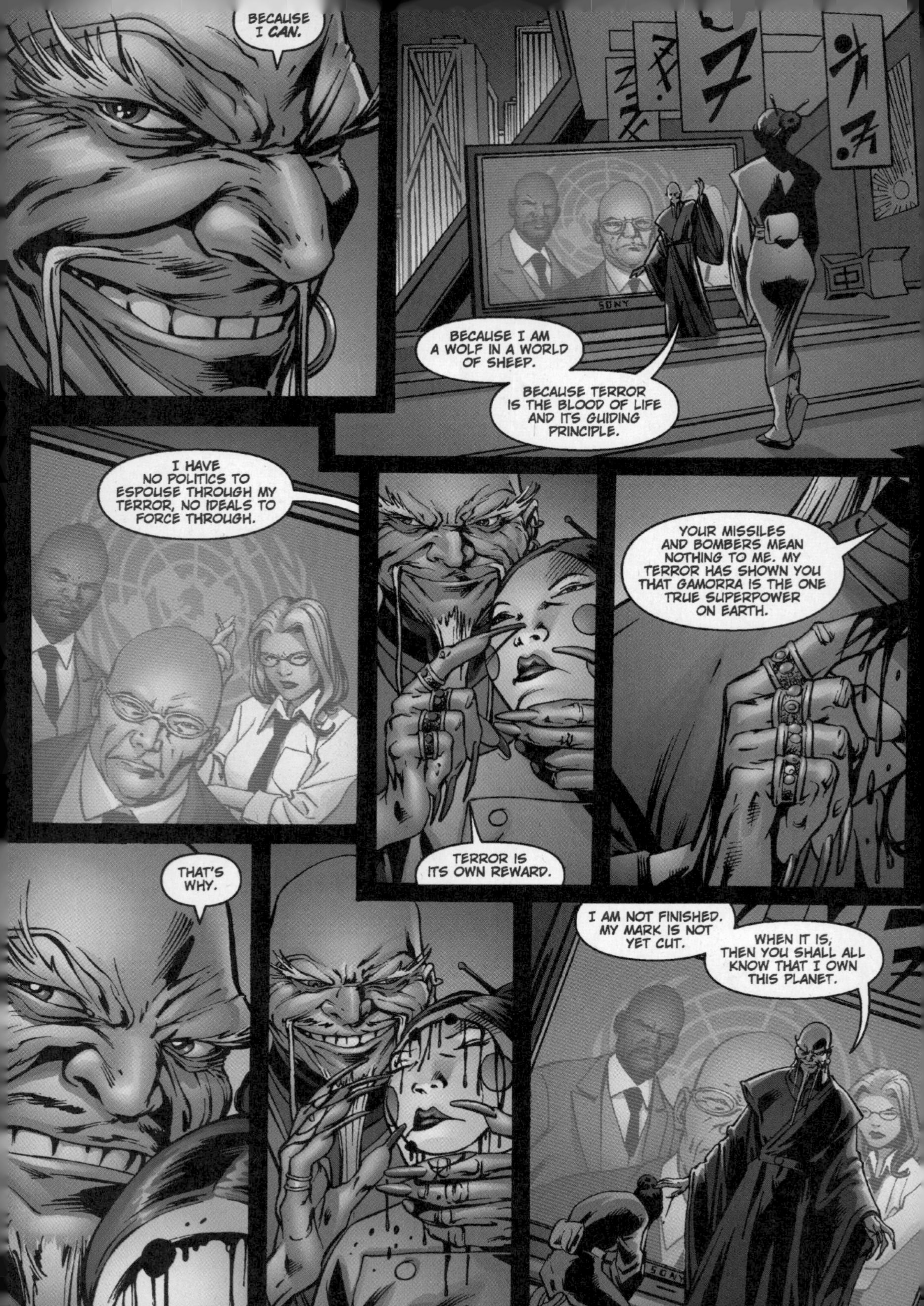
BECAUSE I CAN.
BECAUSE I AM A WOLF IN A WORLD OF SHEEP.
BECAUSE TERROR IS THE BLOOD OF LIFE AND ITS GUIDING PRINCIPLE.
I HAVE NO POLITICS TO ESPOUSE THROUGH MY TERROR, NO IDEALS TO FORCE THROUGH.
TERROR IS ITS OWN REWARD.
YOUR MISSILES AND BOMBERS MEAN NOTHING TO ME. MY TERROR HAS SHOWN YOU THAT GAMORRA IS THE ONE TRUE SUPERPOWER ON EARTH.
THAT'S WHY.
I AM NOT FINISHED. MY MARK IS NOT YET CUT.
WHEN IT IS, THEN YOU SHALL ALL KNOW THAT I OWN THIS PLANET.

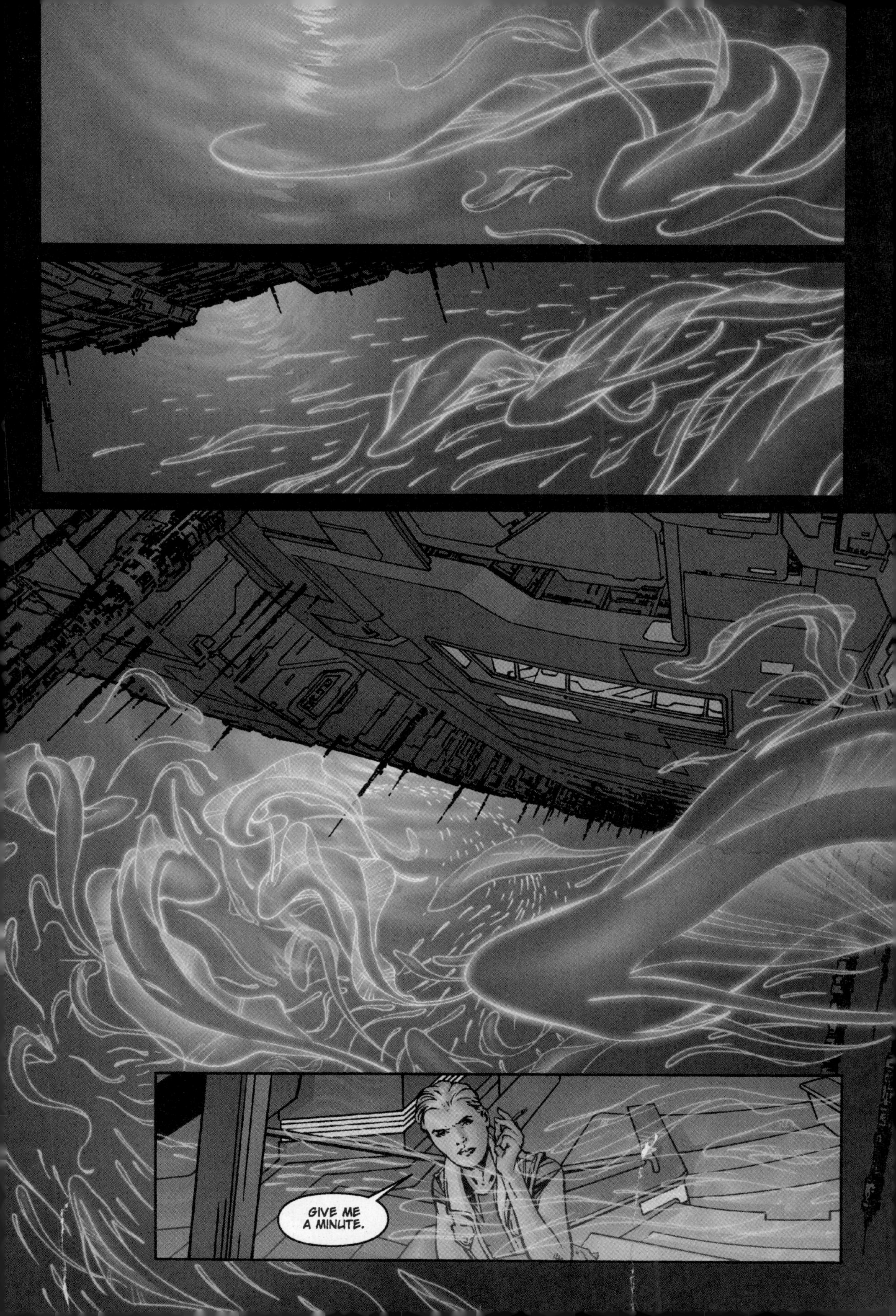
GIVE ME A MINUTE.

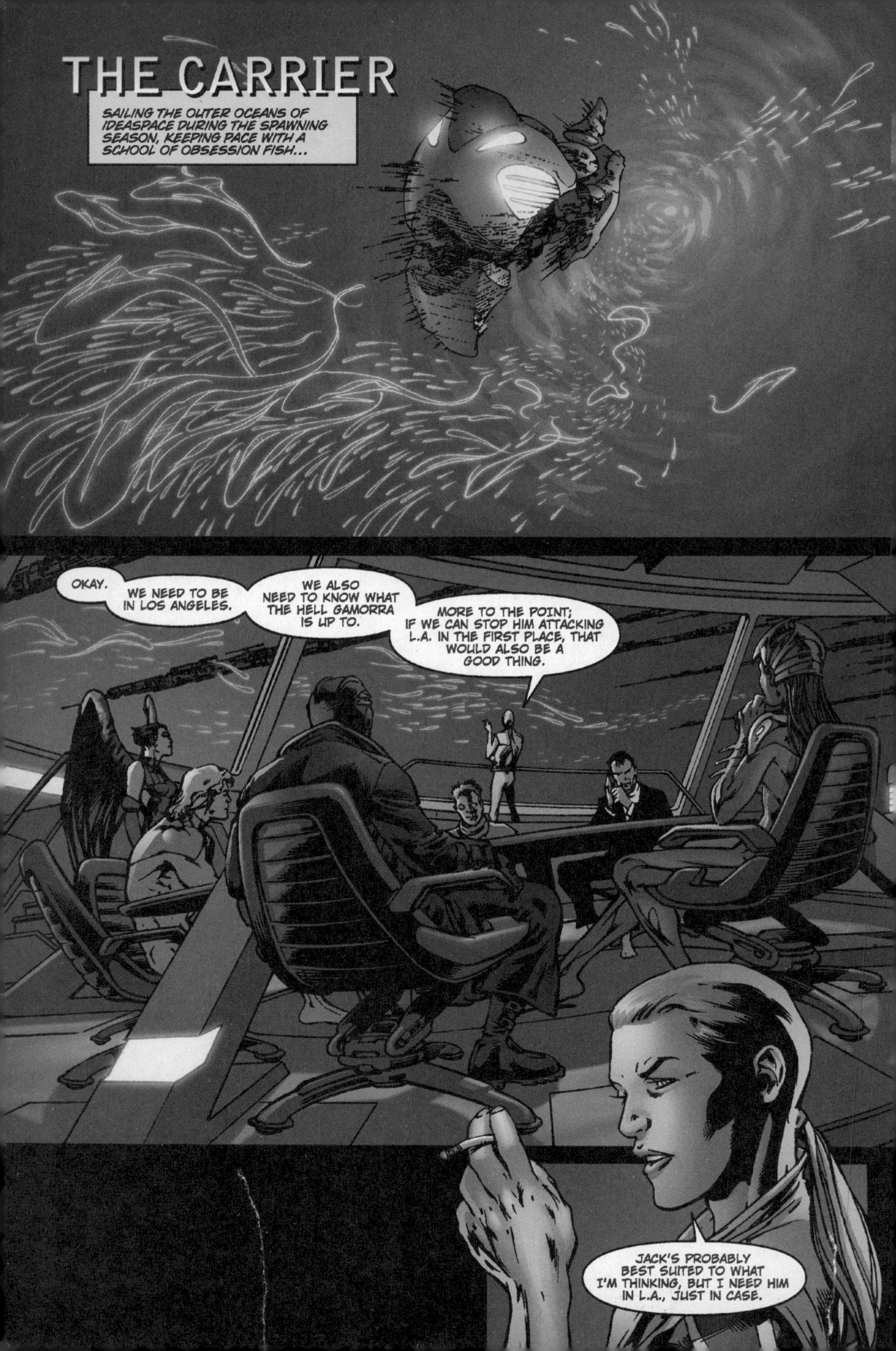
THE CARRIER
SAILING THE OUTER OCEANS OF IDEASPACE DURING THE SPAWNING SEASON, KEEPING PACE WITH A SCHOOL OF OBSESSION FISH...
OKAY.
WE NEED TO BE IN LOS ANGELES.
WE ALSO NEED TO KNOW WHAT THE HELL GAMORRA IS UP TO.
MORE TO THE POINT; IF WE CAN STOP HIM ATTACKING L.A. IN THE FIRST PLACE, THAT WOULD ALSO BE A GOOD THING.
JACK'S PROBABLY BEST SUITED TO WHAT I'M THINKING, BUT I NEED HIM IN L.A., JUST IN CASE.

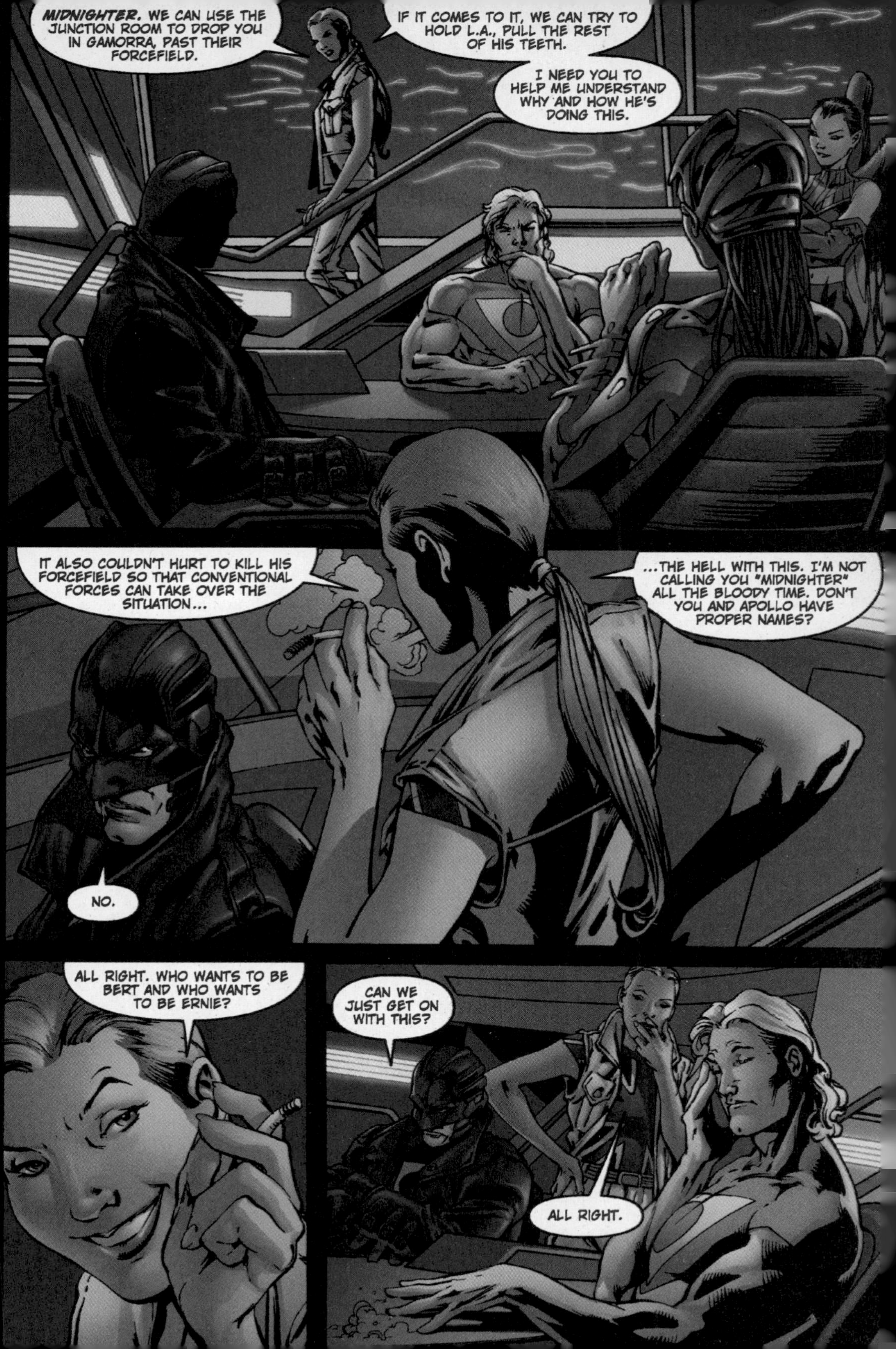
MIDNIGHTER. WE CAN USE THE JUNCTION ROOM TO DROP YOU IN GAMORRA, PAST THEIR FORCEFIELD.
IF IT COMES TO IT, WE CAN TRY TO HOLD L.A., PULL THE REST OF HIS TEETH.
I NEED YOU TO HELP ME UNDERSTAND WHY AND HOW HE'S DOING THIS.
IT ALSO COULDN'T HURT TO KILL HIS FORCEFIELD SO THAT CONVENTIONAL FORCES CAN TAKE OVER THE SITUATION...
NO.
...THE HELL WITH THIS. I'M NOT CALLING YOU "MIDNIGHTER" ALL THE BLOODY TIME. DON'T YOU AND APOLLO HAVE PROPER NAMES?
ALL RIGHT. WHO WANTS TO BE BERT AND WHO WANTS TO BE ERNIE?
CAN WE JUST GET ON WITH THIS?
ALL RIGHT.

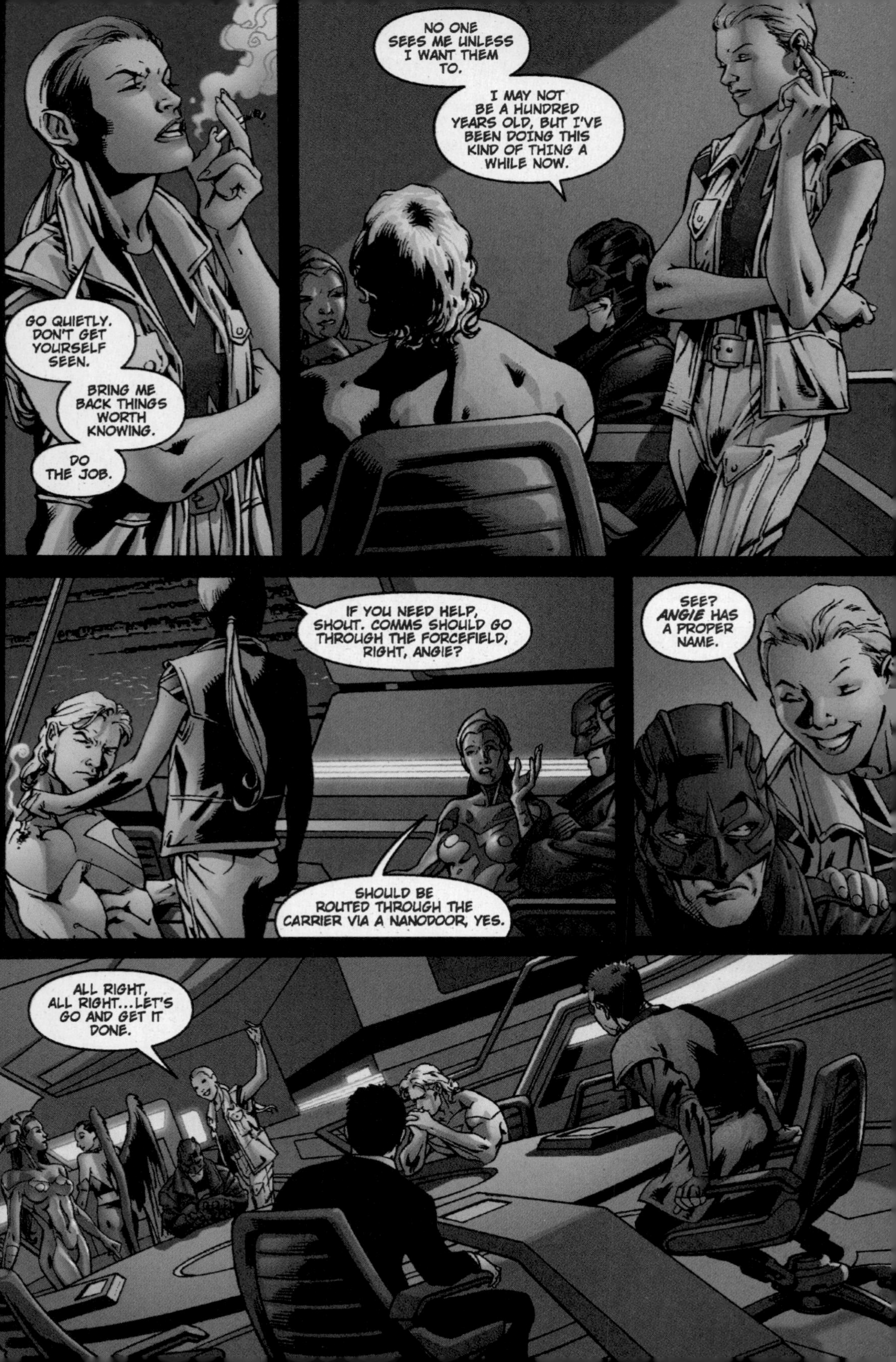
GO QUIETLY. DON'T GET YOURSELF SEEN.
BRING ME BACK THINGS WORTH KNOWING.
DO THE JOB.
NO ONE SEES ME UNLESS I WANT THEM TO.
I MAY NOT BE A HUNDRED YEARS OLD, BUT I'VE BEEN DOING THIS KIND OF THING A WHILE NOW.
IF YOU NEED HELP, SHOUT. COMMS SHOULD GO THROUGH THE FORCEFIELD, RIGHT, ANGIE?
SHOULD BE ROUTED THROUGH THE CARRIER VIA A NANODOOR, YES.
SEE? *ANGIE* HAS A PROPER NAME.
ALL RIGHT, ALL RIGHT...LET'S GO AND GET IT DONE.

ENGINEER. I HAVE A QUESTION.

WHO *FLIES* THIS THING?

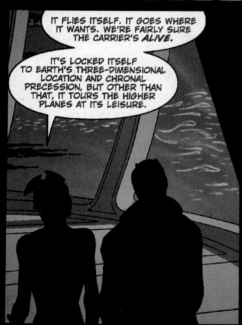

IT FLIES ITSELF. IT GOES WHERE IT WANTS. WE'RE FAIRLY SURE THE CARRIER'S *ALIVE*.

IT'S LOCKED ITSELF TO EARTH'S THREE-DIMENSIONAL LOCATION AND CHRONAL PRECESSION, BUT OTHER THAN THAT, IT TOURS THE HIGHER PLANES AT ITS LEISURE.

CHRONAL PRECESSION?

SORRY. TIME ON THE CARRIER MOVES AT THE SAME SPEED IT DOES ON EARTH.

IT'S NOT LIKE WE COULDN'T TAKE CONTROL IF WE WANTED, THOUGH. TO AN EXTENT, ANYWAY.

CARRIER; TACK INTO THE BLEED?

THERE WE GO, WE GOT RED...THAT'S THE BLEED, THE ARTERY WALL BETWEEN PARALLEL UNIVERSES.

THE ONLY THING WE COULDN'T DO IS LEAVE EARTHSPACE. IT SEEMS TO WANT TO STAY WITH EARTH.

I JUST WISH WE REALLY UNDERSTOOD WHAT THE CARRIER WAS. IT'S SOMETHING THE DOCTOR'S GOING TO WORK ON.

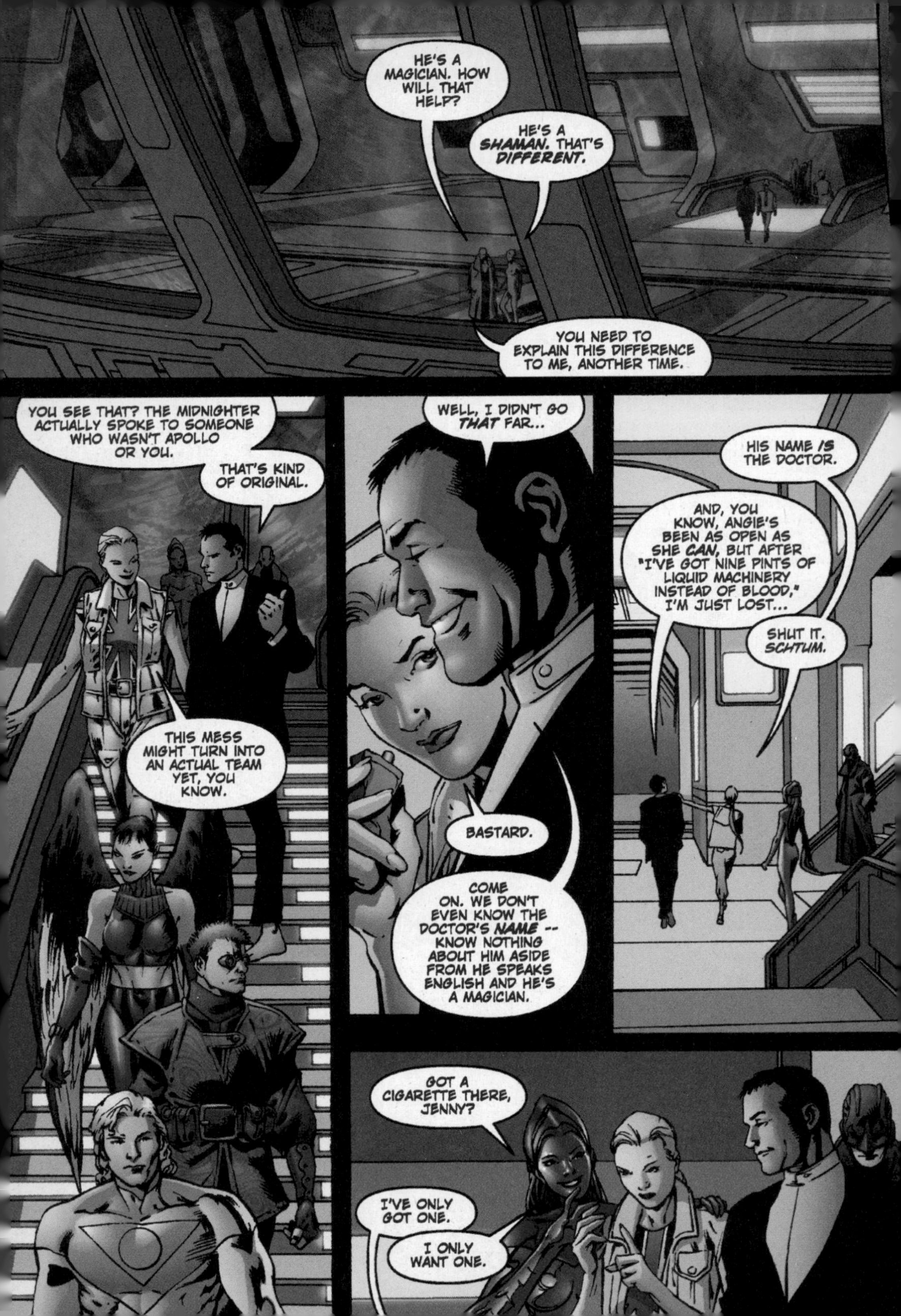
HE'S A MAGICIAN. HOW WILL THAT HELP?
HE'S A SHAMAN. THAT'S DIFFERENT.
YOU NEED TO EXPLAIN THIS DIFFERENCE TO ME, ANOTHER TIME.
YOU SEE THAT? THE MIDNIGHTER ACTUALLY SPOKE TO SOMEONE WHO WASN'T APOLLO OR YOU.
THAT'S KIND OF ORIGINAL.
THIS MESS MIGHT TURN INTO AN ACTUAL TEAM YET, YOU KNOW.
WELL, I DIDN'T GO THAT FAR...
BASTARD.
COME ON. WE DON'T EVEN KNOW THE DOCTOR'S NAME -- KNOW NOTHING ABOUT HIM ASIDE FROM HE SPEAKS ENGLISH AND HE'S A MAGICIAN.
HIS NAME IS THE DOCTOR.
AND, YOU KNOW, ANGIE'S BEEN AS OPEN AS SHE CAN, BUT AFTER "I'VE GOT NINE PINTS OF LIQUID MACHINERY INSTEAD OF BLOOD," I'M JUST LOST...
SHUT IT. SCHTUM.
GOT A CIGARETTE THERE, JENNY?
I'VE ONLY GOT ONE.
I ONLY WANT ONE.

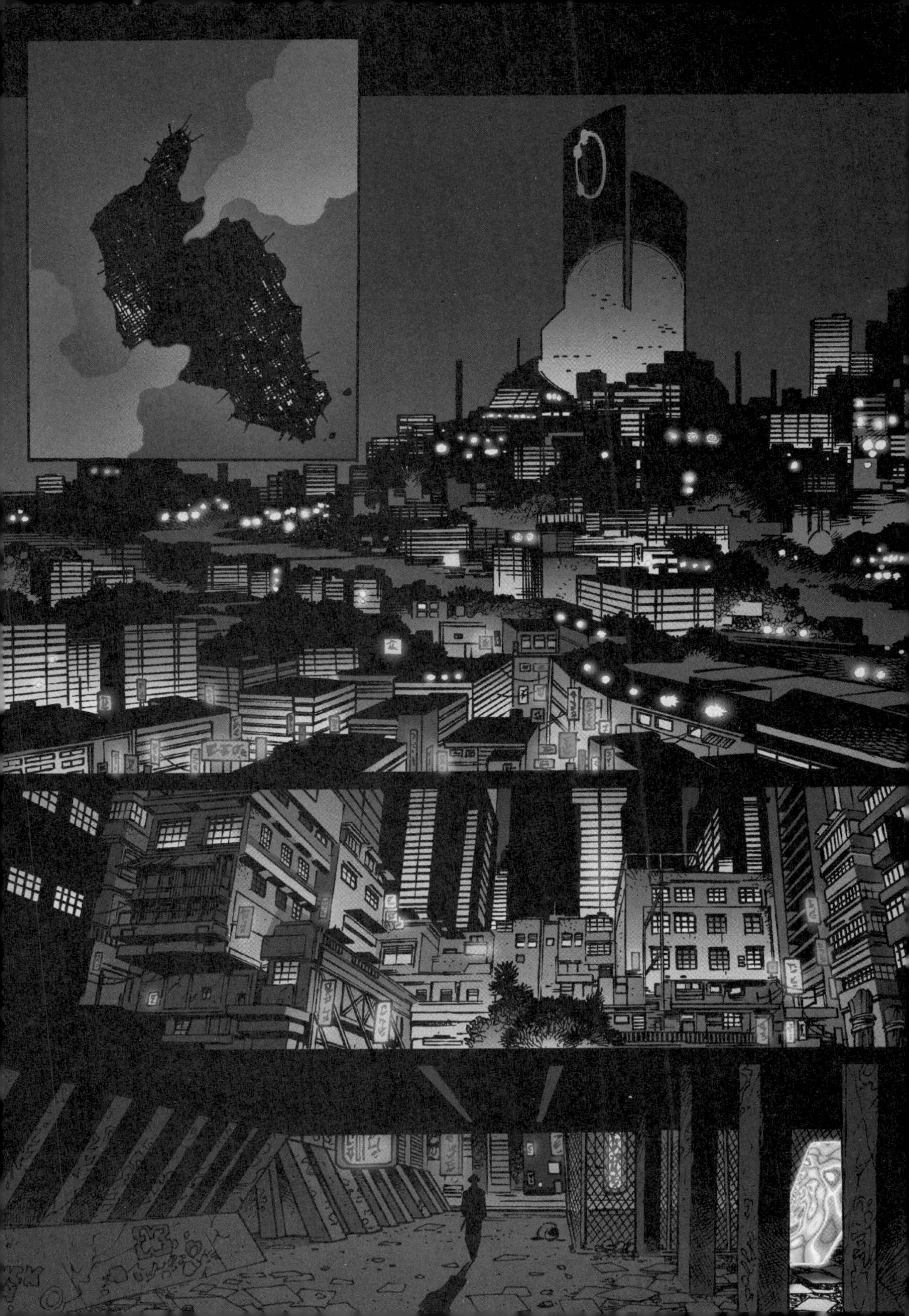

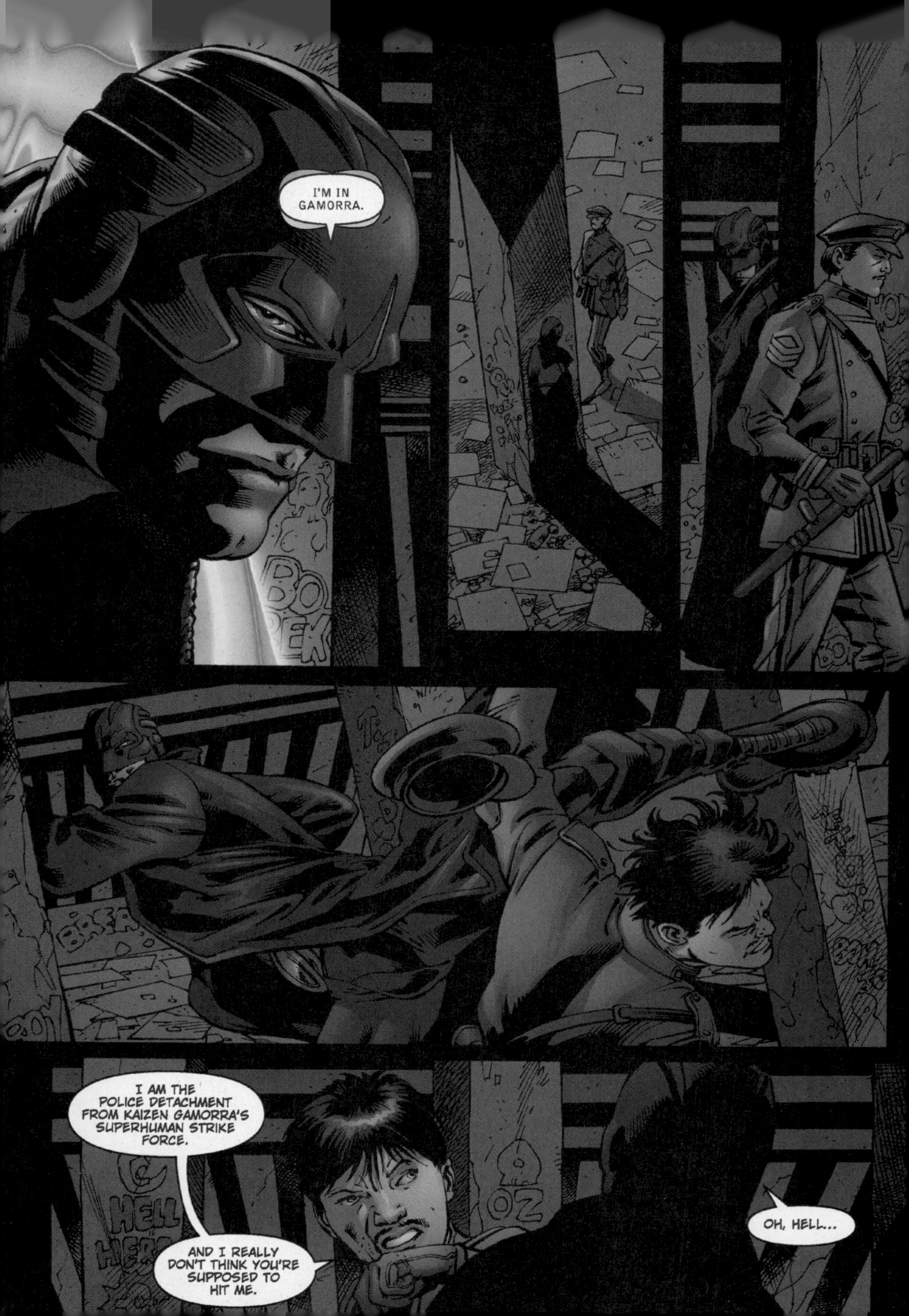
I'M IN GAMORRA.
I AM THE POLICE DETACHMENT FROM KAIZEN GAMORRA'S SUPERHUMAN STRIKE FORCE.
AND I REALLY DON'T THINK YOU'RE SUPPOSED TO HIT ME.
OH, HELL...

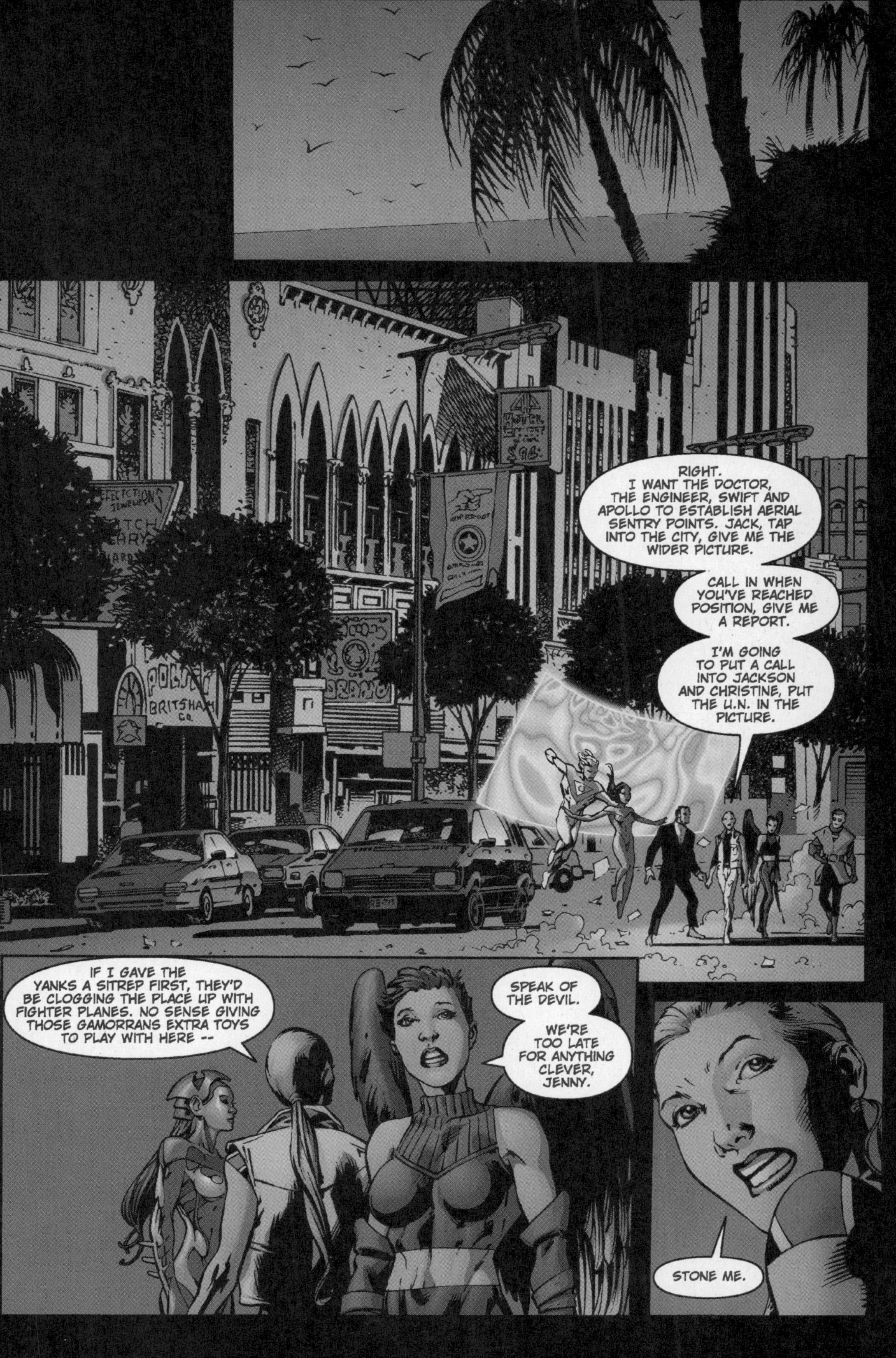
RIGHT. I WANT THE DOCTOR, THE ENGINEER, SWIFT AND APOLLO TO ESTABLISH AERIAL SENTRY POINTS. JACK, TAP INTO THE CITY, GIVE ME THE WIDER PICTURE.
CALL IN WHEN YOU'VE REACHED POSITION, GIVE ME A REPORT.
I'M GOING TO PUT A CALL INTO JACKSON AND CHRISTINE, PUT THE U.N. IN THE PICTURE.
IF I GAVE THE YANKS A SITREP FIRST, THEY'D BE CLOGGING THE PLACE UP WITH FIGHTER PLANES. NO SENSE GIVING THOSE GAMORRANS EXTRA TOYS TO PLAY WITH HERE --
SPEAK OF THE DEVIL.
WE'RE TOO LATE FOR ANYTHING CLEVER, JENNY.
STONE ME.

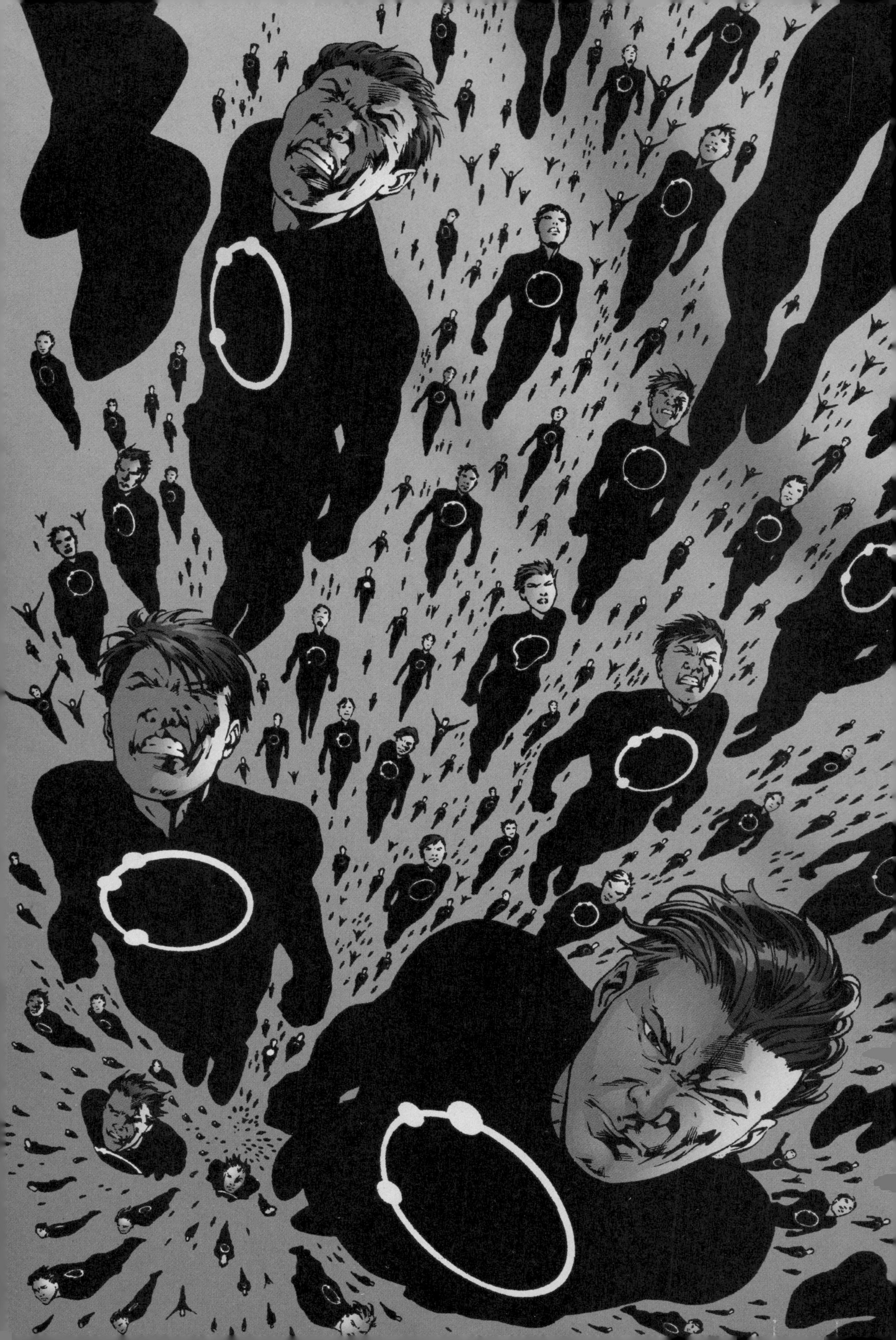

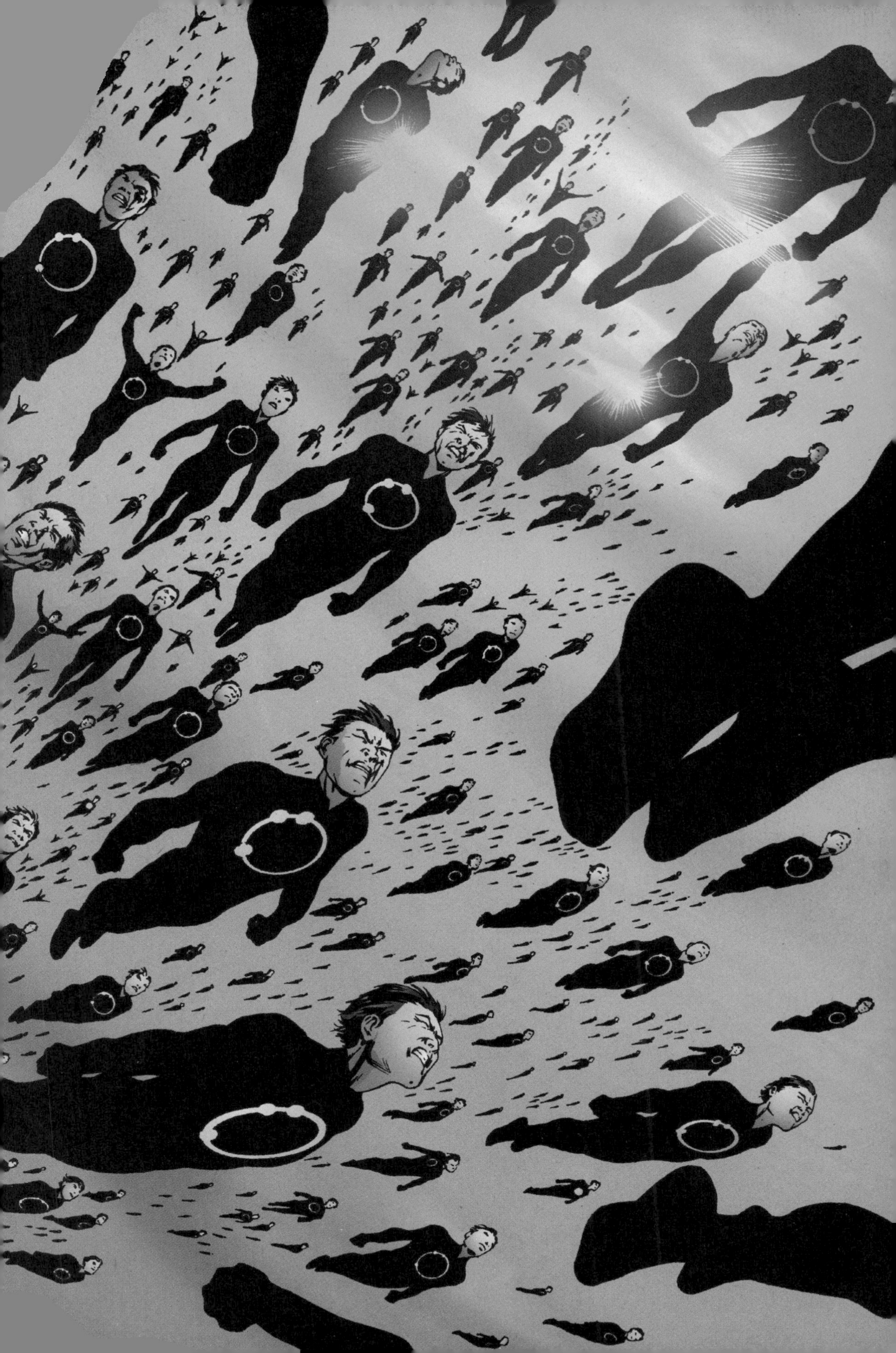

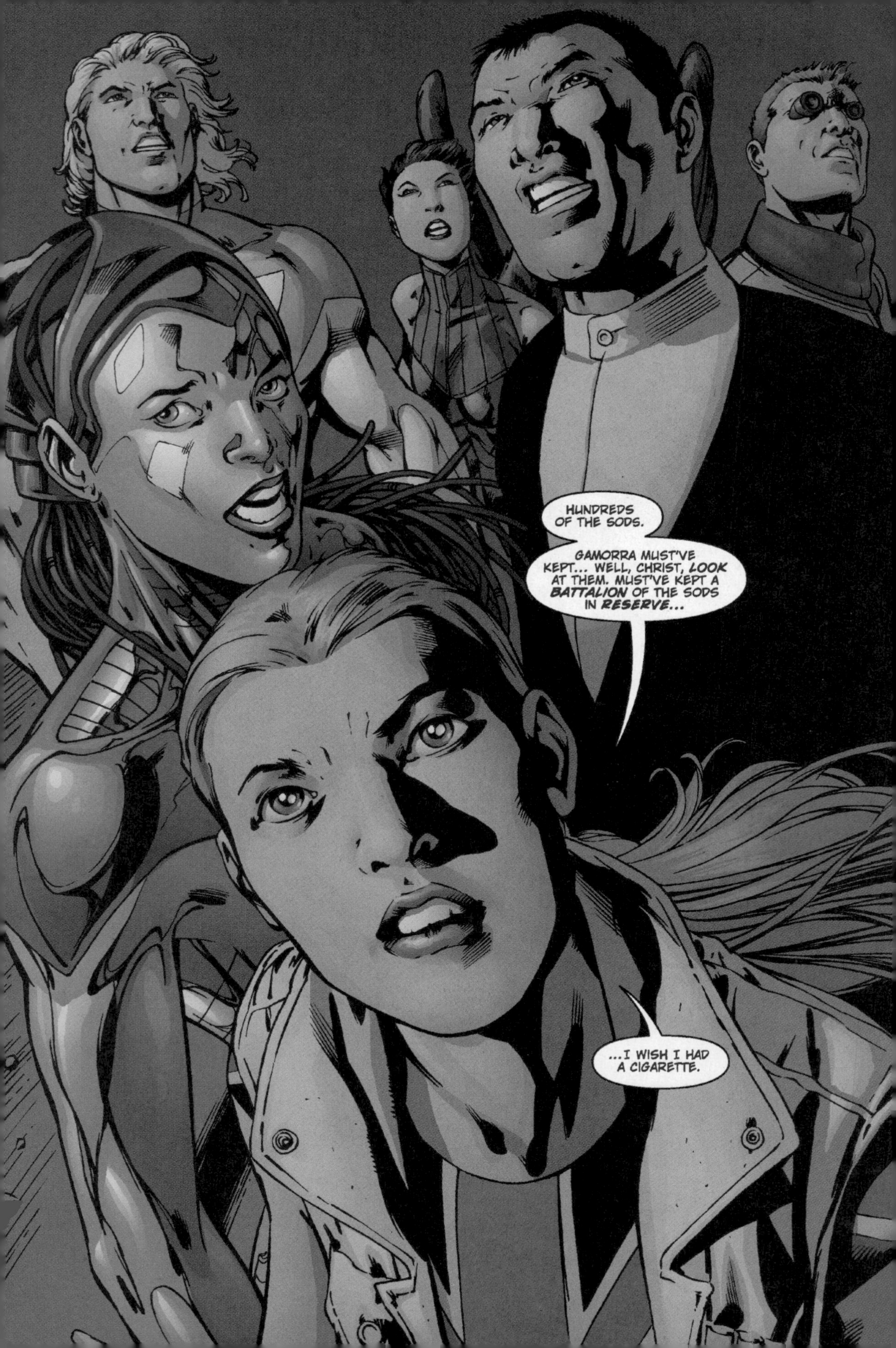
HUNDREDS OF THE SODS.
GAMORRA MUST'VE KEPT... WELL, CHRIST, *LOOK* AT THEM. MUST'VE KEPT A *BATTALION* OF THE SODS IN *RESERVE*...
...I WISH I HAD A CIGARETTE.

GAMORRA:

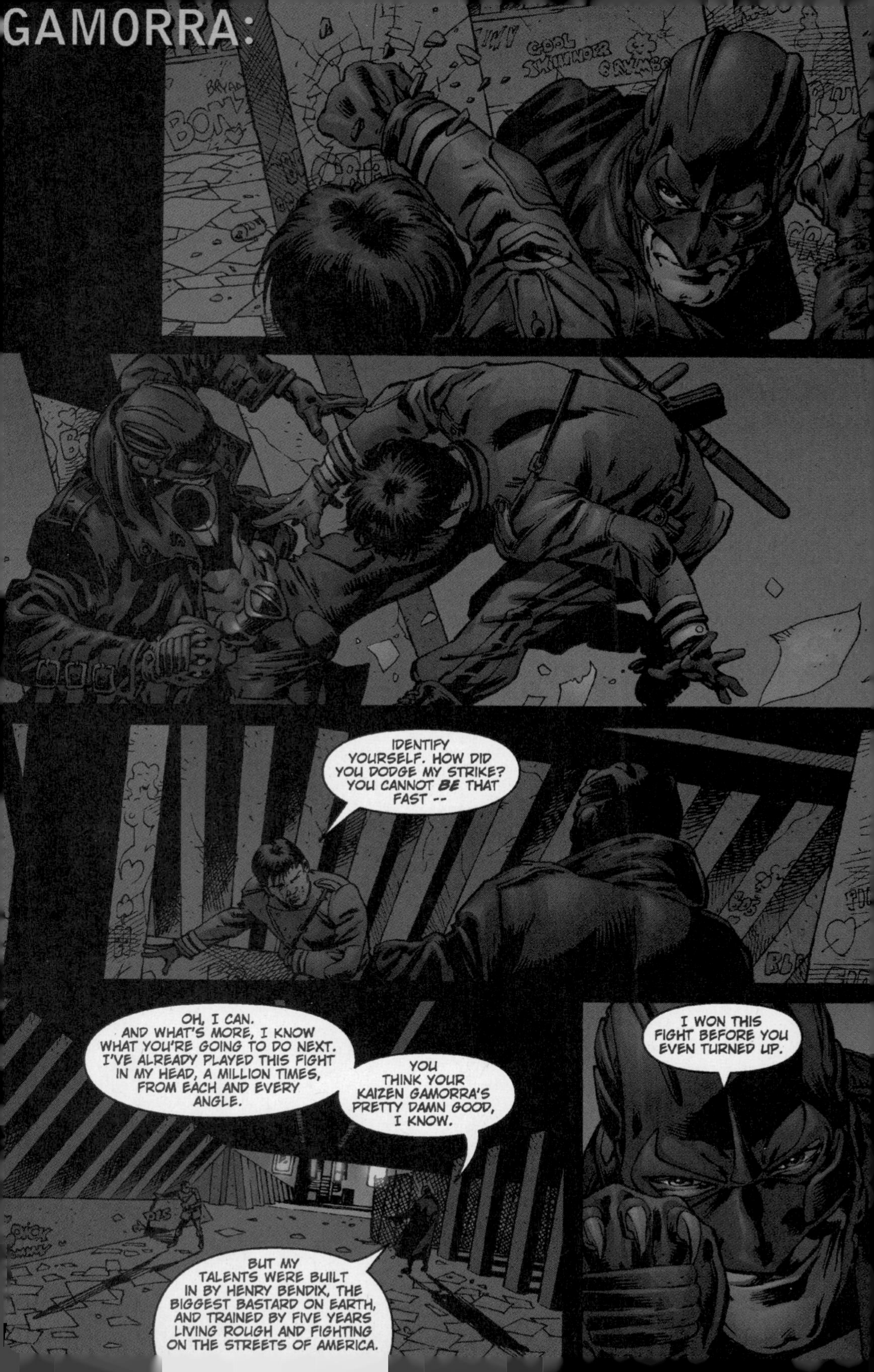
IDENTIFY YOURSELF. HOW DID YOU DODGE MY STRIKE? YOU CANNOT *BE* THAT FAST --
OH, I CAN. AND WHAT'S MORE, I KNOW WHAT YOU'RE GOING TO DO NEXT. I'VE ALREADY PLAYED THIS FIGHT IN MY HEAD, A MILLION TIMES, FROM EACH AND EVERY ANGLE.
YOU THINK YOUR KAIZEN GAMORRA'S PRETTY DAMN GOOD, I KNOW.
BUT MY TALENTS WERE BUILT IN BY HENRY BENDIX, THE BIGGEST BASTARD ON EARTH, AND TRAINED BY FIVE YEARS LIVING ROUGH AND FIGHTING ON THE STREETS OF AMERICA.
I WON THIS FIGHT BEFORE YOU EVEN TURNED UP.

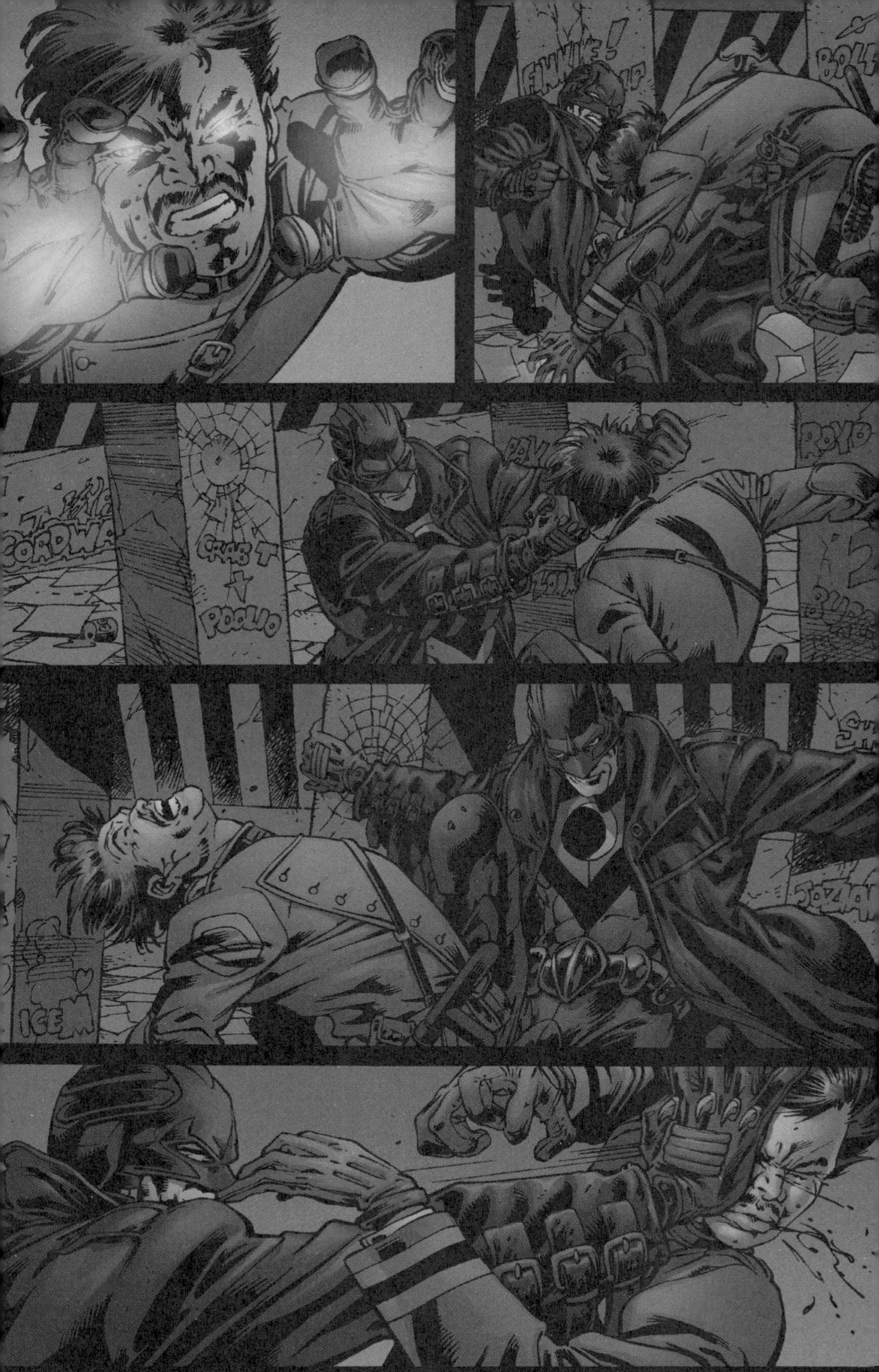
CORDWA
CRAB T
POOLIO
ICE M

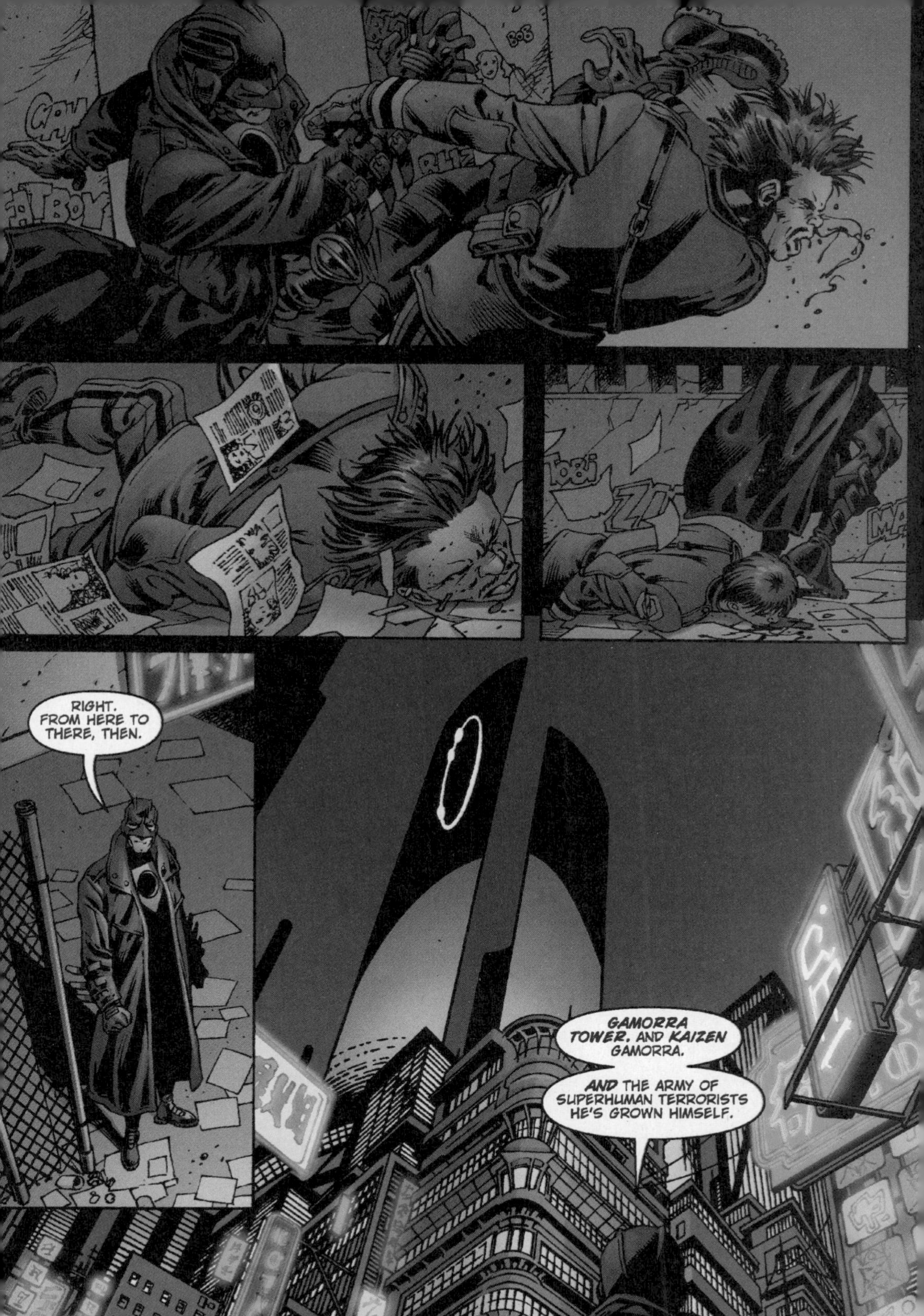
RIGHT. FROM HERE TO THERE, THEN.
GAMORRA TOWER. AND KAIZEN GAMORRA.
AND THE ARMY OF SUPERHUMAN TERRORISTS HE'S GROWN HIMSELF.

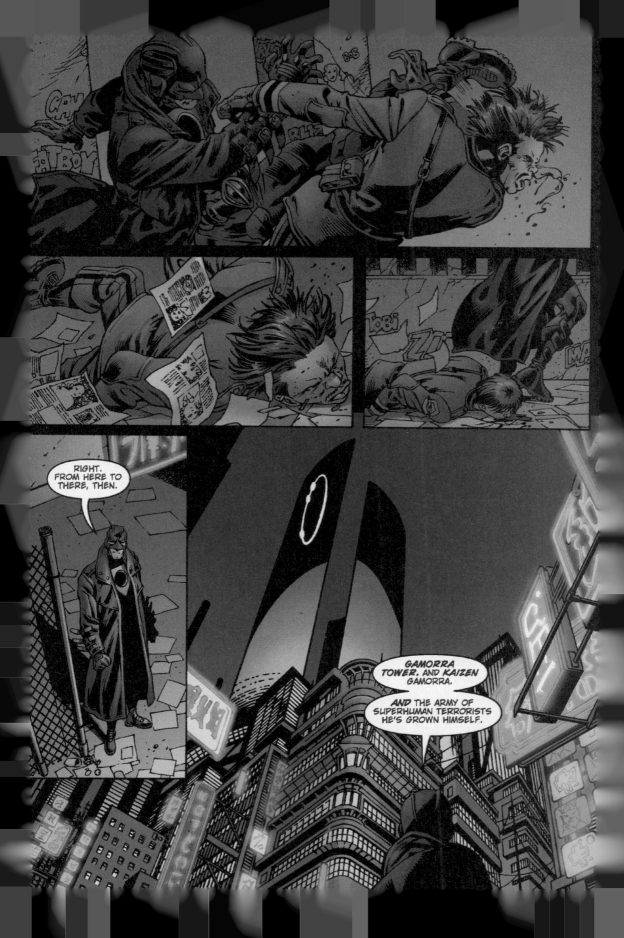

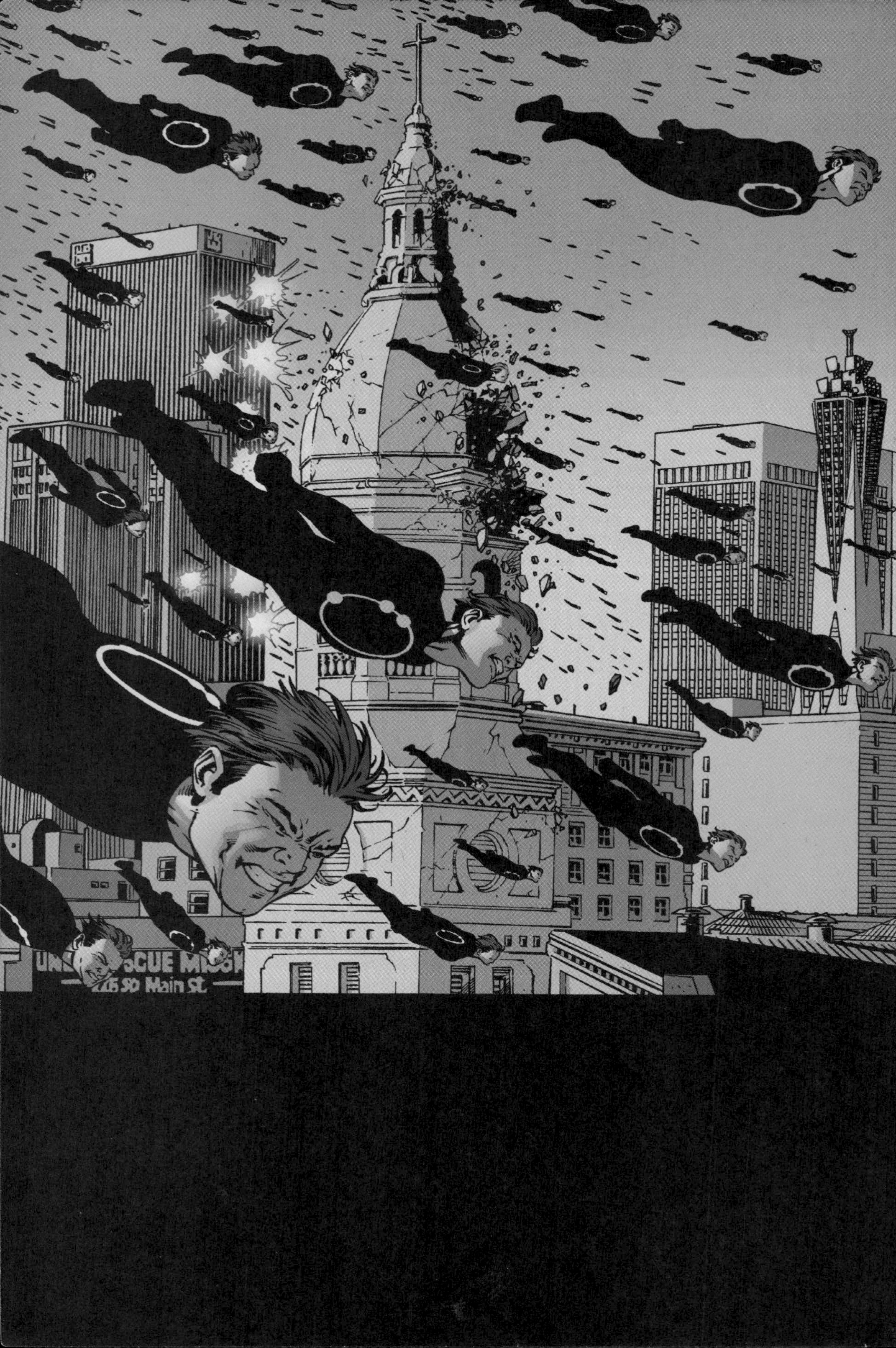
So Main St.

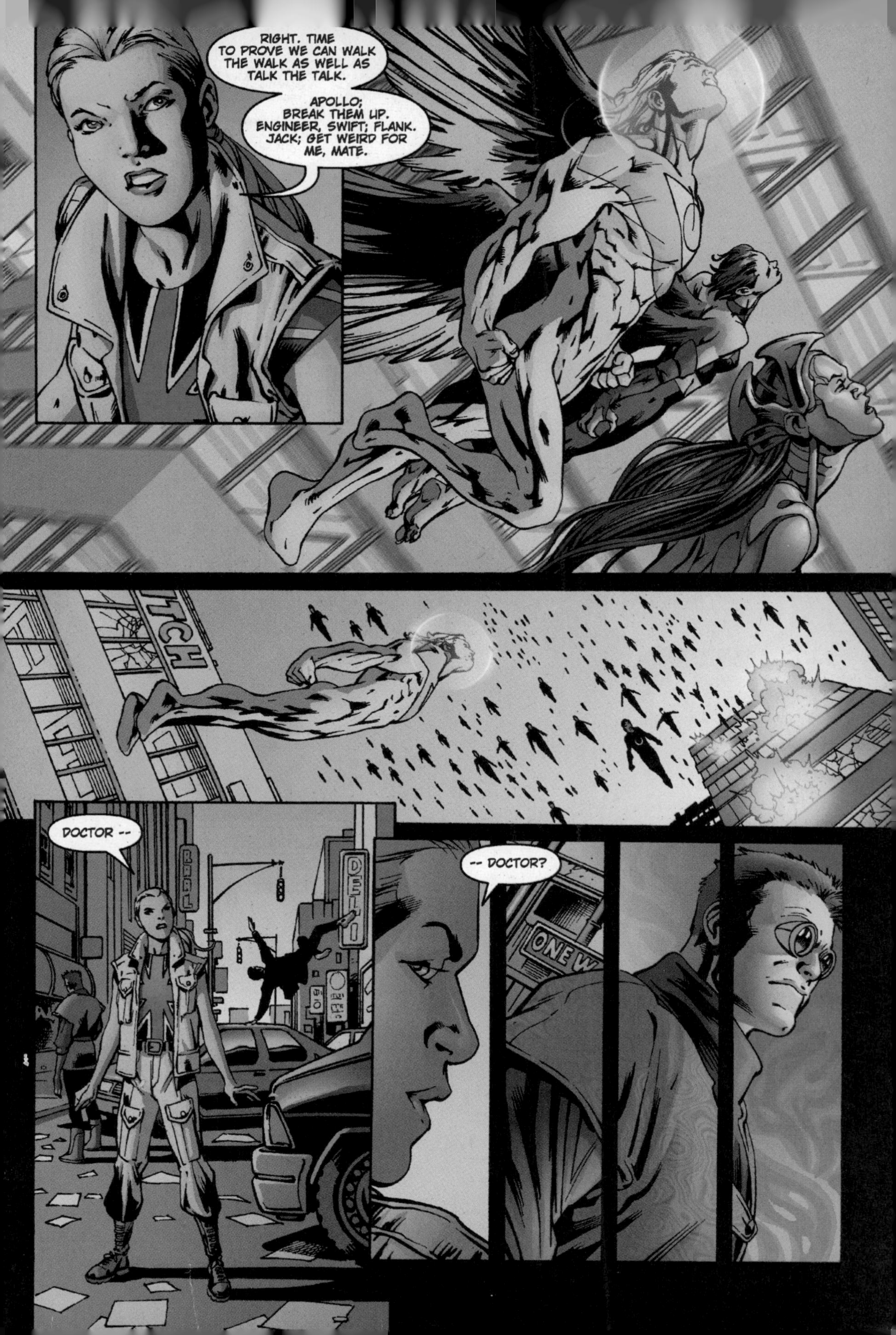
RIGHT. TIME TO PROVE WE CAN WALK THE WALK AS WELL AS TALK THE TALK.
APOLLO; BREAK THEM UP. ENGINEER, SWIFT; FLANK. JACK; GET WEIRD FOR ME, MATE.
DOCTOR --
-- DOCTOR?

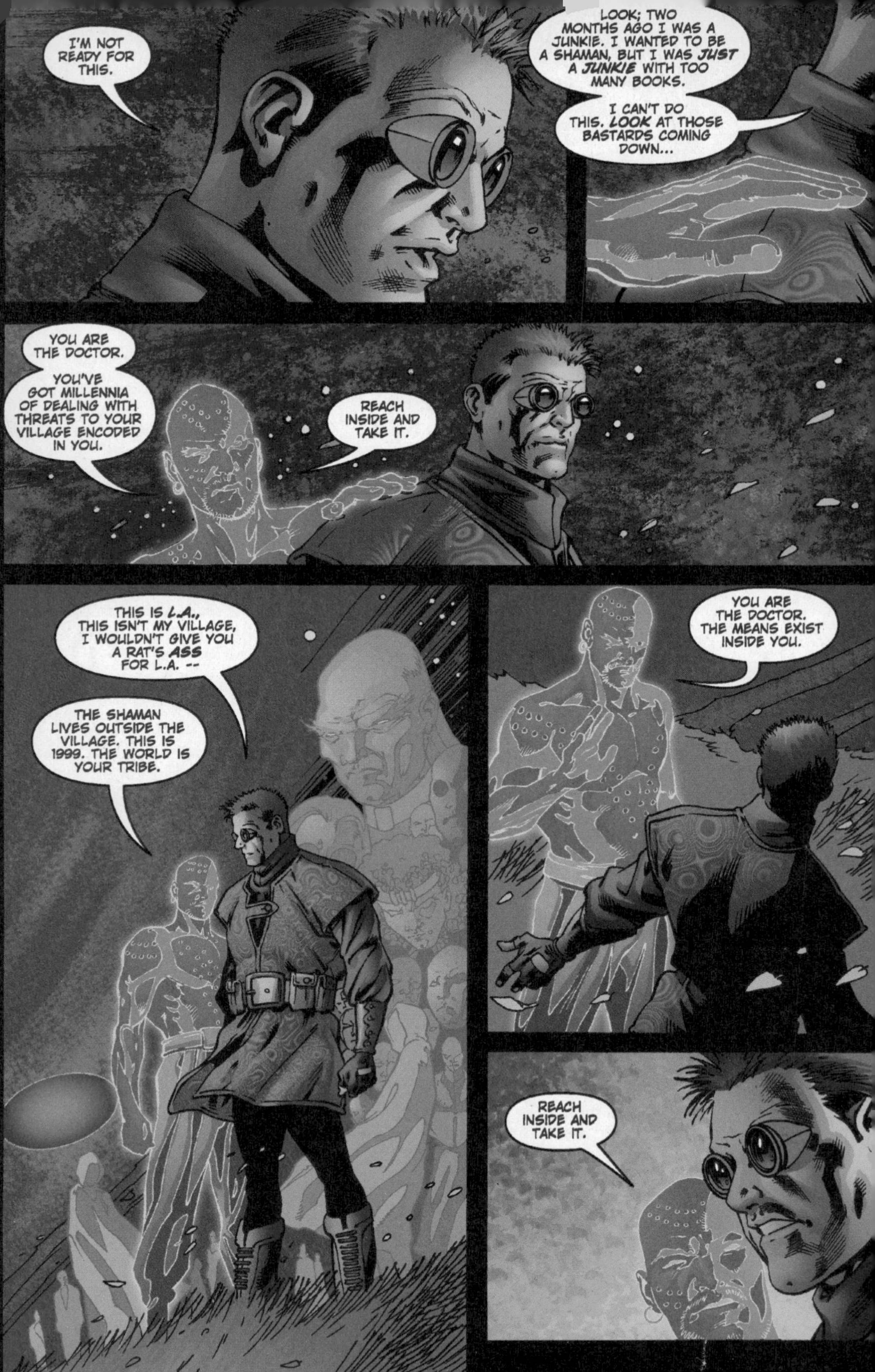
I'M NOT READY FOR THIS.
LOOK; TWO MONTHS AGO I WAS A JUNKIE. I WANTED TO BE A SHAMAN, BUT I WAS JUST A JUNKIE WITH TOO MANY BOOKS.
I CAN'T DO THIS. LOOK AT THOSE BASTARDS COMING DOWN...
YOU ARE THE DOCTOR.
YOU'VE GOT MILLENNIA OF DEALING WITH THREATS TO YOUR VILLAGE ENCODED IN YOU.
REACH INSIDE AND TAKE IT.
THIS IS L.A., THIS ISN'T MY VILLAGE, I WOULDN'T GIVE YOU A RAT'S ASS FOR L.A. --
THE SHAMAN LIVES OUTSIDE THE VILLAGE. THIS IS 1999. THE WORLD IS YOUR TRIBE.
YOU ARE THE DOCTOR. THE MEANS EXIST INSIDE YOU.
REACH INSIDE AND TAKE IT.

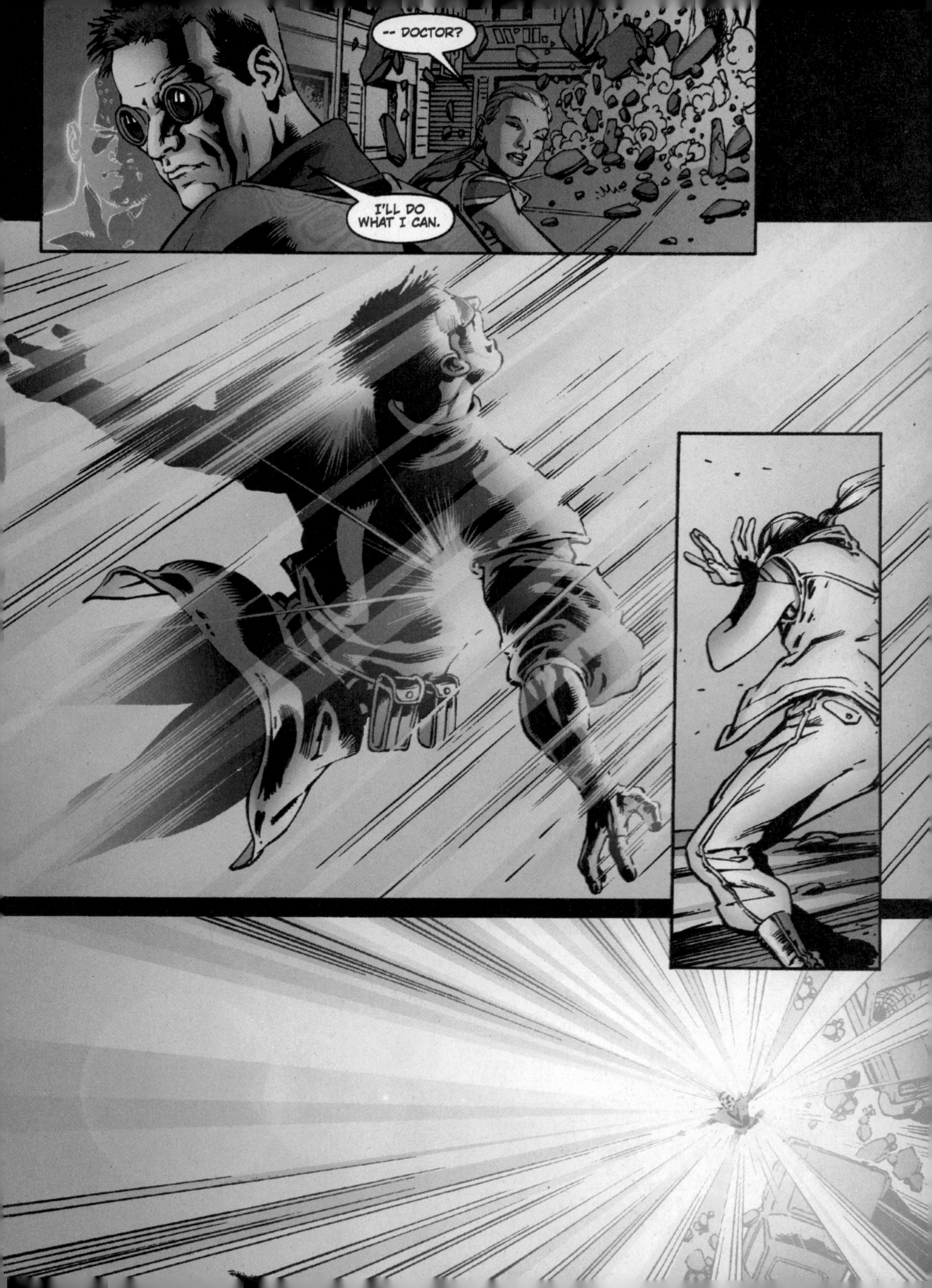
-- DOCTOR?
I'LL DO WHAT I CAN.

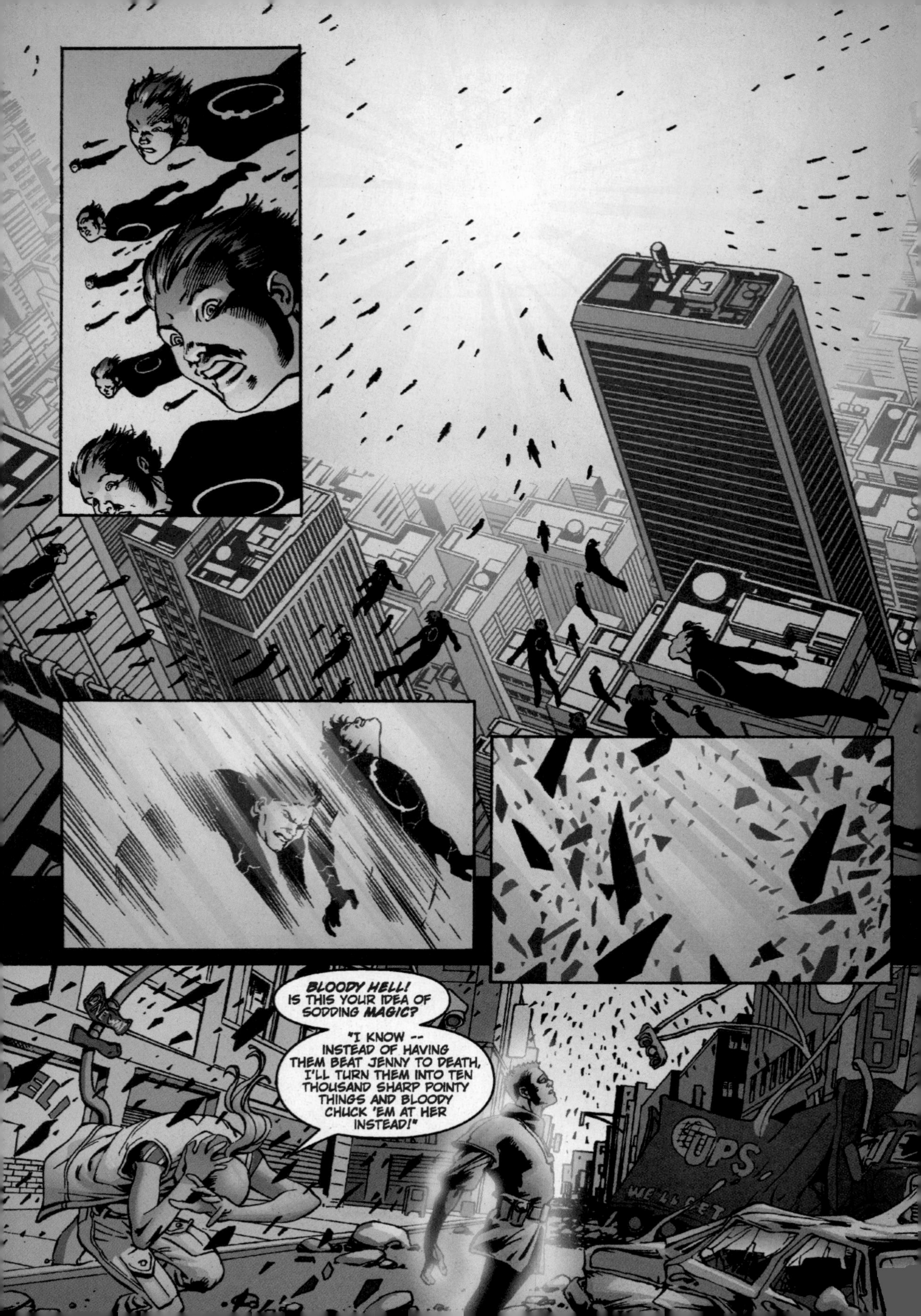

BLOODY HELL! IS THIS YOUR IDEA OF SODDING MAGIC?
"I KNOW -- INSTEAD OF HAVING THEM BEAT JENNY TO DEATH, I'LL TURN THEM INTO TEN THOUSAND SHARP POINTY THINGS AND BLOODY CHUCK 'EM AT HER INSTEAD!"
UPS

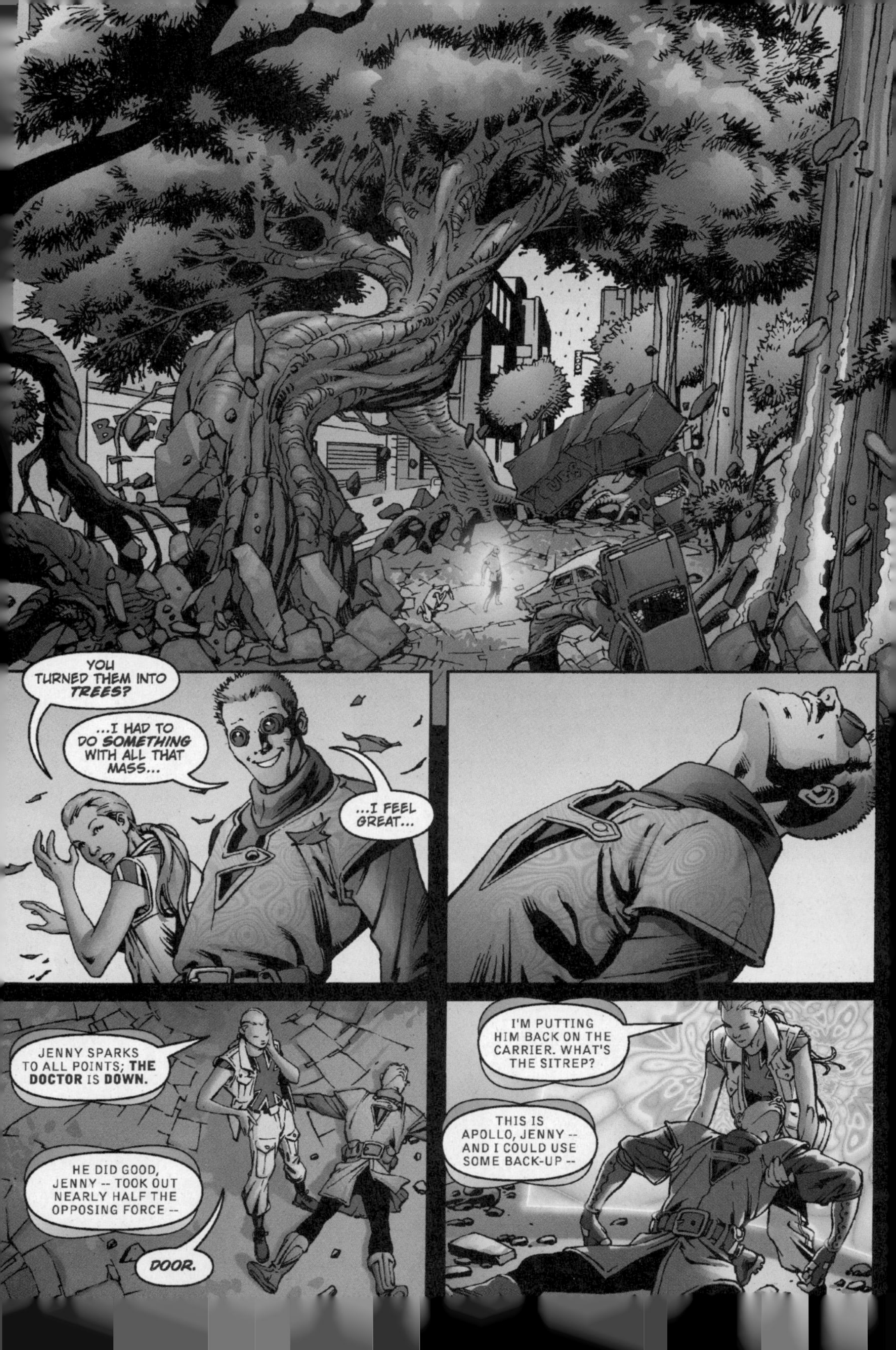

YOU TURNED THEM INTO TREES?
...I HAD TO DO SOMETHING WITH ALL THAT MASS...
...I FEEL GREAT...
JENNY SPARKS TO ALL POINTS; THE DOCTOR IS DOWN.
HE DID GOOD, JENNY -- TOOK OUT NEARLY HALF THE OPPOSING FORCE --
DOOR.
I'M PUTTING HIM BACK ON THE CARRIER. WHAT'S THE SITREP?
THIS IS APOLLO, JENNY -- AND I COULD USE SOME BACK-UP --

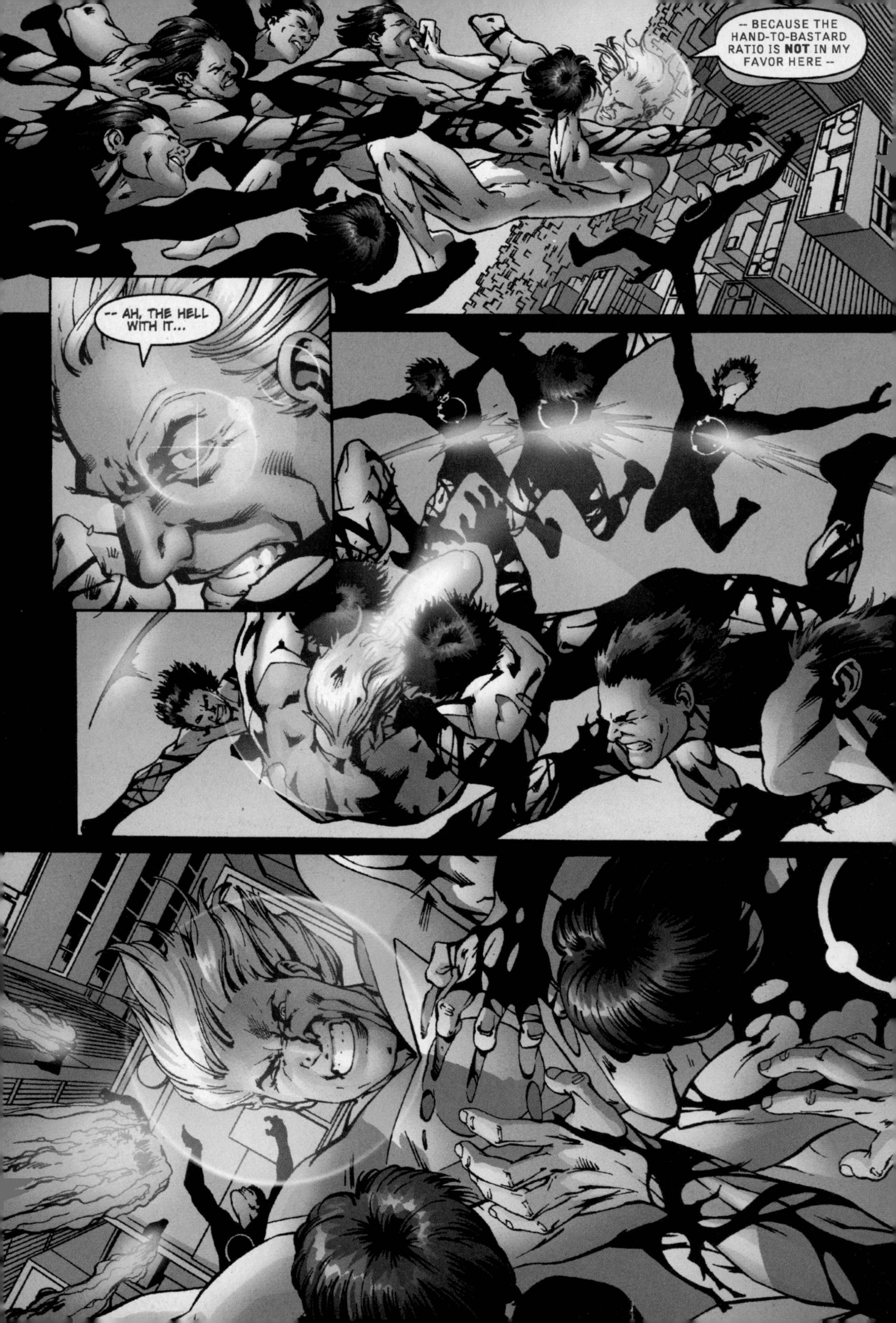
-- BECAUSE THE HAND-TO-BASTARD RATIO IS **NOT** IN MY FAVOR HERE --
-- AH, THE HELL WITH IT...

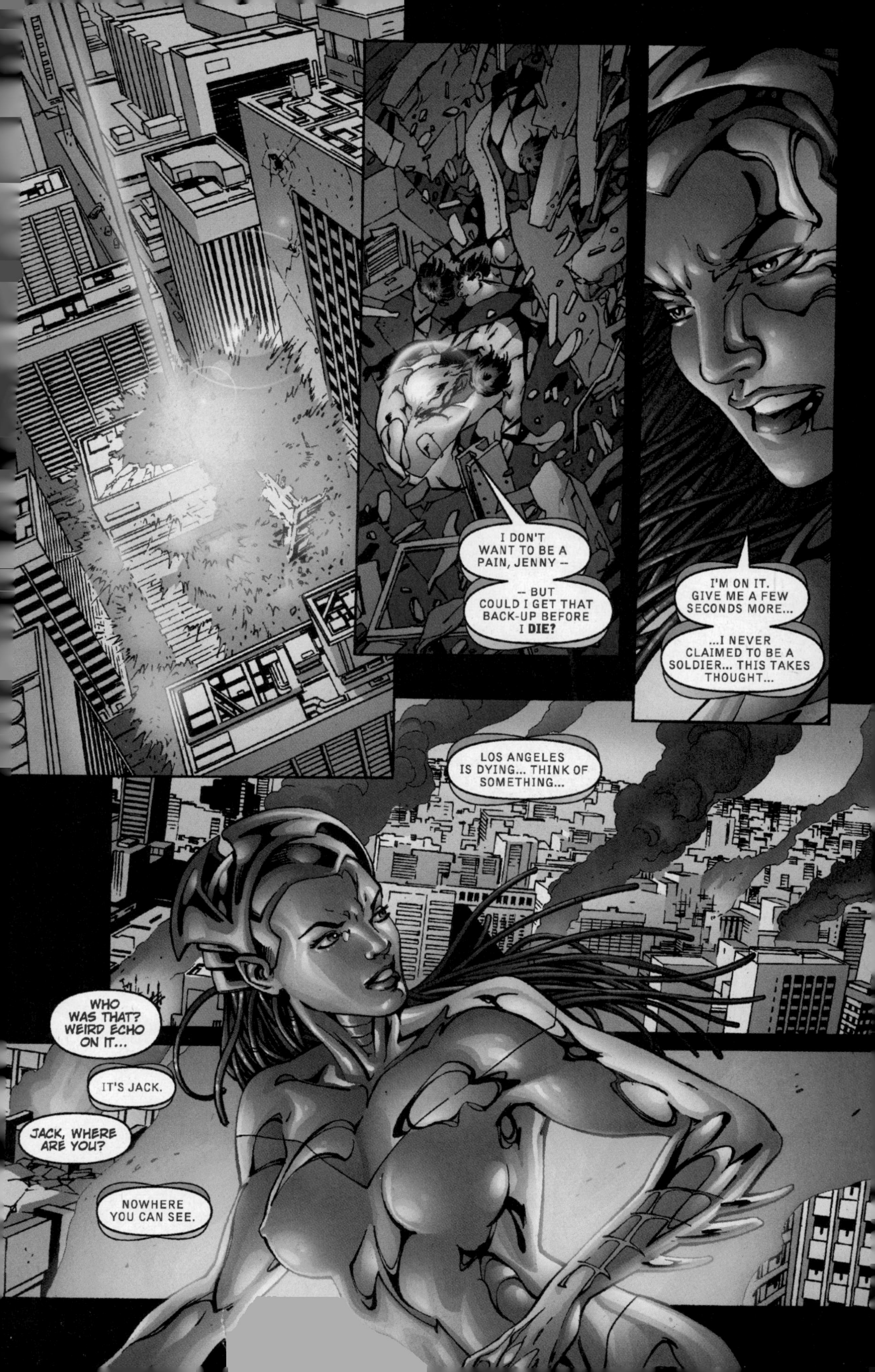
I DON'T WANT TO BE A PAIN, JENNY --
-- BUT COULD I GET THAT BACK-UP BEFORE I DIE?
I'M ON IT. GIVE ME A FEW SECONDS MORE...
...I NEVER CLAIMED TO BE A SOLDIER... THIS TAKES THOUGHT...
LOS ANGELES IS DYING... THINK OF SOMETHING...
WHO WAS THAT? WEIRD ECHO ON IT...
IT'S JACK.
JACK, WHERE ARE YOU?
NOWHERE YOU CAN SEE.

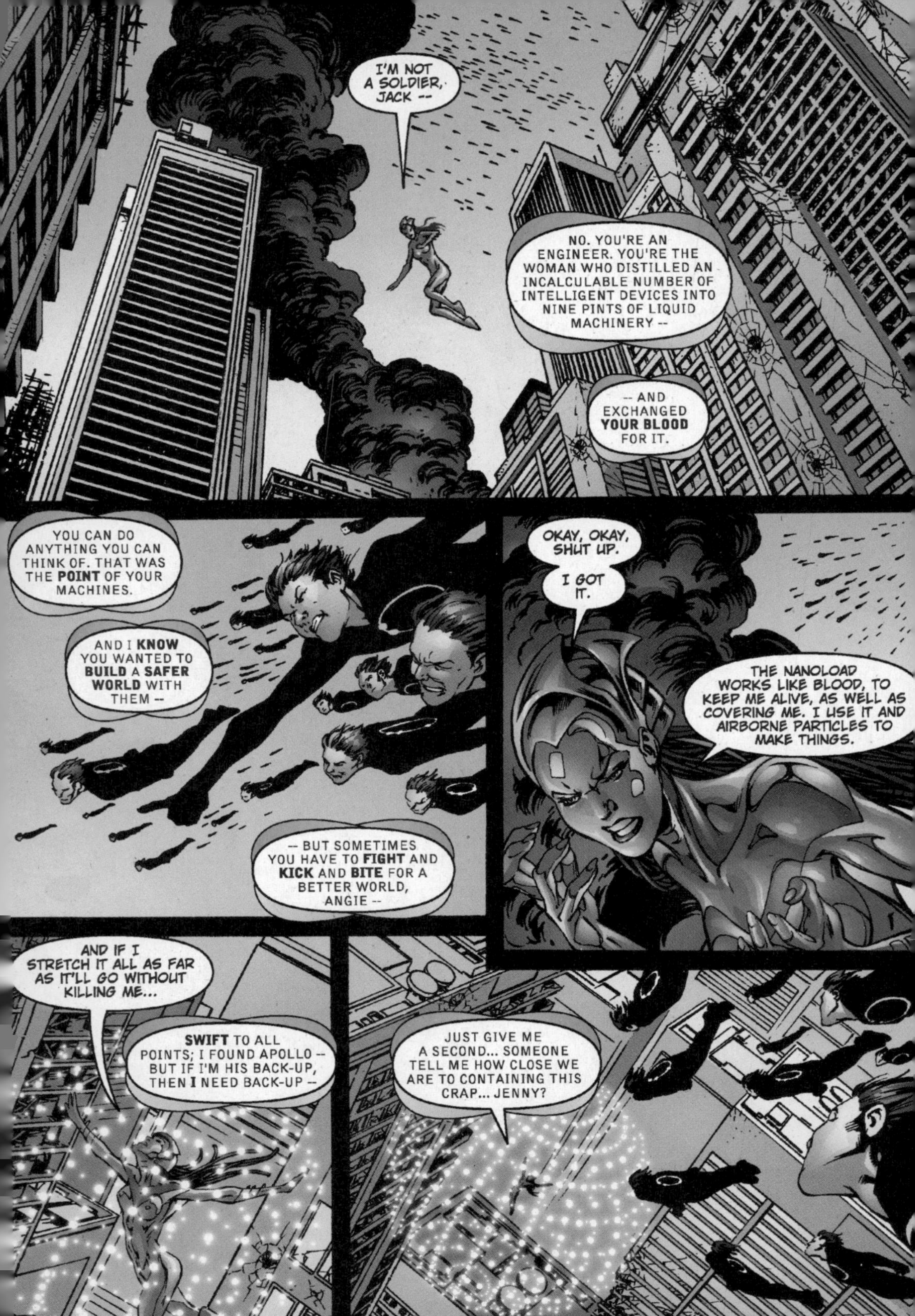
I'M NOT A SOLDIER, JACK --
NO. YOU'RE AN ENGINEER. YOU'RE THE WOMAN WHO DISTILLED AN INCALCULABLE NUMBER OF INTELLIGENT DEVICES INTO NINE PINTS OF LIQUID MACHINERY --
-- AND EXCHANGED YOUR BLOOD FOR IT.
YOU CAN DO ANYTHING YOU CAN THINK OF. THAT WAS THE POINT OF YOUR MACHINES.
AND I KNOW YOU WANTED TO BUILD A SAFER WORLD WITH THEM --
-- BUT SOMETIMES YOU HAVE TO FIGHT AND KICK AND BITE FOR A BETTER WORLD, ANGIE --
OKAY, OKAY, SHUT UP.
I GOT IT.
THE NANOLOAD WORKS LIKE BLOOD, TO KEEP ME ALIVE, AS WELL AS COVERING ME. I USE IT AND AIRBORNE PARTICLES TO MAKE THINGS.
AND IF I STRETCH IT ALL AS FAR AS IT'LL GO WITHOUT KILLING ME...
SWIFT TO ALL POINTS; I FOUND APOLLO -- BUT IF I'M HIS BACK-UP, THEN I NEED BACK-UP --
JUST GIVE ME A SECOND... SOMEONE TELL ME HOW CLOSE WE ARE TO CONTAINING THIS CRAP... JENNY?

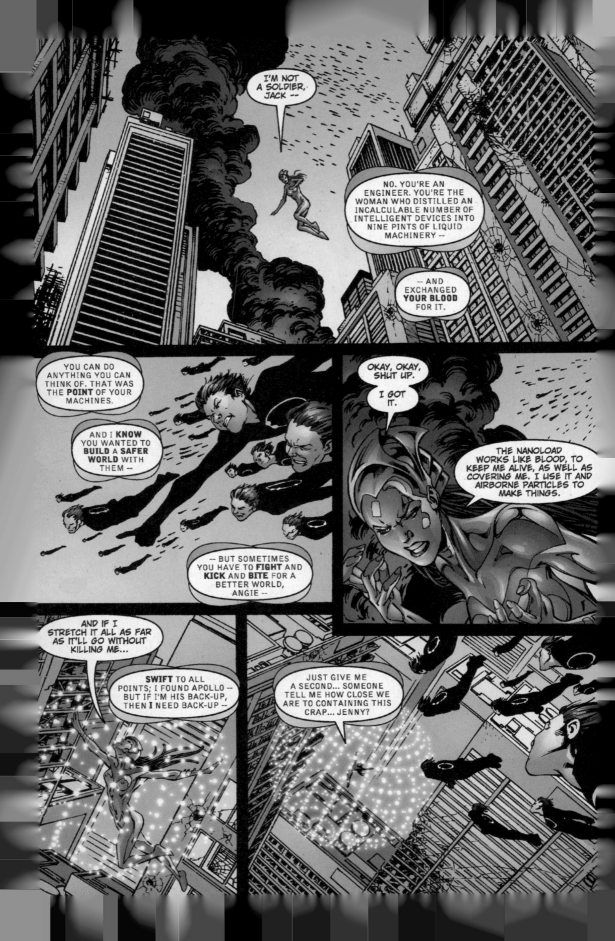

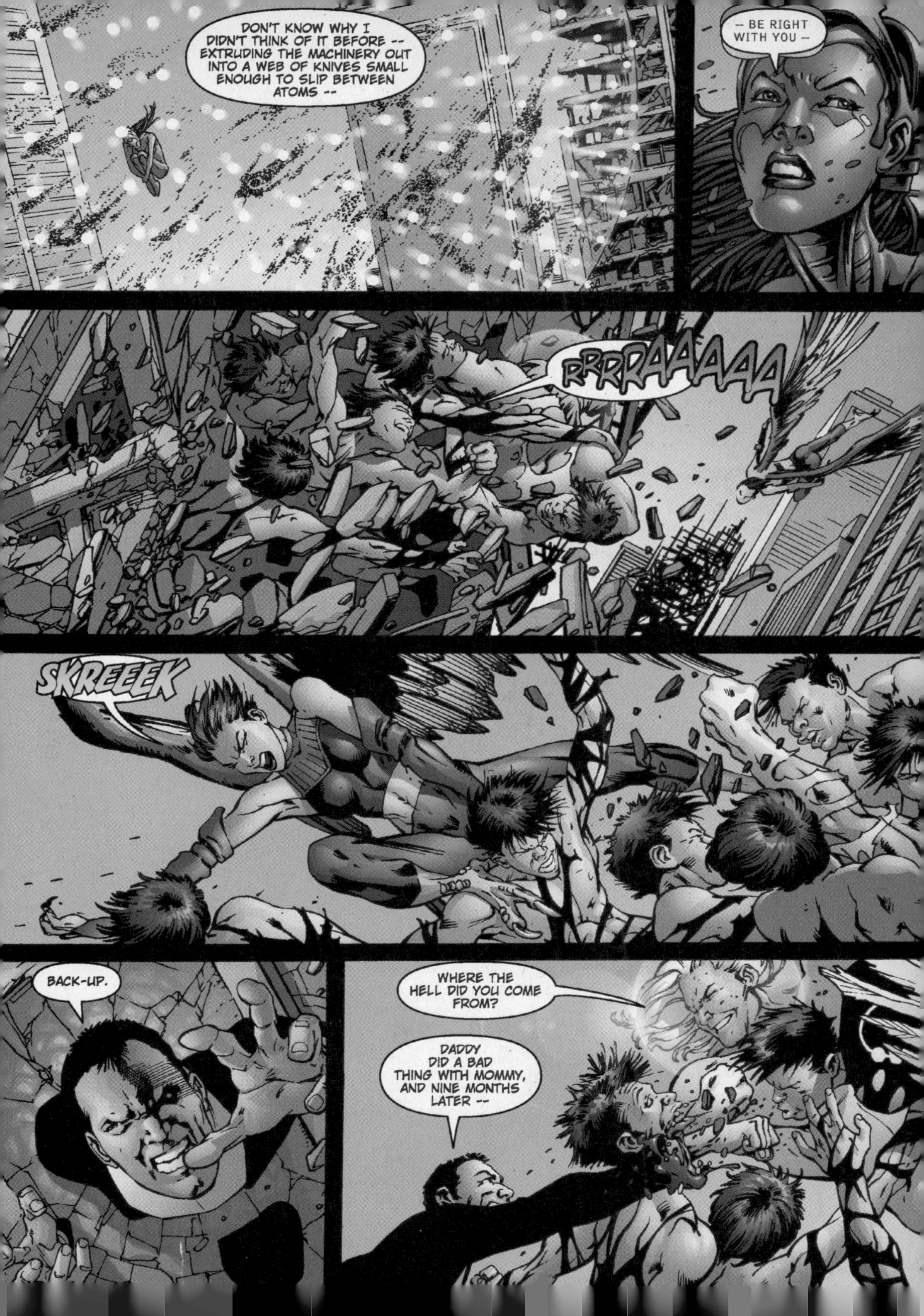
DON'T KNOW WHY I DIDN'T THINK OF IT BEFORE -- EXTRUDING THE MACHINERY OUT INTO A WEB OF KNIVES SMALL ENOUGH TO SLIP BETWEEN ATOMS --
-- BE RIGHT WITH YOU --
RRRRAAAAAA
SKREEEK
BACK-UP.
WHERE THE HELL DID YOU COME FROM?
DADDY DID A BAD THING WITH MOMMY, AND NINE MONTHS LATER --

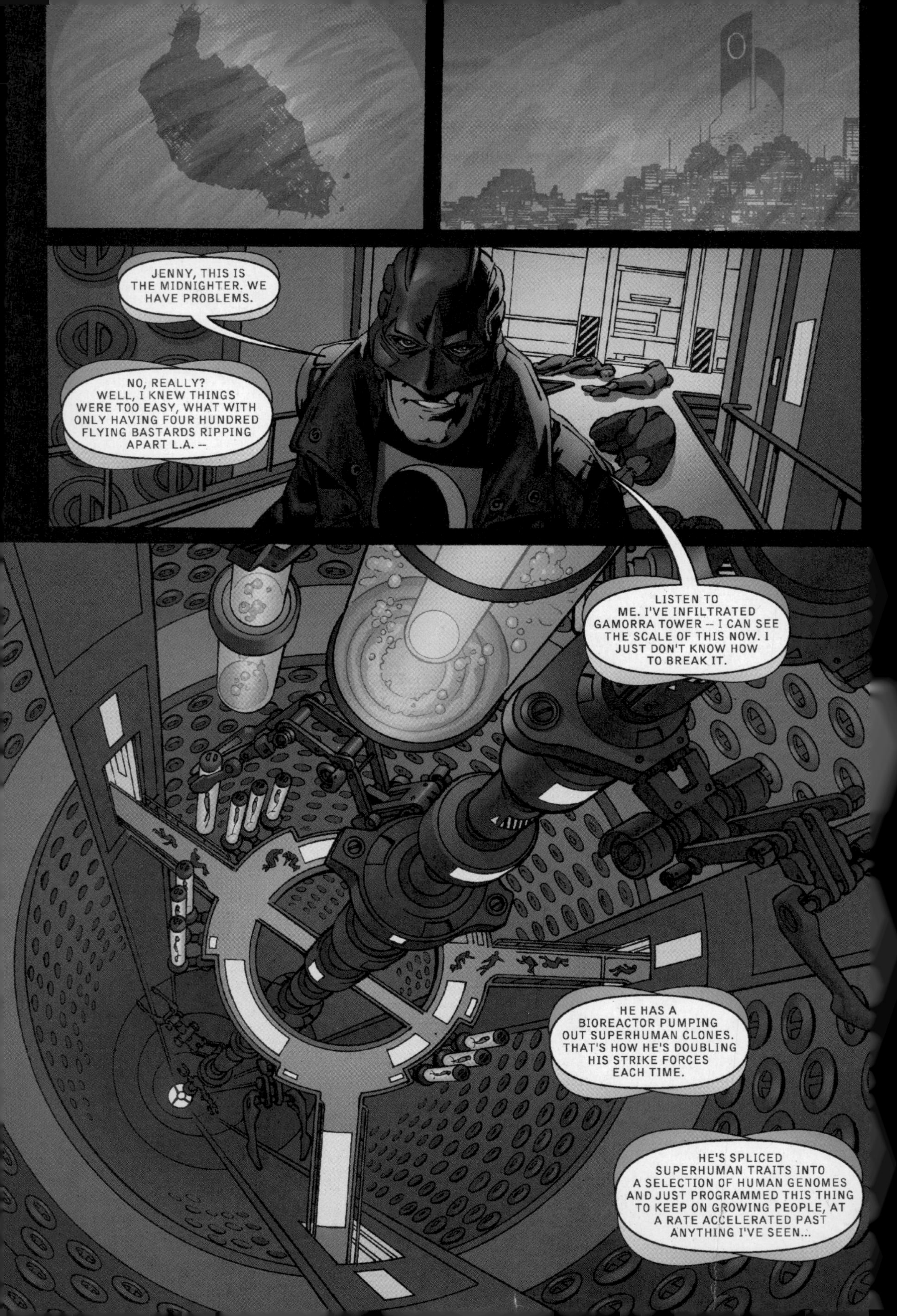
JENNY, THIS IS THE MIDNIGHTER. WE HAVE PROBLEMS.
NO, REALLY? WELL, I KNEW THINGS WERE TOO EASY, WHAT WITH ONLY HAVING FOUR HUNDRED FLYING BASTARDS RIPPING APART L.A. --
LISTEN TO ME. I'VE INFILTRATED GAMORRA TOWER -- I CAN SEE THE SCALE OF THIS NOW. I JUST DON'T KNOW HOW TO BREAK IT.
HE HAS A BIOREACTOR PUMPING OUT SUPERHUMAN CLONES. THAT'S HOW HE'S DOUBLING HIS STRIKE FORCES EACH TIME.
HE'S SPLICED SUPERHUMAN TRAITS INTO A SELECTION OF HUMAN GENOMES AND JUST PROGRAMMED THIS THING TO KEEP ON GROWING PEOPLE, AT A RATE ACCELERATED PAST ANYTHING I'VE SEEN...

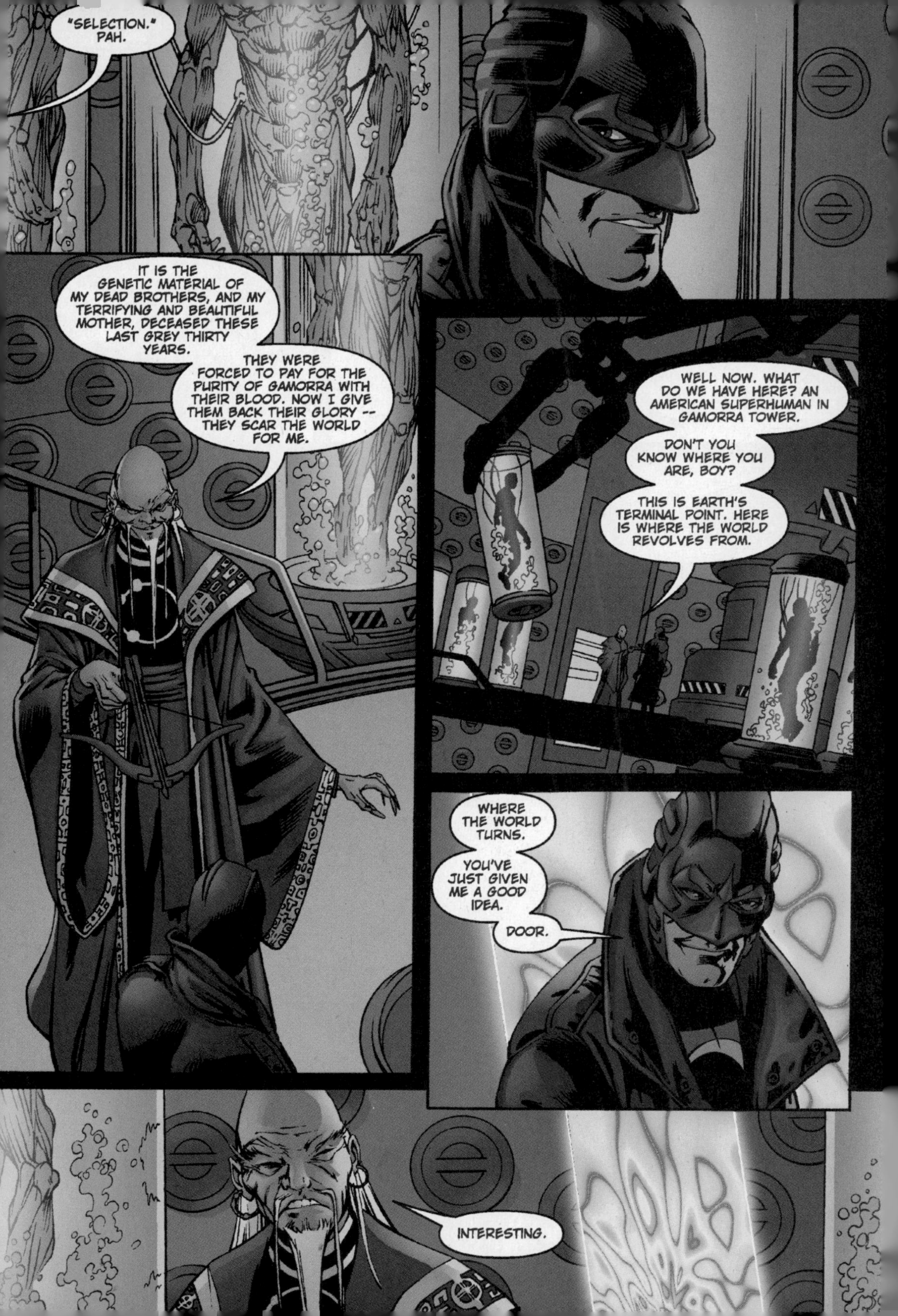
"SELECTION." PAH.
IT IS THE GENETIC MATERIAL OF MY DEAD BROTHERS, AND MY TERRIFYING AND BEAUTIFUL MOTHER, DECEASED THESE LAST GREY THIRTY YEARS.
THEY WERE FORCED TO PAY FOR THE PURITY OF GAMORRA WITH THEIR BLOOD. NOW I GIVE THEM BACK THEIR GLORY -- THEY SCAR THE WORLD FOR ME.
WELL NOW. WHAT DO WE HAVE HERE? AN AMERICAN SUPERHUMAN IN GAMORRA TOWER.
DON'T YOU KNOW WHERE YOU ARE, BOY?
THIS IS EARTH'S TERMINAL POINT. HERE IS WHERE THE WORLD REVOLVES FROM.
WHERE THE WORLD TURNS.
YOU'VE JUST GIVEN ME A GOOD IDEA.
DOOR.
INTERESTING.

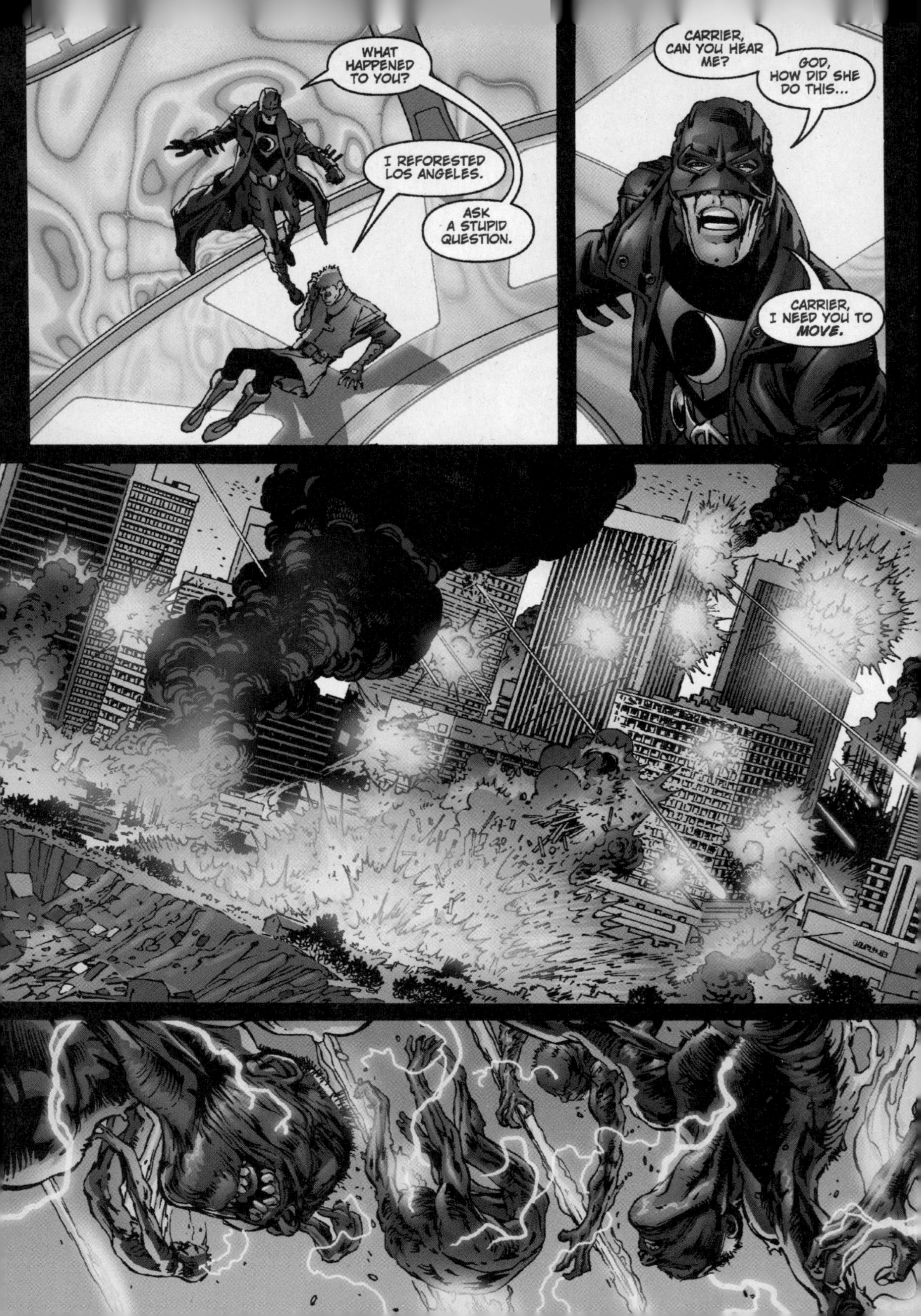
WHAT HAPPENED TO YOU?
I REFORESTED LOS ANGELES.
ASK A STUPID QUESTION.
CARRIER, CAN YOU HEAR ME?
GOD, HOW DID SHE DO THIS...
CARRIER, I NEED YOU TO *MOVE.*

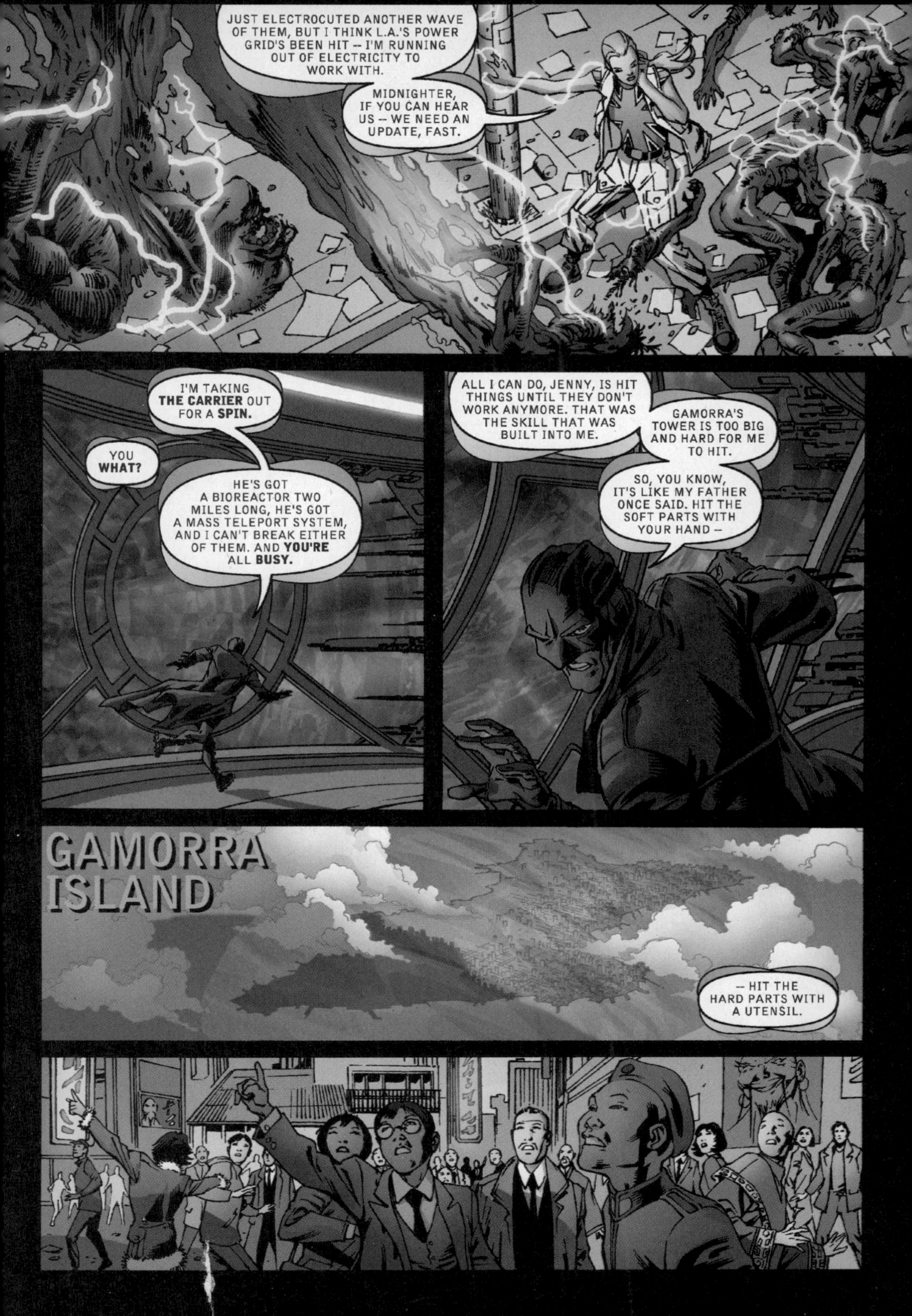
JUST ELECTROCUTED ANOTHER WAVE OF THEM, BUT I THINK L.A.'S POWER GRID'S BEEN HIT -- I'M RUNNING OUT OF ELECTRICITY TO WORK WITH.
MIDNIGHTER, IF YOU CAN HEAR US -- WE NEED AN UPDATE, FAST.
I'M TAKING THE CARRIER OUT FOR A SPIN.
YOU WHAT?
HE'S GOT A BIOREACTOR TWO MILES LONG, HE'S GOT A MASS TELEPORT SYSTEM, AND I CAN'T BREAK EITHER OF THEM. AND YOU'RE ALL BUSY.
ALL I CAN DO, JENNY, IS HIT THINGS UNTIL THEY DON'T WORK ANYMORE. THAT WAS THE SKILL THAT WAS BUILT INTO ME.
GAMORRA'S TOWER IS TOO BIG AND HARD FOR ME TO HIT.
SO, YOU KNOW, IT'S LIKE MY FATHER ONCE SAID. HIT THE SOFT PARTS WITH YOUR HAND --
GAMORRA ISLAND
-- HIT THE HARD PARTS WITH A UTENSIL.

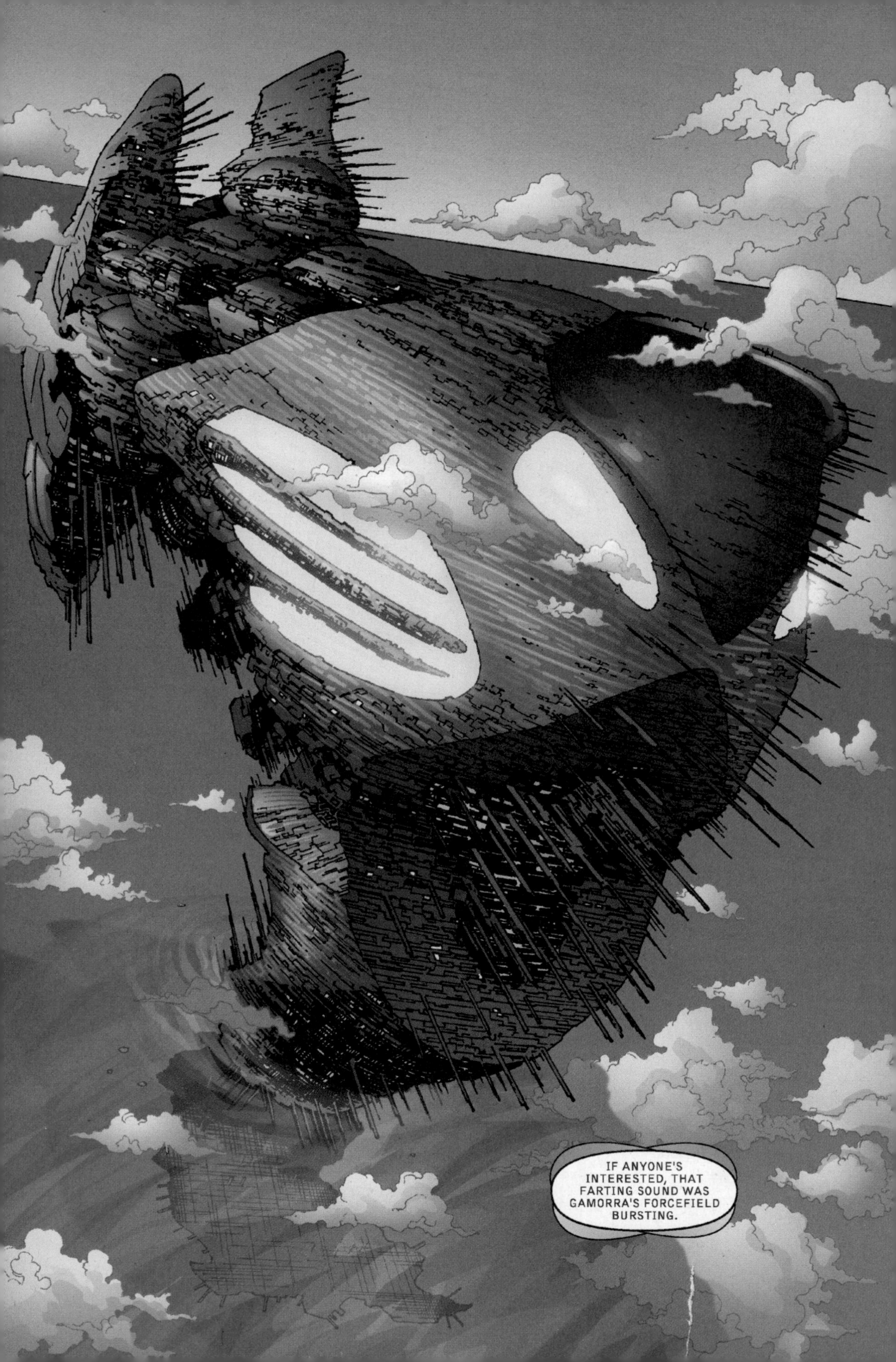
IF ANYONE'S INTERESTED, THAT FARTING SOUND WAS GAMORRA'S FORCEFIELD BURSTING.

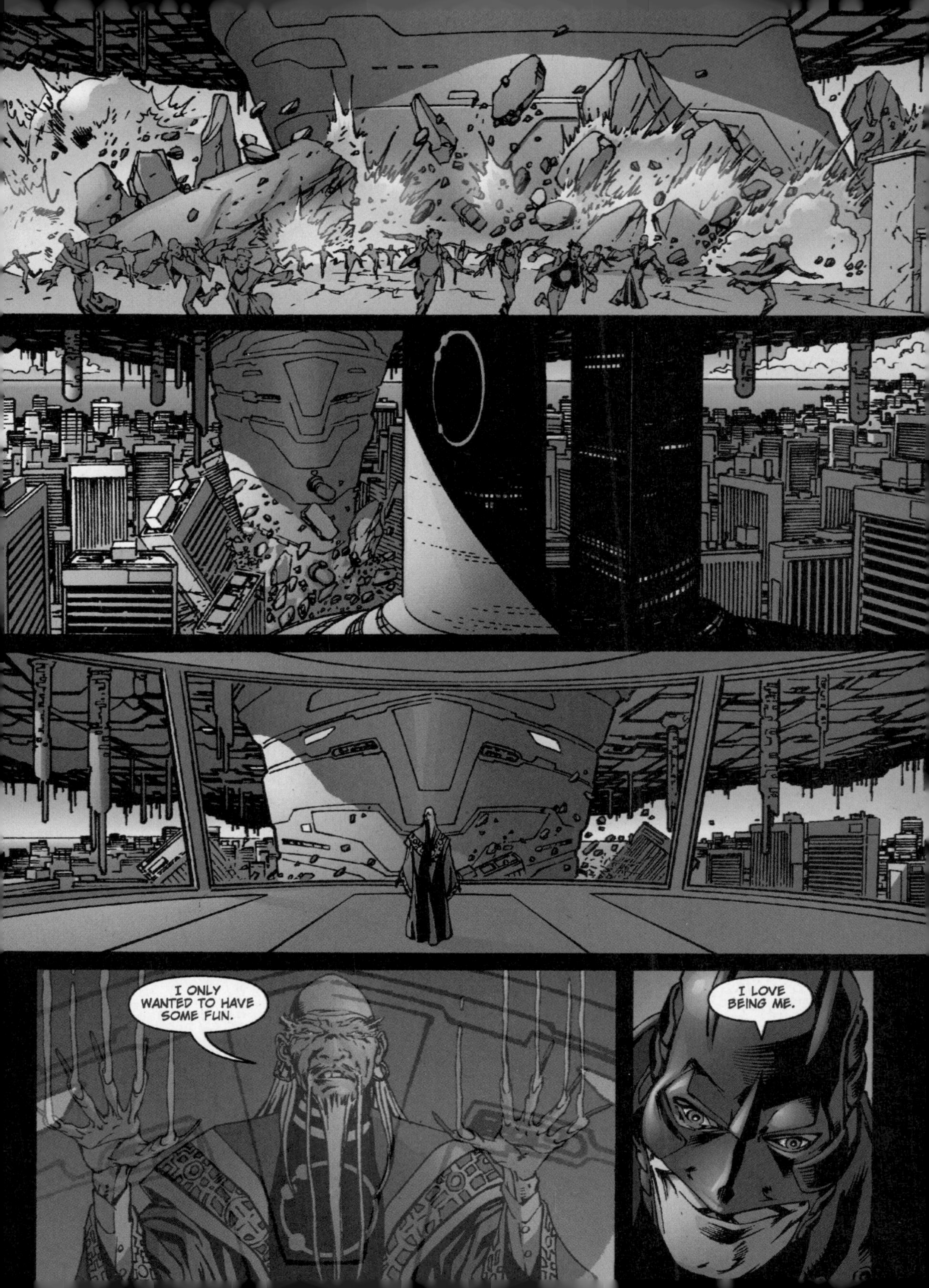
I ONLY WANTED TO HAVE SOME FUN.
I LOVE BEING ME.

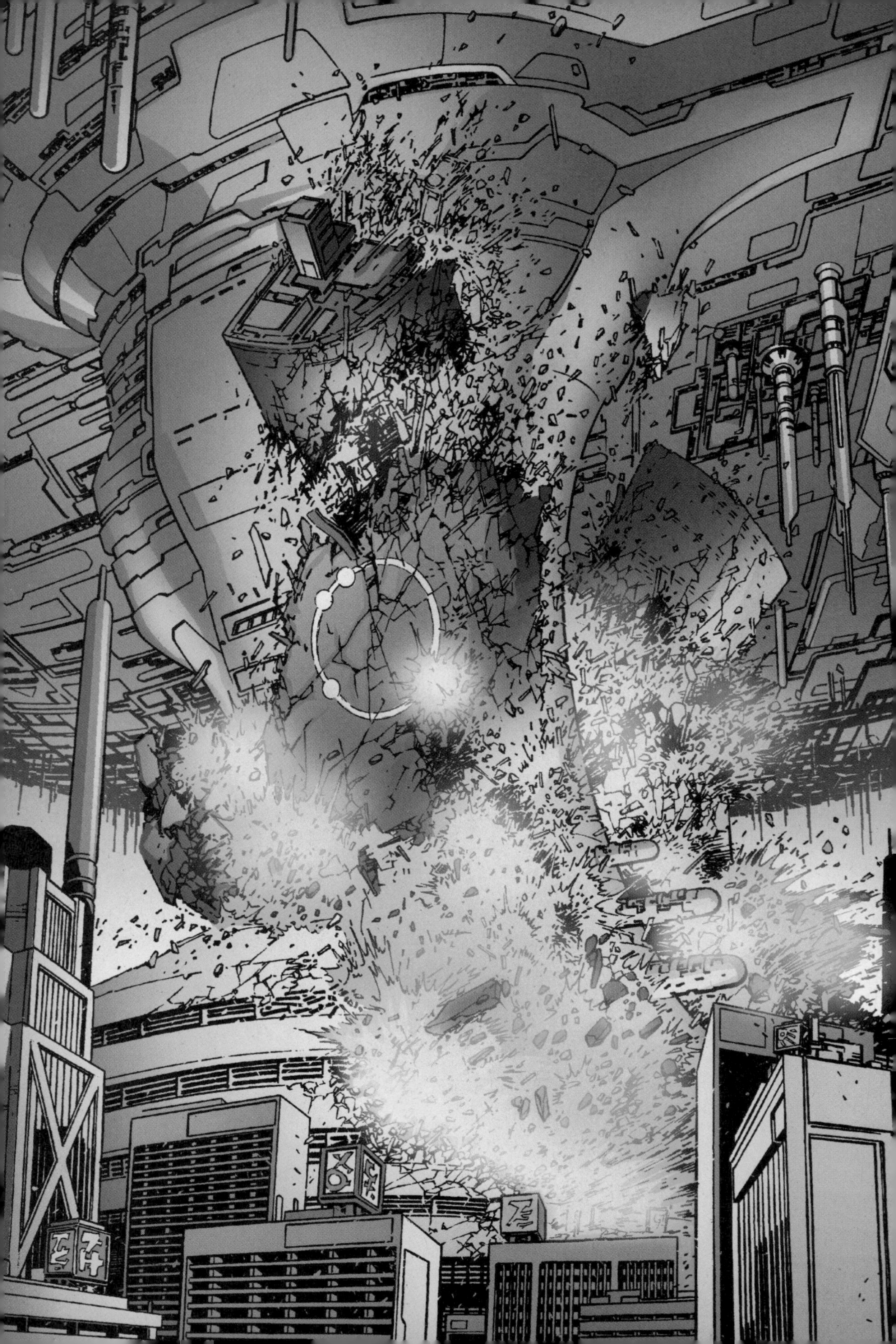

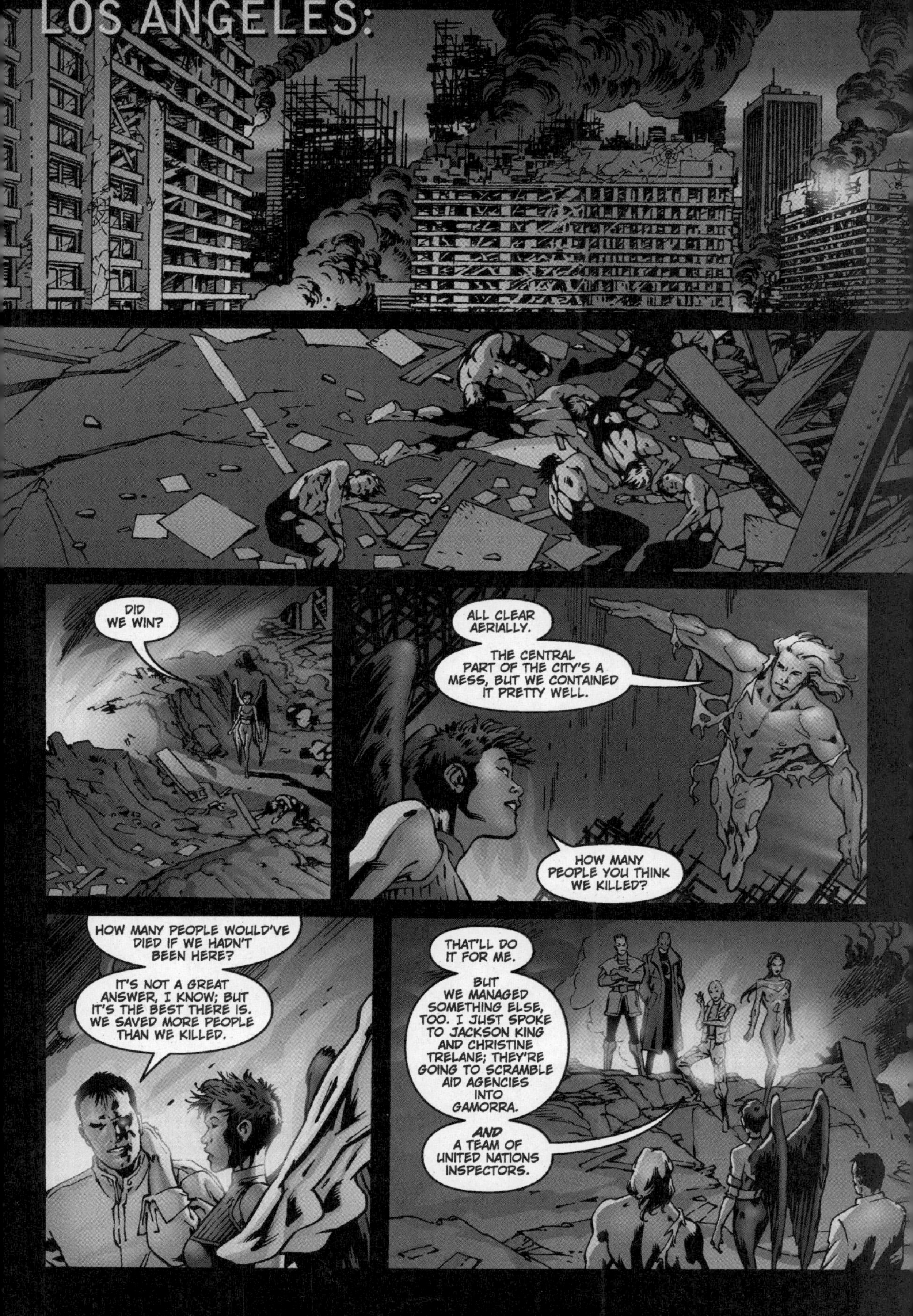
LOS ANGELES:
DID WE WIN?
ALL CLEAR AERIALLY.
THE CENTRAL PART OF THE CITY'S A MESS, BUT WE CONTAINED IT PRETTY WELL.
HOW MANY PEOPLE YOU THINK WE KILLED?
HOW MANY PEOPLE WOULD'VE DIED IF WE HADN'T BEEN HERE?
IT'S NOT A GREAT ANSWER, I KNOW; BUT IT'S THE BEST THERE IS. WE SAVED MORE PEOPLE THAN WE KILLED.
THAT'LL DO IT FOR ME.
BUT WE MANAGED SOMETHING ELSE, TOO. I JUST SPOKE TO JACKSON KING AND CHRISTINE TRELANE; THEY'RE GOING TO SCRAMBLE AID AGENCIES INTO GAMORRA.
AND A TEAM OF UNITED NATIONS INSPECTORS.

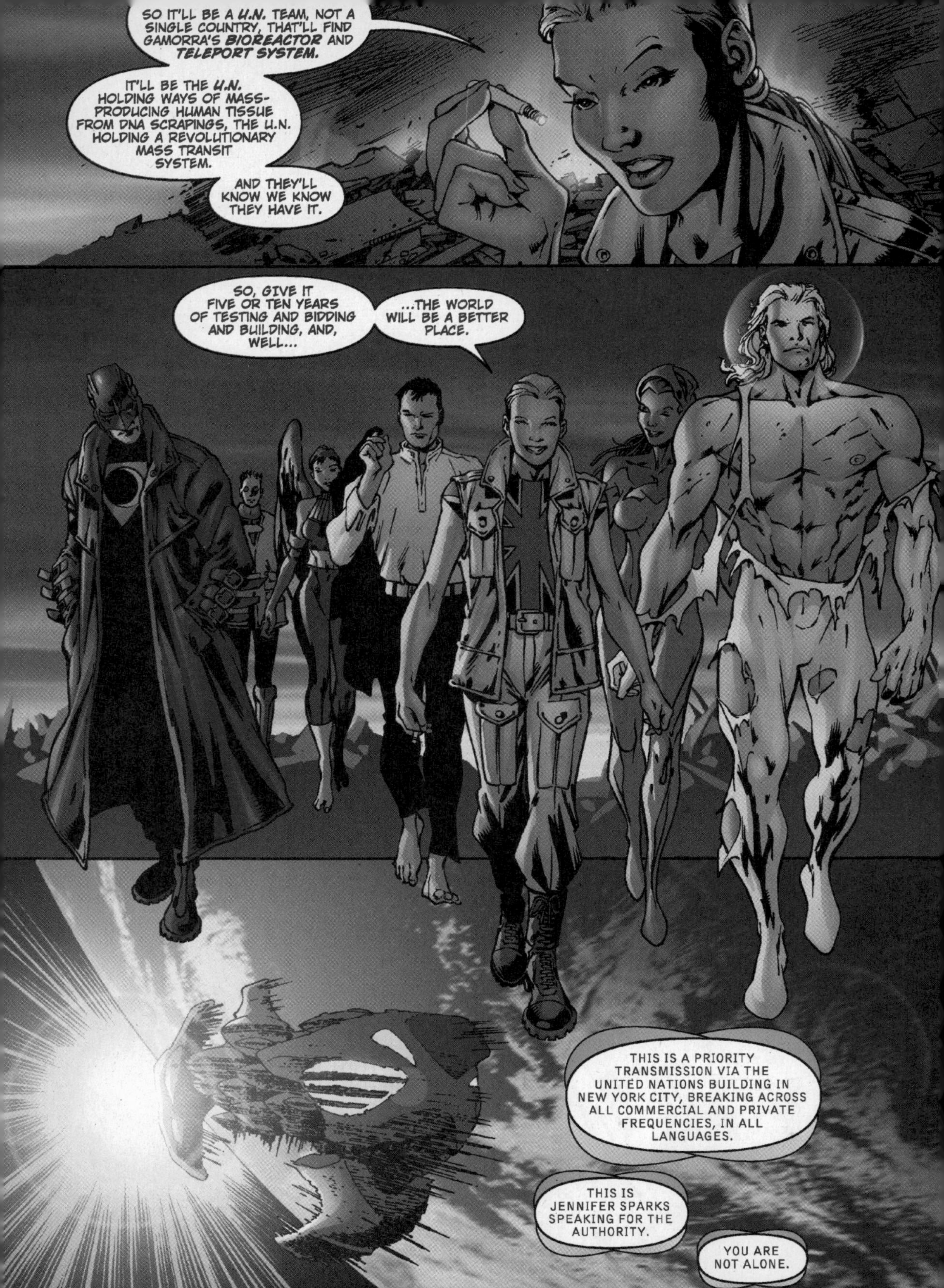
SO IT'LL BE A U.N. TEAM, NOT A SINGLE COUNTRY, THAT'LL FIND GAMORRA'S BIOREACTOR AND TELEPORT SYSTEM.
IT'LL BE THE U.N. HOLDING WAYS OF MASS-PRODUCING HUMAN TISSUE FROM DNA SCRAPINGS, THE U.N. HOLDING A REVOLUTIONARY MASS TRANSIT SYSTEM.
AND THEY'LL KNOW WE KNOW THEY HAVE IT.
SO, GIVE IT FIVE OR TEN YEARS OF TESTING AND BIDDING AND BUILDING, AND, WELL...
...THE WORLD WILL BE A BETTER PLACE.
THIS IS A PRIORITY TRANSMISSION VIA THE UNITED NATIONS BUILDING IN NEW YORK CITY, BREAKING ACROSS ALL COMMERCIAL AND PRIVATE FREQUENCIES, IN ALL LANGUAGES.
THIS IS JENNIFER SPARKS SPEAKING FOR THE AUTHORITY.
YOU ARE NOT ALONE.

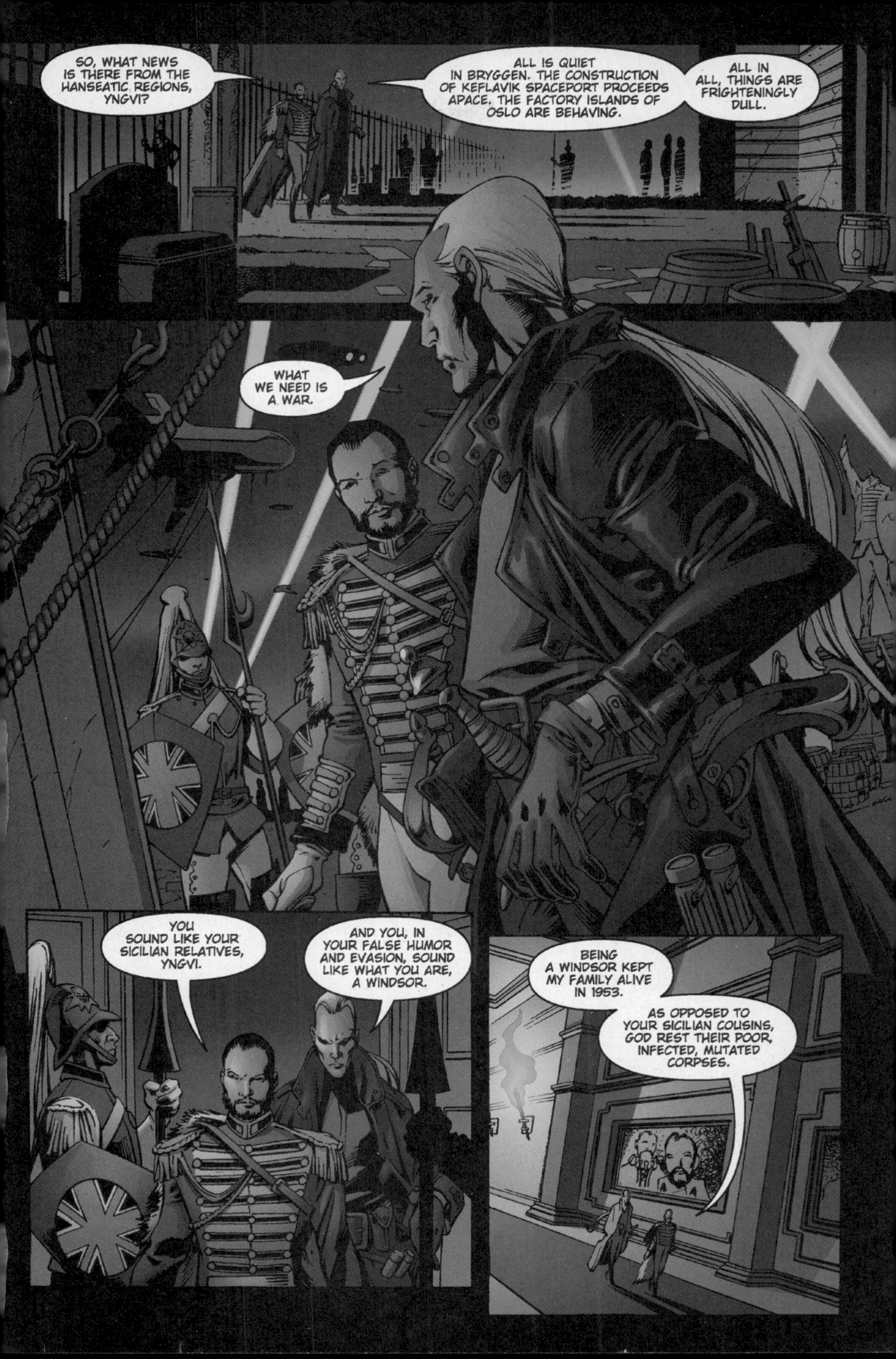
SO, WHAT NEWS IS THERE FROM THE HANSEATIC REGIONS, YNGVI?
ALL IS QUIET IN BRYGGEN. THE CONSTRUCTION OF KEFLAVIK SPACEPORT PROCEEDS APACE. THE FACTORY ISLANDS OF OSLO ARE BEHAVING.
ALL IN ALL, THINGS ARE FRIGHTENINGLY DULL.
WHAT WE NEED IS A WAR.
YOU SOUND LIKE YOUR SICILIAN RELATIVES, YNGVI.
AND YOU, IN YOUR FALSE HUMOR AND EVASION, SOUND LIKE WHAT YOU ARE, A WINDSOR.
BEING A WINDSOR KEPT MY FAMILY ALIVE IN 1953.
AS OPPOSED TO YOUR SICILIAN COUSINS, GOD REST THEIR POOR, INFECTED, MUTATED CORPSES.

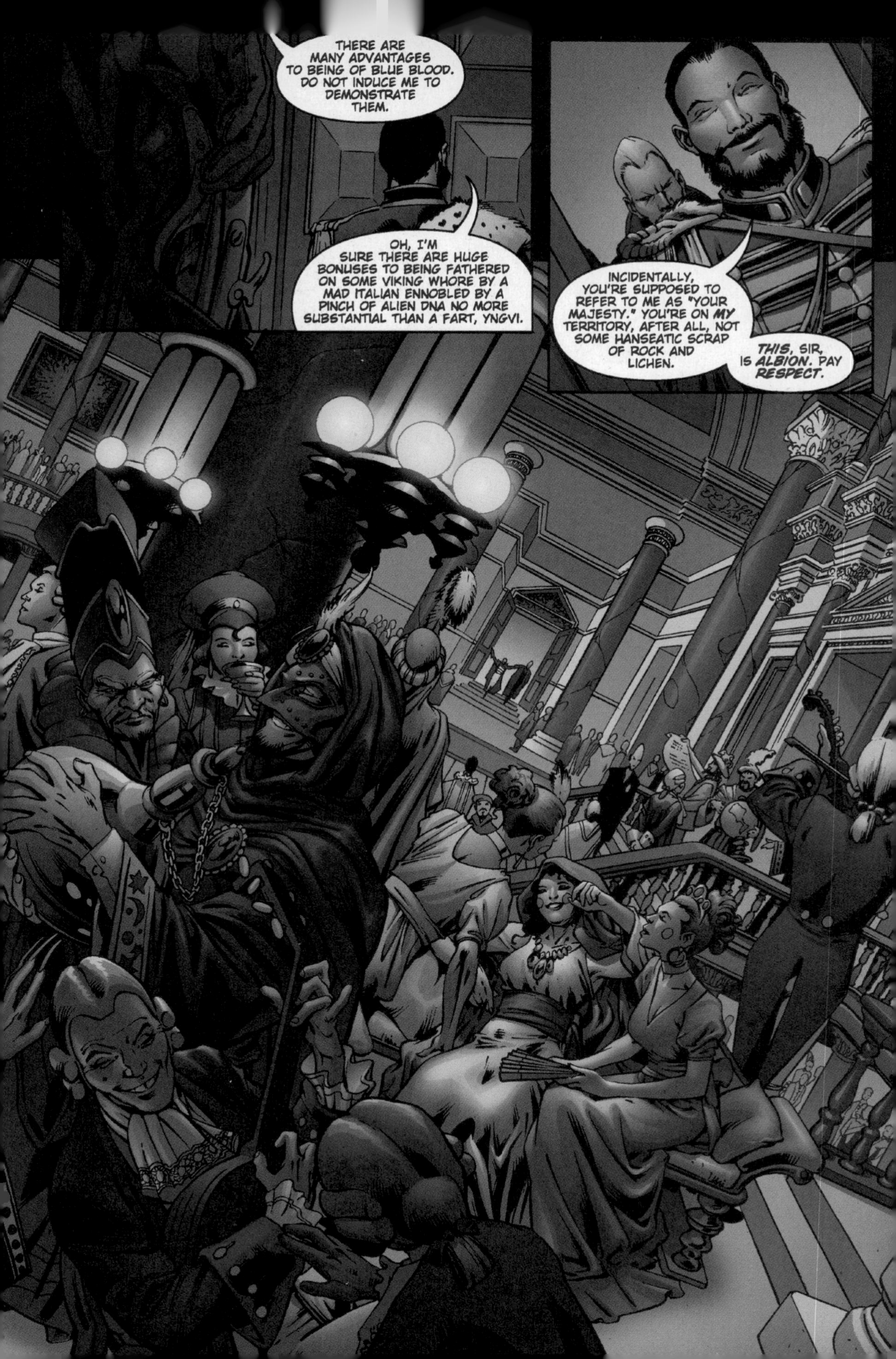
THERE ARE MANY ADVANTAGES TO BEING OF BLUE BLOOD. DO NOT INDUCE ME TO DEMONSTRATE THEM.
OH, I'M SURE THERE ARE HUGE BONUSES TO BEING FATHERED ON SOME VIKING WHORE BY A MAD ITALIAN ENNOBLED BY A PINCH OF ALIEN DNA NO MORE SUBSTANTIAL THAN A FART, YNGVI.
INCIDENTALLY, YOU'RE SUPPOSED TO REFER TO ME AS "YOUR MAJESTY." YOU'RE ON *MY* TERRITORY, AFTER ALL, NOT SOME HANSEATIC SCRAP OF ROCK AND LICHEN.
THIS, SIR, IS *ALBION*. PAY *RESPECT*.

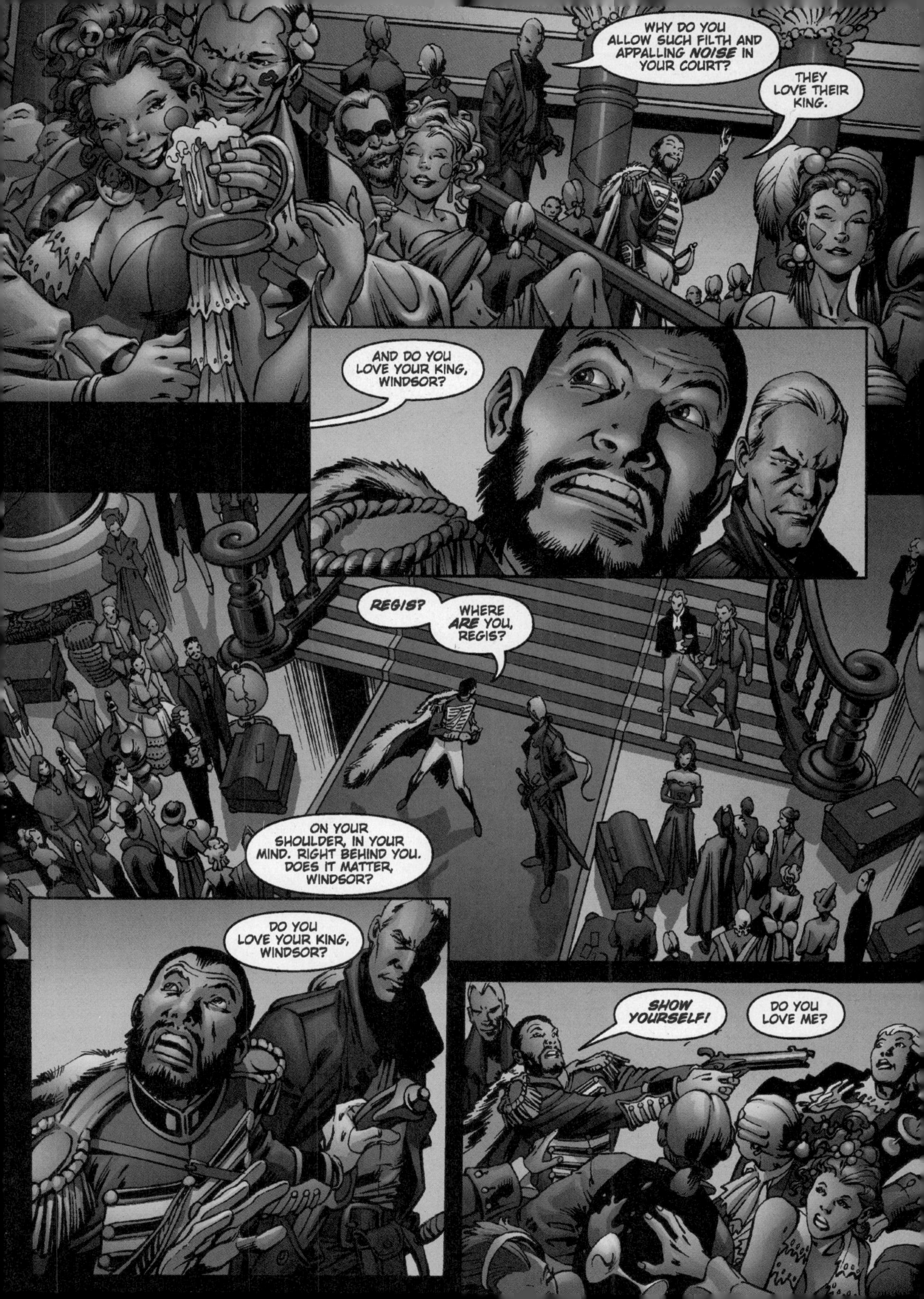
WHY DO YOU ALLOW SUCH FILTH AND APPALLING NOISE IN YOUR COURT?
THEY LOVE THEIR KING.
AND DO YOU LOVE YOUR KING, WINDSOR?
REGIS?
WHERE ARE YOU, REGIS?
ON YOUR SHOULDER, IN YOUR MIND. RIGHT BEHIND YOU. DOES IT MATTER, WINDSOR?
DO YOU LOVE YOUR KING, WINDSOR?
SHOW YOURSELF!
DO YOU LOVE ME?

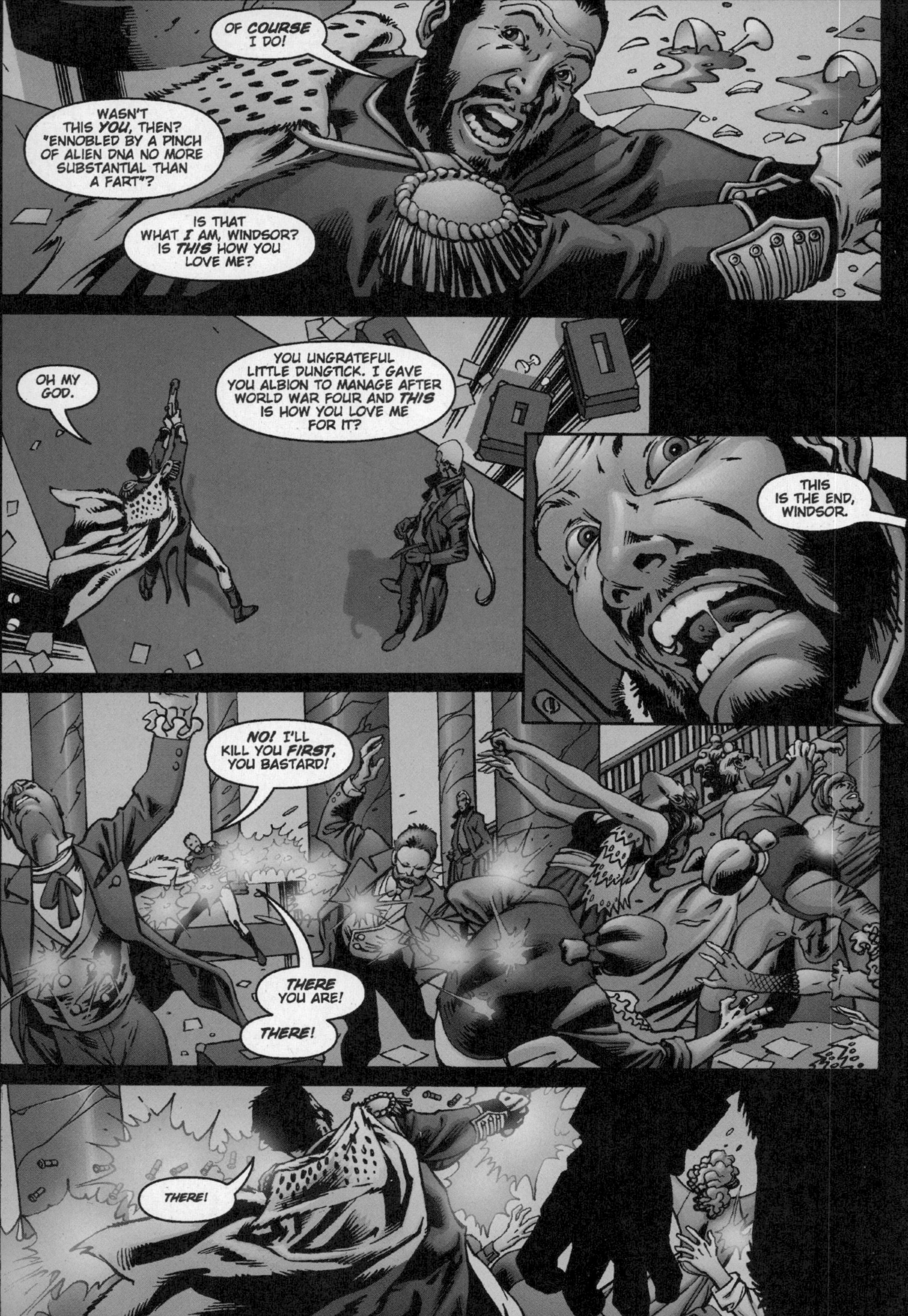
OF *COURSE* I DO!
WASN'T THIS *YOU*, THEN? "ENNOBLED BY A PINCH OF ALIEN DNA NO MORE SUBSTANTIAL THAN A FART"?
IS THAT WHAT *I* AM, WINDSOR? IS *THIS* HOW YOU LOVE ME?
OH MY GOD.
YOU UNGRATEFUL LITTLE DUNGTICK. I GAVE YOU ALBION TO MANAGE AFTER WORLD WAR FOUR AND *THIS* IS HOW YOU LOVE ME FOR IT?
THIS IS THE END, WINDSOR.
NO! I'LL KILL YOU *FIRST*, YOU BASTARD!
THERE YOU ARE!
THERE!
THERE!

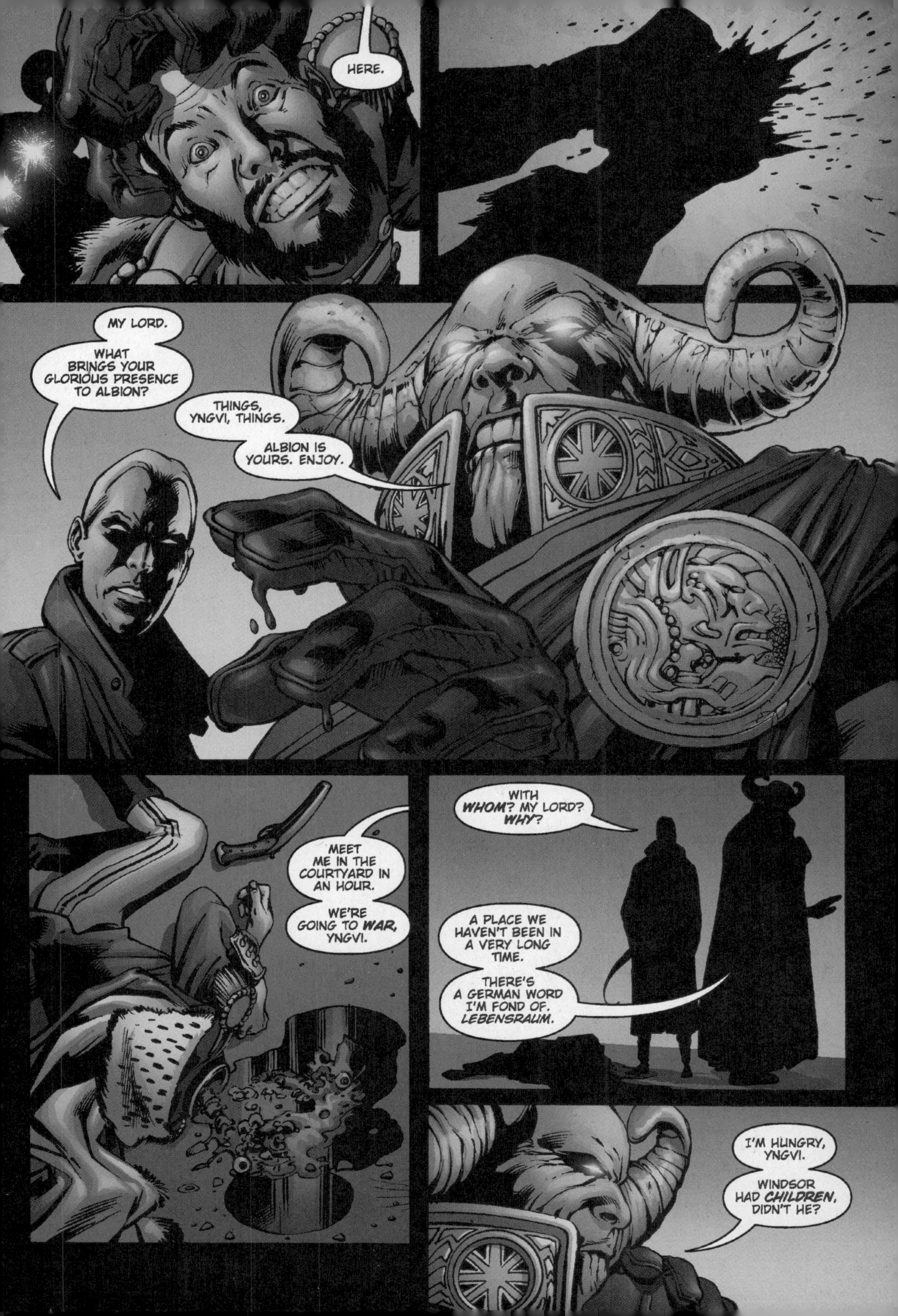
HERE.
MY LORD.
WHAT BRINGS YOUR GLORIOUS PRESENCE TO ALBION?
THINGS, YNGVI, THINGS.
ALBION IS YOURS. ENJOY.
MEET ME IN THE COURTYARD IN AN HOUR.
WE'RE GOING TO **WAR**, YNGVI.
WITH **WHOM**? MY LORD? **WHY**?
A PLACE WE HAVEN'T BEEN IN A VERY LONG TIME.
THERE'S A GERMAN WORD I'M FOND OF. *LEBENSRAUM*.
I'M HUNGRY, YNGVI.
WINDSOR HAD **CHILDREN**, DIDN'T HE?

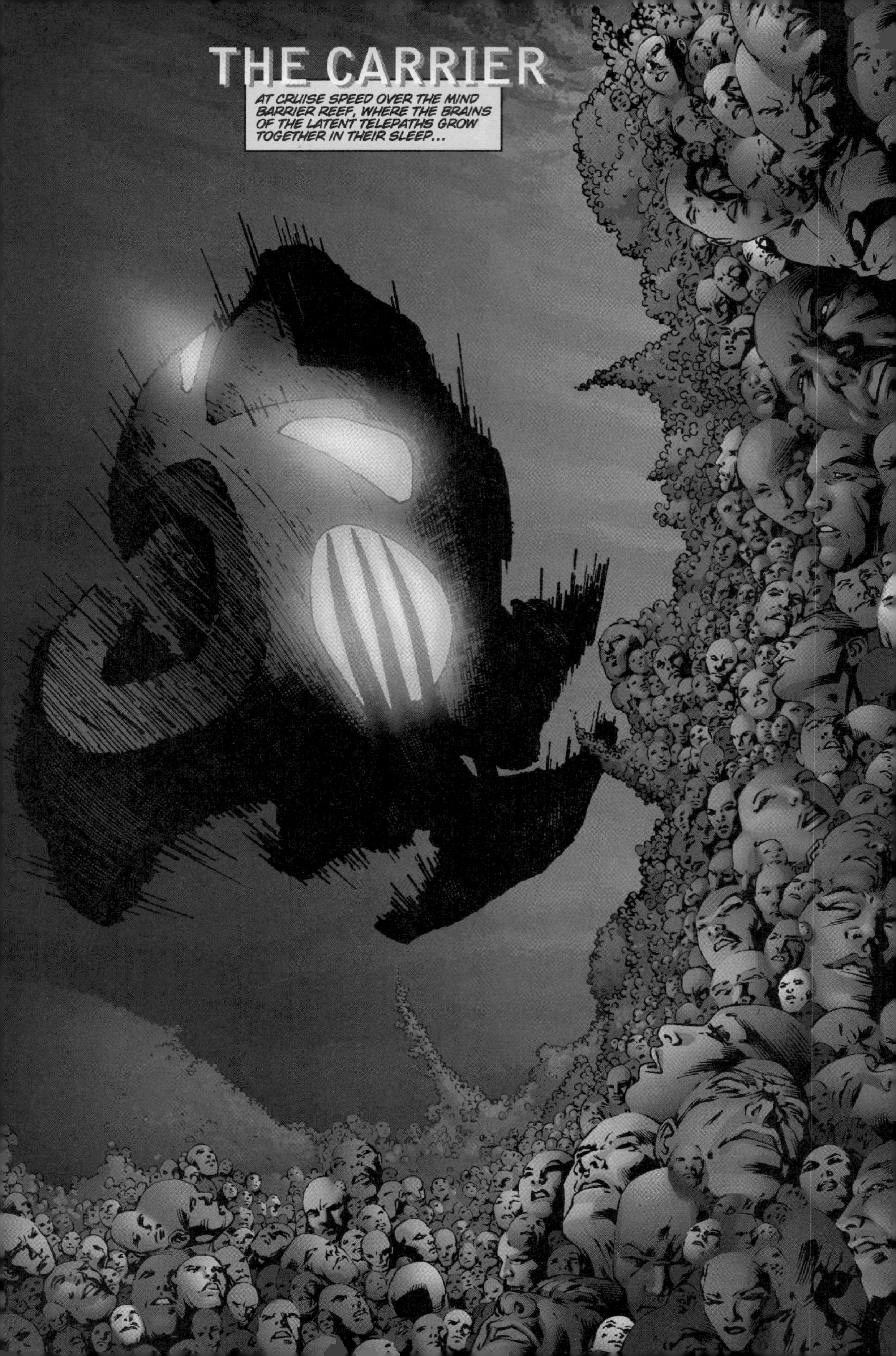
THE CARRIER
AT CRUISE SPEED OVER THE MIND BARRIER REEF, WHERE THE BRAINS OF THE LATENT TELEPATHS GROW TOGETHER IN THEIR SLEEP...

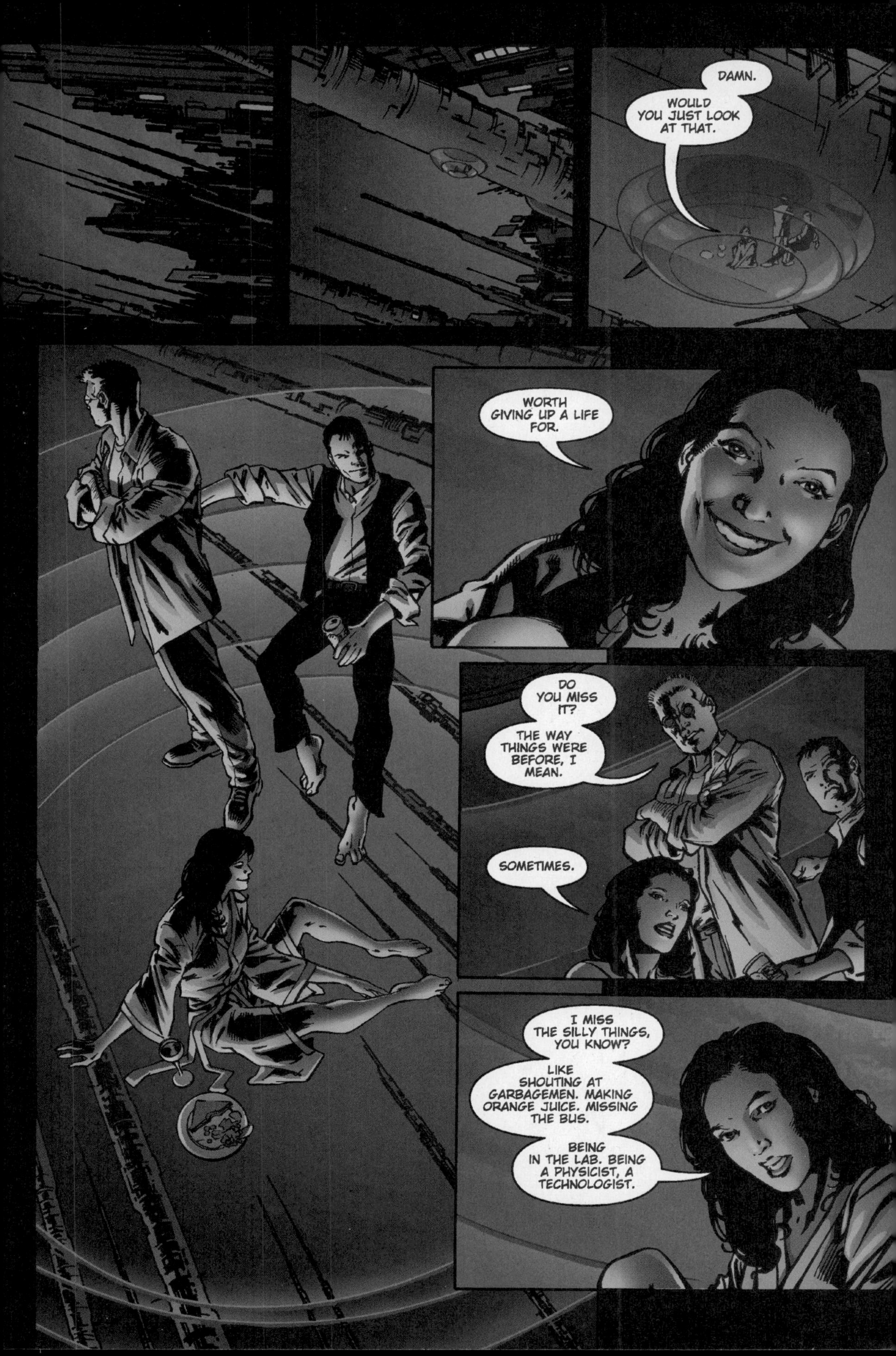
DAMN.
WOULD YOU JUST LOOK AT THAT.
WORTH GIVING UP A LIFE FOR.
DO YOU MISS IT?
THE WAY THINGS WERE BEFORE, I MEAN.
SOMETIMES.
I MISS THE SILLY THINGS, YOU KNOW?
LIKE SHOUTING AT GARBAGEMEN. MAKING ORANGE JUICE. MISSING THE BUS.
BEING IN THE LAB. BEING A PHYSICIST, A TECHNOLOGIST.

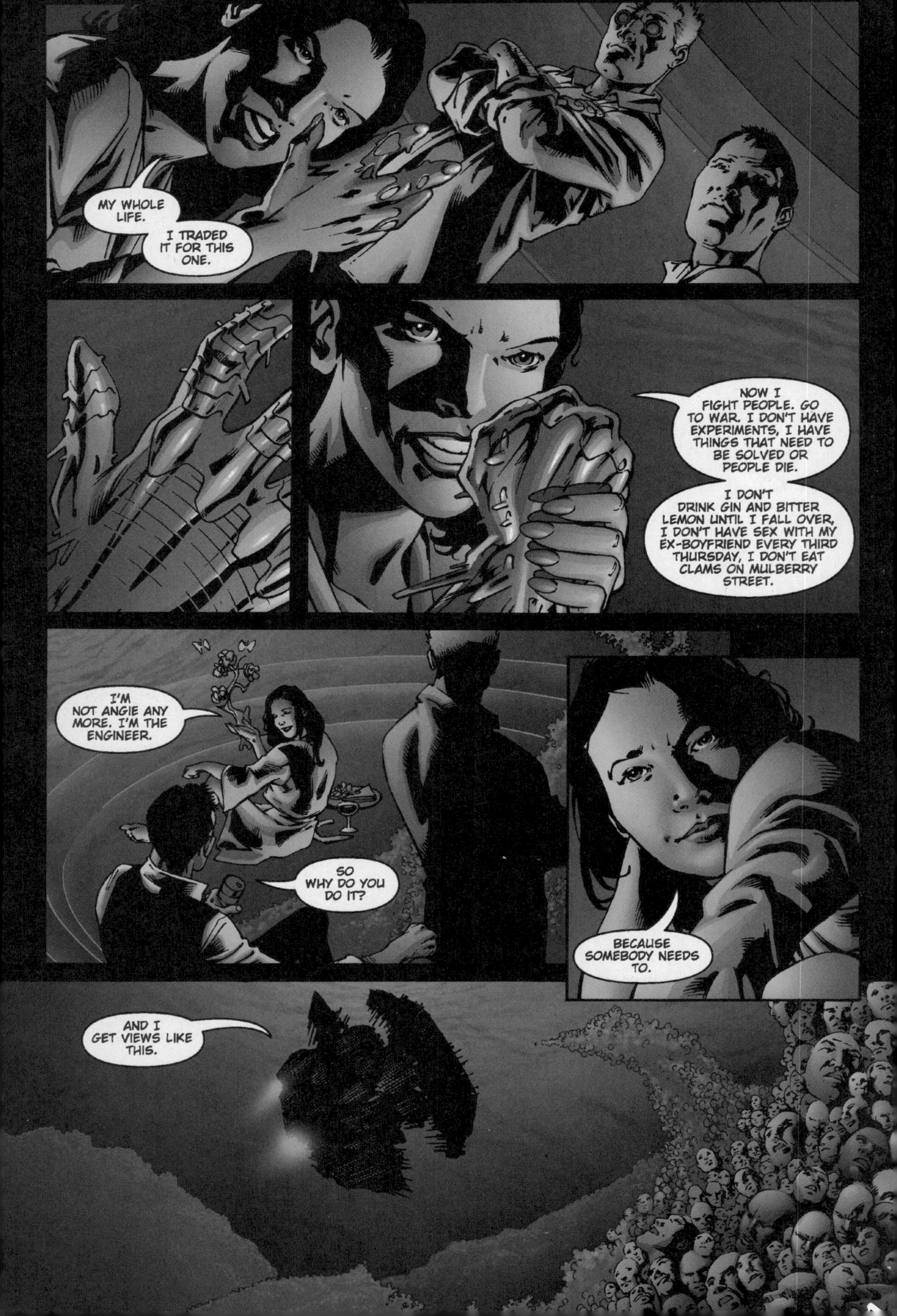
MY WHOLE LIFE.
I TRADED IT FOR THIS ONE.
NOW I FIGHT PEOPLE. GO TO WAR. I DON'T HAVE EXPERIMENTS, I HAVE THINGS THAT NEED TO BE SOLVED OR PEOPLE DIE.
I DON'T DRINK GIN AND BITTER LEMON UNTIL I FALL OVER, I DON'T HAVE SEX WITH MY EX-BOYFRIEND EVERY THIRD THURSDAY, I DON'T EAT CLAMS ON MULBERRY STREET.
I'M NOT ANGIE ANY MORE. I'M THE ENGINEER.
SO WHY DO YOU DO IT?
BECAUSE SOMEBODY NEEDS TO.
AND I GET VIEWS LIKE THIS.

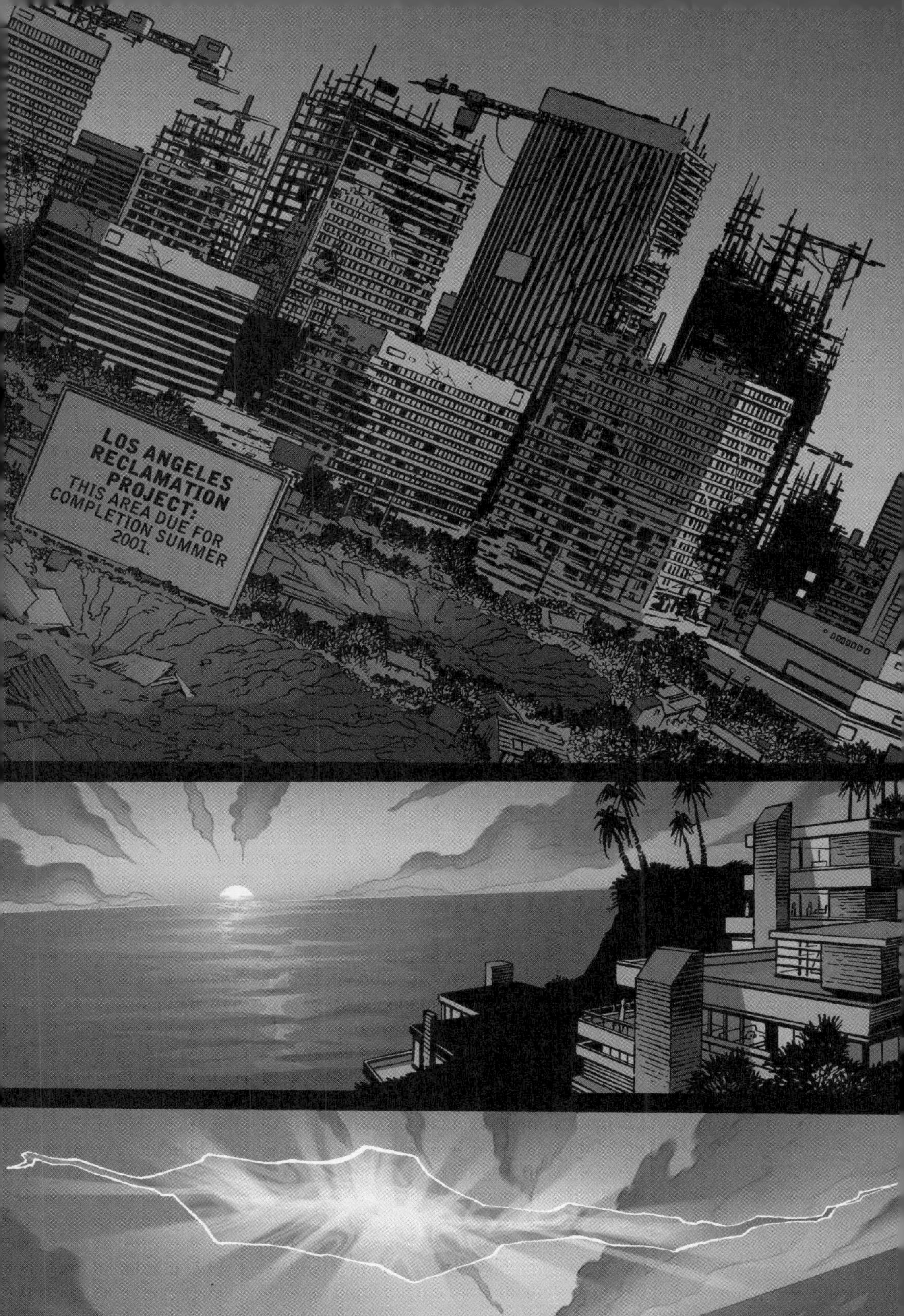
LOS ANGELES
RECLAMATION
PROJECT:
THIS AREA DUE FOR
COMPLETION SUMMER
2001.

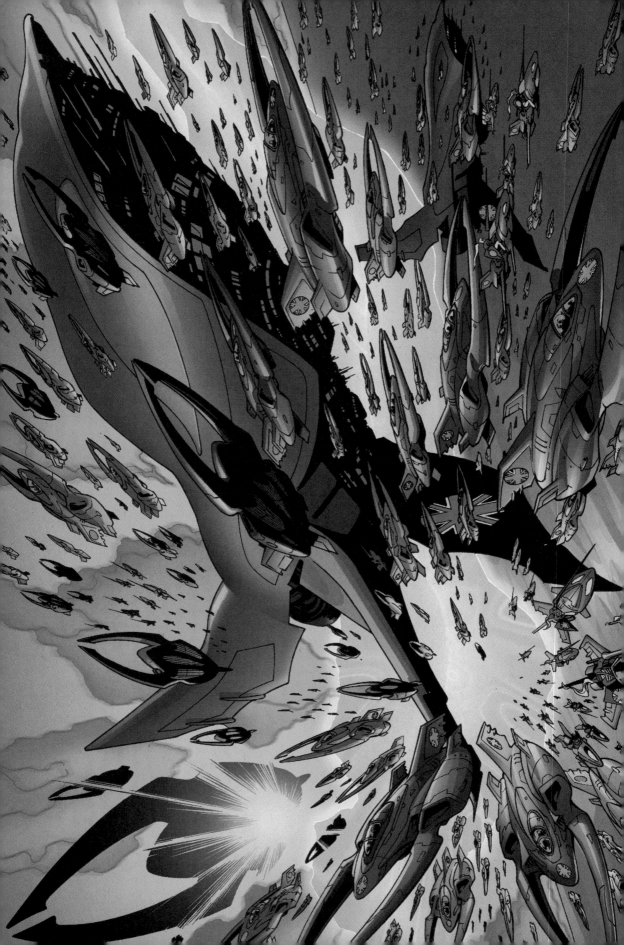

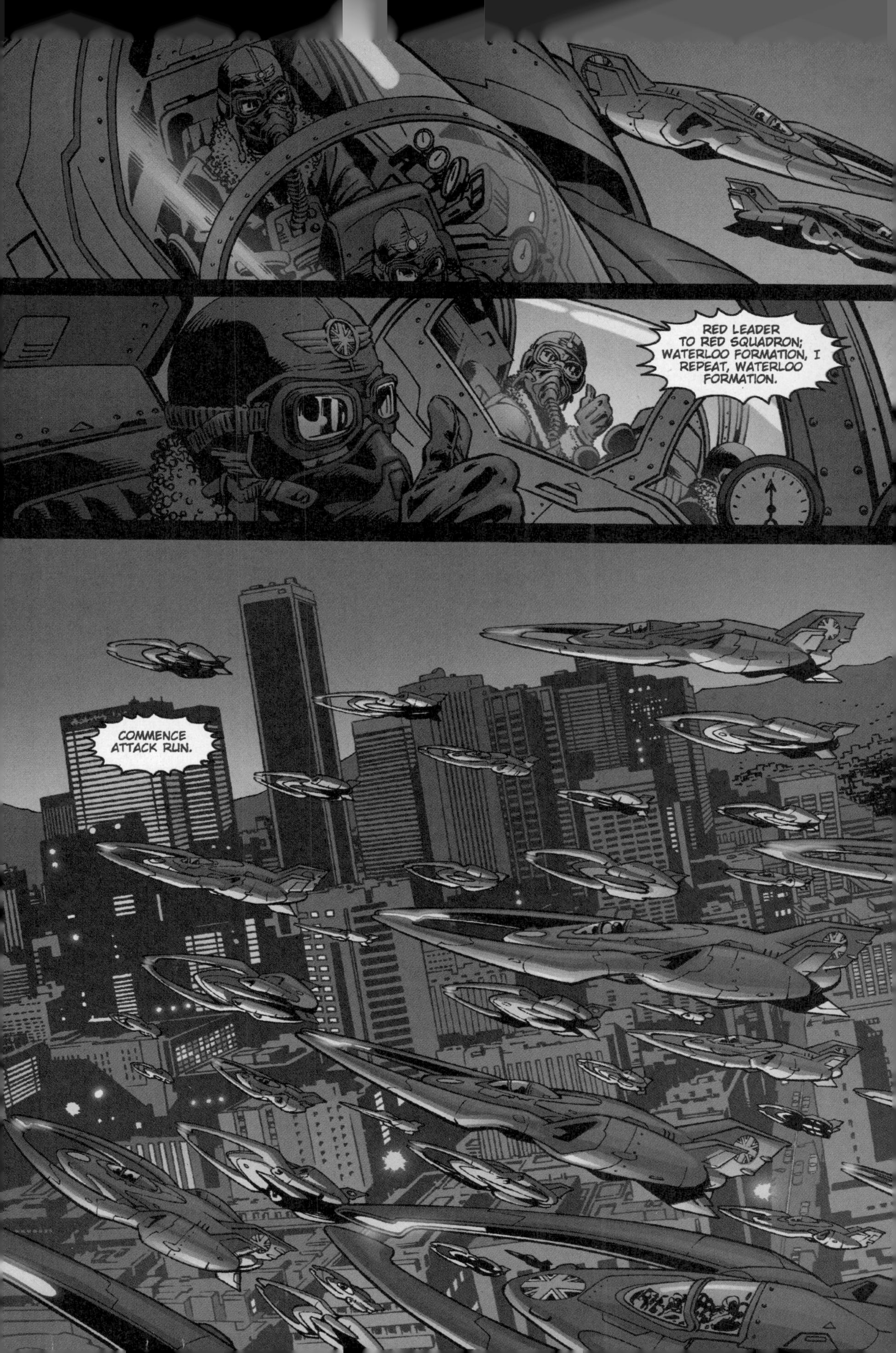
RED LEADER TO RED SQUADRON; WATERLOO FORMATION, I REPEAT, WATERLOO FORMATION.
COMMENCE ATTACK RUN.

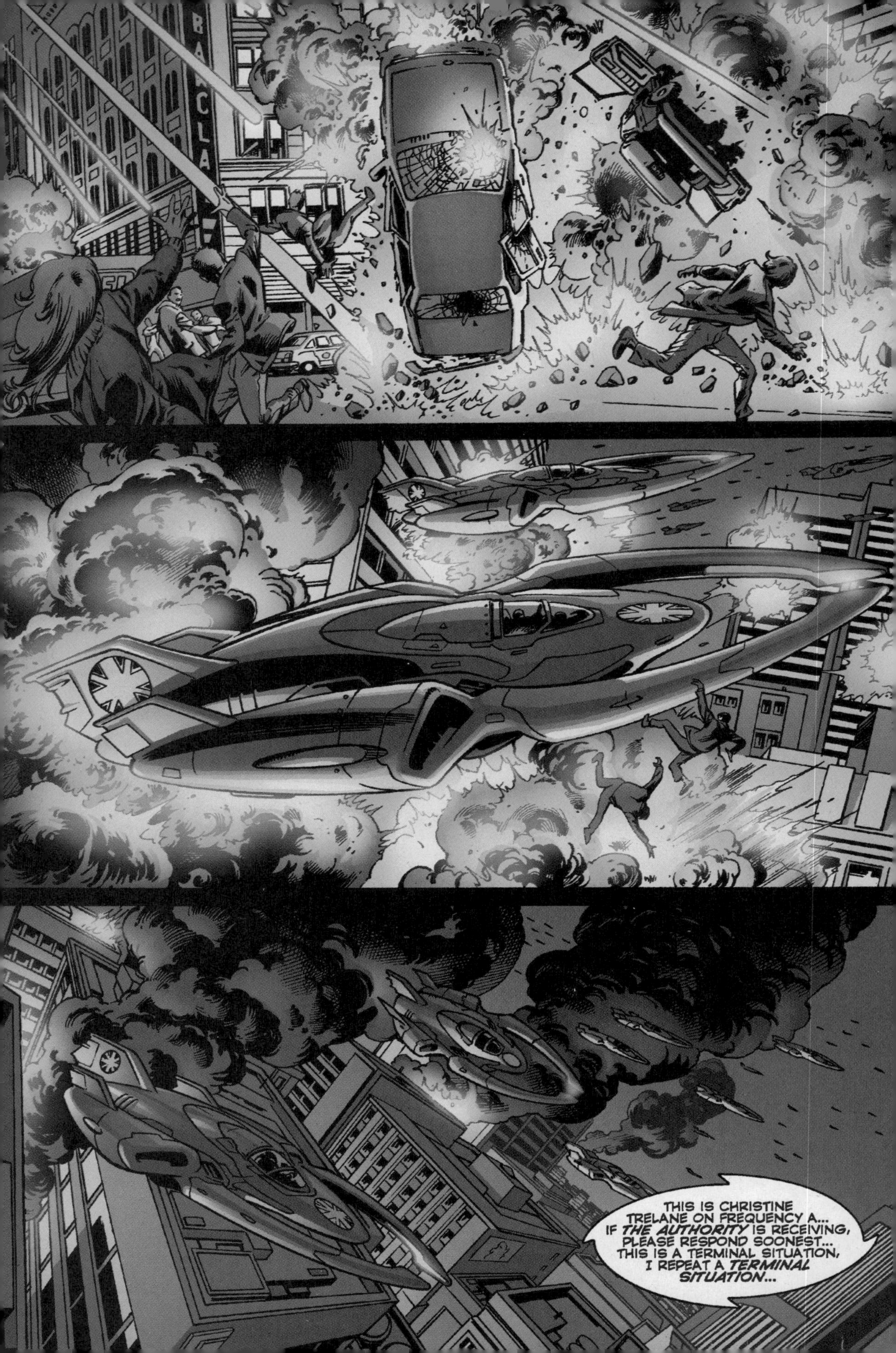
THIS IS CHRISTINE TRELANE ON FREQUENCY A... IF THE AUTHORITY IS RECEIVING, PLEASE RESPOND SOONEST... THIS IS A TERMINAL SITUATION, I REPEAT A TERMINAL SITUATION...

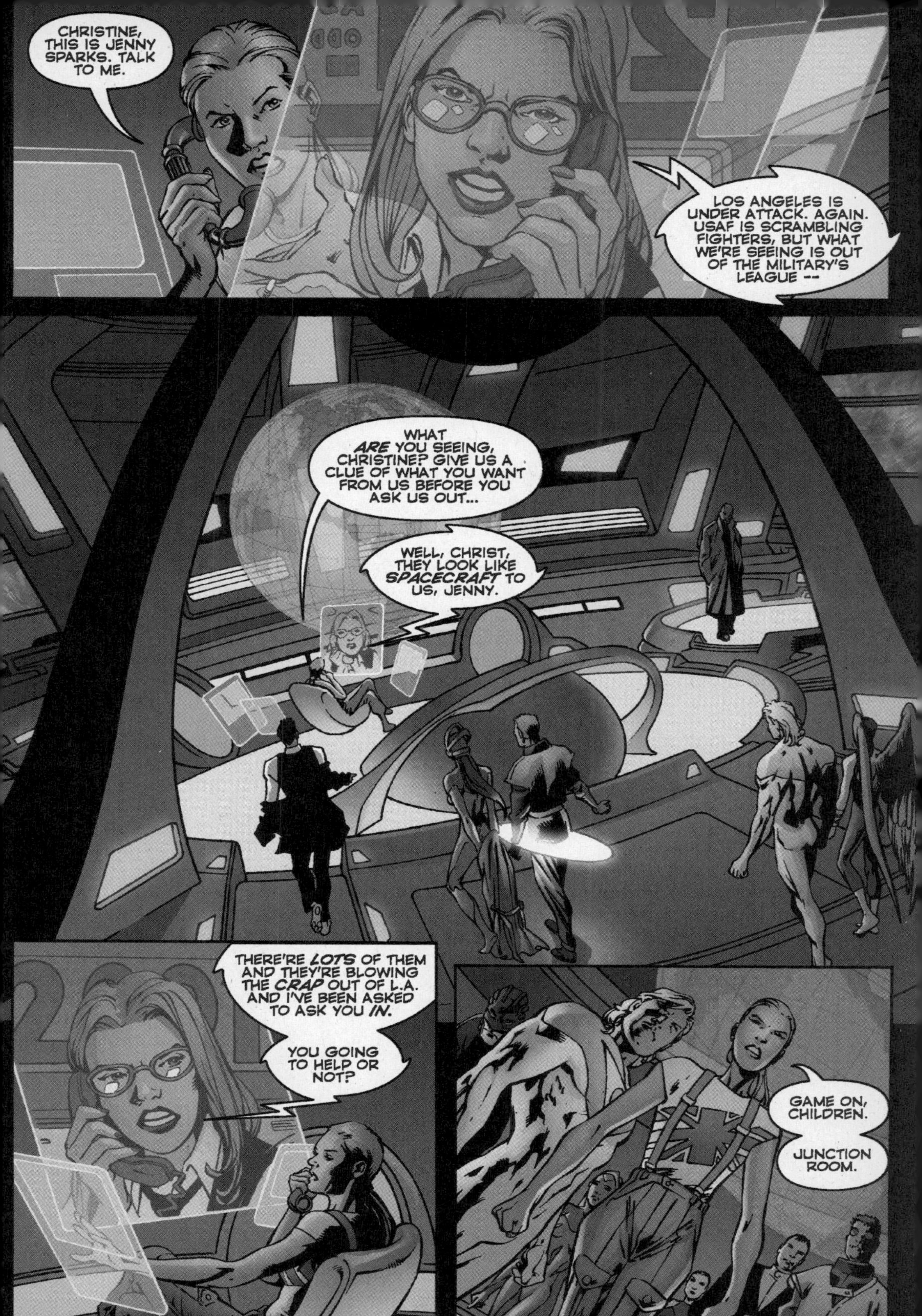
CHRISTINE, THIS IS JENNY SPARKS. TALK TO ME.
LOS ANGELES IS UNDER ATTACK. AGAIN. USAF IS SCRAMBLING FIGHTERS, BUT WHAT WE'RE SEEING IS OUT OF THE MILITARY'S LEAGUE --
WHAT *ARE* YOU SEEING, CHRISTINE? GIVE US A CLUE OF WHAT YOU WANT FROM US BEFORE YOU ASK US OUT...
WELL, CHRIST, THEY LOOK LIKE *SPACECRAFT* TO US, JENNY.
THERE'RE *LOTS* OF THEM AND THEY'RE BLOWING THE *CRAP* OUT OF L.A. AND I'VE BEEN ASKED TO ASK YOU *IN*.
YOU GOING TO HELP OR NOT?
GAME ON, CHILDREN.
JUNCTION ROOM.

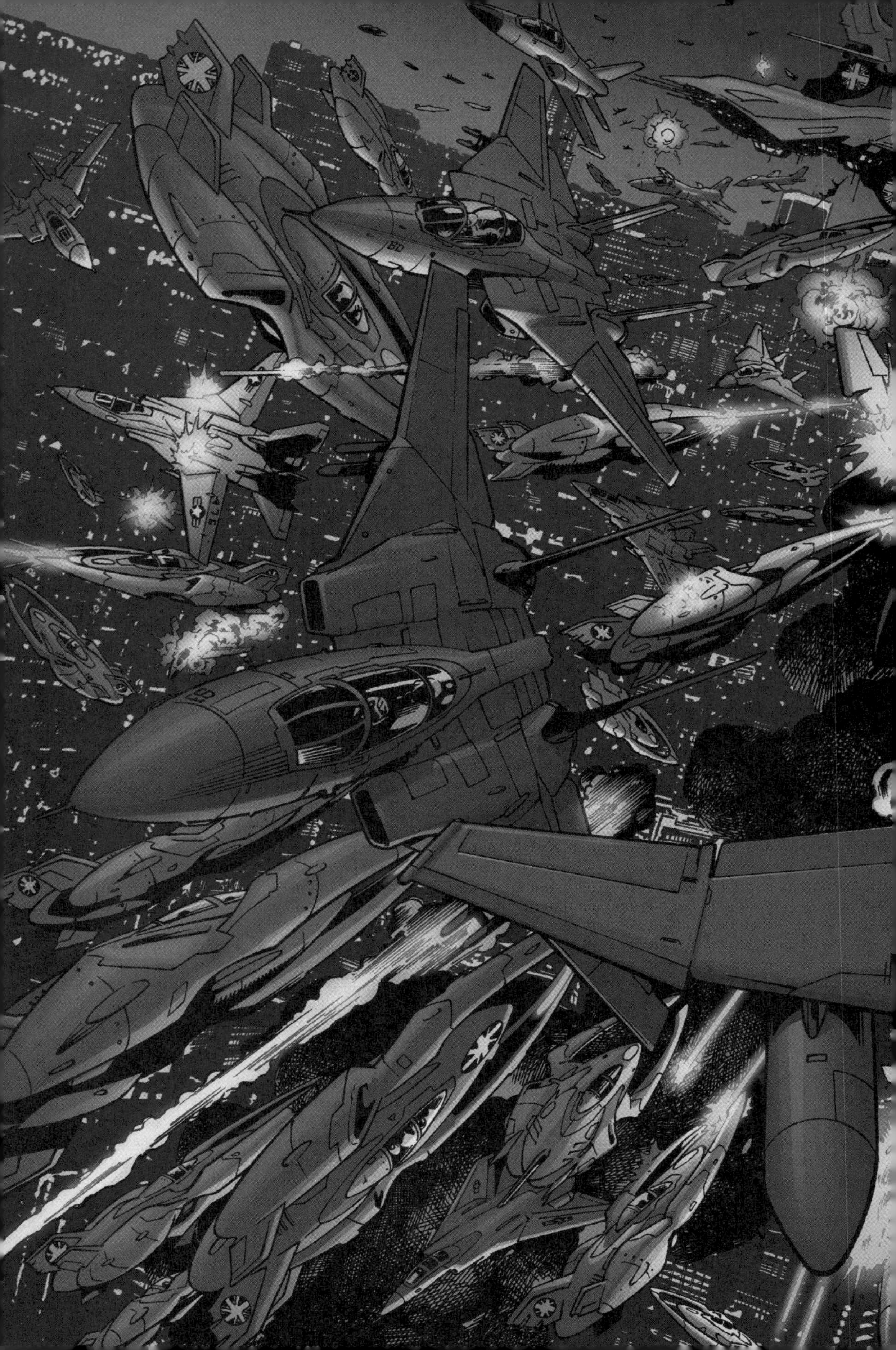

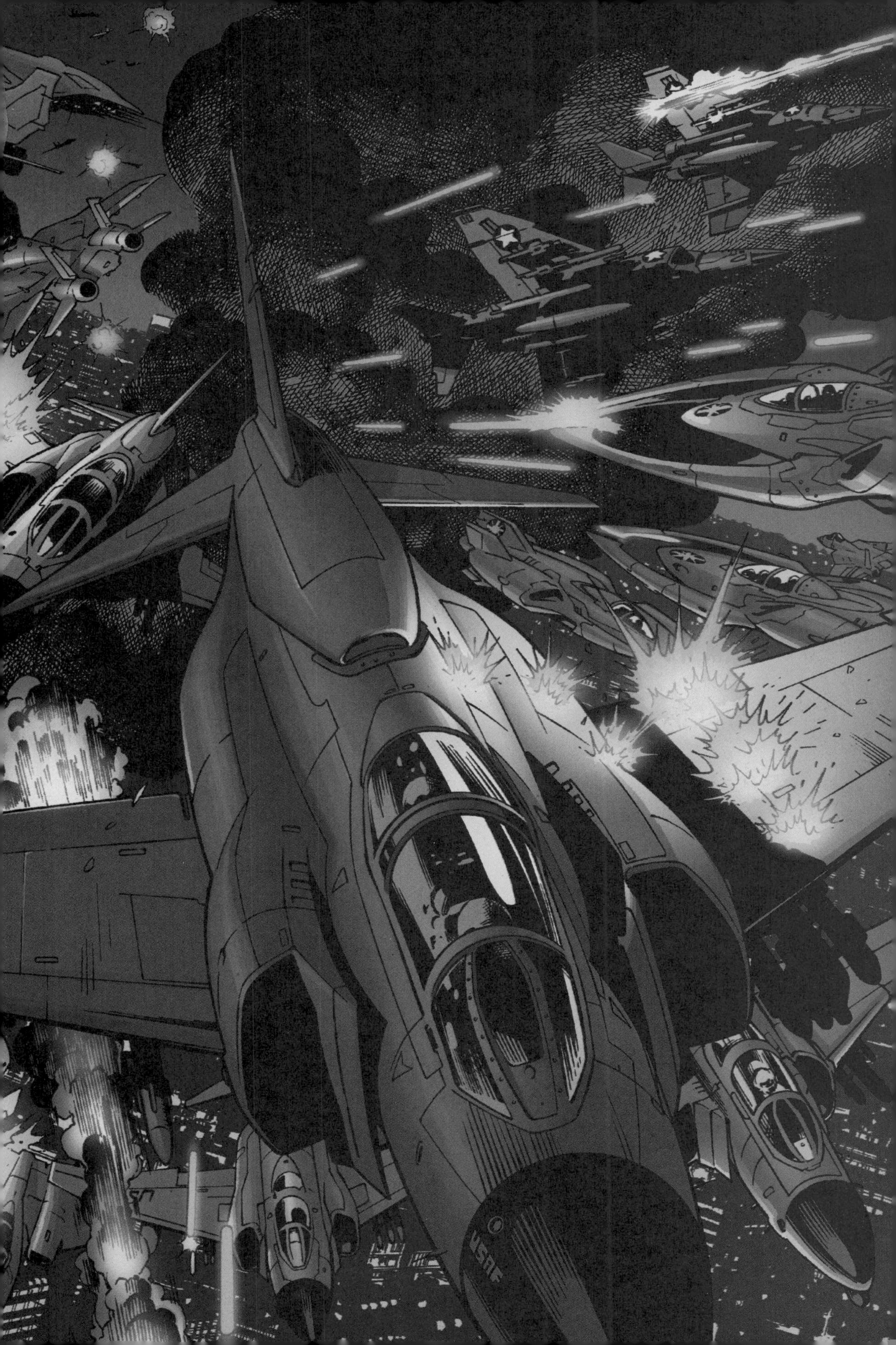
USAF

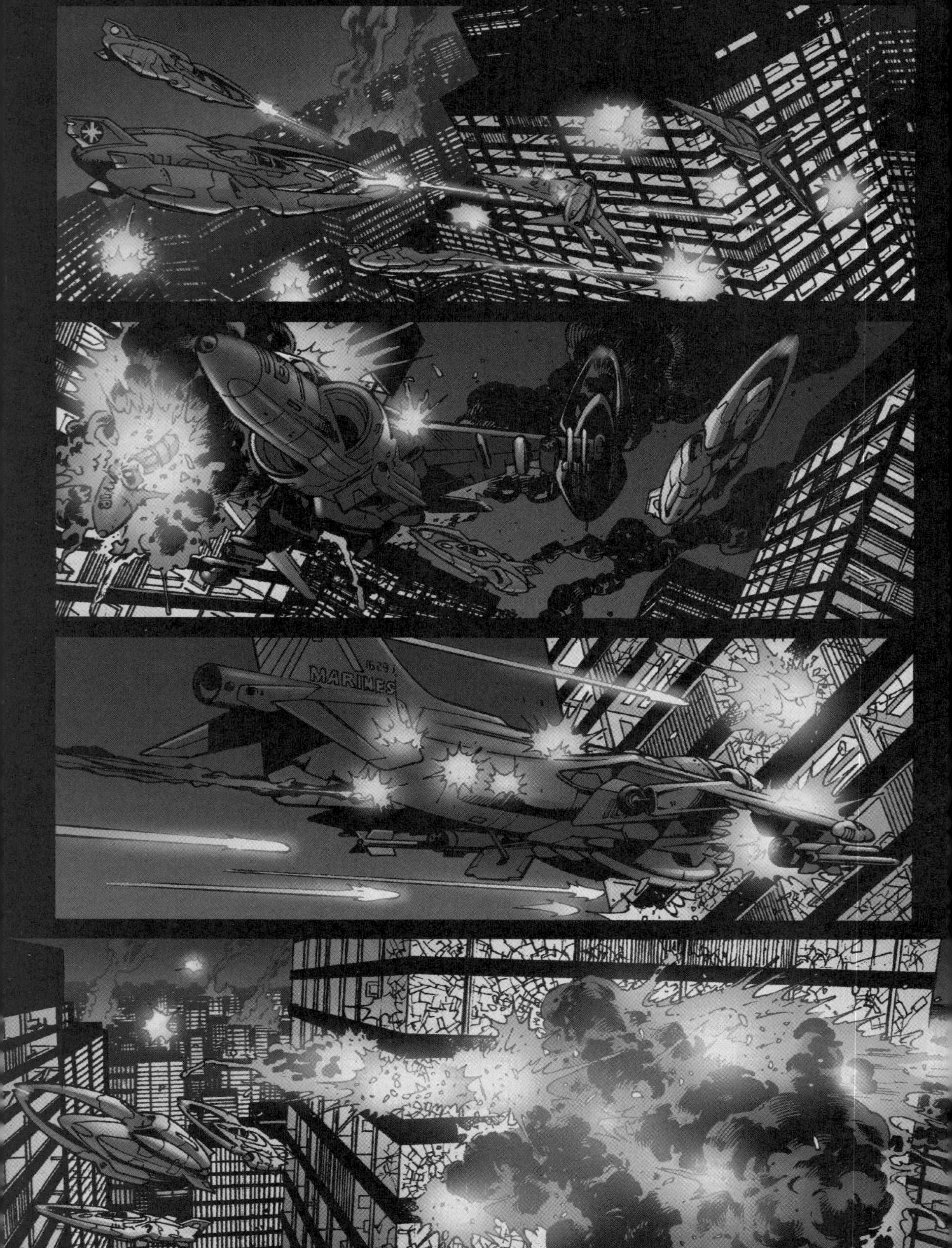
MARINES

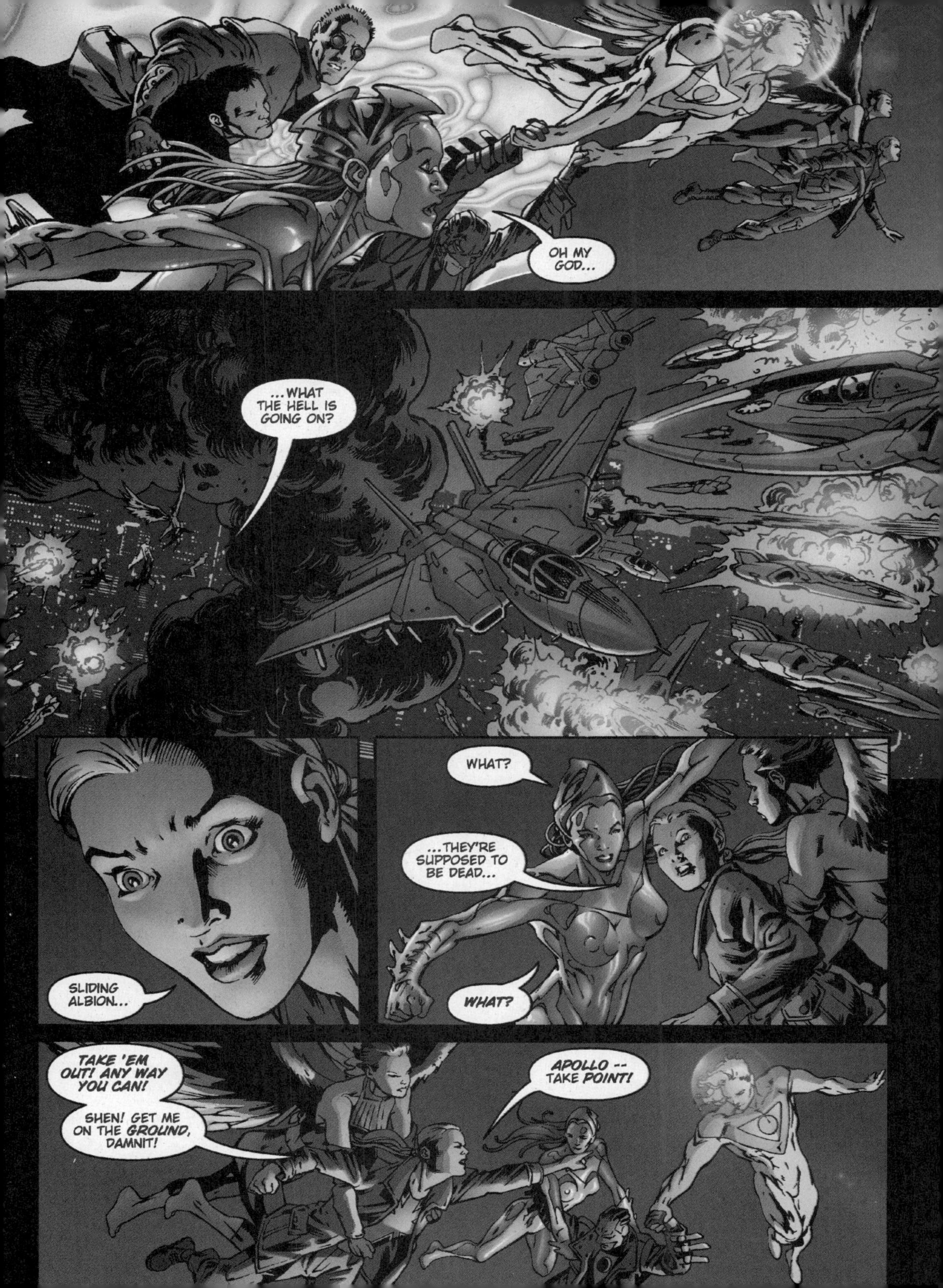
OH MY GOD...
...WHAT THE HELL IS GOING ON?
SLIDING ALBION...
WHAT?
...THEY'RE SUPPOSED TO BE DEAD...
WHAT?
TAKE 'EM OUT! ANY WAY YOU CAN!
SHEN! GET ME ON THE GROUND, DAMNIT!
APOLLO -- TAKE POINT!

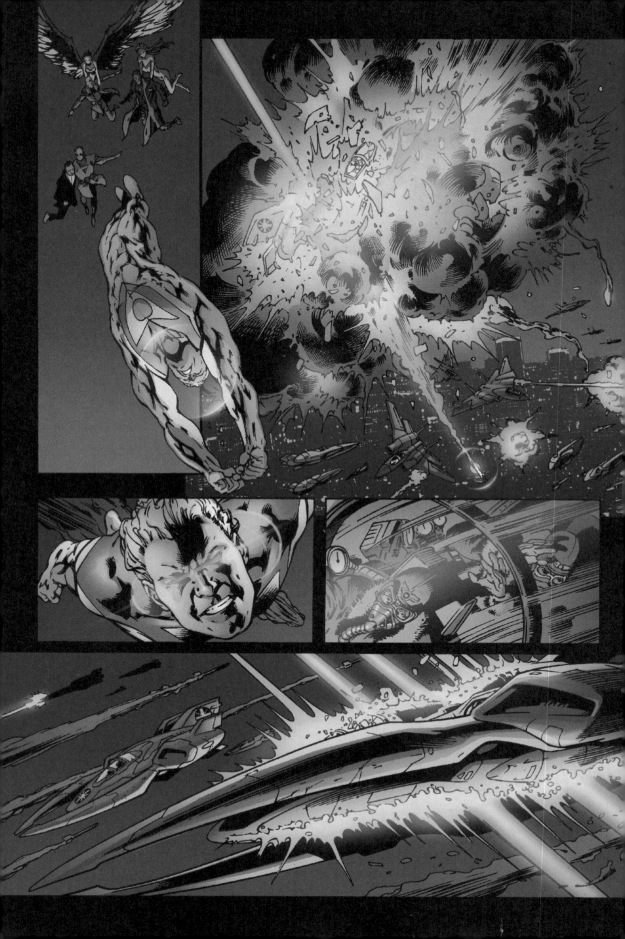

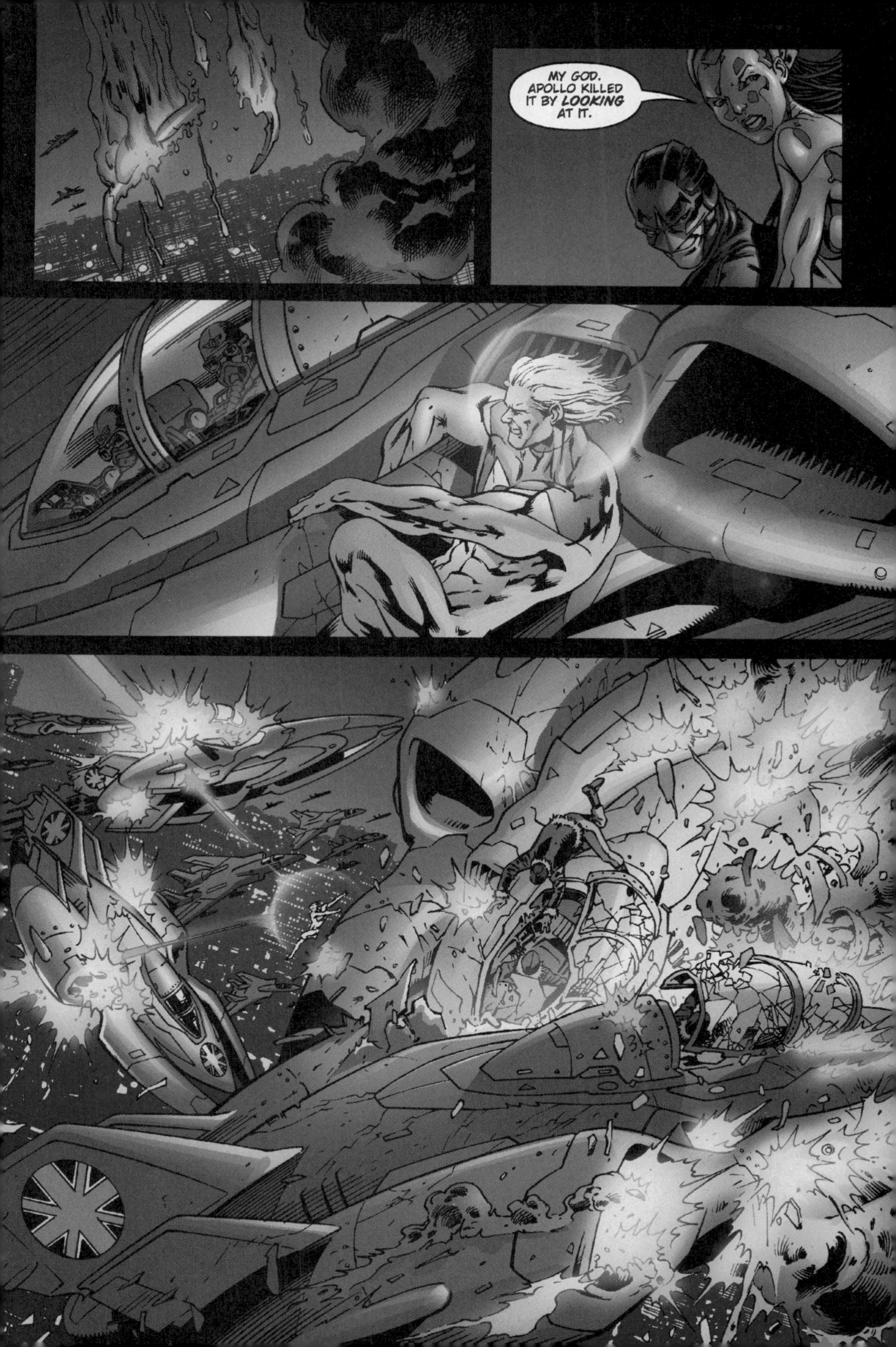
MY GOD. APOLLO KILLED IT BY LOOKING AT IT.

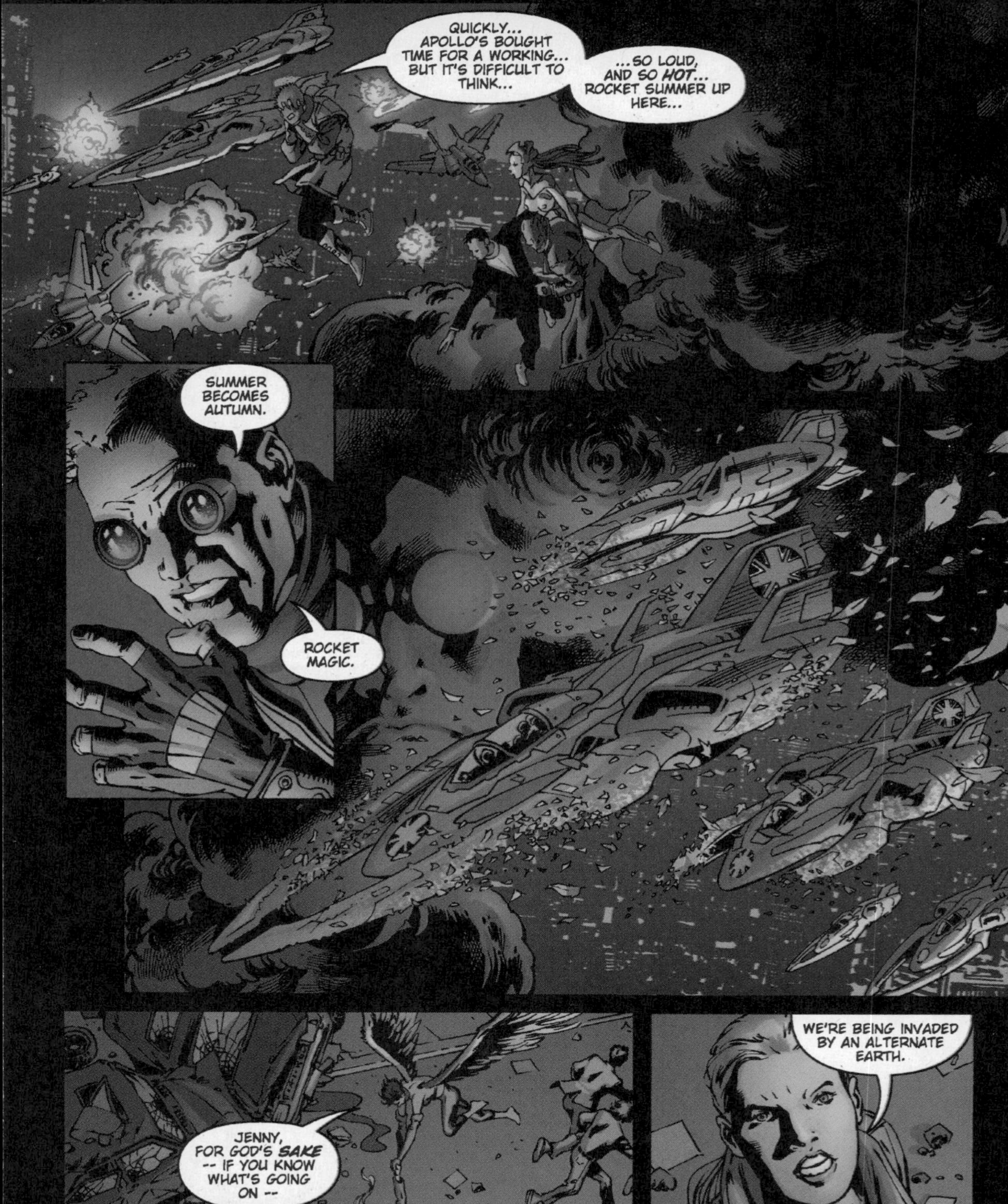
QUICKLY... APOLLO'S BOUGHT TIME FOR A WORKING... BUT IT'S DIFFICULT TO THINK...
...SO LOUD, AND SO HOT... ROCKET SUMMER UP HERE...
SUMMER BECOMES AUTUMN.
ROCKET MAGIC.
JENNY, FOR GOD'S SAKE -- IF YOU KNOW WHAT'S GOING ON --
OF COURSE I KNOW WHAT'S BLOODY GOING ON.
WE'RE BEING INVADED BY AN ALTERNATE EARTH.

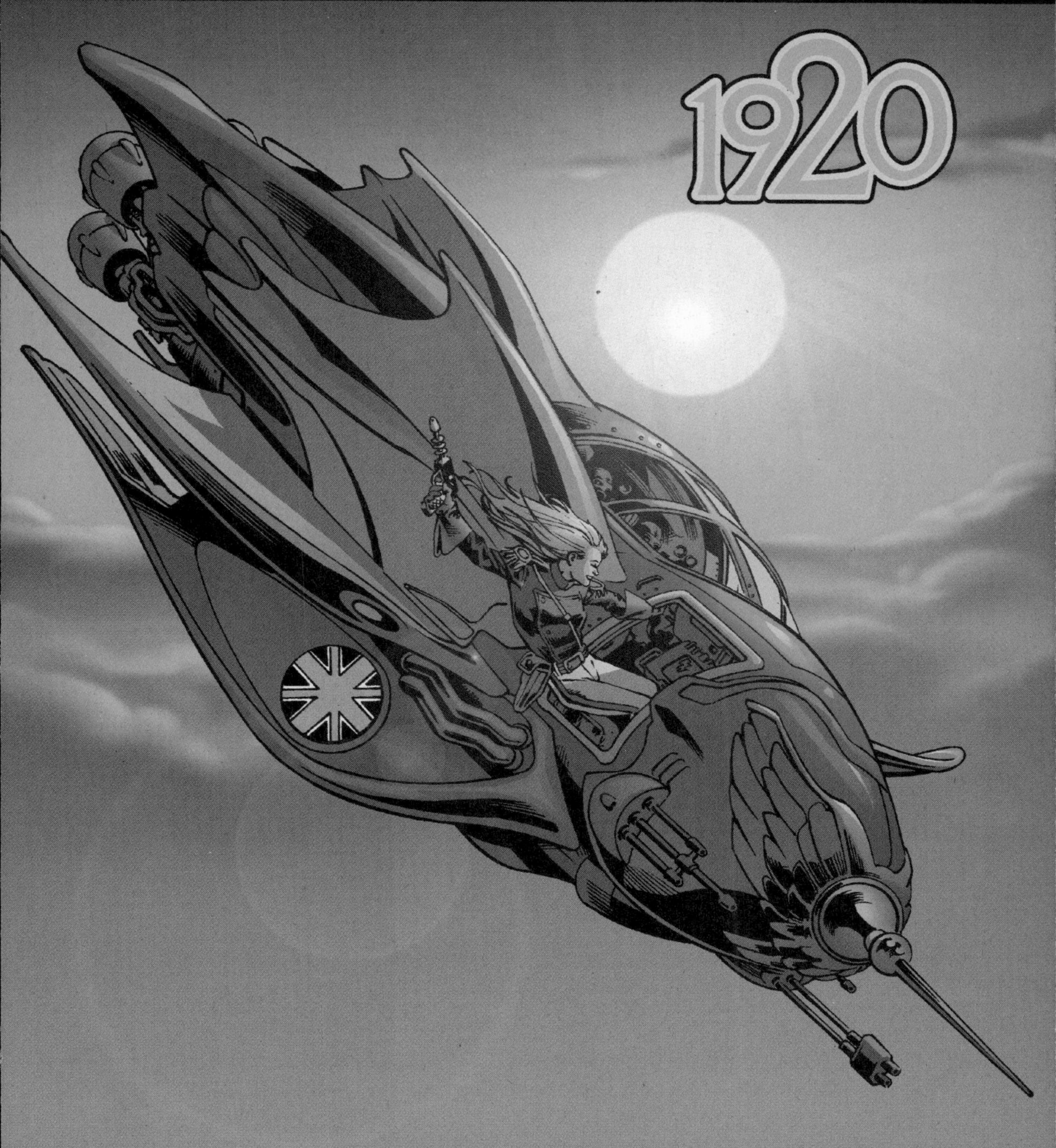
1920

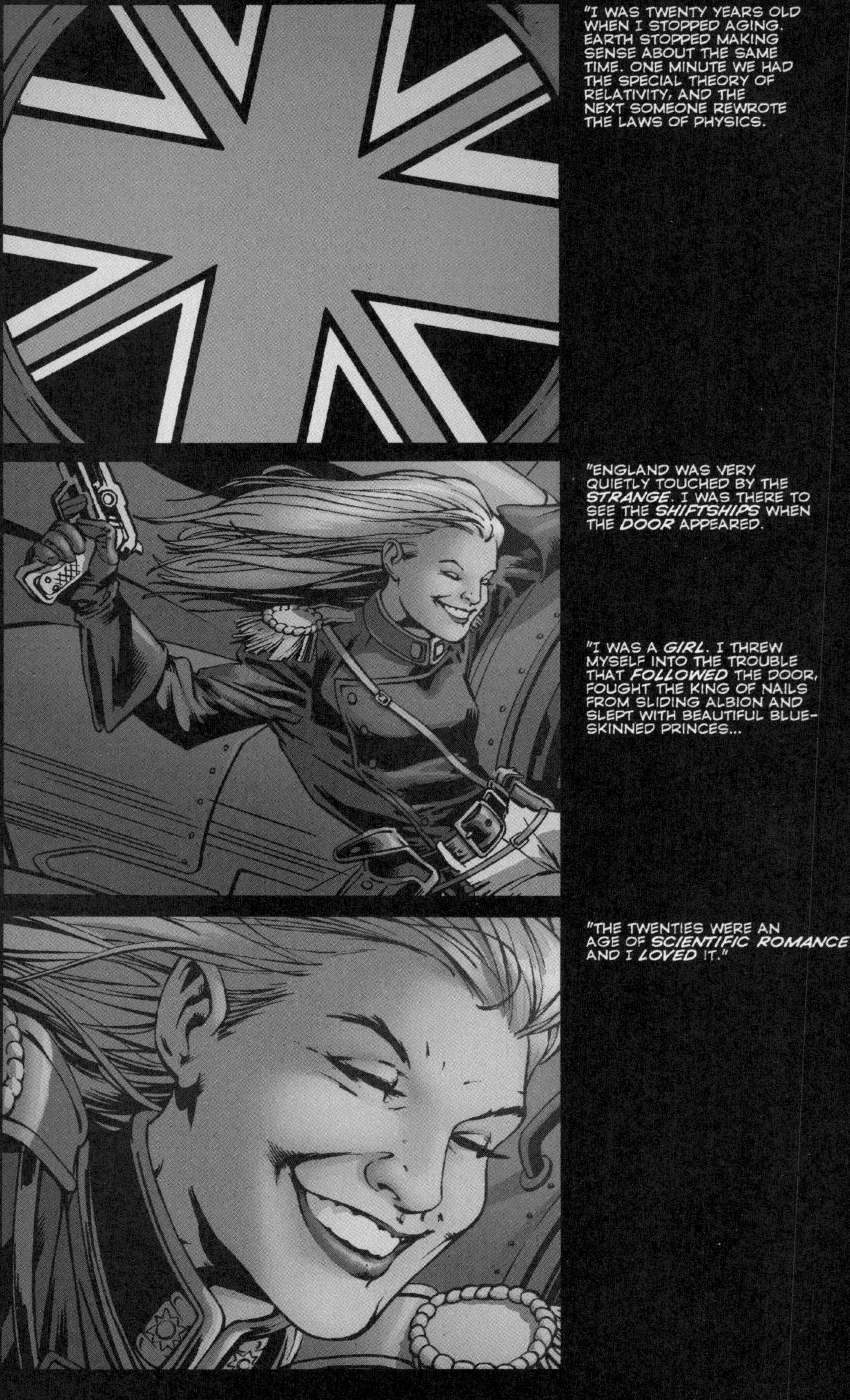
"I WAS TWENTY YEARS OLD WHEN I STOPPED AGING. EARTH STOPPED MAKING SENSE ABOUT THE SAME TIME. ONE MINUTE WE HAD THE SPECIAL THEORY OF RELATIVITY, AND THE NEXT SOMEONE REWROTE THE LAWS OF PHYSICS.
"ENGLAND WAS VERY QUIETLY TOUCHED BY THE STRANGE. I WAS THERE TO SEE THE SHIFTSHIPS WHEN THE DOOR APPEARED.
"I WAS A GIRL. I THREW MYSELF INTO THE TROUBLE THAT FOLLOWED THE DOOR, FOUGHT THE KING OF NAILS FROM SLIDING ALBION AND SLEPT WITH BEAUTIFUL BLUE-SKINNED PRINCES...
"THE TWENTIES WERE AN AGE OF SCIENTIFIC ROMANCE AND I LOVED IT."

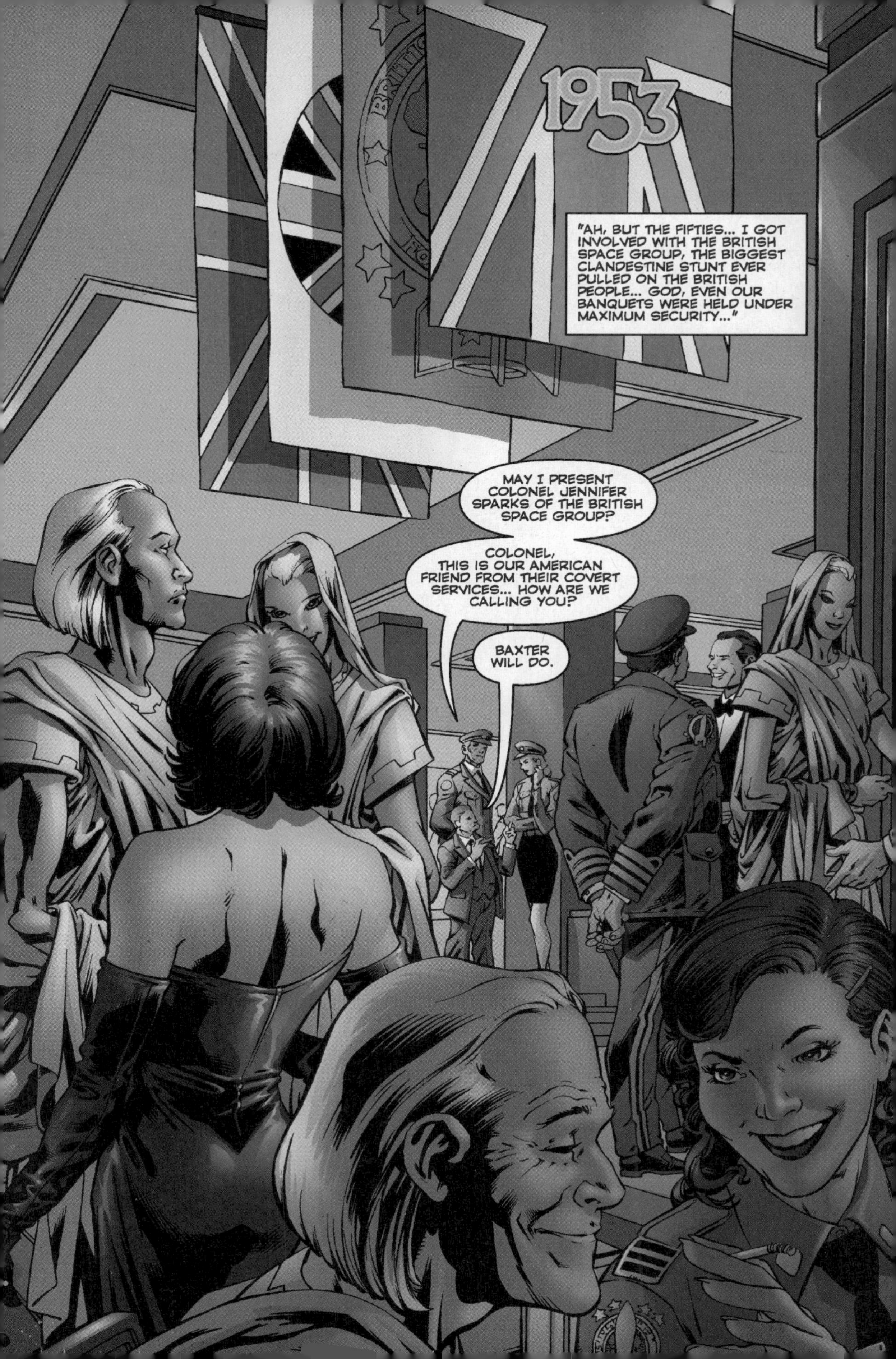
1953
"AH, BUT THE FIFTIES... I GOT INVOLVED WITH THE BRITISH SPACE GROUP, THE BIGGEST CLANDESTINE STUNT EVER PULLED ON THE BRITISH PEOPLE... GOD, EVEN OUR BANQUETS WERE HELD UNDER MAXIMUM SECURITY..."
MAY I PRESENT COLONEL JENNIFER SPARKS OF THE BRITISH SPACE GROUP?
COLONEL, THIS IS OUR AMERICAN FRIEND FROM THEIR COVERT SERVICES... HOW ARE WE CALLING YOU?
BAXTER WILL DO.

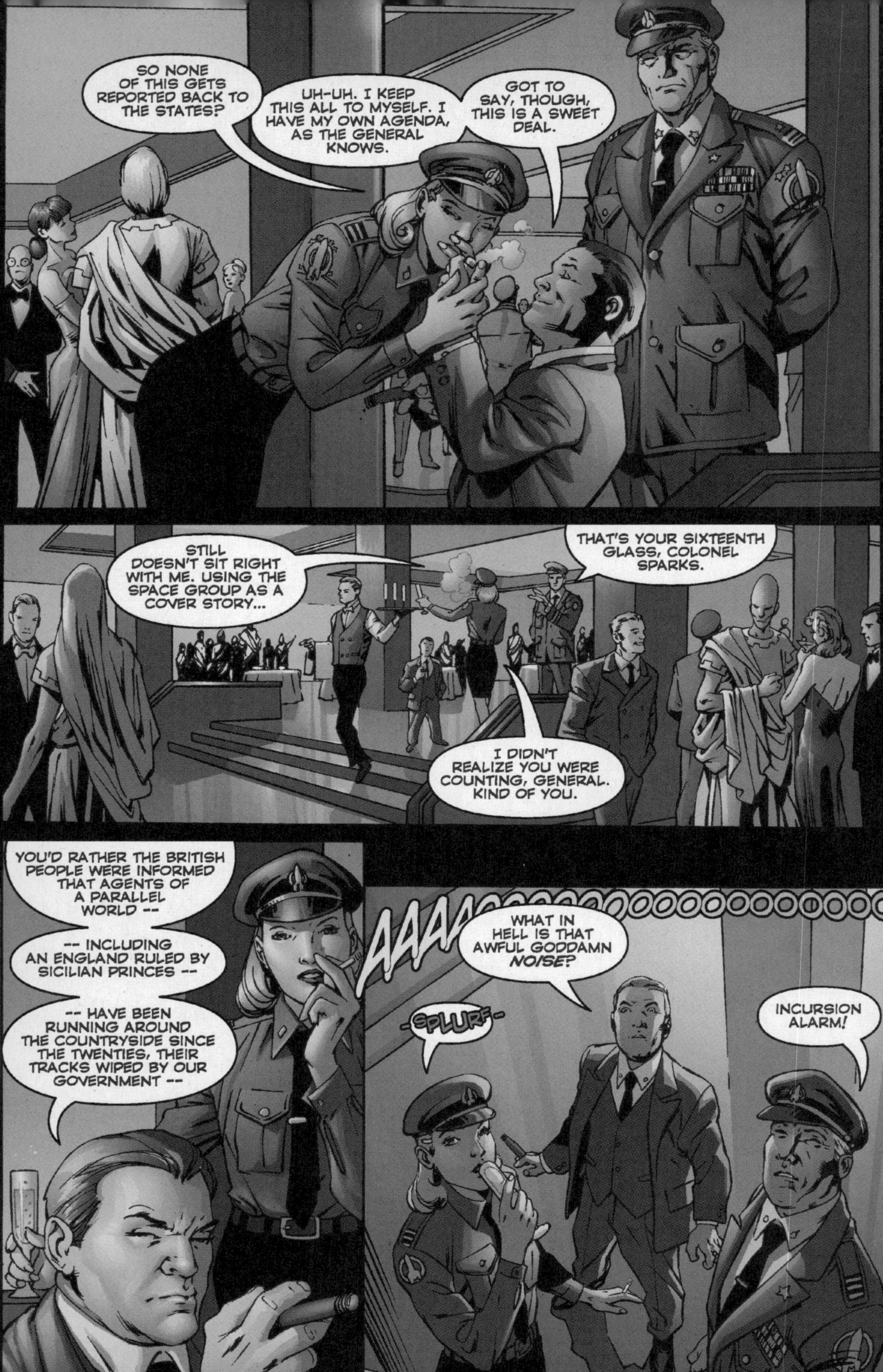
SO NONE OF THIS GETS REPORTED BACK TO THE STATES?
UH-UH. I KEEP THIS ALL TO MYSELF. I HAVE MY OWN AGENDA, AS THE GENERAL KNOWS.
GOT TO SAY, THOUGH, THIS IS A SWEET DEAL.
STILL DOESN'T SIT RIGHT WITH ME. USING THE SPACE GROUP AS A COVER STORY...
THAT'S YOUR SIXTEENTH GLASS, COLONEL SPARKS.
I DIDN'T REALIZE YOU WERE COUNTING, GENERAL. KIND OF YOU.
YOU'D RATHER THE BRITISH PEOPLE WERE INFORMED THAT AGENTS OF A PARALLEL WORLD --
-- INCLUDING AN ENGLAND RULED BY SICILIAN PRINCES --
-- HAVE BEEN RUNNING AROUND THE COUNTRYSIDE SINCE THE TWENTIES, THEIR TRACKS WIPED BY OUR GOVERNMENT --
AAAAOOOOOOOOOOOOOOOOOOOO
WHAT IN HELL IS THAT AWFUL GODDAMN *NOISE*?
-SPLURF-
INCURSION ALARM!

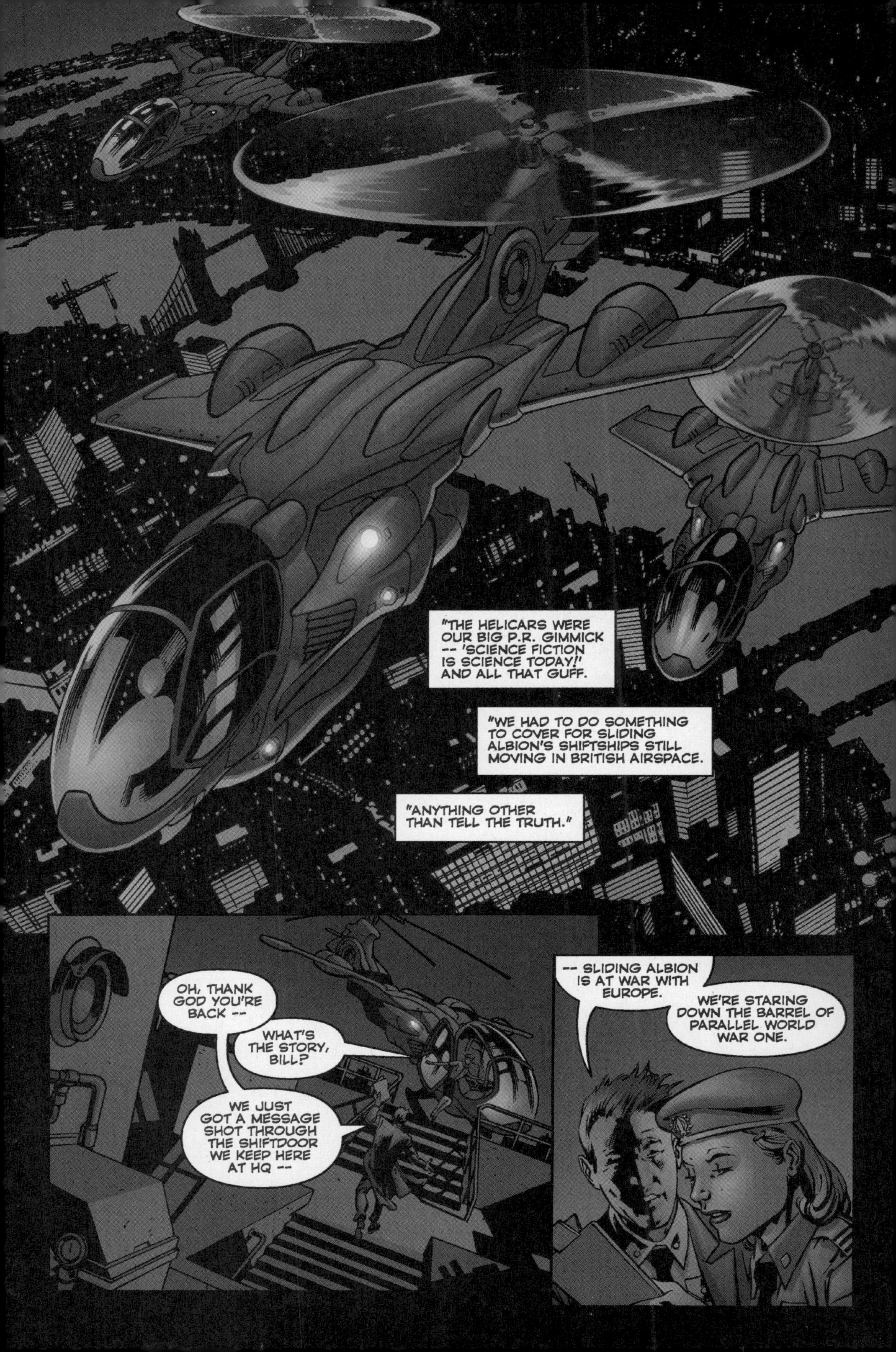
"THE HELICARS WERE OUR BIG P.R. GIMMICK -- 'SCIENCE FICTION IS SCIENCE TODAY!' AND ALL THAT GUFF.
"WE HAD TO DO SOMETHING TO COVER FOR SLIDING ALBION'S SHIFTSHIPS STILL MOVING IN BRITISH AIRSPACE.
"ANYTHING OTHER THAN TELL THE TRUTH."
OH, THANK GOD YOU'RE BACK --
WHAT'S THE STORY, BILL?
WE JUST GOT A MESSAGE SHOT THROUGH THE SHIFTDOOR WE KEEP HERE AT HQ --
-- SLIDING ALBION IS AT WAR WITH EUROPE.
WE'RE STARING DOWN THE BARREL OF PARALLEL WORLD WAR ONE.

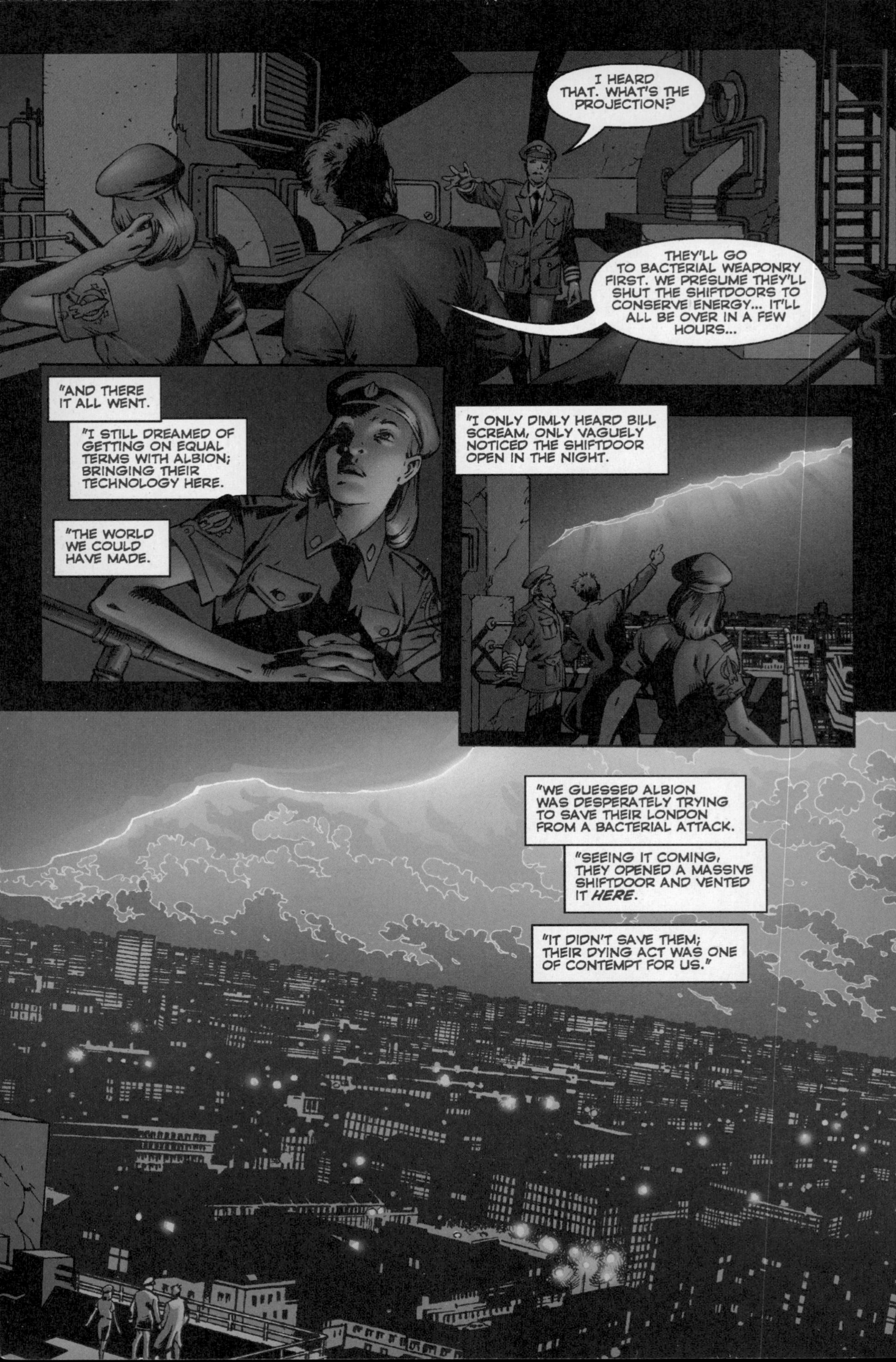
I HEARD THAT. WHAT'S THE PROJECTION?
THEY'LL GO TO BACTERIAL WEAPONRY FIRST. WE PRESUME THEY'LL SHUT THE SHIFTDOORS TO CONSERVE ENERGY... IT'LL ALL BE OVER IN A FEW HOURS...
"AND THERE IT ALL WENT.
"I STILL DREAMED OF GETTING ON EQUAL TERMS WITH ALBION; BRINGING THEIR TECHNOLOGY HERE.
"THE WORLD WE COULD HAVE MADE.
"I ONLY DIMLY HEARD BILL SCREAM, ONLY VAGUELY NOTICED THE SHIFTDOOR OPEN IN THE NIGHT.
"WE GUESSED ALBION WAS DESPERATELY TRYING TO SAVE THEIR LONDON FROM A BACTERIAL ATTACK.
"SEEING IT COMING, THEY OPENED A MASSIVE SHIFTDOOR AND VENTED IT *HERE*.
"IT DIDN'T SAVE THEM; THEIR DYING ACT WAS ONE OF CONTEMPT FOR US."

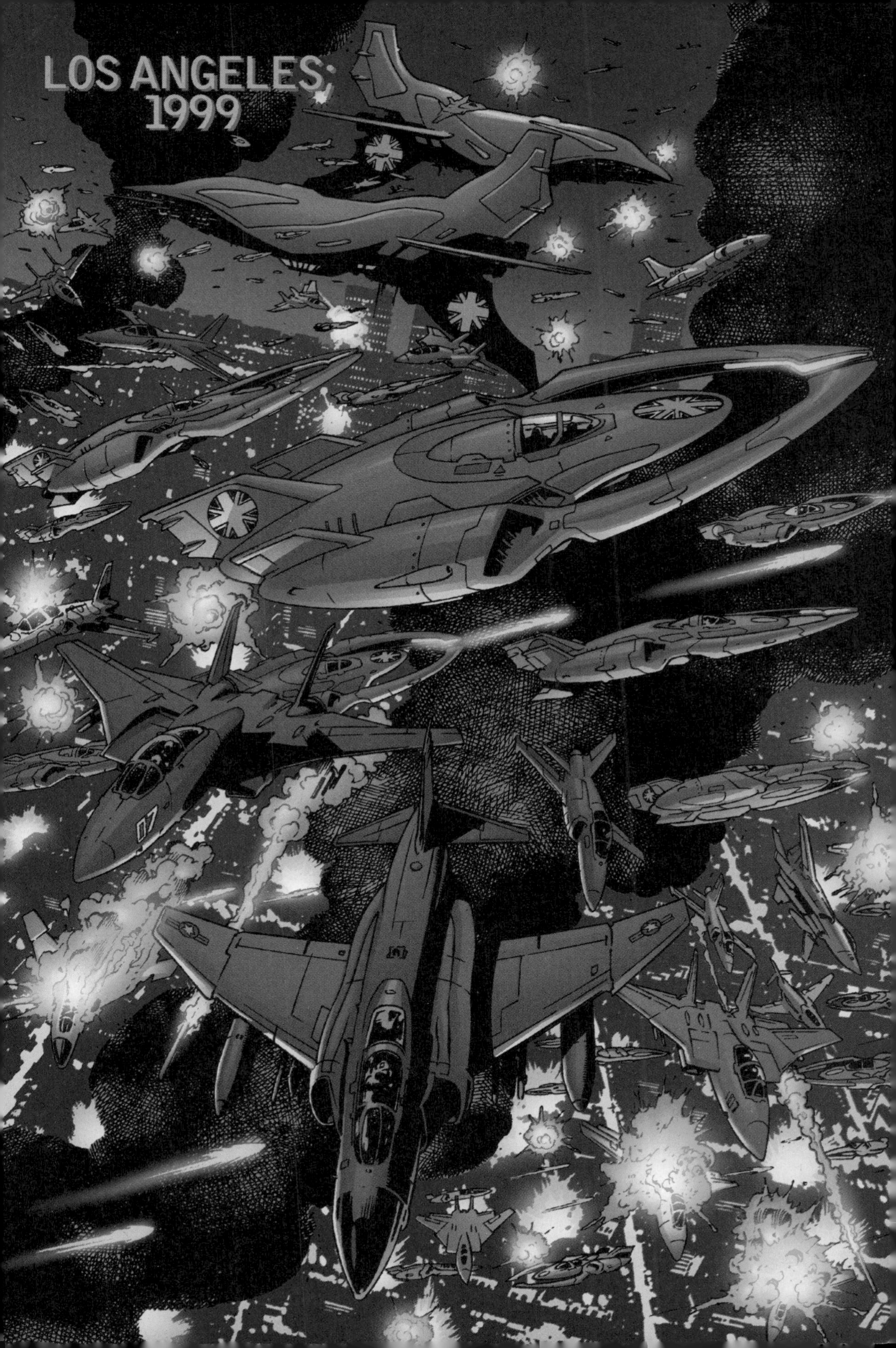
LOS ANGELES:
1999
07

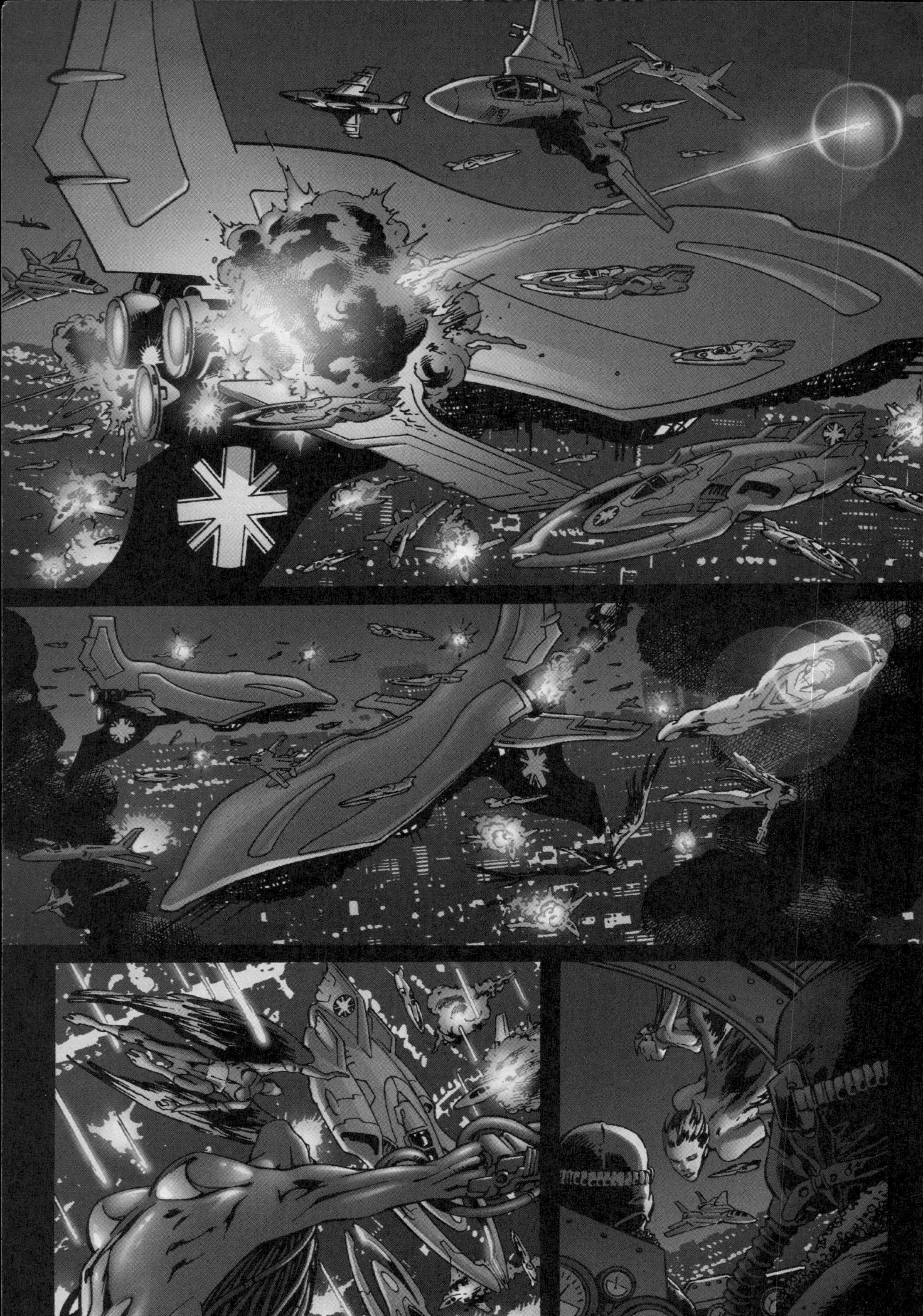

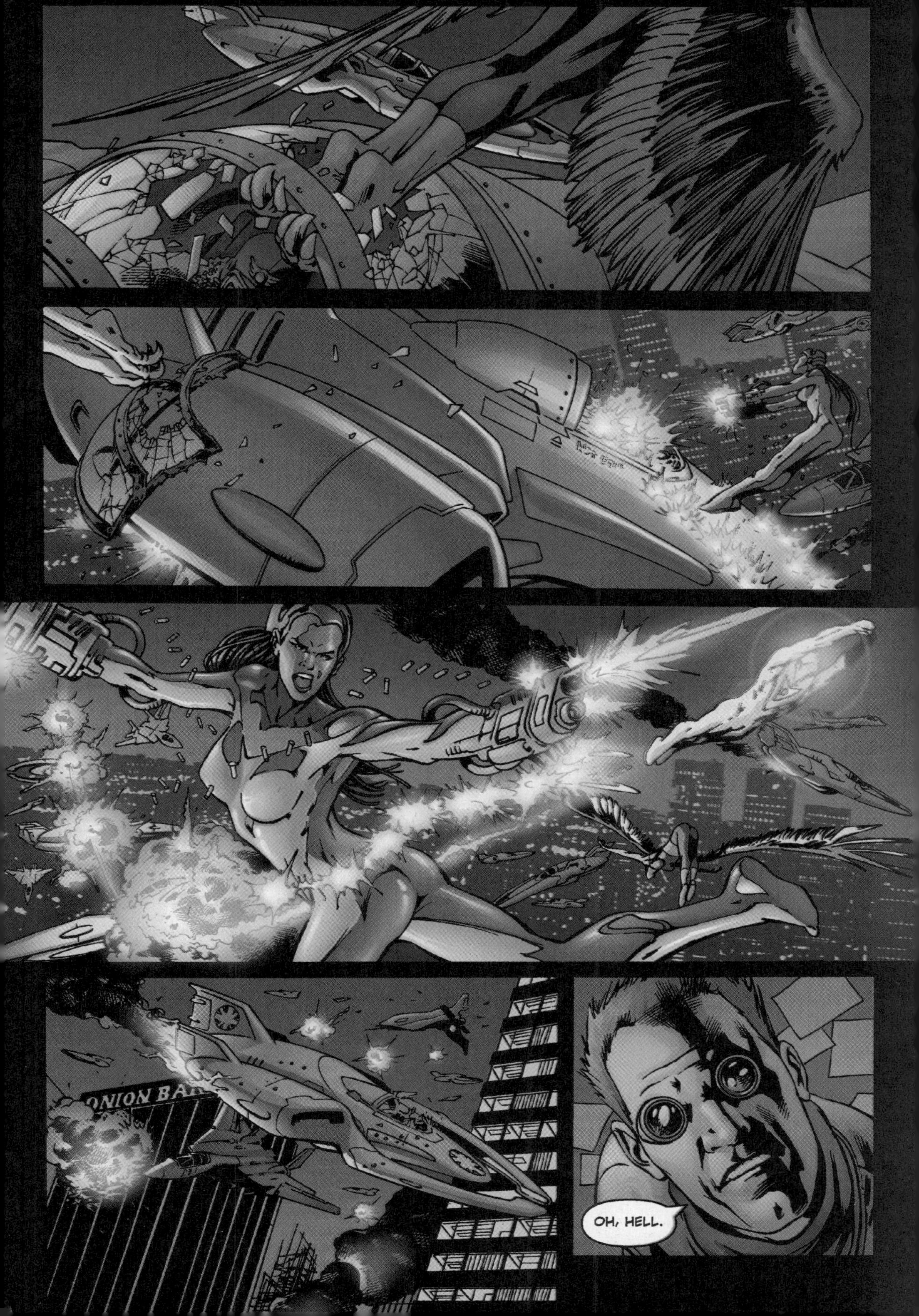
ONION BA
OH, HELL.

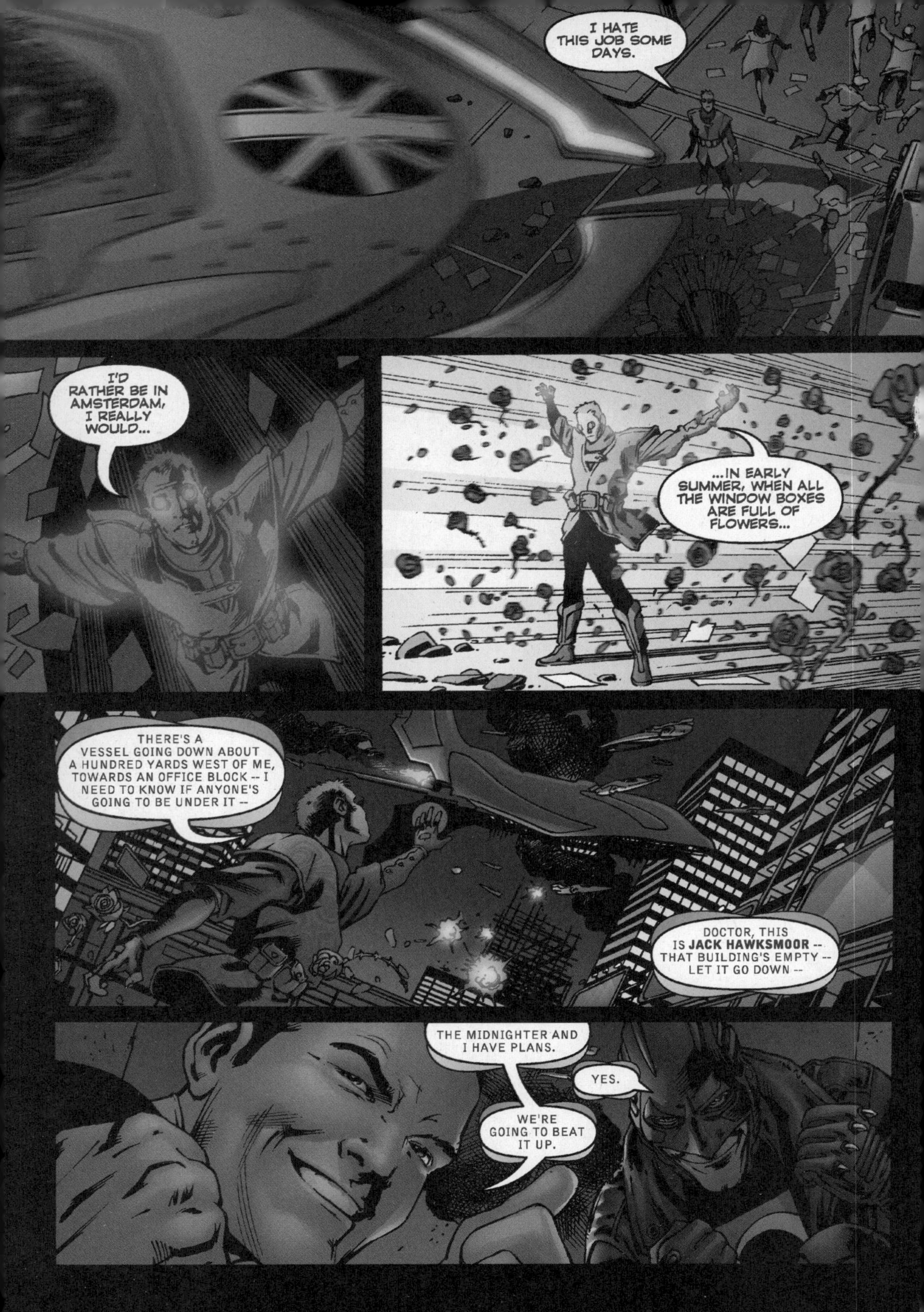

I HATE THIS JOB SOME DAYS.
I'D RATHER BE IN AMSTERDAM, I REALLY WOULD...
...IN EARLY SUMMER, WHEN ALL THE WINDOW BOXES ARE FULL OF FLOWERS...
THERE'S A VESSEL GOING DOWN ABOUT A HUNDRED YARDS WEST OF ME, TOWARDS AN OFFICE BLOCK -- I NEED TO KNOW IF ANYONE'S GOING TO BE UNDER IT --
DOCTOR, THIS IS JACK HAWKSMOOR -- THAT BUILDING'S EMPTY -- LET IT GO DOWN --
THE MIDNIGHTER AND I HAVE PLANS.
YES.
WE'RE GOING TO BEAT IT UP.

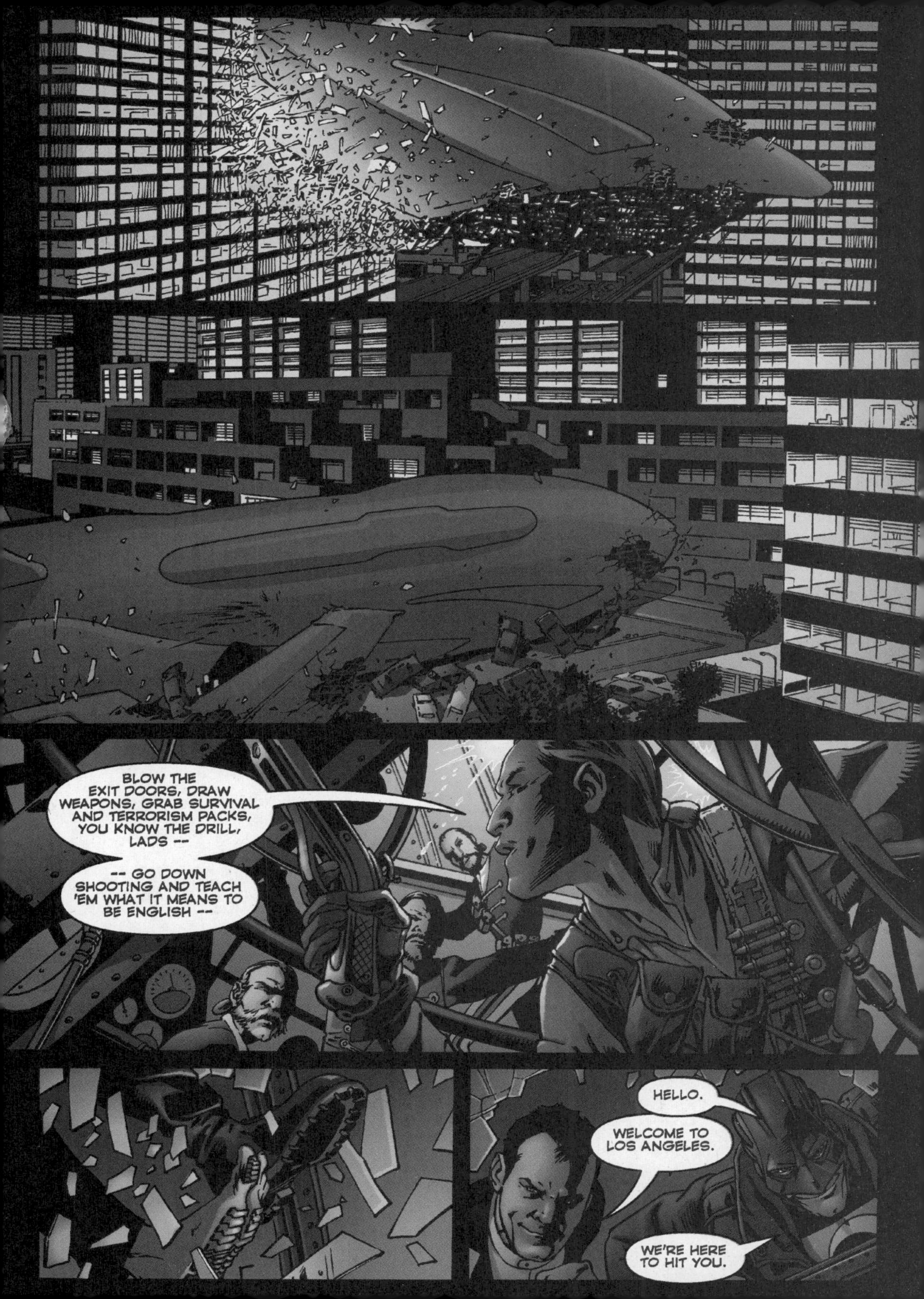
BLOW THE EXIT DOORS, DRAW WEAPONS, GRAB SURVIVAL AND TERRORISM PACKS, YOU KNOW THE DRILL, LADS --
-- GO DOWN SHOOTING AND TEACH 'EM WHAT IT MEANS TO BE ENGLISH --
HELLO.
WELCOME TO LOS ANGELES.
WE'RE HERE TO HIT YOU.

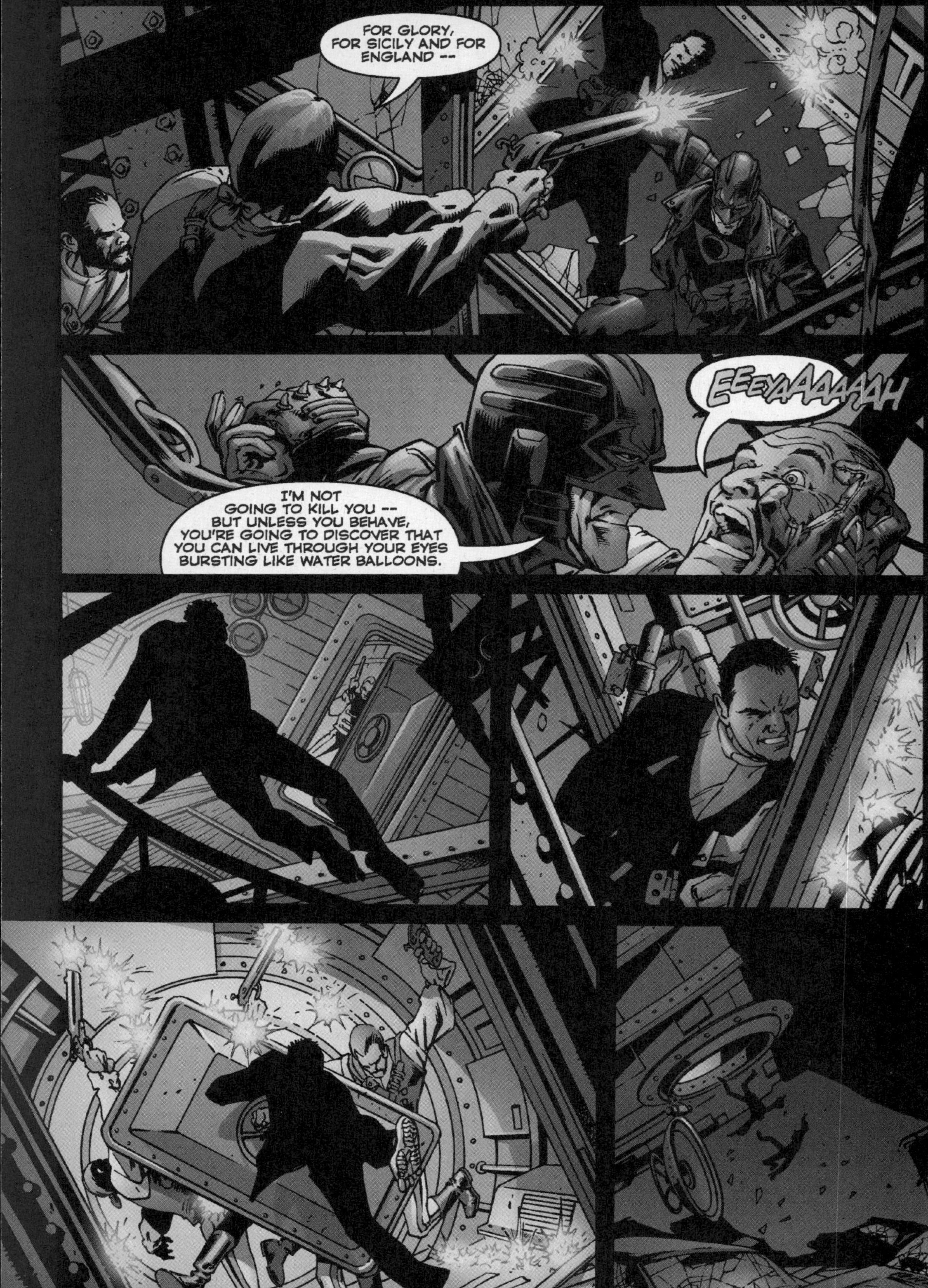
FOR GLORY, FOR SICILY AND FOR ENGLAND --
EEEYAAAAAAH
I'M NOT GOING TO KILL YOU -- BUT UNLESS YOU BEHAVE, YOU'RE GOING TO DISCOVER THAT YOU CAN LIVE THROUGH YOUR EYES BURSTING LIKE WATER BALLOONS.

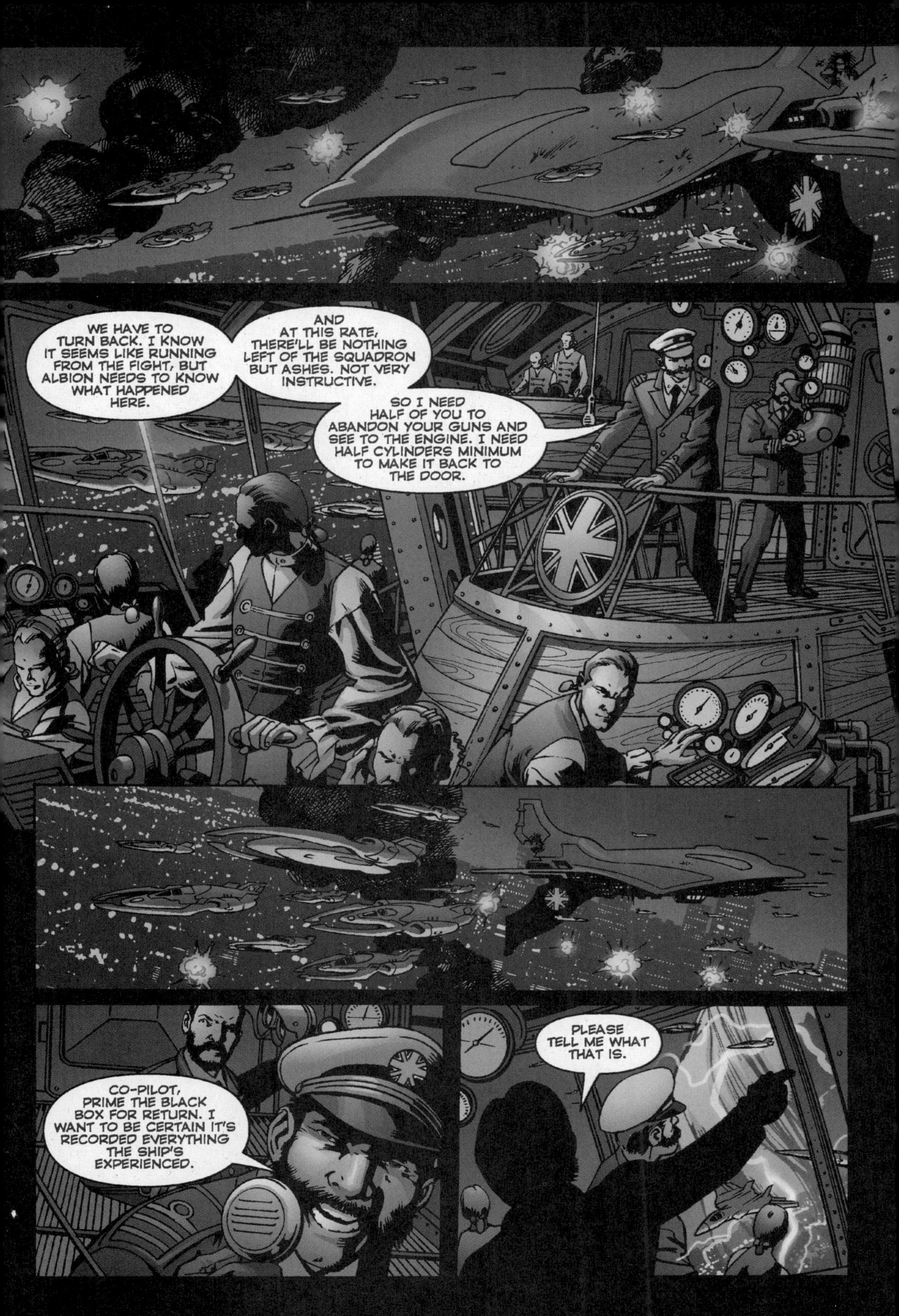
WE HAVE TO TURN BACK. I KNOW IT SEEMS LIKE RUNNING FROM THE FIGHT, BUT ALBION NEEDS TO KNOW WHAT HAPPENED HERE.
AND AT THIS RATE, THERE'LL BE NOTHING LEFT OF THE SQUADRON BUT ASHES. NOT VERY INSTRUCTIVE.
SO I NEED HALF OF YOU TO ABANDON YOUR GUNS AND SEE TO THE ENGINE. I NEED HALF CYLINDERS MINIMUM TO MAKE IT BACK TO THE DOOR.
CO-PILOT, PRIME THE BLACK BOX FOR RETURN. I WANT TO BE CERTAIN IT'S RECORDED EVERYTHING THE SHIP'S EXPERIENCED.
PLEASE TELL ME WHAT THAT IS.

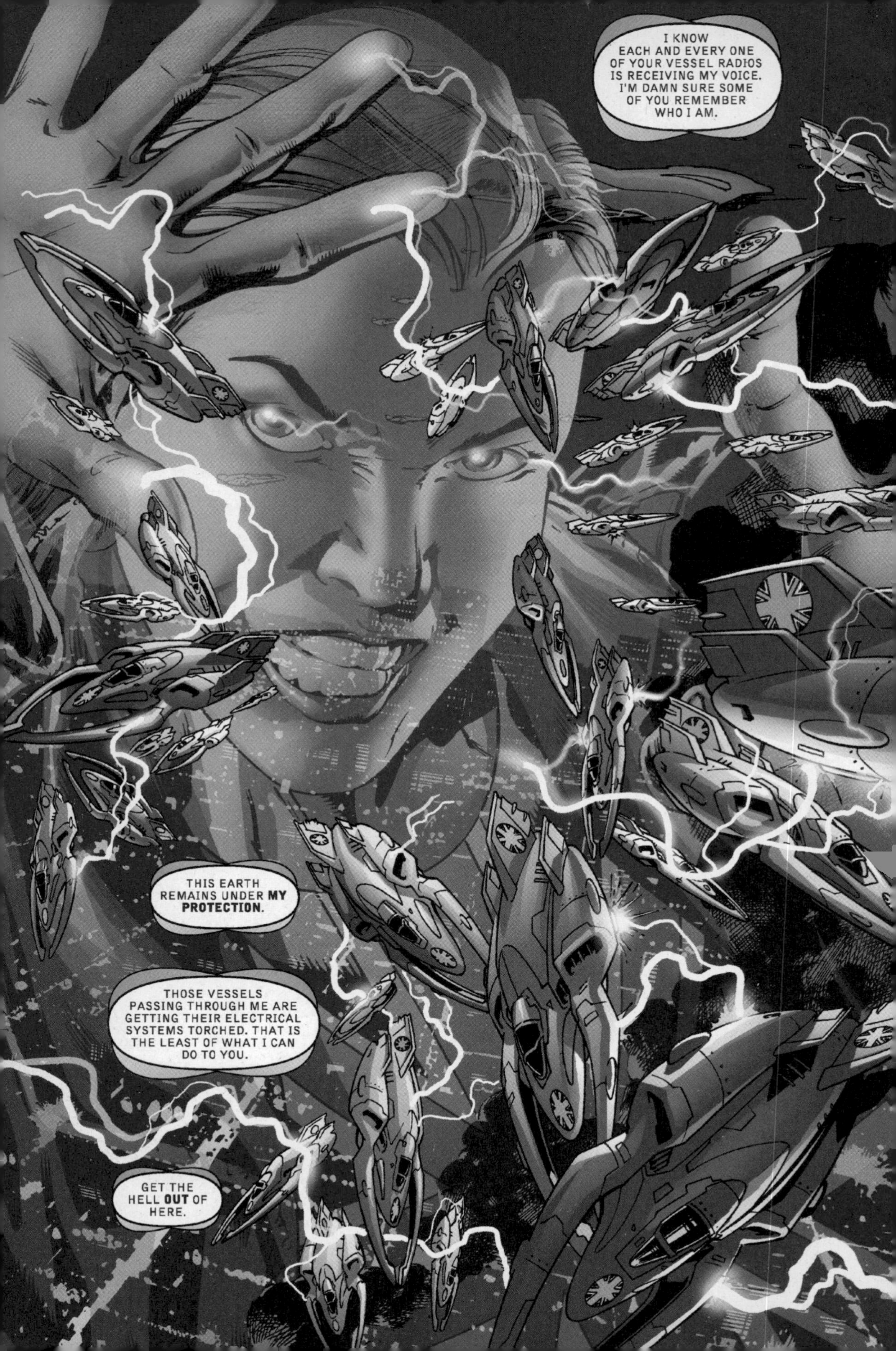
I KNOW EACH AND EVERY ONE OF YOUR VESSEL RADIOS IS RECEIVING MY VOICE. I'M DAMN SURE SOME OF YOU REMEMBER WHO I AM.
THIS EARTH REMAINS UNDER MY PROTECTION.
THOSE VESSELS PASSING THROUGH ME ARE GETTING THEIR ELECTRICAL SYSTEMS TORCHED. THAT IS THE LEAST OF WHAT I CAN DO TO YOU.
GET THE HELL OUT OF HERE.

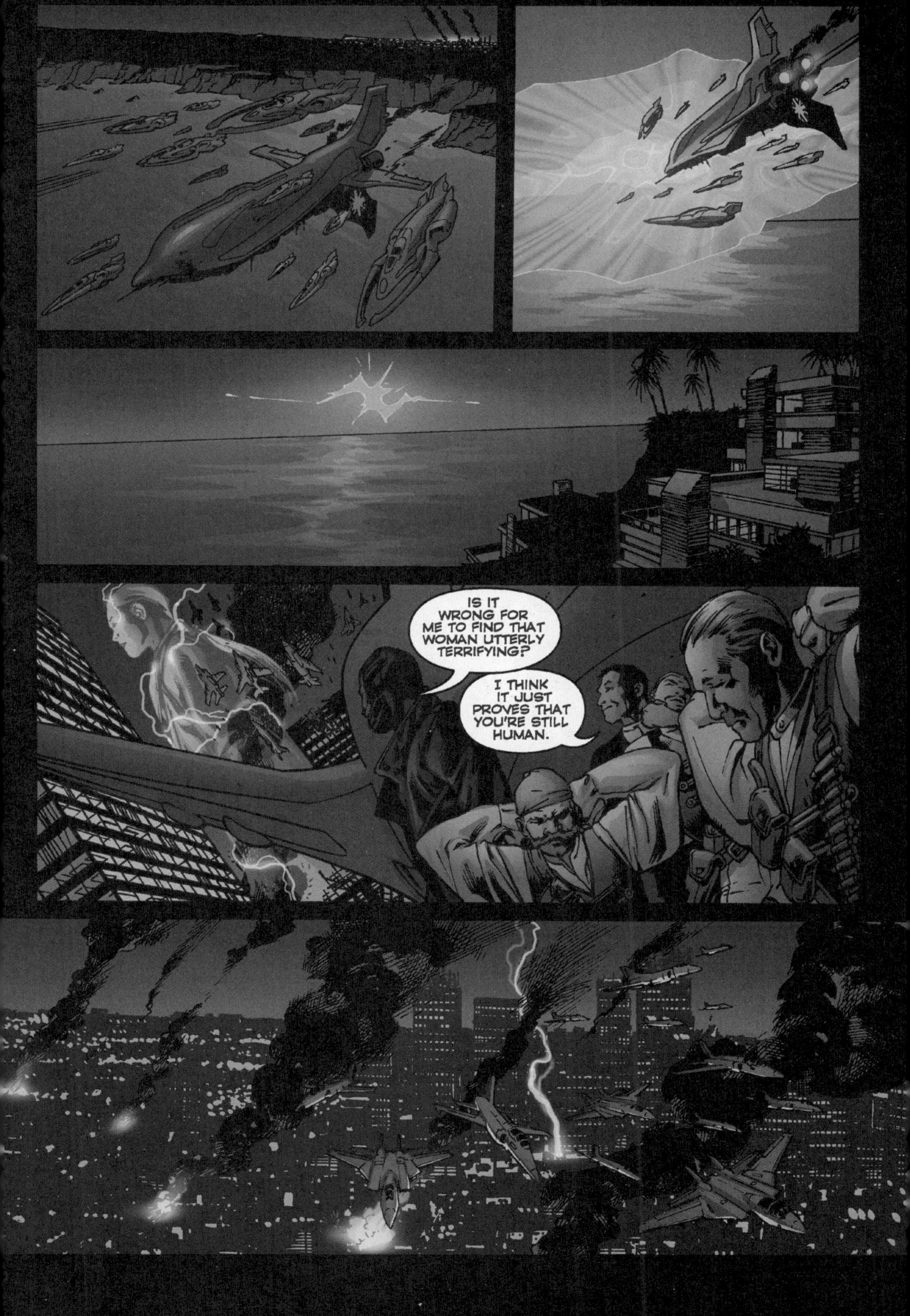
IS IT WRONG FOR ME TO FIND THAT WOMAN UTTERLY TERRIFYING?
I THINK IT JUST PROVES THAT YOU'RE STILL HUMAN.

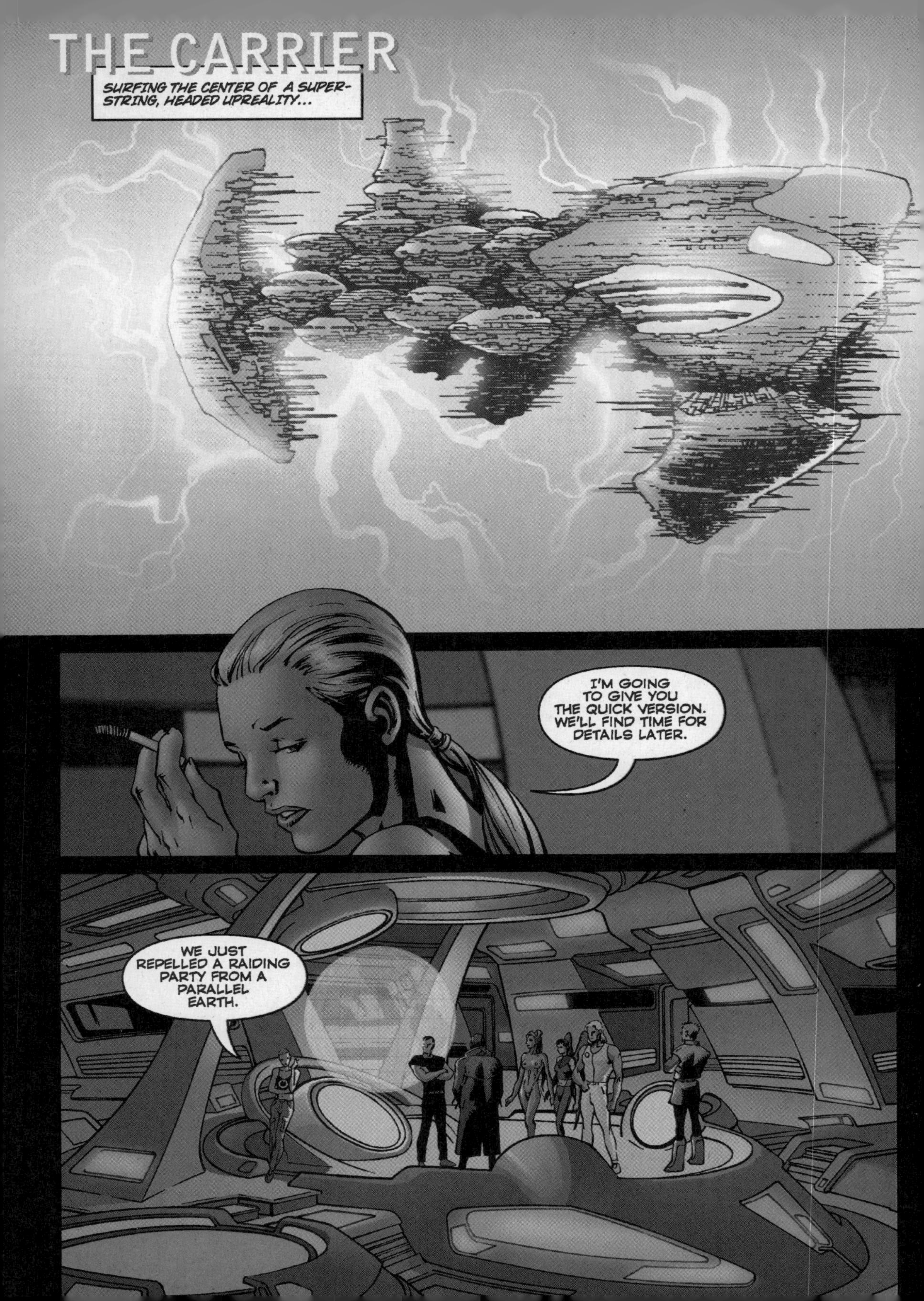
THE CARRIER
SURFING THE CENTER OF A SUPER-STRING, HEADED UPREALITY...
I'M GOING TO GIVE YOU THE QUICK VERSION. WE'LL FIND TIME FOR DETAILS LATER.
WE JUST REPELLED A RAIDING PARTY FROM A PARALLEL EARTH.

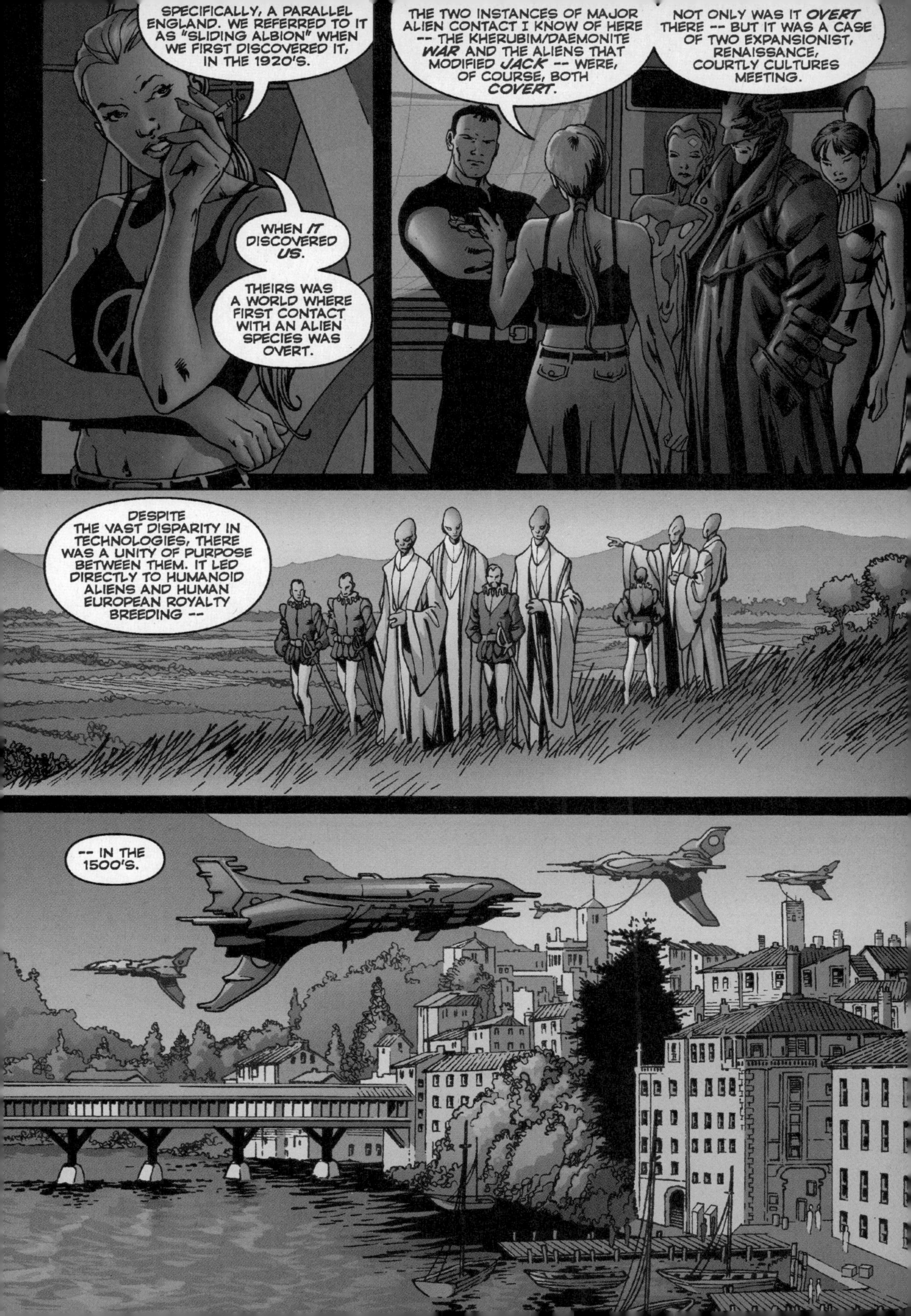
SPECIFICALLY, A PARALLEL ENGLAND. WE REFERRED TO IT AS "SLIDING ALBION" WHEN WE FIRST DISCOVERED IT, IN THE 1920'S.
WHEN *IT* DISCOVERED *US*.
THEIRS WAS A WORLD WHERE FIRST CONTACT WITH AN ALIEN SPECIES WAS OVERT.
THE TWO INSTANCES OF MAJOR ALIEN CONTACT I KNOW OF HERE -- THE KHERUBIM/DAEMONITE *WAR* AND THE ALIENS THAT MODIFIED *JACK* -- WERE, OF COURSE, BOTH *COVERT*.
NOT ONLY WAS IT *OVERT* THERE -- BUT IT WAS A CASE OF TWO EXPANSIONIST, RENAISSANCE, COURTLY CULTURES MEETING.
DESPITE THE VAST DISPARITY IN TECHNOLOGIES, THERE WAS A UNITY OF PURPOSE BETWEEN THEM. IT LED DIRECTLY TO HUMANOID ALIENS AND HUMAN EUROPEAN ROYALTY BREEDING --
-- IN THE 1500'S.

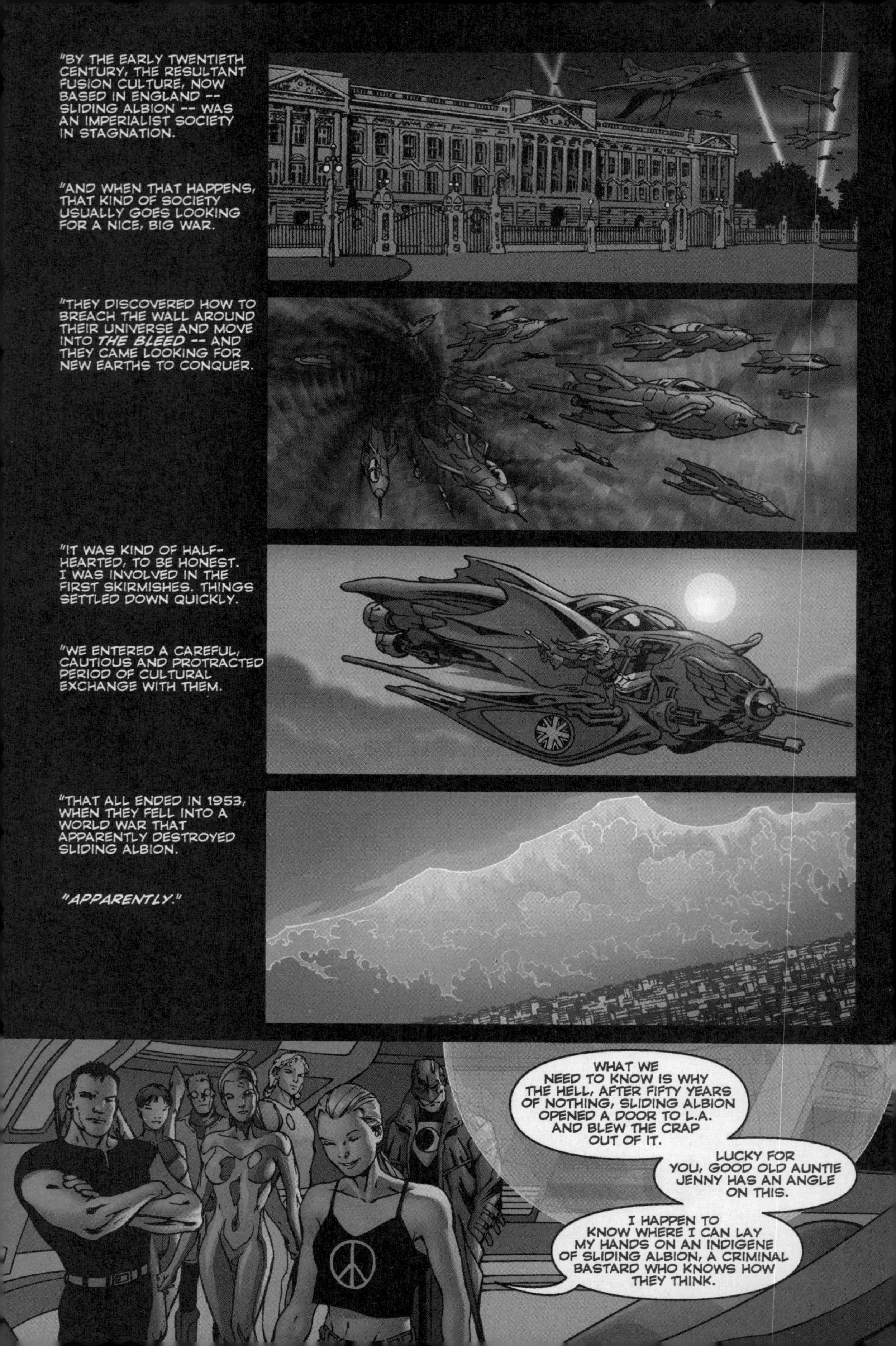
"BY THE EARLY TWENTIETH CENTURY, THE RESULTANT FUSION CULTURE, NOW BASED IN ENGLAND -- SLIDING ALBION -- WAS AN IMPERIALIST SOCIETY IN STAGNATION.
"AND WHEN THAT HAPPENS, THAT KIND OF SOCIETY USUALLY GOES LOOKING FOR A NICE, BIG WAR.
"THEY DISCOVERED HOW TO BREACH THE WALL AROUND THEIR UNIVERSE AND MOVE INTO *THE BLEED* -- AND THEY CAME LOOKING FOR NEW EARTHS TO CONQUER.
"IT WAS KIND OF HALF-HEARTED, TO BE HONEST. I WAS INVOLVED IN THE FIRST SKIRMISHES. THINGS SETTLED DOWN QUICKLY.
"WE ENTERED A CAREFUL, CAUTIOUS AND PROTRACTED PERIOD OF CULTURAL EXCHANGE WITH THEM.
"THAT ALL ENDED IN 1953, WHEN THEY FELL INTO A WORLD WAR THAT APPARENTLY DESTROYED SLIDING ALBION.
"APPARENTLY."
WHAT WE NEED TO KNOW IS WHY THE HELL, AFTER FIFTY YEARS OF NOTHING, SLIDING ALBION OPENED A DOOR TO L.A. AND BLEW THE CRAP OUT OF IT.
LUCKY FOR YOU, GOOD OLD AUNTIE JENNY HAS AN ANGLE ON THIS.
I HAPPEN TO KNOW WHERE I CAN LAY MY HANDS ON AN INDIGENE OF SLIDING ALBION, A CRIMINAL BASTARD WHO KNOWS HOW THEY THINK.

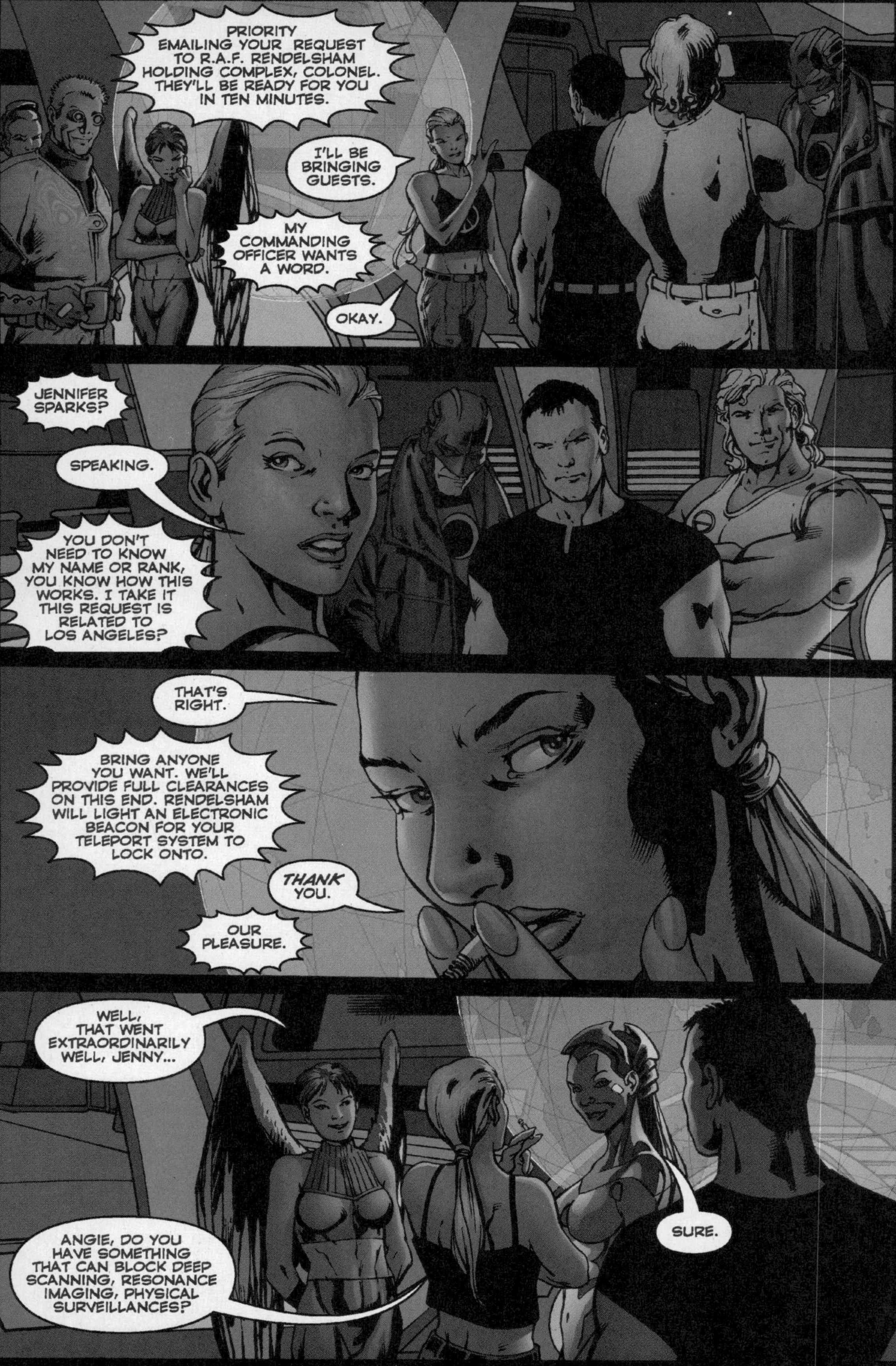

PRIORITY EMAILING YOUR REQUEST TO R.A.F. RENDELSHAM HOLDING COMPLEX, COLONEL. THEY'LL BE READY FOR YOU IN TEN MINUTES.
I'LL BE BRINGING GUESTS.
MY COMMANDING OFFICER WANTS A WORD.
OKAY.
JENNIFER SPARKS?
SPEAKING.
YOU DON'T NEED TO KNOW MY NAME OR RANK, YOU KNOW HOW THIS WORKS. I TAKE IT THIS REQUEST IS RELATED TO LOS ANGELES?
THAT'S RIGHT.
BRING ANYONE YOU WANT. WE'LL PROVIDE FULL CLEARANCES ON THIS END. RENDELSHAM WILL LIGHT AN ELECTRONIC BEACON FOR YOUR TELEPORT SYSTEM TO LOCK ONTO.
THANK YOU.
OUR PLEASURE.
WELL, THAT WENT EXTRAORDINARILY WELL, JENNY...
ANGIE, DO YOU HAVE SOMETHING THAT CAN BLOCK DEEP SCANNING, RESONANCE IMAGING, PHYSICAL SURVEILLANCES?
SURE.

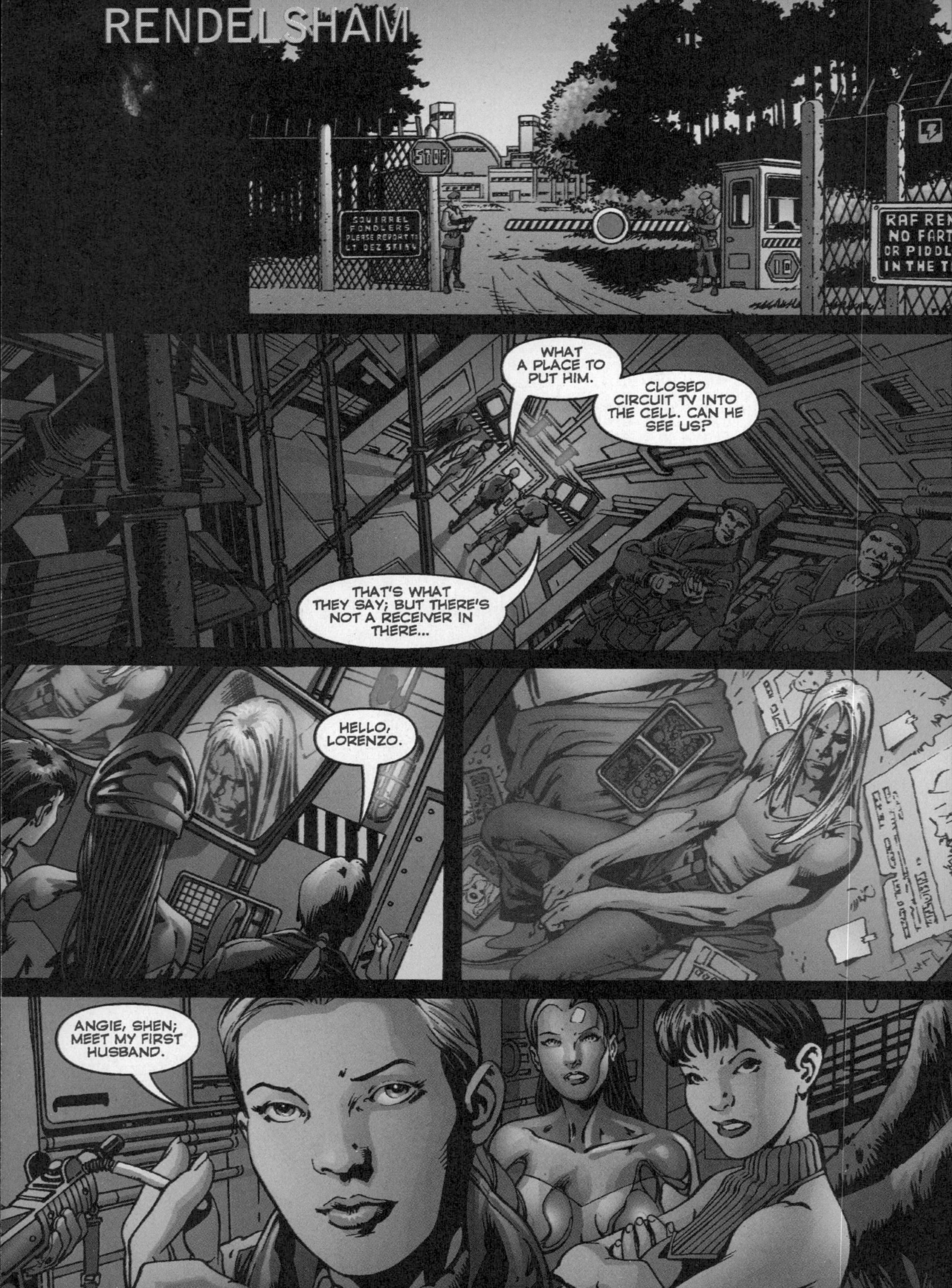
RENDELSHAM
STOP
SQUIRREL FONDLERS PLEASE REPORT TO
WHAT A PLACE TO PUT HIM.
CLOSED CIRCUIT TV INTO THE CELL. CAN HE SEE US?
THAT'S WHAT THEY SAY; BUT THERE'S NOT A RECEIVER IN THERE...
HELLO, LORENZO.
ANGIE, SHEN; MEET MY FIRST HUSBAND.

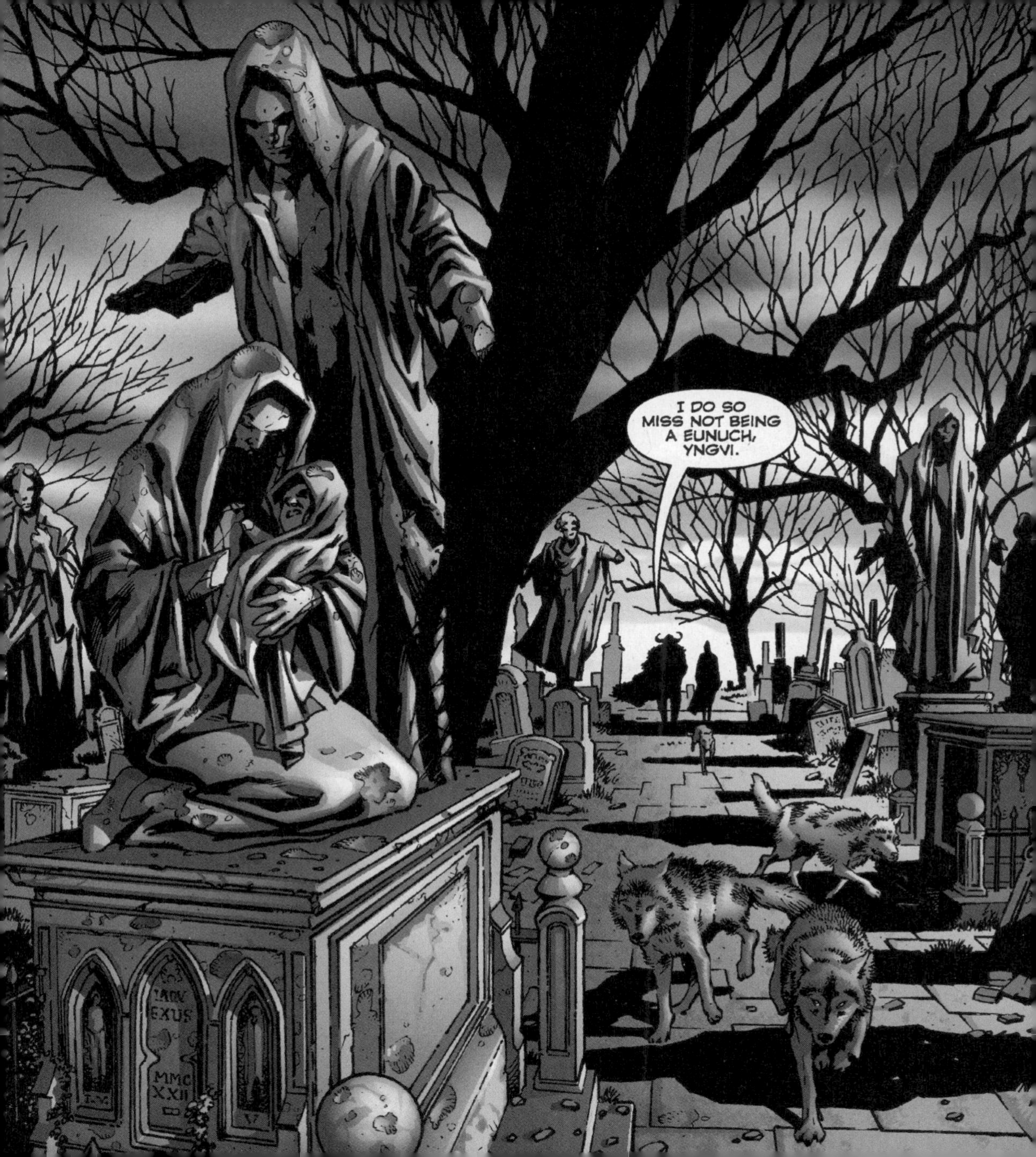
I DO SO MISS NOT BEING A EUNUCH, YNGVI.
IAN EXUS
MMC XXII

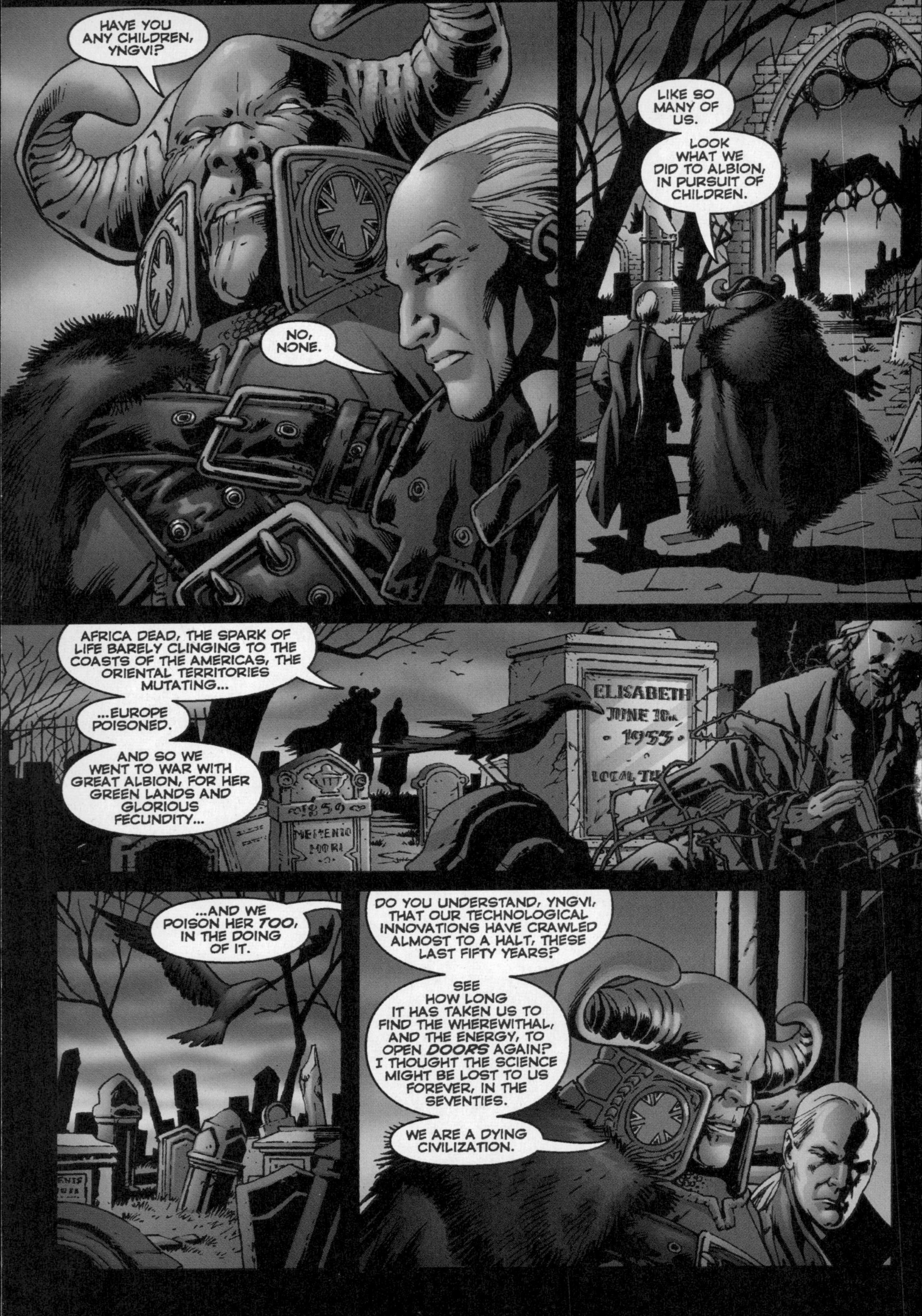
HAVE YOU ANY CHILDREN, YNGVI?
NO, NONE.
LIKE SO MANY OF US.
LOOK WHAT WE DID TO ALBION, IN PURSUIT OF CHILDREN.
AFRICA DEAD, THE SPARK OF LIFE BARELY CLINGING TO THE COASTS OF THE AMERICAS, THE ORIENTAL TERRITORIES MUTATING...
...EUROPE POISONED.
AND SO WE WENT TO WAR WITH GREAT ALBION, FOR HER GREEN LANDS AND GLORIOUS FECUNDITY...
ELISABETH
...AND WE POISON HER *TOO*, IN THE DOING OF IT.
DO YOU UNDERSTAND, YNGVI, THAT OUR TECHNOLOGICAL INNOVATIONS HAVE CRAWLED ALMOST TO A HALT, THESE LAST FIFTY YEARS?
SEE HOW LONG IT HAS TAKEN US TO FIND THE WHEREWITHAL, AND THE ENERGY, TO OPEN *DOORS* AGAIN? I THOUGHT THE SCIENCE MIGHT BE LOST TO US FOREVER, IN THE SEVENTIES.
WE ARE A DYING CIVILIZATION.

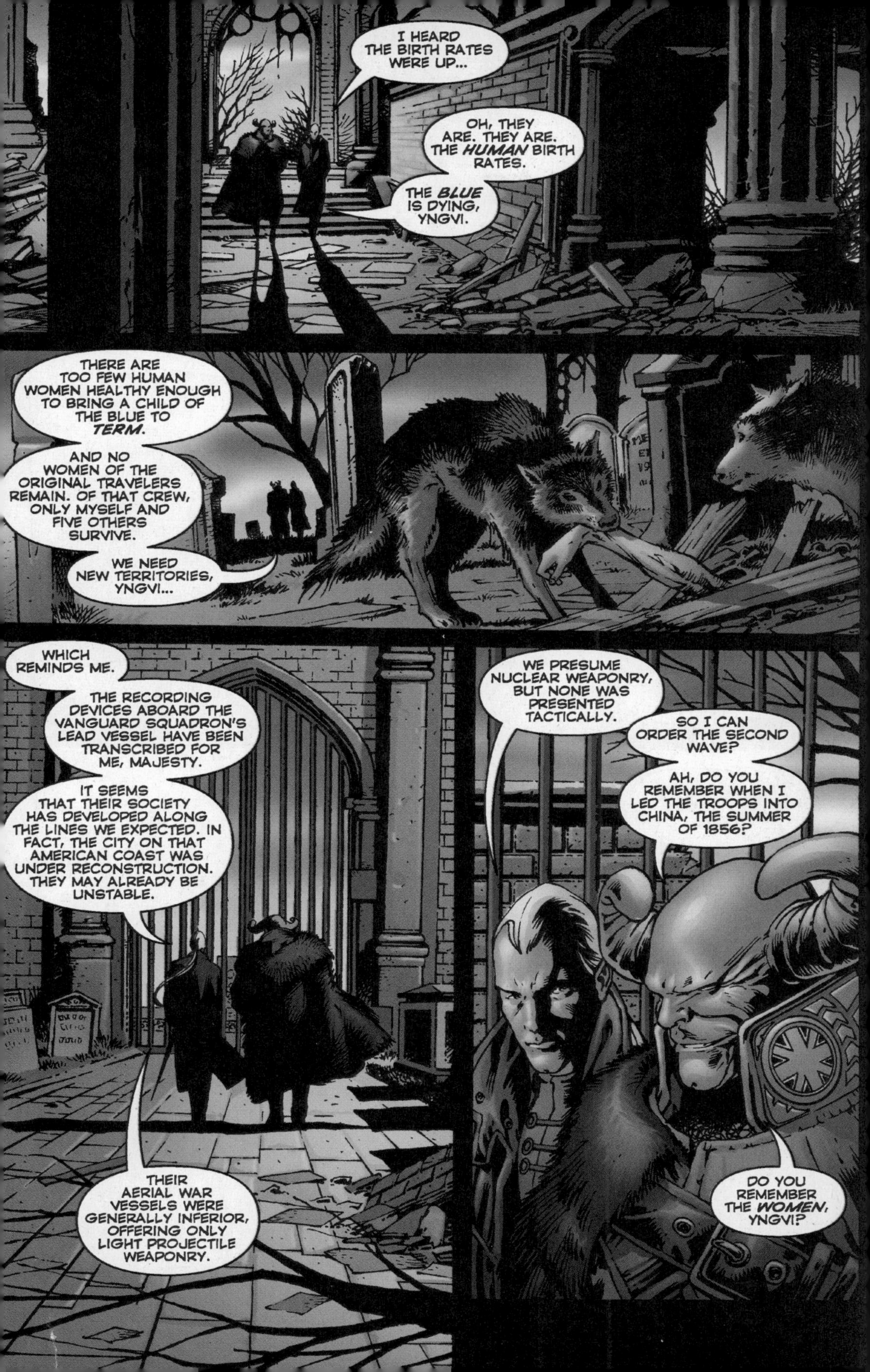
I HEARD THE BIRTH RATES WERE UP...
OH, THEY ARE. THEY ARE. THE *HUMAN* BIRTH RATES.
THE *BLUE* IS DYING, YNGVI.
THERE ARE TOO FEW HUMAN WOMEN HEALTHY ENOUGH TO BRING A CHILD OF THE BLUE TO *TERM*.
AND NO WOMEN OF THE ORIGINAL TRAVELERS REMAIN. OF THAT CREW, ONLY MYSELF AND FIVE OTHERS SURVIVE.
WE NEED NEW TERRITORIES, YNGVI...
WHICH REMINDS ME.
THE RECORDING DEVICES ABOARD THE VANGUARD SQUADRON'S LEAD VESSEL HAVE BEEN TRANSCRIBED FOR ME, MAJESTY.
IT SEEMS THAT THEIR SOCIETY HAS DEVELOPED ALONG THE LINES WE EXPECTED. IN FACT, THE CITY ON THAT AMERICAN COAST WAS UNDER RECONSTRUCTION. THEY MAY ALREADY BE UNSTABLE.
THEIR AERIAL WAR VESSELS WERE GENERALLY INFERIOR, OFFERING ONLY LIGHT PROJECTILE WEAPONRY.
WE PRESUME NUCLEAR WEAPONRY, BUT NONE WAS PRESENTED TACTICALLY.
SO I CAN ORDER THE SECOND WAVE?
AH, DO YOU REMEMBER WHEN I LED THE TROOPS INTO CHINA, THE SUMMER OF 1856?
DO YOU REMEMBER THE *WOMEN*, YNGVI?

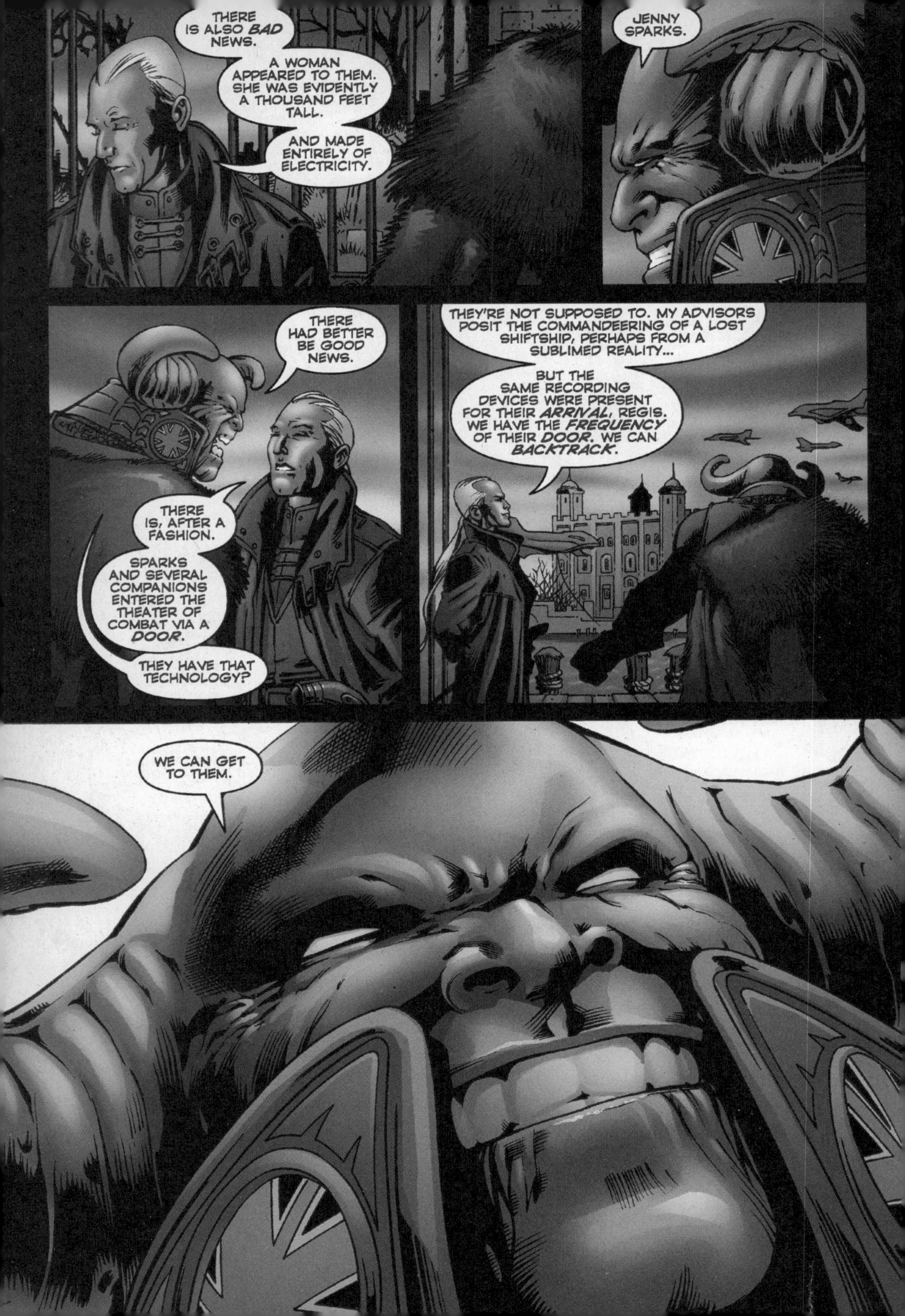

THERE IS ALSO *BAD* NEWS.
A WOMAN APPEARED TO THEM. SHE WAS EVIDENTLY A THOUSAND FEET TALL.
AND MADE ENTIRELY OF ELECTRICITY.
JENNY SPARKS.
THERE HAD BETTER BE GOOD NEWS.
THERE IS, AFTER A FASHION.
SPARKS AND SEVERAL COMPANIONS ENTERED THE THEATER OF COMBAT VIA A *DOOR*.
THEY HAVE THAT TECHNOLOGY?
THEY'RE NOT SUPPOSED TO. MY ADVISORS POSIT THE COMMANDEERING OF A LOST SHIFTSHIP, PERHAPS FROM A SUBLIMED REALITY...
BUT THE SAME RECORDING DEVICES WERE PRESENT FOR THEIR *ARRIVAL*, REGIS. WE HAVE THE *FREQUENCY* OF THEIR *DOOR*. WE CAN *BACKTRACK*.
WE CAN GET TO THEM.

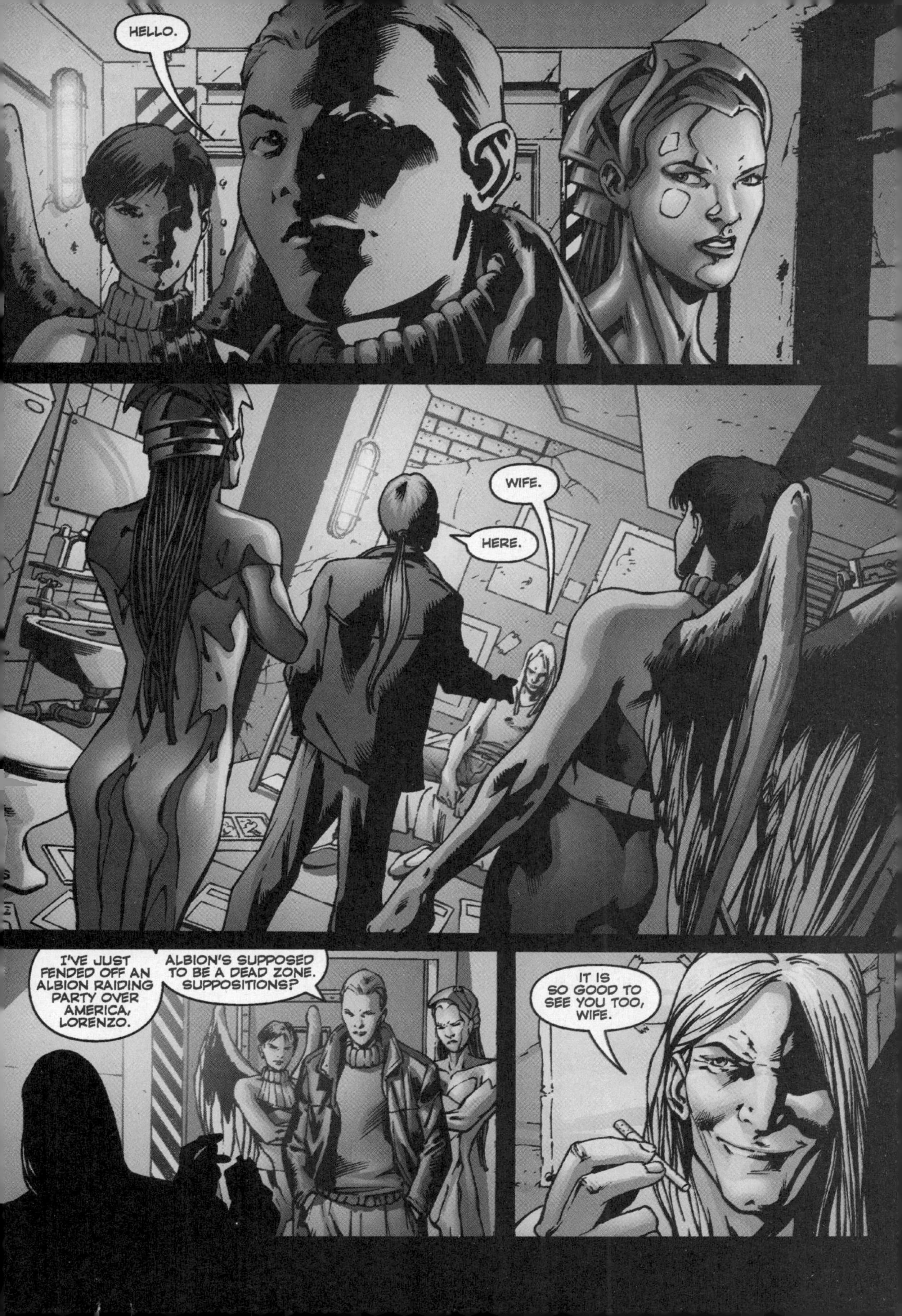
HELLO.
WIFE.
HERE.
I'VE JUST FENDED OFF AN ALBION RAIDING PARTY OVER AMERICA, LORENZO.
ALBION'S SUPPOSED TO BE A DEAD ZONE. SUPPOSITIONS?
IT IS SO GOOD TO SEE YOU TOO, WIFE.

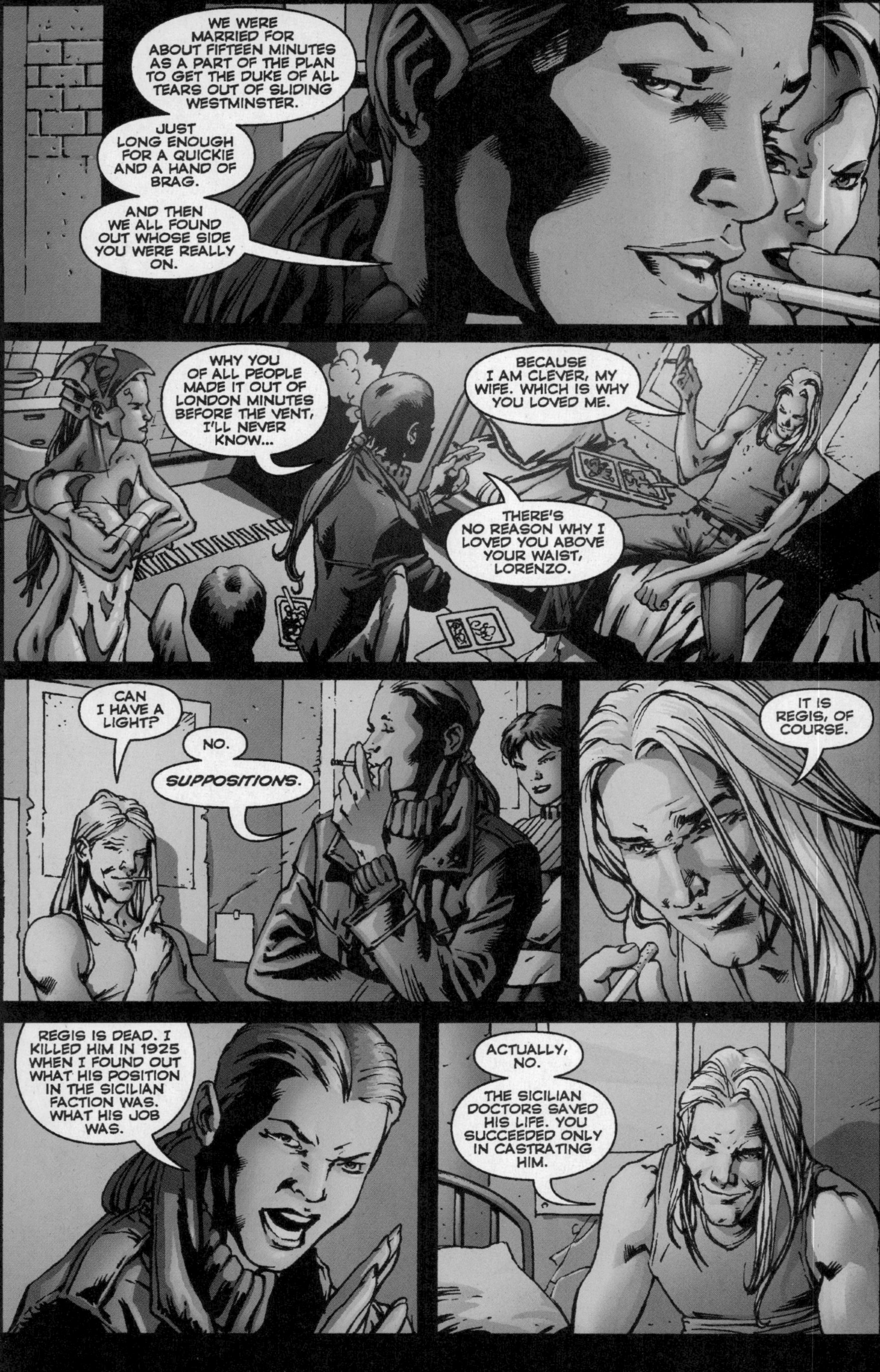
WE WERE MARRIED FOR ABOUT FIFTEEN MINUTES AS A PART OF THE PLAN TO GET THE DUKE OF ALL TEARS OUT OF SLIDING WESTMINSTER.
JUST LONG ENOUGH FOR A QUICKIE AND A HAND OF BRAG.
AND THEN WE ALL FOUND OUT WHOSE SIDE YOU WERE REALLY ON.
WHY YOU OF ALL PEOPLE MADE IT OUT OF LONDON MINUTES BEFORE THE VENT, I'LL NEVER KNOW...
BECAUSE I AM CLEVER, MY WIFE. WHICH IS WHY YOU LOVED ME.
THERE'S NO REASON WHY I LOVED YOU ABOVE YOUR WAIST, LORENZO.
CAN I HAVE A LIGHT?
NO.
SUPPOSITIONS.
IT IS REGIS, OF COURSE.
REGIS IS DEAD. I KILLED HIM IN 1925 WHEN I FOUND OUT WHAT HIS POSITION IN THE SICILIAN FACTION WAS. WHAT HIS JOB WAS.
ACTUALLY, NO.
THE SICILIAN DOCTORS SAVED HIS LIFE. YOU SUCCEEDED ONLY IN CASTRATING HIM.

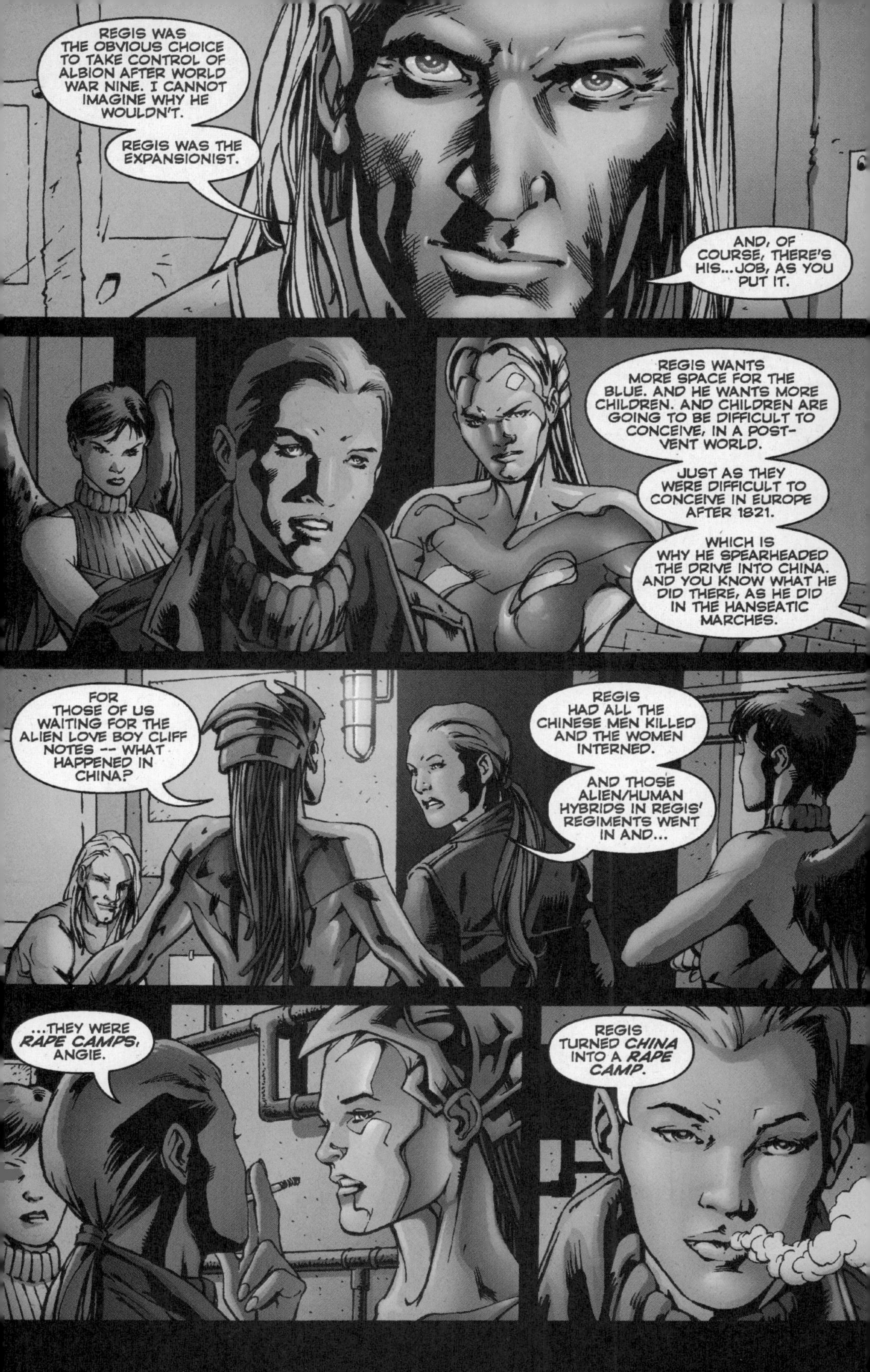
REGIS WAS THE OBVIOUS CHOICE TO TAKE CONTROL OF ALBION AFTER WORLD WAR NINE. I CANNOT IMAGINE WHY HE WOULDN'T.
REGIS WAS THE EXPANSIONIST.
AND, OF COURSE, THERE'S HIS...JOB, AS YOU PUT IT.
REGIS WANTS MORE SPACE FOR THE BLUE. AND HE WANTS MORE CHILDREN. AND CHILDREN ARE GOING TO BE DIFFICULT TO CONCEIVE, IN A POST-VENT WORLD.
JUST AS THEY WERE DIFFICULT TO CONCEIVE IN EUROPE AFTER 1821.
WHICH IS WHY HE SPEARHEADED THE DRIVE INTO CHINA. AND YOU KNOW WHAT HE DID THERE, AS HE DID IN THE HANSEATIC MARCHES.
FOR THOSE OF US WAITING FOR THE ALIEN LOVE BOY CLIFF NOTES -- WHAT HAPPENED IN CHINA?
REGIS HAD ALL THE CHINESE MEN KILLED AND THE WOMEN INTERNED.
AND THOSE ALIEN/HUMAN HYBRIDS IN REGIS' REGIMENTS WENT IN AND...
...THEY WERE *RAPE CAMPS*, ANGIE.
REGIS TURNED *CHINA* INTO A *RAPE CAMP*.

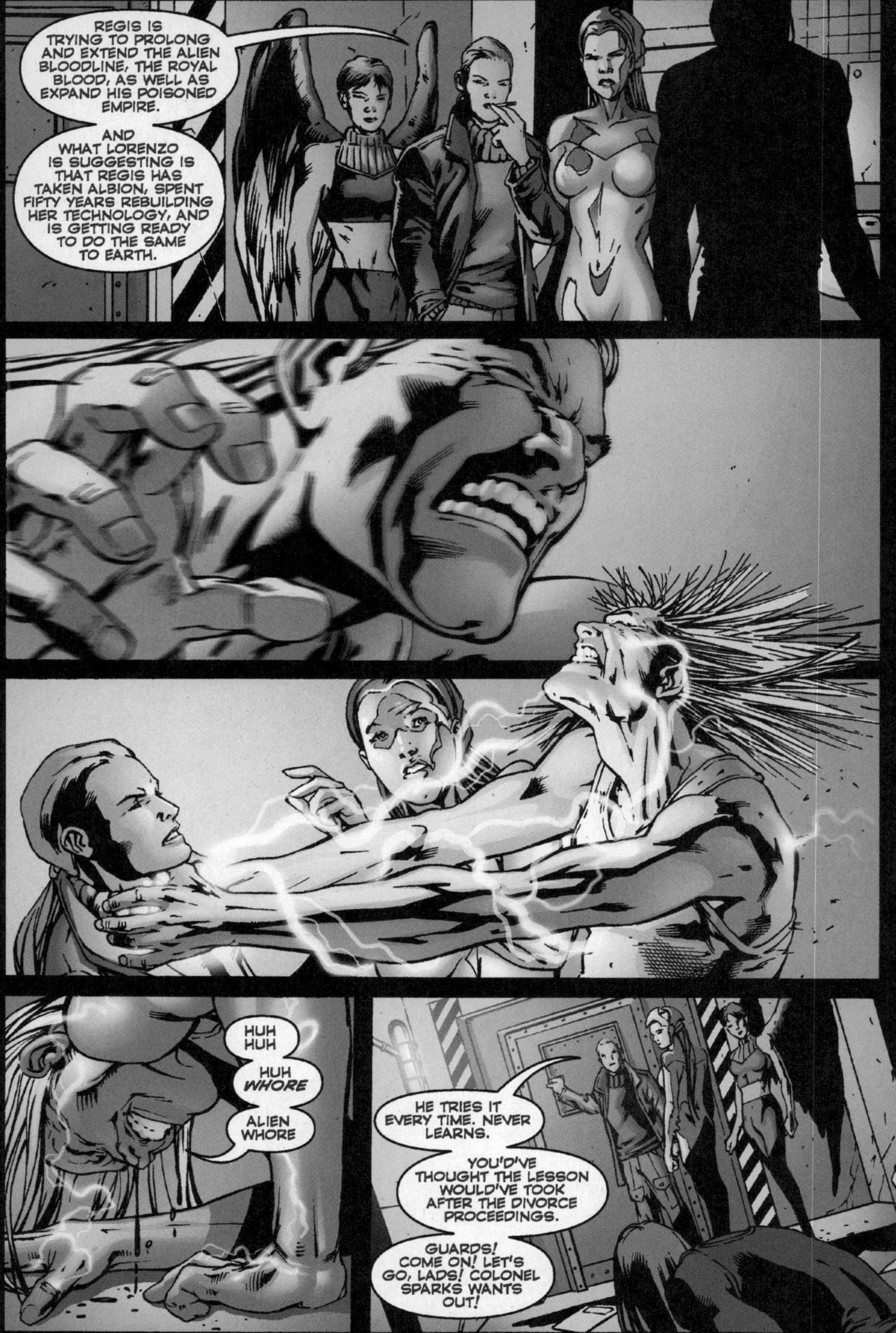
REGIS IS TRYING TO PROLONG AND EXTEND THE ALIEN BLOODLINE, THE ROYAL BLOOD, AS WELL AS EXPAND HIS POISONED EMPIRE.
AND WHAT LORENZO IS SUGGESTING IS THAT REGIS HAS TAKEN ALBION, SPENT FIFTY YEARS REBUILDING HER TECHNOLOGY, AND IS GETTING READY TO DO THE SAME TO EARTH.
HUH HUH
HUH *WHORE*
ALIEN WHORE
HE TRIES IT EVERY TIME. NEVER LEARNS.
YOU'D'VE THOUGHT THE LESSON WOULD'VE TOOK AFTER THE DIVORCE PROCEEDINGS.
GUARDS! COME ON! LET'S GO, LADS! COLONEL SPARKS WANTS OUT!

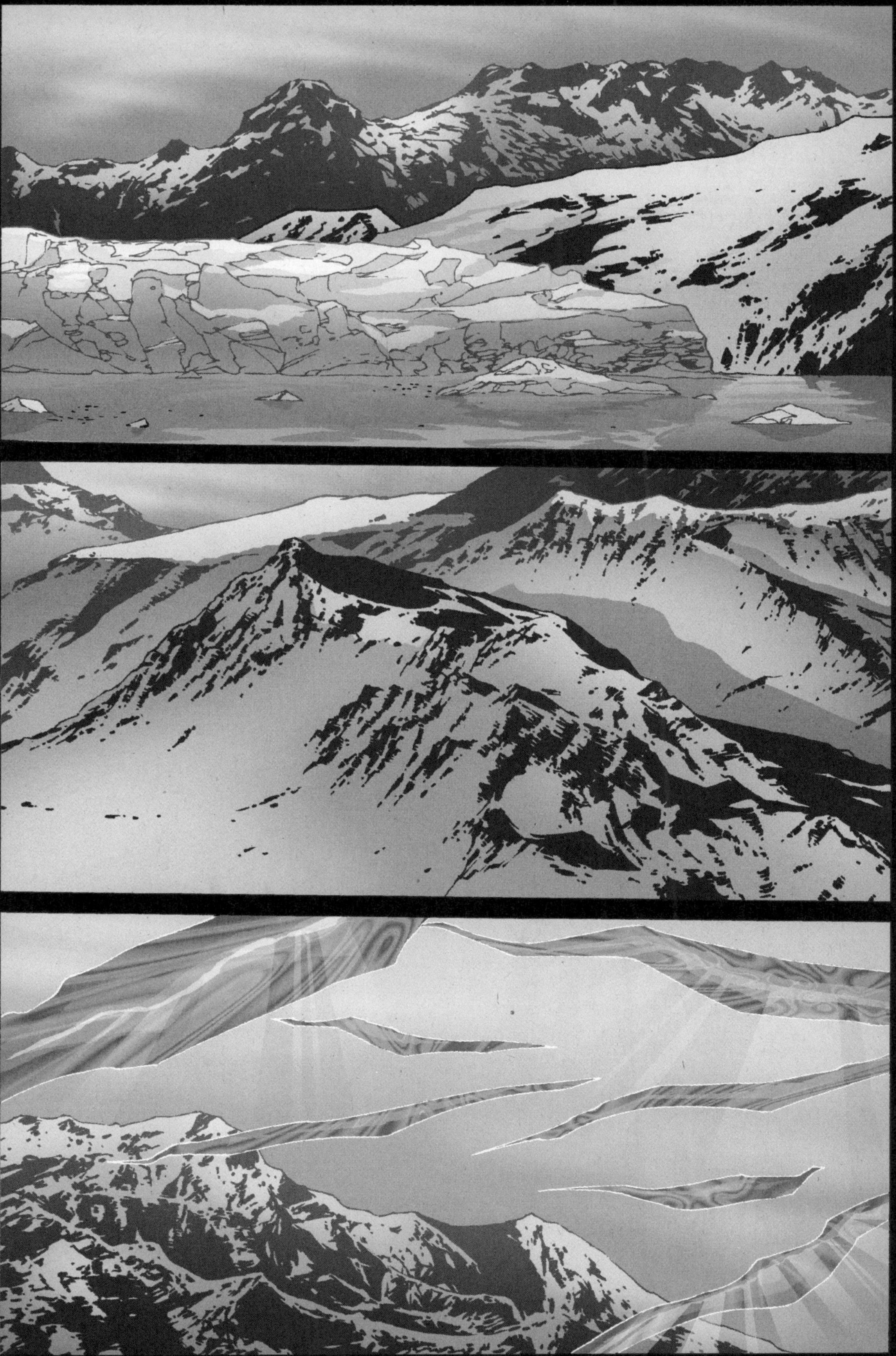

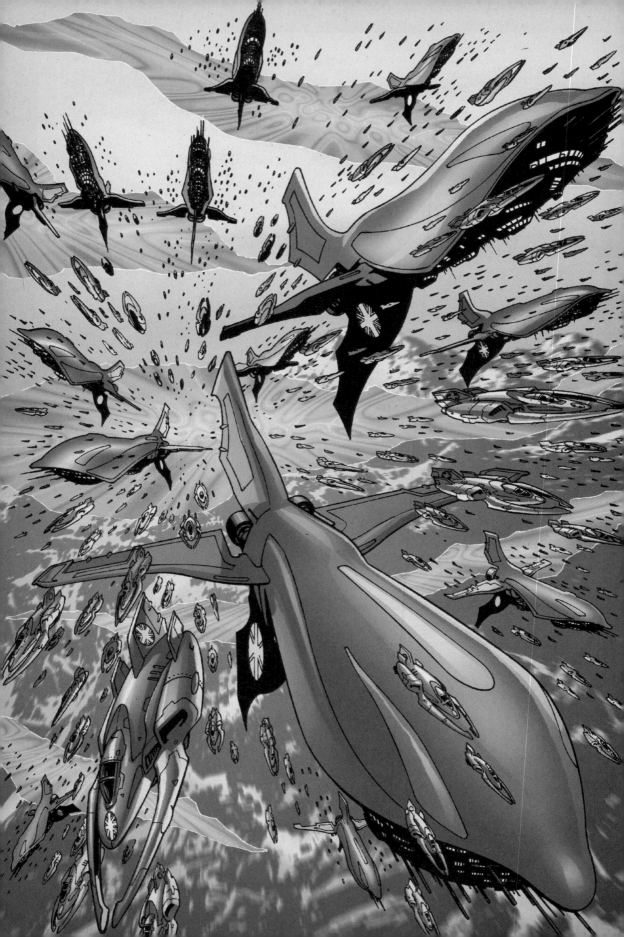

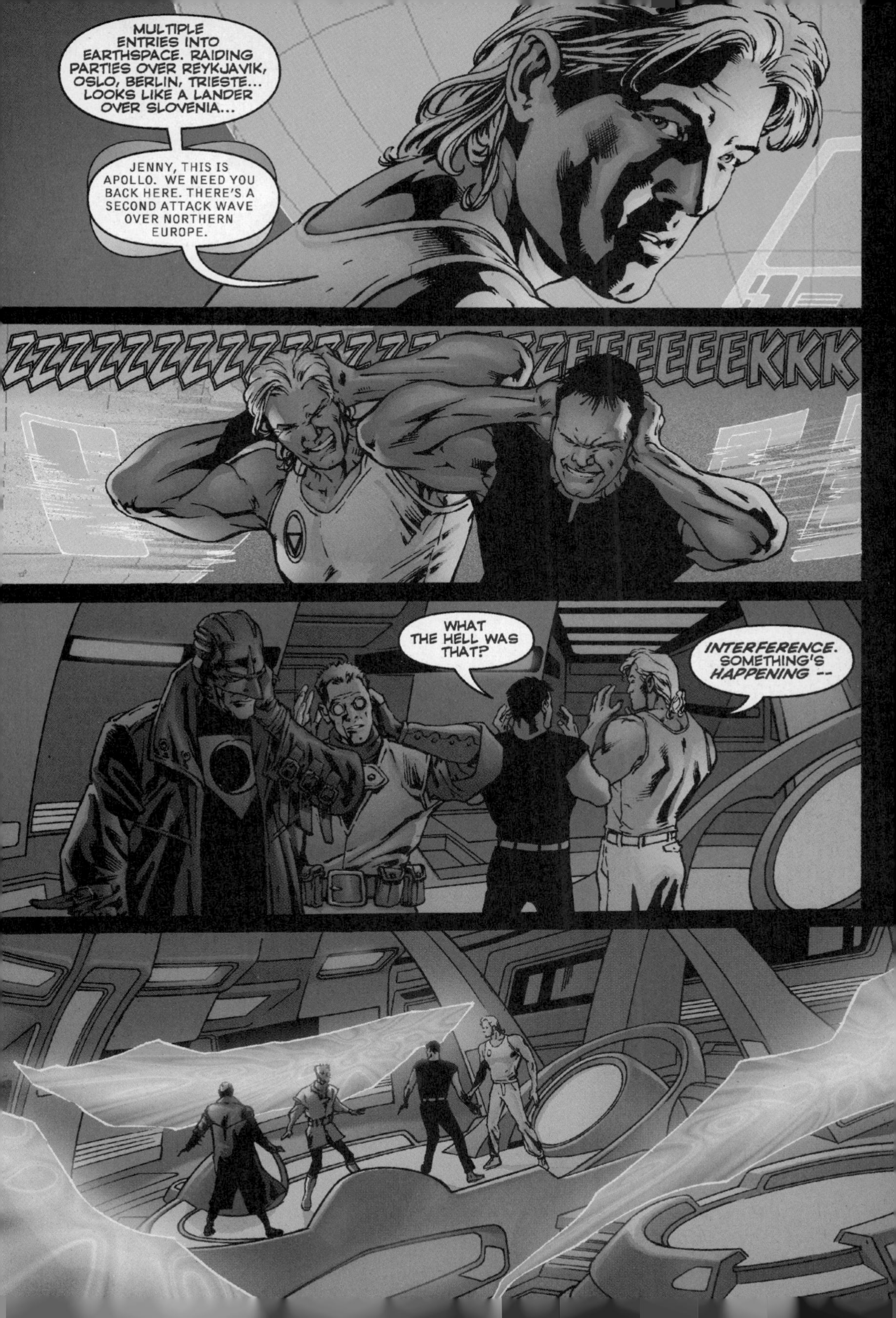
MULTIPLE ENTRIES INTO EARTHSPACE. RAIDING PARTIES OVER REYKJAVIK, OSLO, BERLIN, TRIESTE... LOOKS LIKE A LANDER OVER SLOVENIA...
JENNY, THIS IS APOLLO. WE NEED YOU BACK HERE. THERE'S A SECOND ATTACK WAVE OVER NORTHERN EUROPE.
ZZZZZZZZZZZZZZZZZZEEEEEEKKK
WHAT THE HELL WAS THAT?
INTERFERENCE. SOMETHING'S *HAPPENING* --

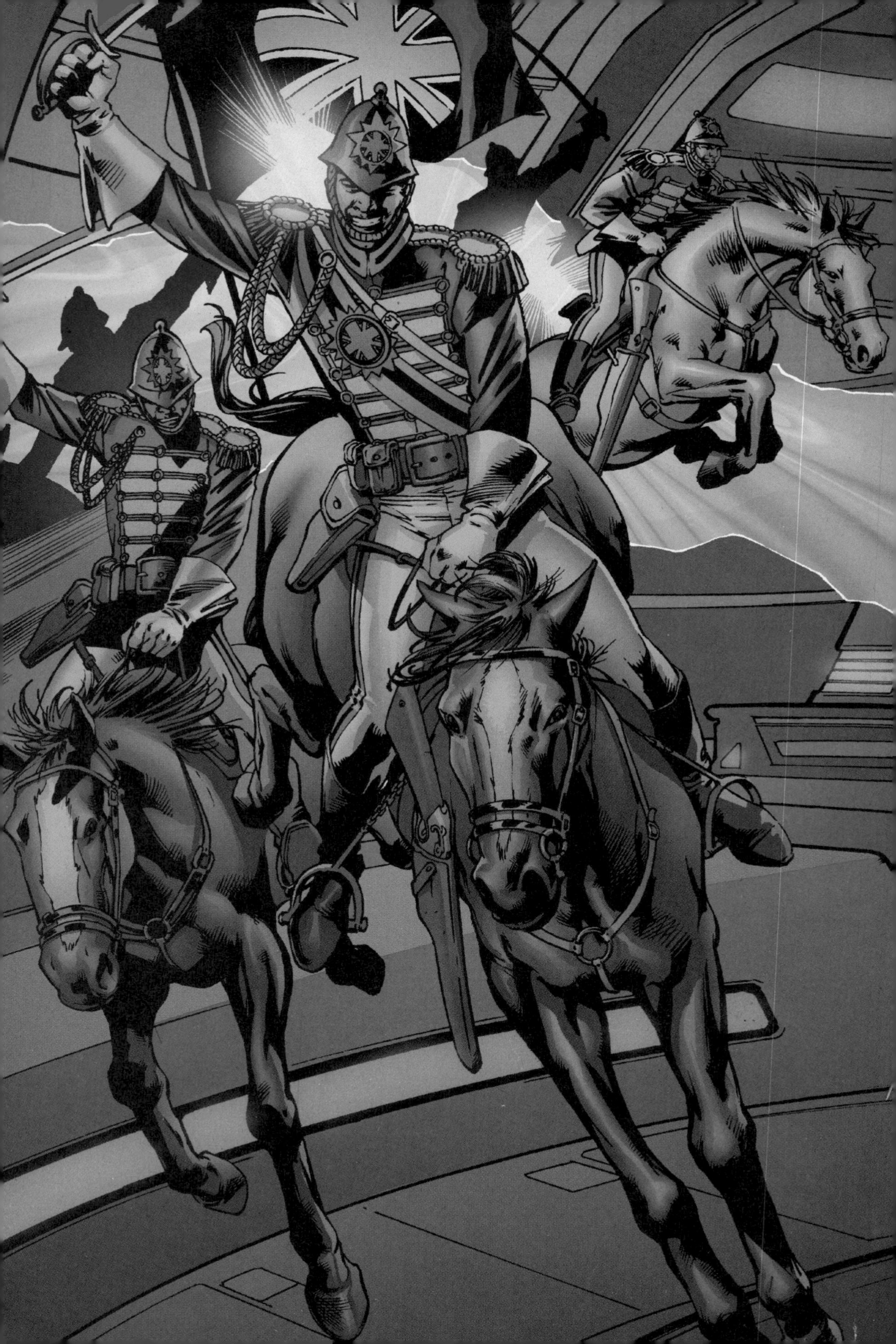

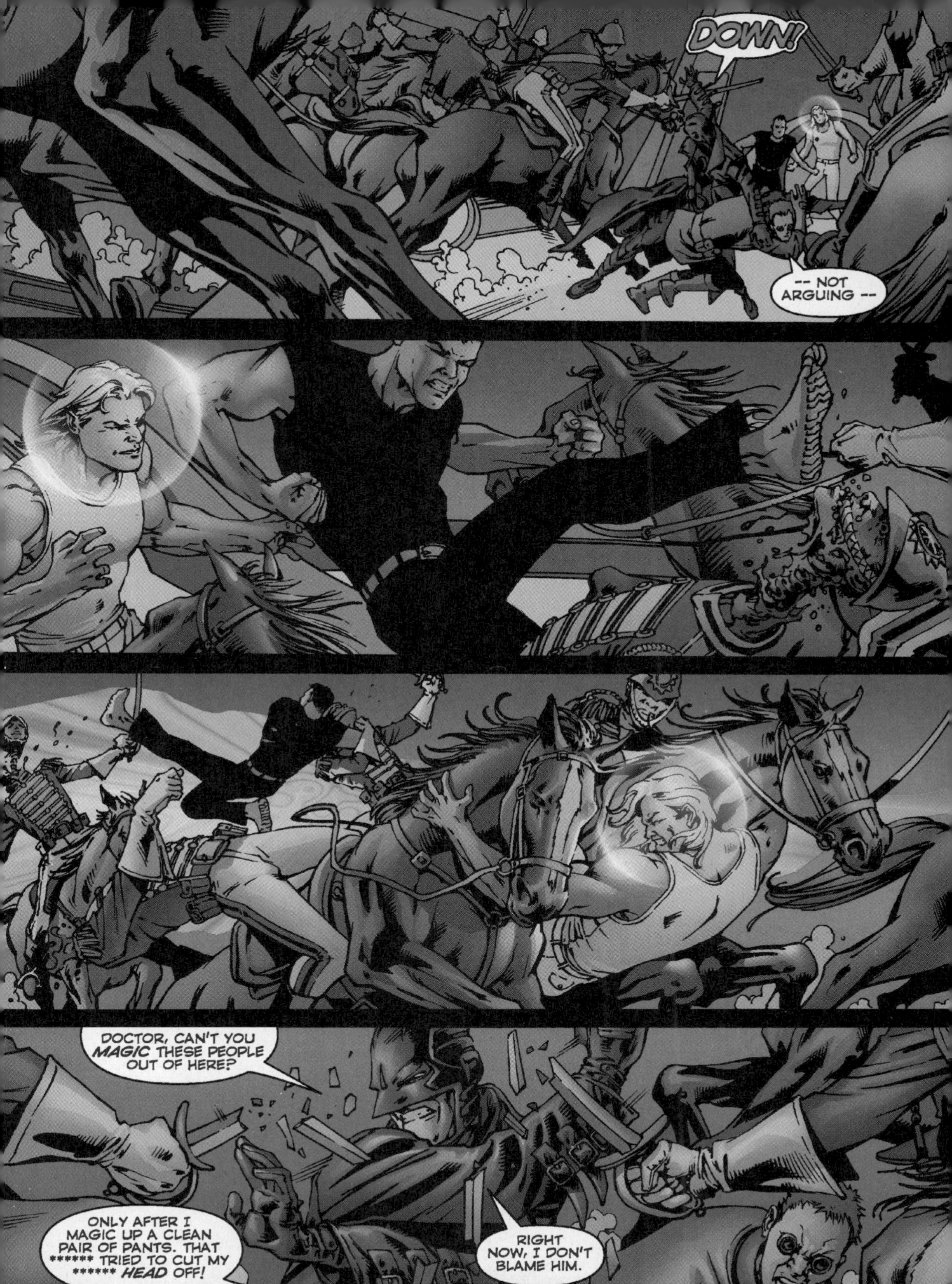

DOWN!
-- NOT ARGUING --
DOCTOR, CAN'T YOU *MAGIC* THESE PEOPLE OUT OF HERE?
ONLY AFTER I MAGIC UP A CLEAN PAIR OF PANTS. THAT ****** TRIED TO CUT MY ****** *HEAD* OFF!
RIGHT NOW, I DON'T BLAME HIM.

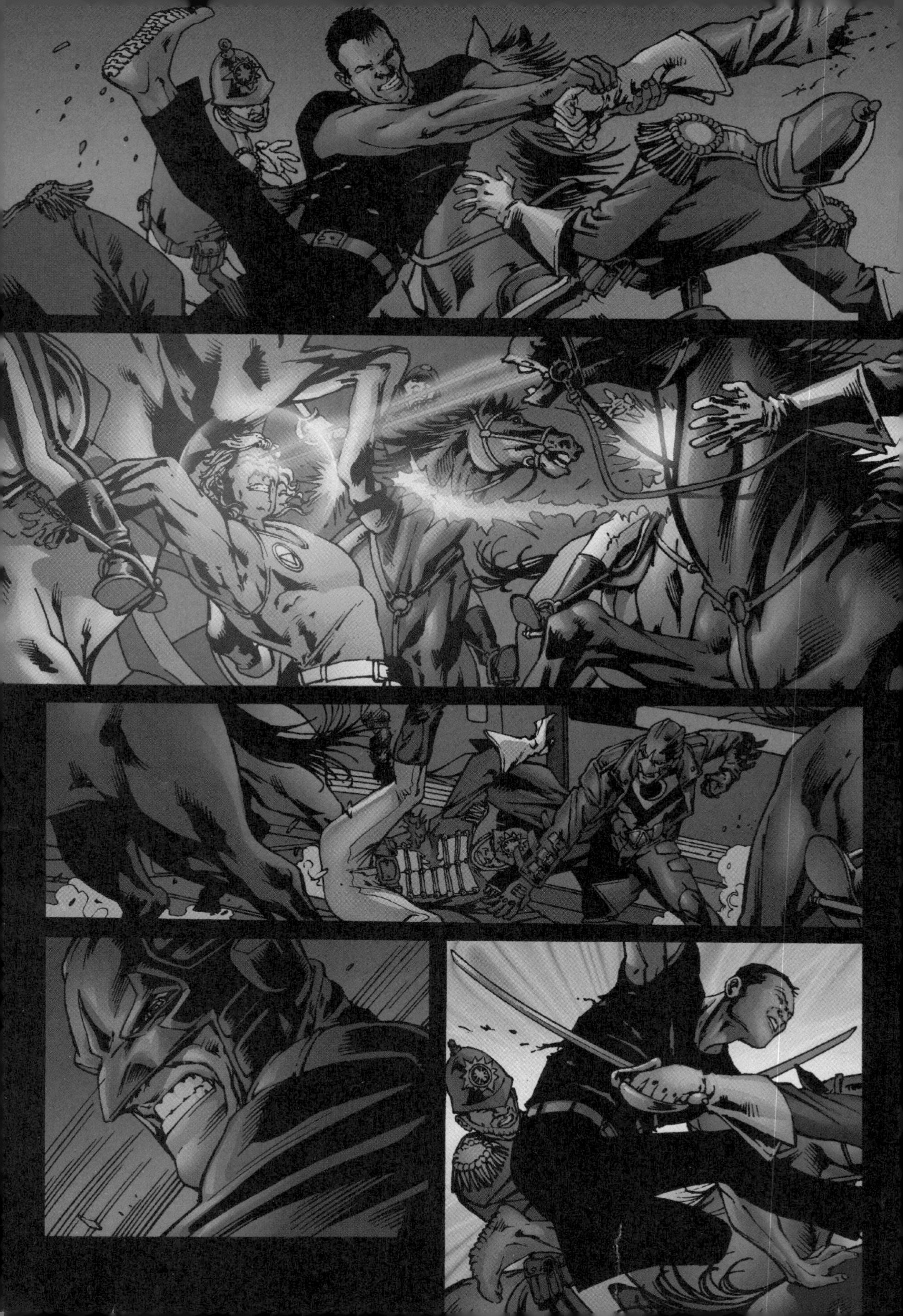

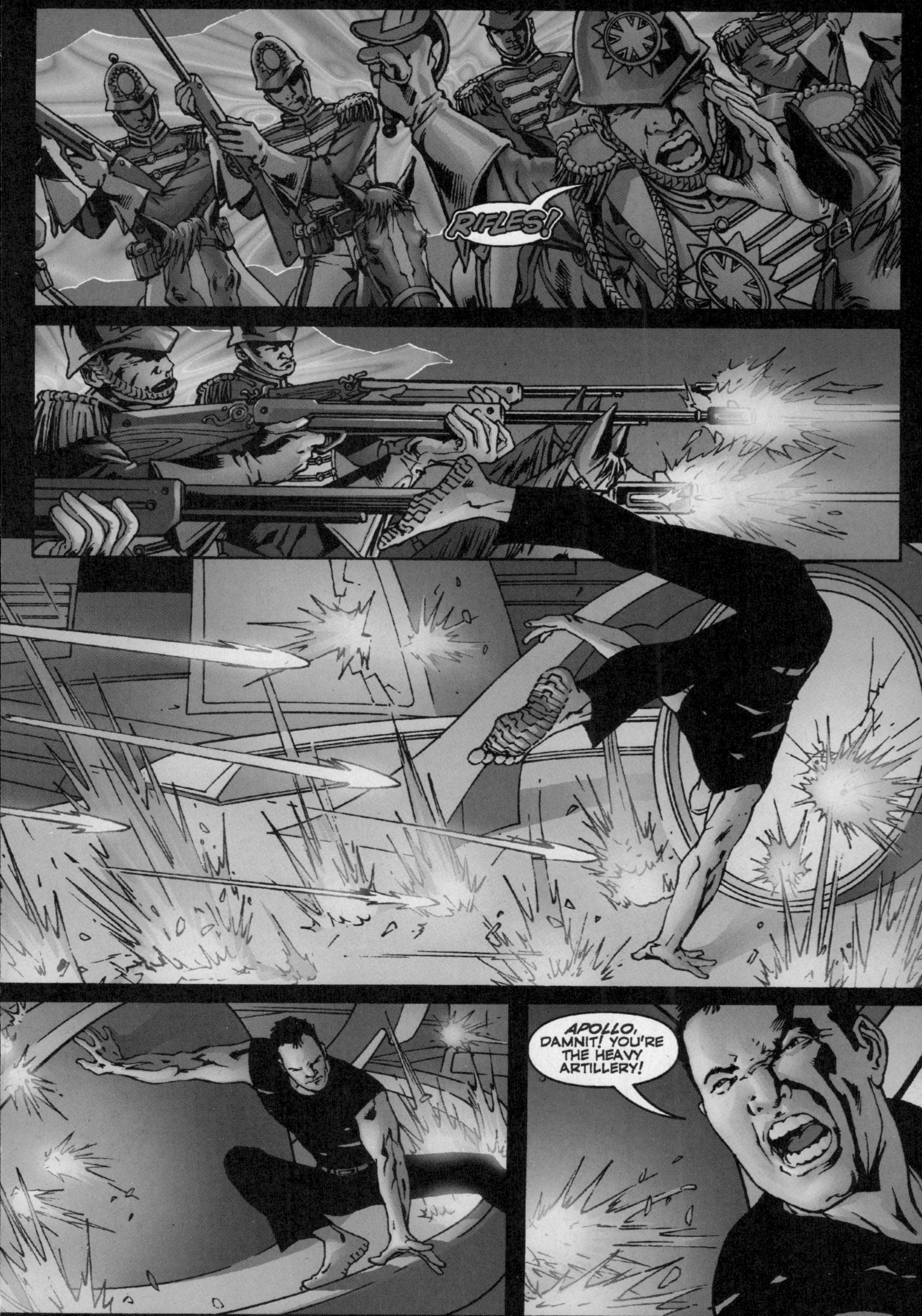
RIFLES!
APOLLO, DAMNIT! YOU'RE THE HEAVY ARTILLERY!

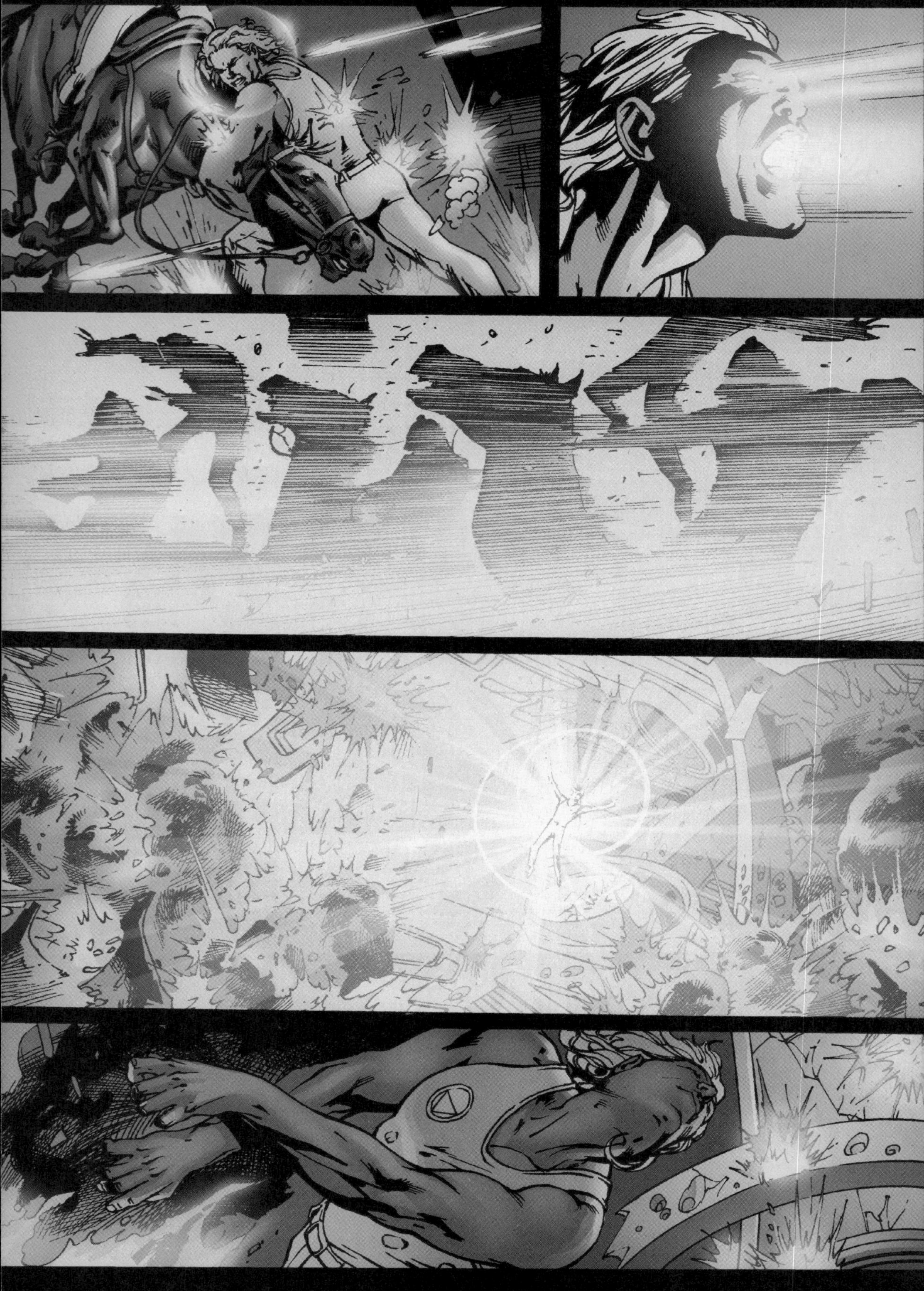

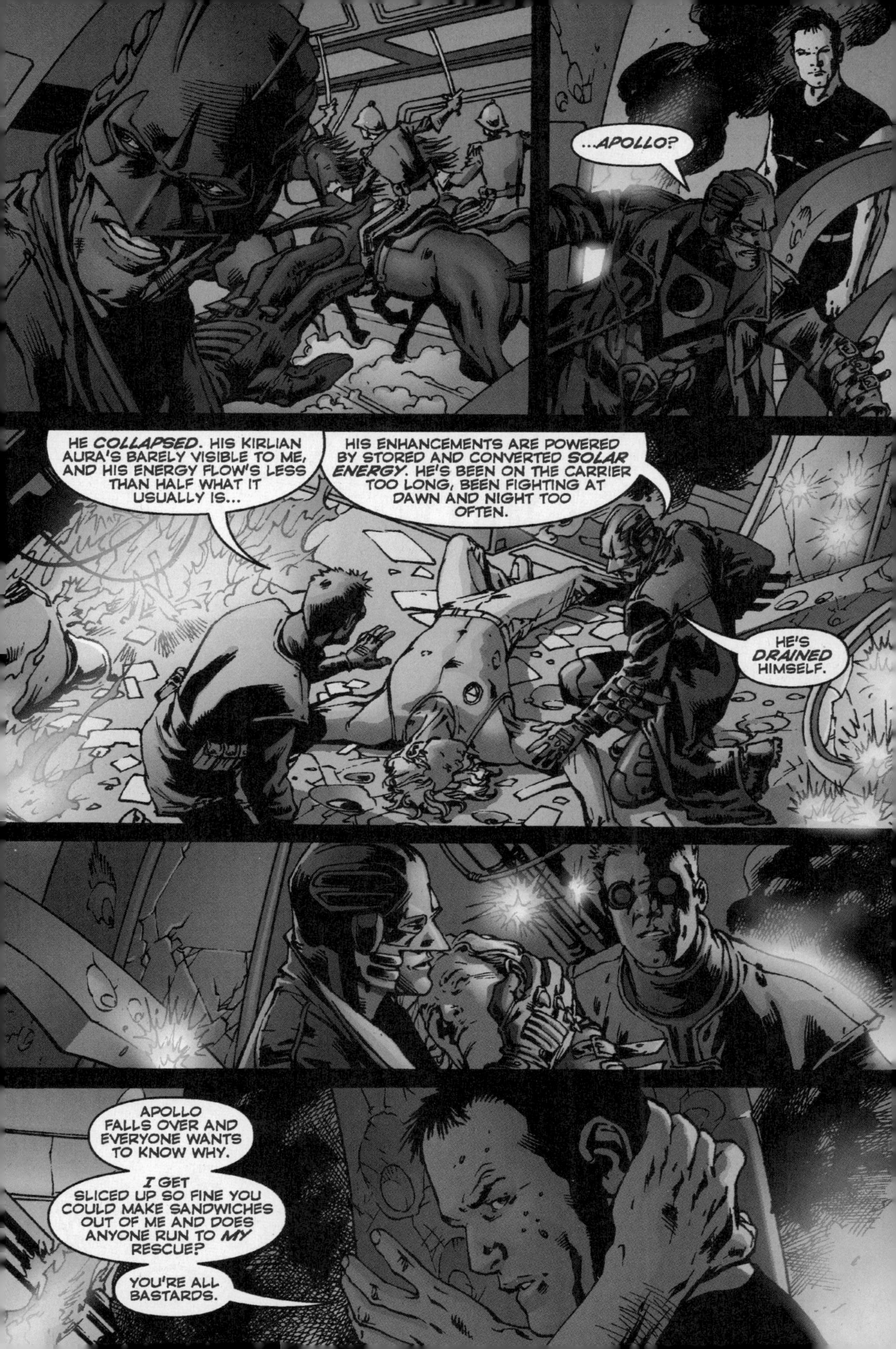
...APOLLO?
HE COLLAPSED. HIS KIRLIAN AURA'S BARELY VISIBLE TO ME, AND HIS ENERGY FLOW'S LESS THAN HALF WHAT IT USUALLY IS...
HIS ENHANCEMENTS ARE POWERED BY STORED AND CONVERTED SOLAR ENERGY. HE'S BEEN ON THE CARRIER TOO LONG, BEEN FIGHTING AT DAWN AND NIGHT TOO OFTEN.
HE'S DRAINED HIMSELF.
APOLLO FALLS OVER AND EVERYONE WANTS TO KNOW WHY.
I GET SLICED UP SO FINE YOU COULD MAKE SANDWICHES OUT OF ME AND DOES ANYONE RUN TO MY RESCUE?
YOU'RE ALL BASTARDS.

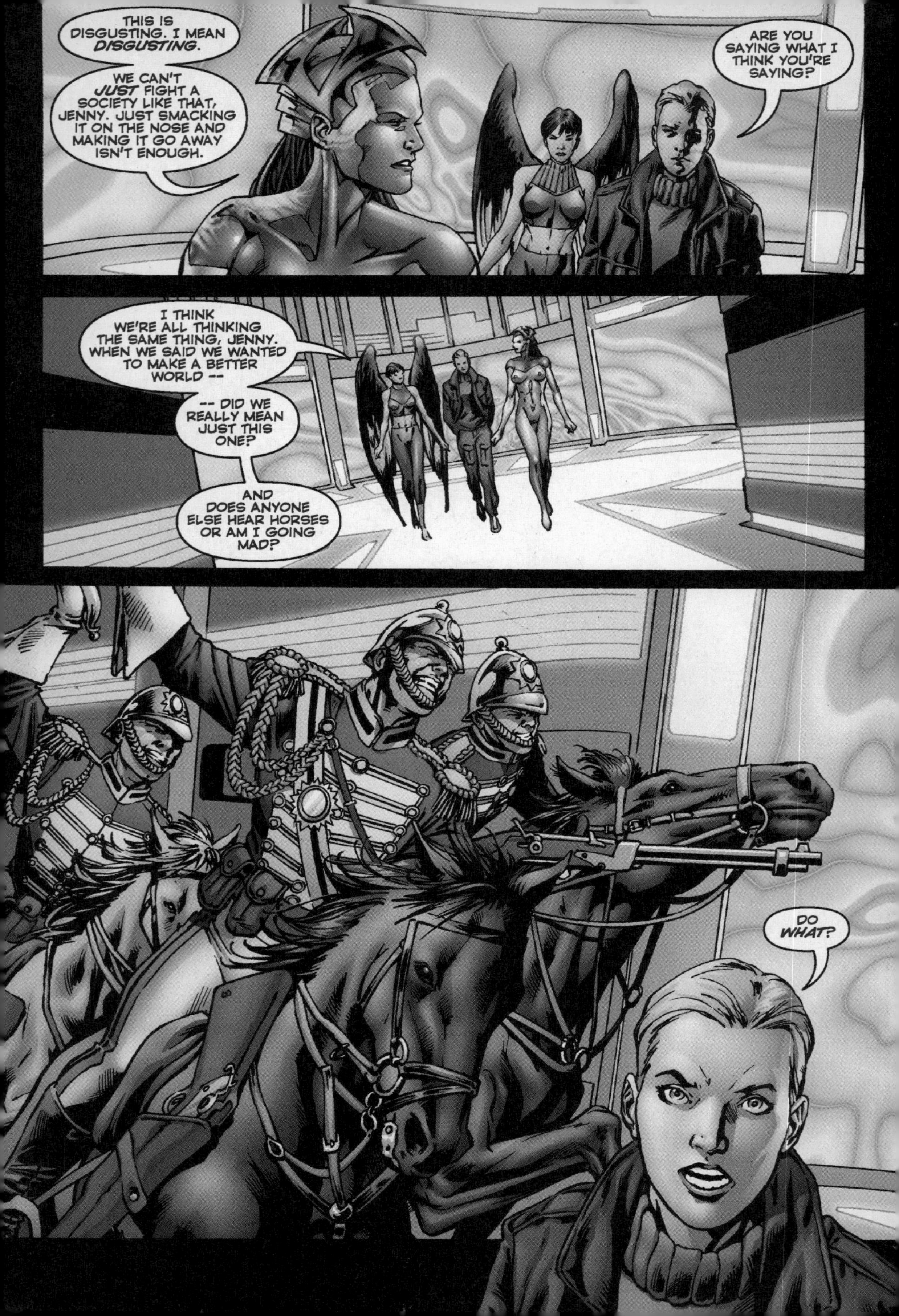
THIS IS DISGUSTING. I MEAN *DISGUSTING*.
WE CAN'T *JUST* FIGHT A SOCIETY LIKE THAT, JENNY. JUST SMACKING IT ON THE NOSE AND MAKING IT GO AWAY ISN'T ENOUGH.
ARE YOU SAYING WHAT I THINK YOU'RE SAYING?
I THINK WE'RE ALL THINKING THE SAME THING, JENNY. WHEN WE SAID WE WANTED TO MAKE A BETTER WORLD --
-- DID WE REALLY MEAN JUST THIS ONE?
AND DOES ANYONE ELSE HEAR HORSES OR AM I GOING MAD?
DO *WHAT*?

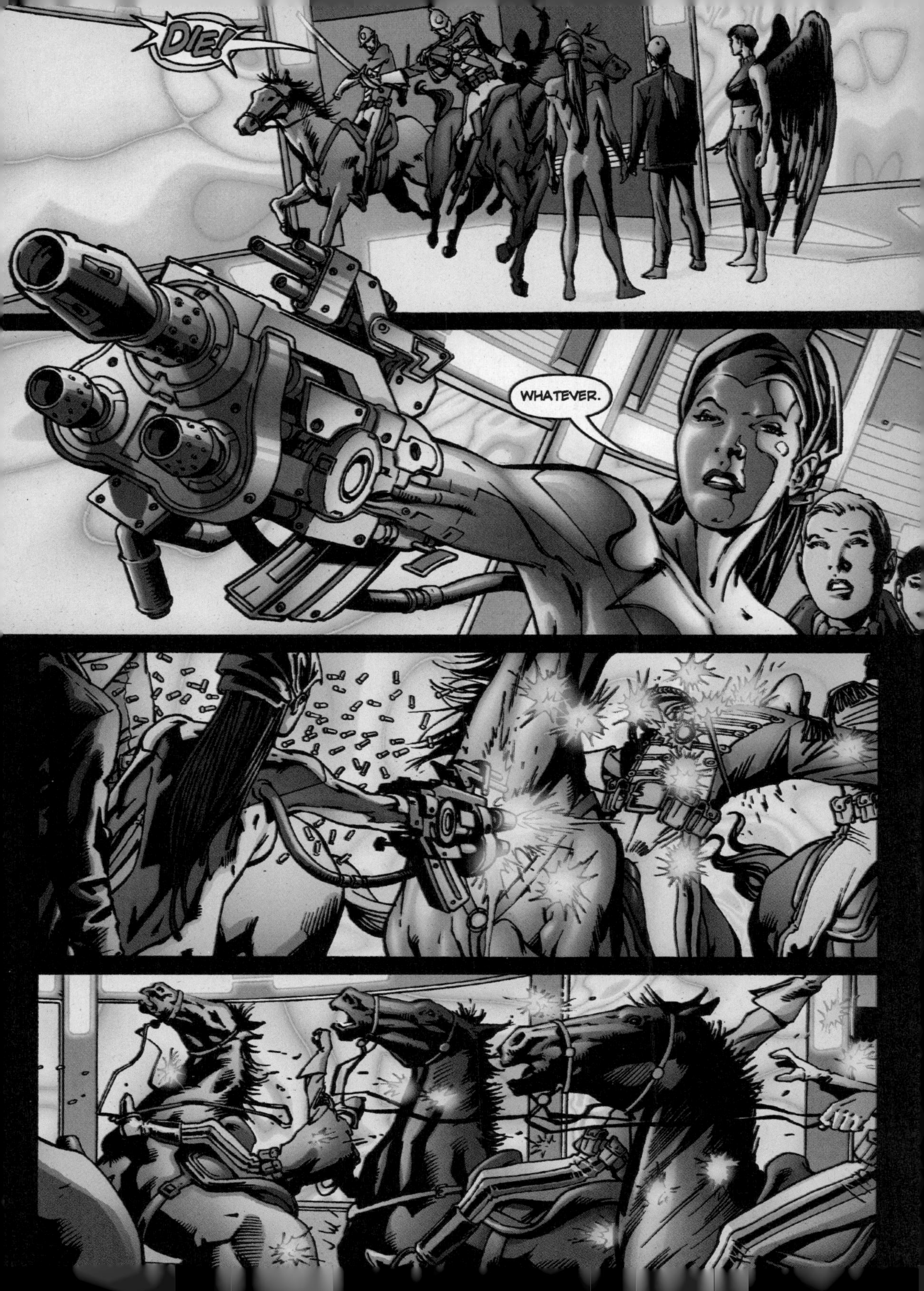
DIE!
WHATEVER.

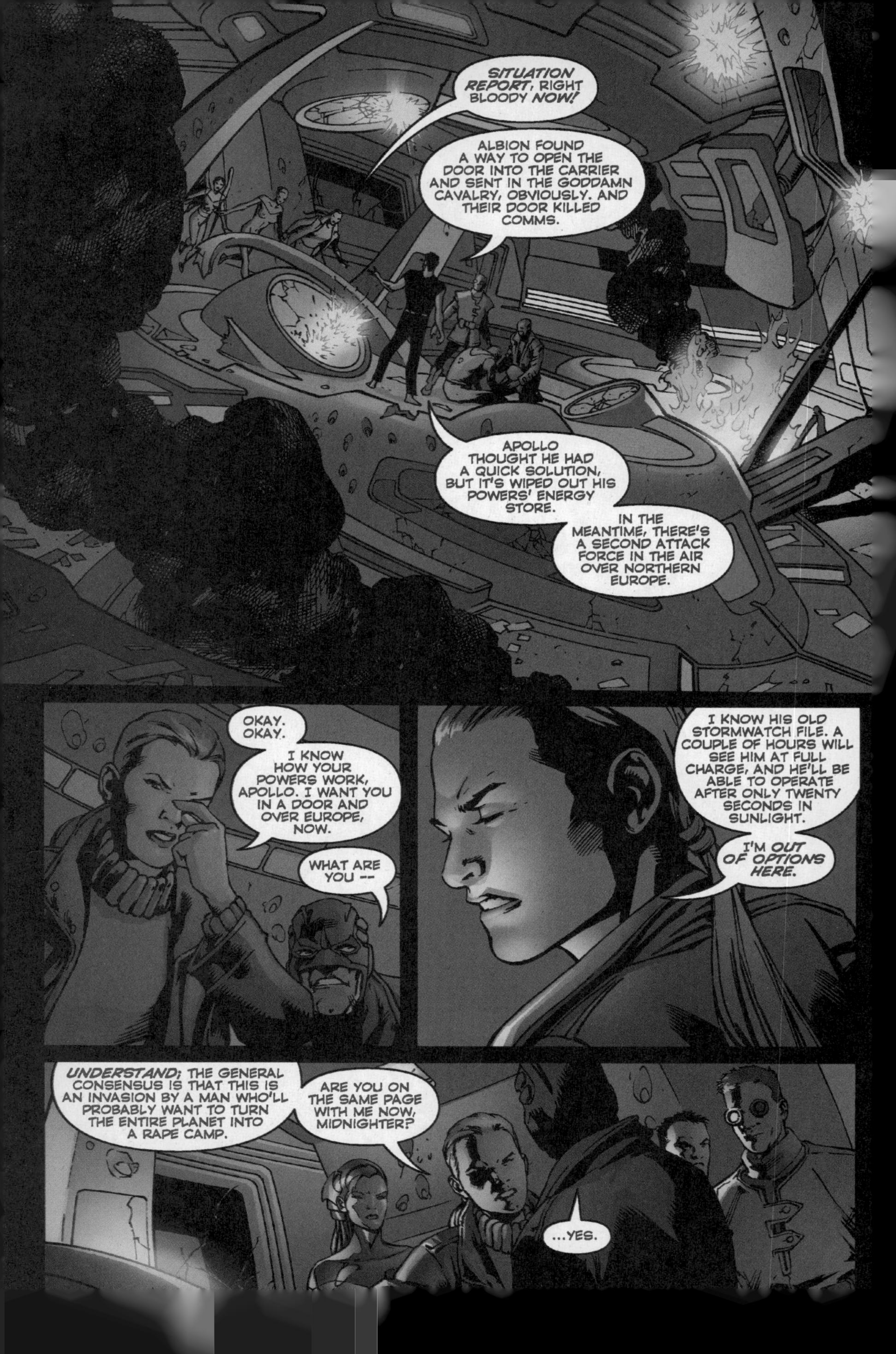
SITUATION REPORT, RIGHT BLOODY NOW!
ALBION FOUND A WAY TO OPEN THE DOOR INTO THE CARRIER AND SENT IN THE GODDAMN CAVALRY, OBVIOUSLY. AND THEIR DOOR KILLED COMMS.
APOLLO THOUGHT HE HAD A QUICK SOLUTION, BUT IT'S WIPED OUT HIS POWERS' ENERGY STORE.
IN THE MEANTIME, THERE'S A SECOND ATTACK FORCE IN THE AIR OVER NORTHERN EUROPE.
OKAY. OKAY.
I KNOW HOW YOUR POWERS WORK, APOLLO. I WANT YOU IN A DOOR AND OVER EUROPE, NOW.
WHAT ARE YOU --
I KNOW HIS OLD STORMWATCH FILE. A COUPLE OF HOURS WILL SEE HIM AT FULL CHARGE, AND HE'LL BE ABLE TO OPERATE AFTER ONLY TWENTY SECONDS IN SUNLIGHT.
I'M OUT OF OPTIONS HERE.
UNDERSTAND; THE GENERAL CONSENSUS IS THAT THIS IS AN INVASION BY A MAN WHO'LL PROBABLY WANT TO TURN THE ENTIRE PLANET INTO A RAPE CAMP.
ARE YOU ON THE SAME PAGE WITH ME NOW, MIDNIGHTER?
...YES.

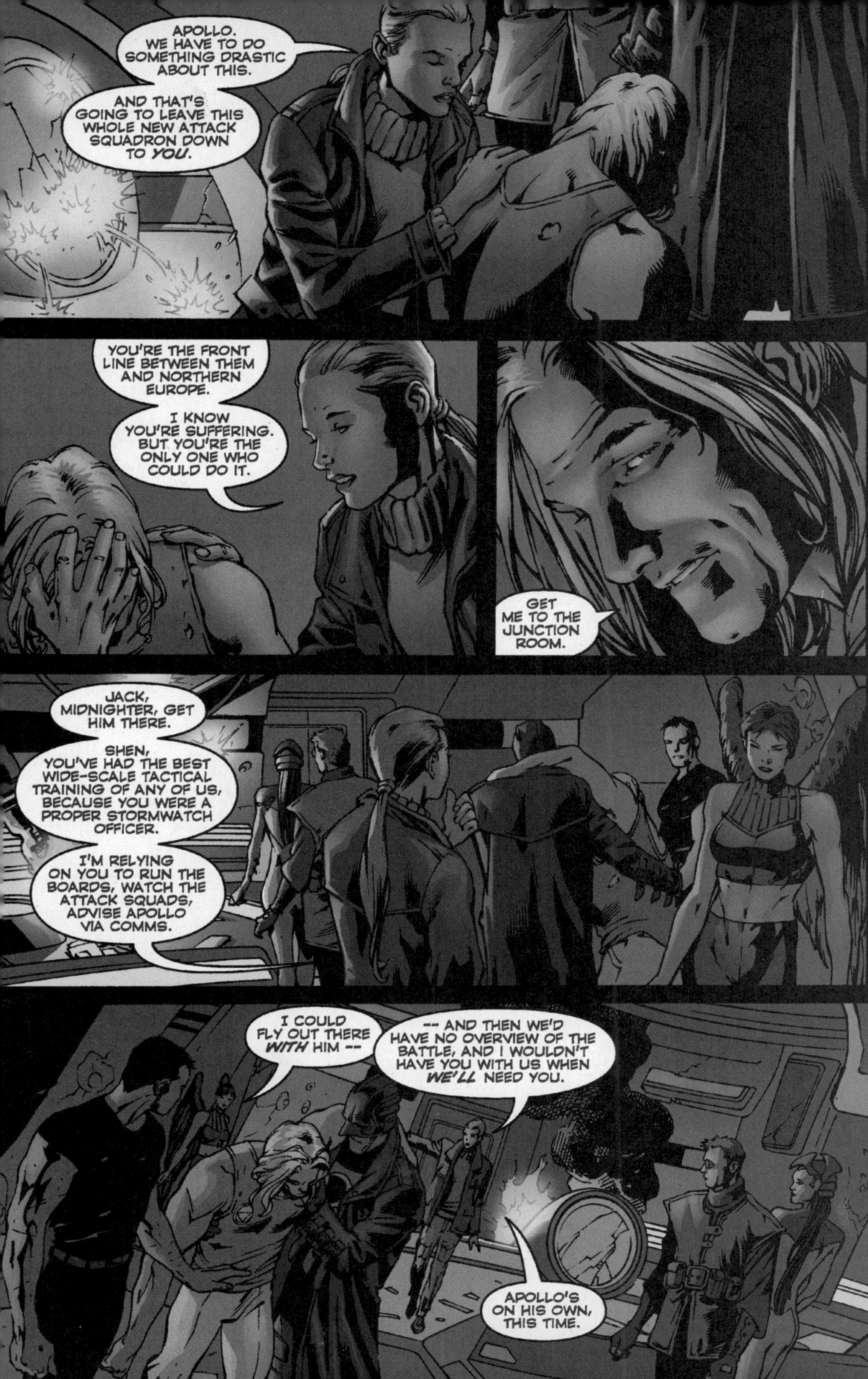
APOLLO. WE HAVE TO DO SOMETHING DRASTIC ABOUT THIS.
AND THAT'S GOING TO LEAVE THIS WHOLE NEW ATTACK SQUADRON DOWN TO *YOU*.
YOU'RE THE FRONT LINE BETWEEN THEM AND NORTHERN EUROPE.
I KNOW YOU'RE SUFFERING. BUT YOU'RE THE ONLY ONE WHO COULD DO IT.
GET ME TO THE JUNCTION ROOM.
JACK, MIDNIGHTER, GET HIM THERE.
SHEN, YOU'VE HAD THE BEST WIDE-SCALE TACTICAL TRAINING OF ANY OF US, BECAUSE YOU WERE A PROPER STORMWATCH OFFICER.
I'M RELYING ON YOU TO RUN THE BOARDS, WATCH THE ATTACK SQUADS, ADVISE APOLLO VIA COMMS.
I COULD FLY OUT THERE *WITH* HIM --
-- AND THEN WE'D HAVE NO OVERVIEW OF THE BATTLE, AND I WOULDN'T HAVE YOU WITH US WHEN *WE'LL* NEED YOU.
APOLLO'S ON HIS OWN, THIS TIME.

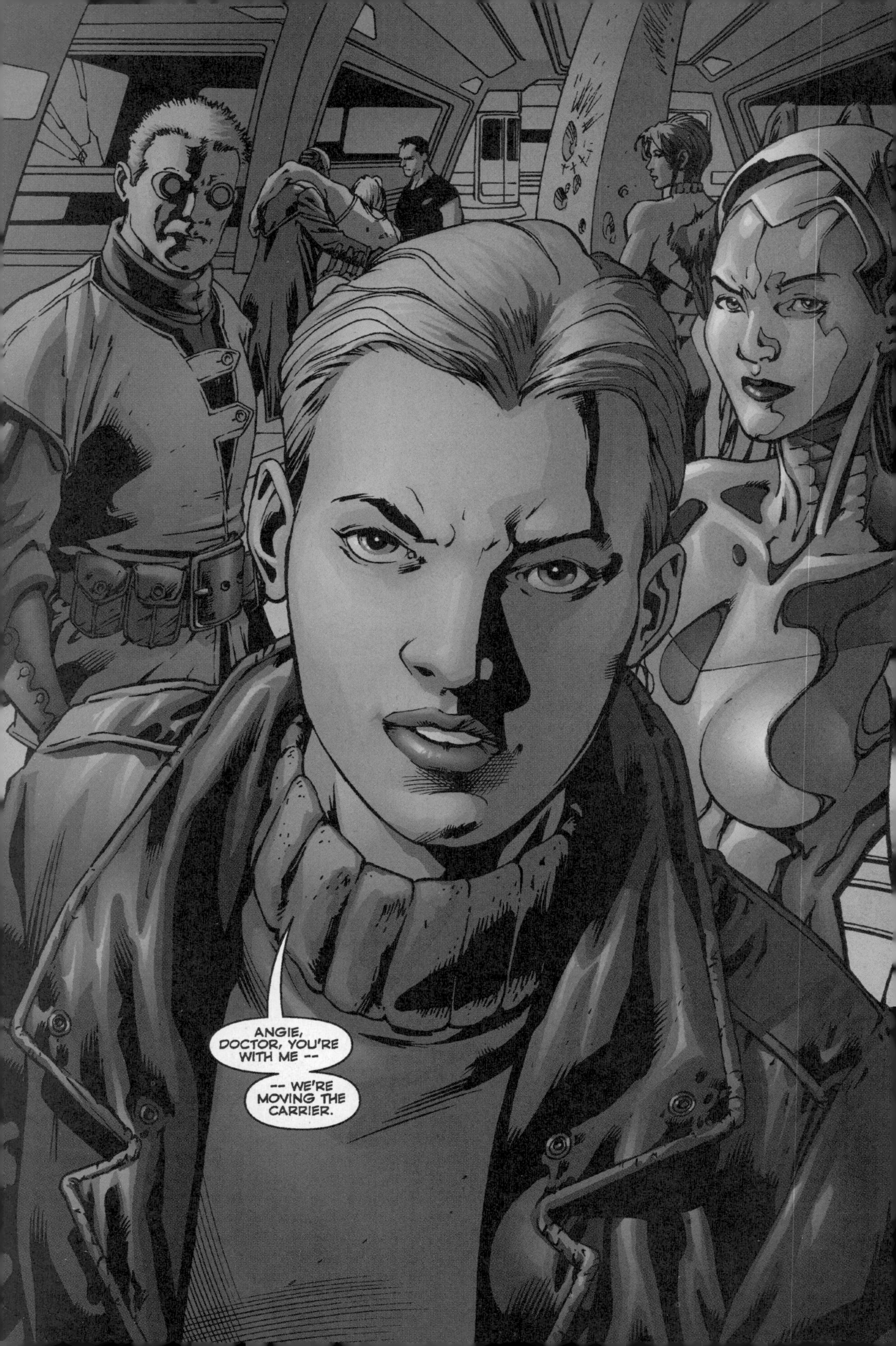
ANGIE, DOCTOR, YOU'RE WITH ME --
-- WE'RE MOVING THE CARRIER.

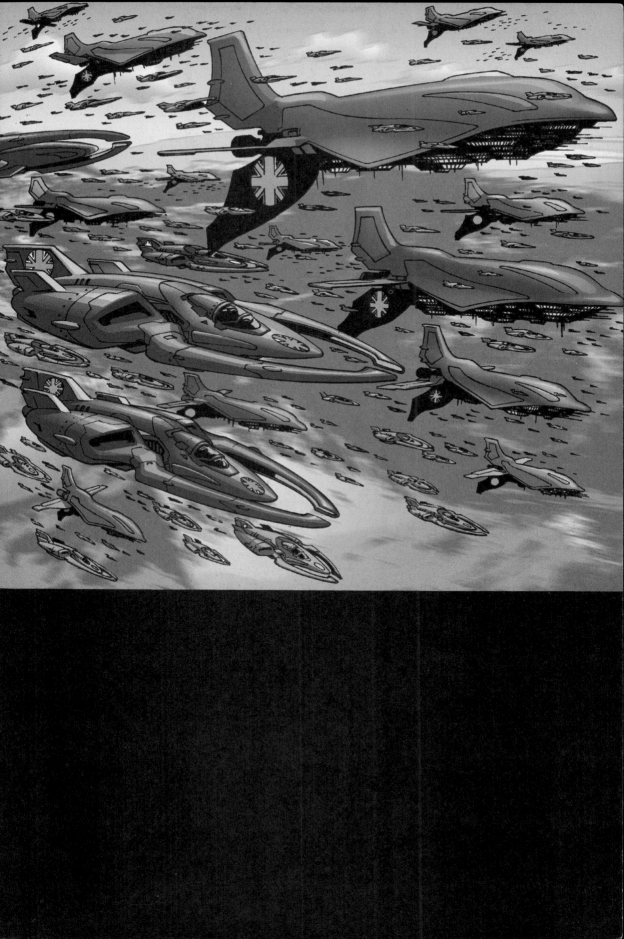

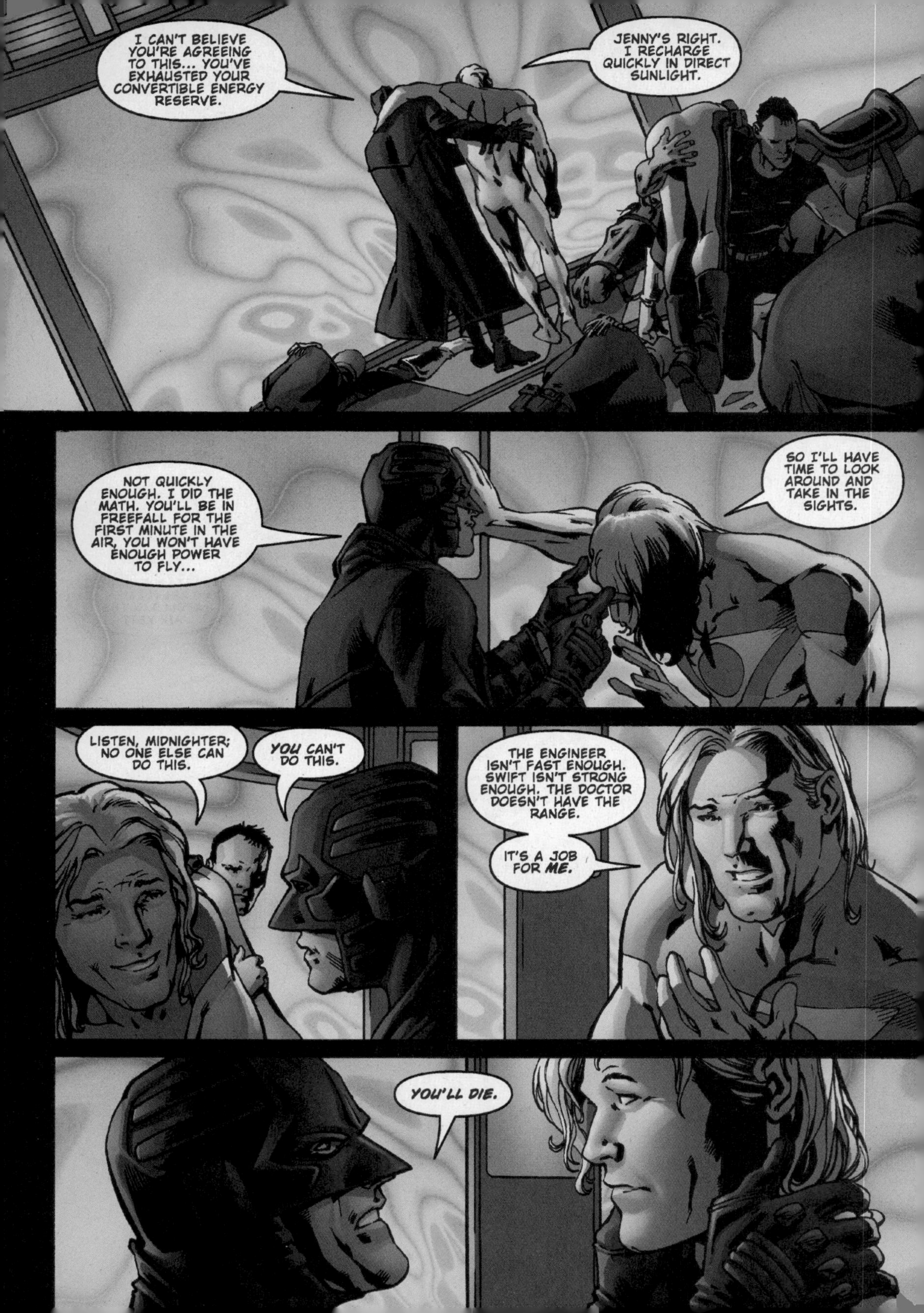
I CAN'T BELIEVE YOU'RE AGREEING TO THIS... YOU'VE EXHAUSTED YOUR CONVERTIBLE ENERGY RESERVE.
JENNY'S RIGHT. I RECHARGE QUICKLY IN DIRECT SUNLIGHT.
NOT QUICKLY ENOUGH. I DID THE MATH. YOU'LL BE IN FREEFALL FOR THE FIRST MINUTE IN THE AIR, YOU WON'T HAVE ENOUGH POWER TO FLY...
SO I'LL HAVE TIME TO LOOK AROUND AND TAKE IN THE SIGHTS.
LISTEN, MIDNIGHTER; NO ONE ELSE CAN DO THIS.
YOU CAN'T DO THIS.
THE ENGINEER ISN'T FAST ENOUGH. SWIFT ISN'T STRONG ENOUGH. THE DOCTOR DOESN'T HAVE THE RANGE.
IT'S A JOB FOR ME.
YOU'LL DIE.

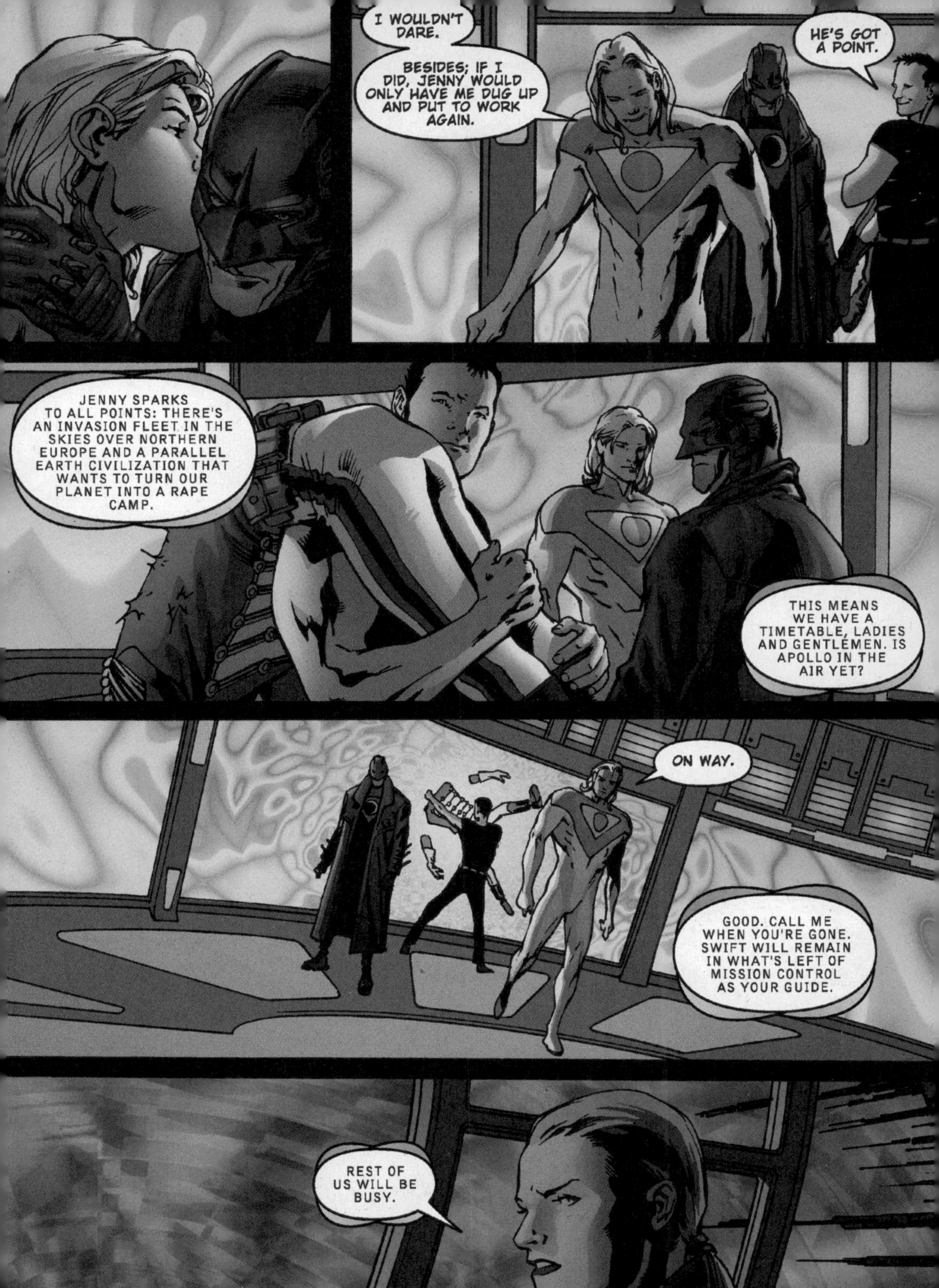
I WOULDN'T DARE.
BESIDES; IF I DID, JENNY WOULD ONLY HAVE ME DUG UP AND PUT TO WORK AGAIN.
HE'S GOT A POINT.
JENNY SPARKS TO ALL POINTS: THERE'S AN INVASION FLEET IN THE SKIES OVER NORTHERN EUROPE AND A PARALLEL EARTH CIVILIZATION THAT WANTS TO TURN OUR PLANET INTO A RAPE CAMP.
THIS MEANS WE HAVE A TIMETABLE, LADIES AND GENTLEMEN. IS APOLLO IN THE AIR YET?
ON WAY.
GOOD. CALL ME WHEN YOU'RE GONE. SWIFT WILL REMAIN IN WHAT'S LEFT OF MISSION CONTROL AS YOUR GUIDE.
REST OF US WILL BE BUSY.

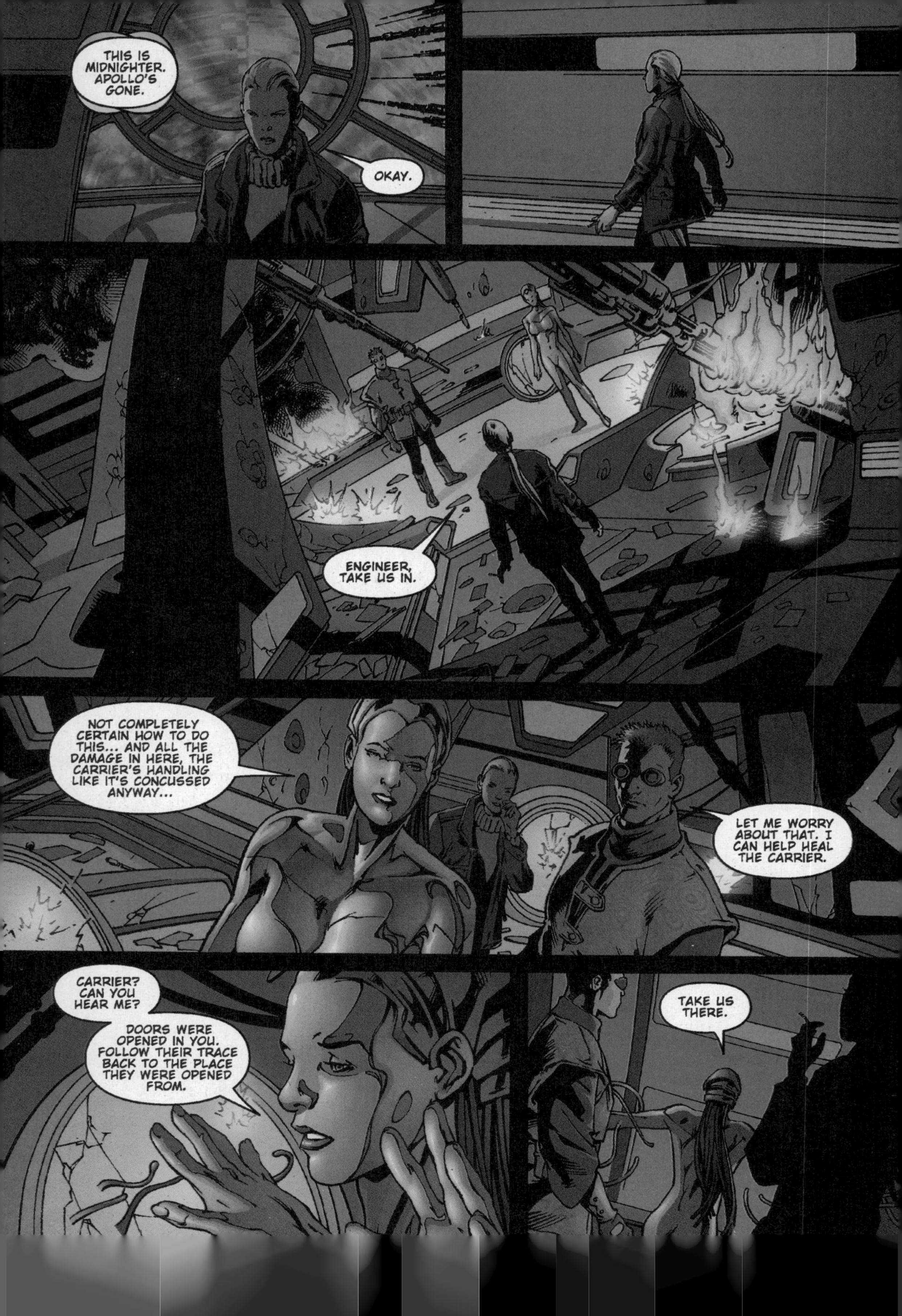
THIS IS MIDNIGHTER. APOLLO'S GONE.
OKAY.
ENGINEER, TAKE US IN.
NOT COMPLETELY CERTAIN HOW TO DO THIS... AND ALL THE DAMAGE IN HERE, THE CARRIER'S HANDLING LIKE IT'S CONCUSSED ANYWAY...
LET ME WORRY ABOUT THAT. I CAN HELP HEAL THE CARRIER.
CARRIER? CAN YOU HEAR ME?
DOORS WERE OPENED IN YOU. FOLLOW THEIR TRACE BACK TO THE PLACE THEY WERE OPENED FROM.
TAKE US THERE.

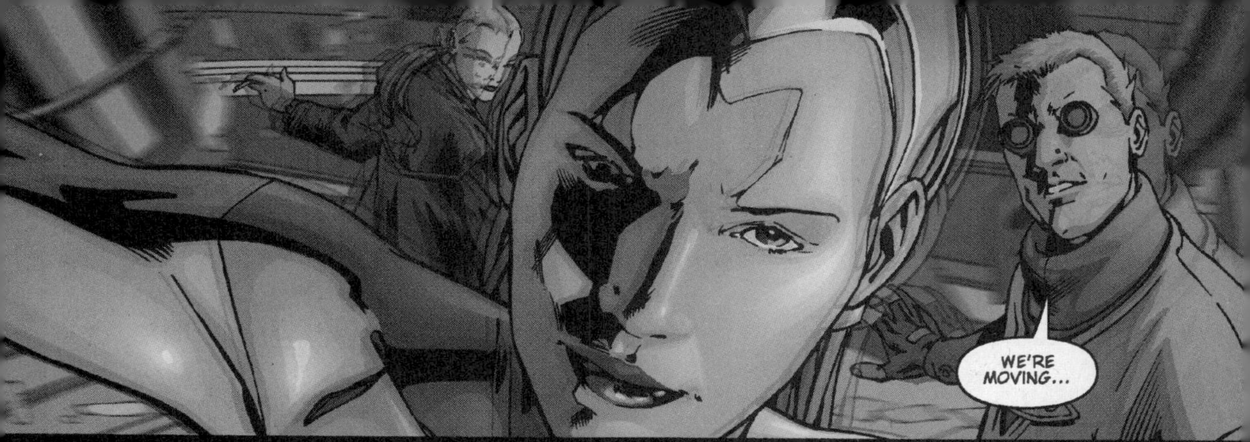
WE'RE MOVING...
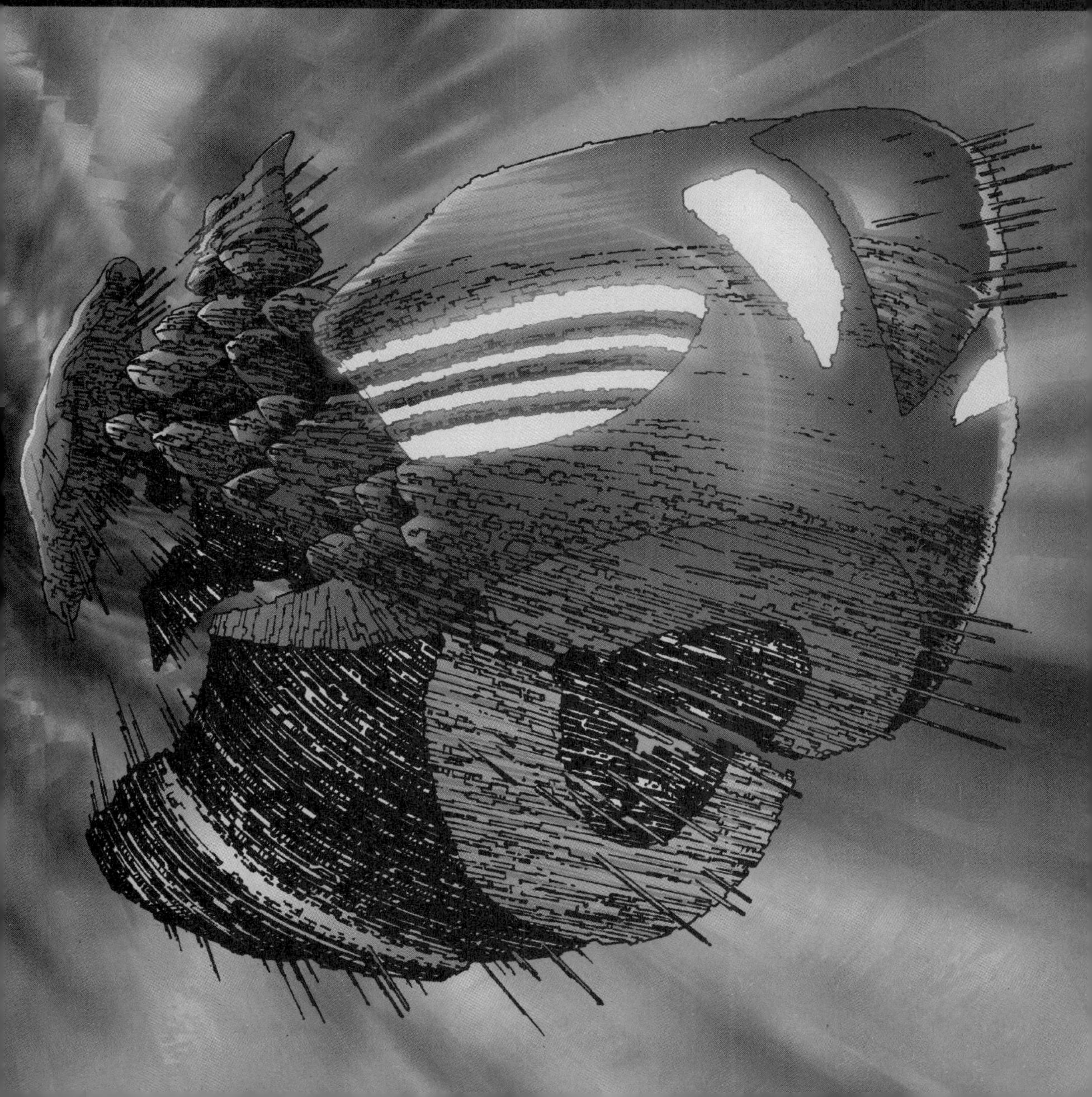

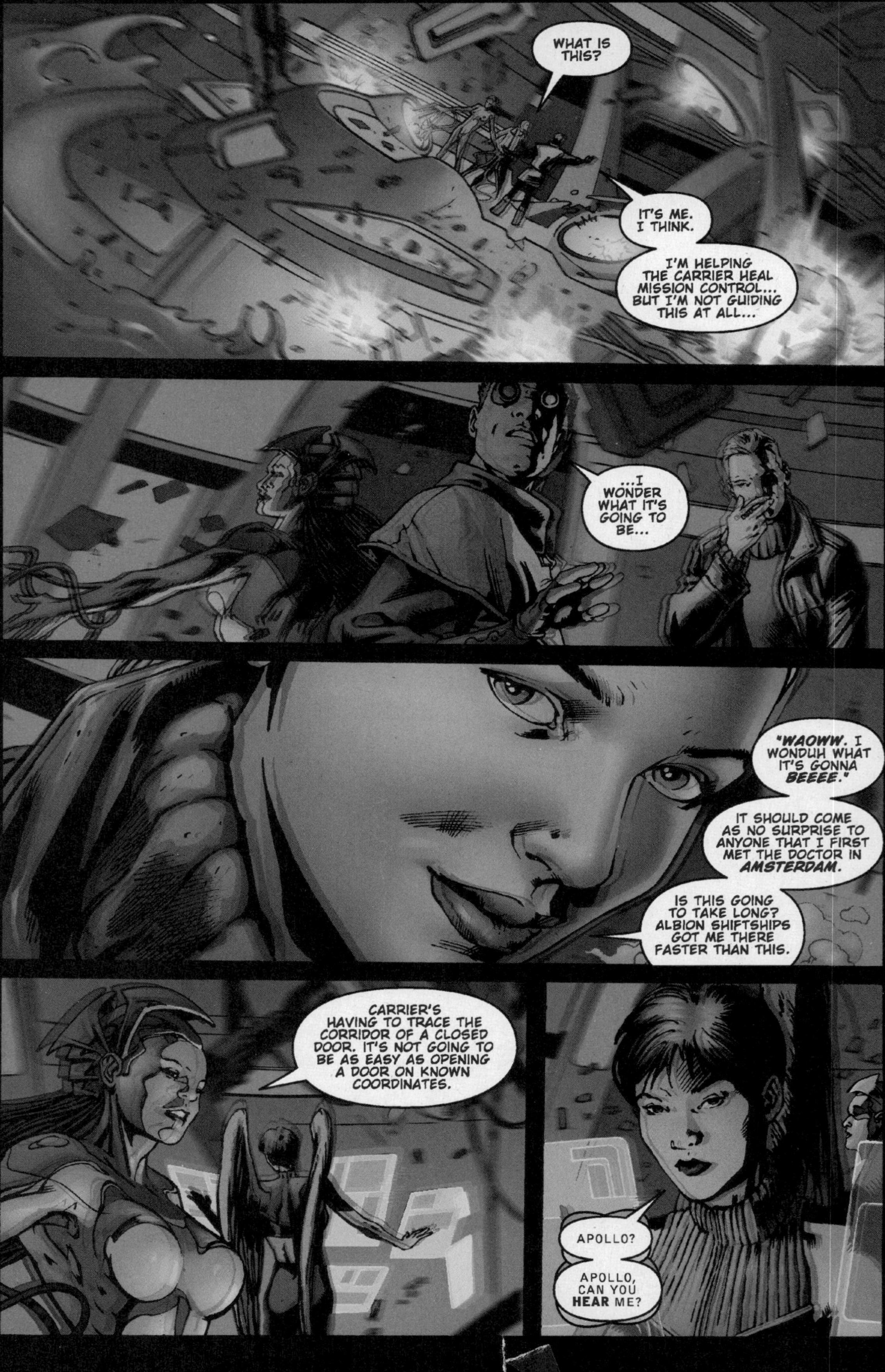
WHAT IS THIS?
IT'S ME. I THINK.
I'M HELPING THE CARRIER HEAL MISSION CONTROL... BUT I'M NOT GUIDING THIS AT ALL...
...I WONDER WHAT IT'S GOING TO BE...
"WAOWW. I WONDUH WHAT IT'S GONNA BEEEE."
IT SHOULD COME AS NO SURPRISE TO ANYONE THAT I FIRST MET THE DOCTOR IN AMSTERDAM.
IS THIS GOING TO TAKE LONG? ALBION SHIFTSHIPS GOT ME THERE FASTER THAN THIS.
CARRIER'S HAVING TO TRACE THE CORRIDOR OF A CLOSED DOOR. IT'S NOT GOING TO BE AS EASY AS OPENING A DOOR ON KNOWN COORDINATES.
APOLLO?
APOLLO, CAN YOU HEAR ME?

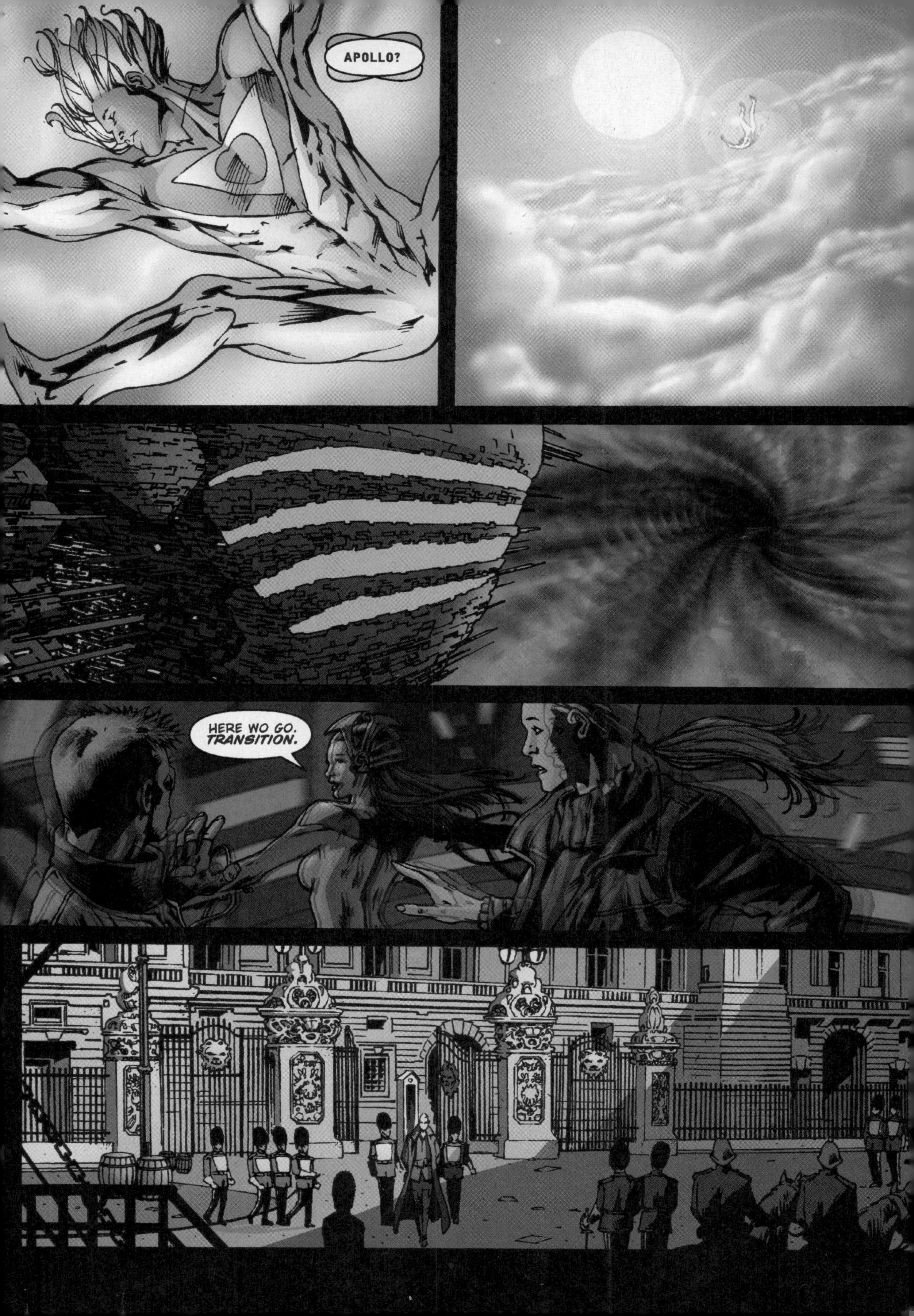
APOLLO?
HERE WO GO. TRANSITION.

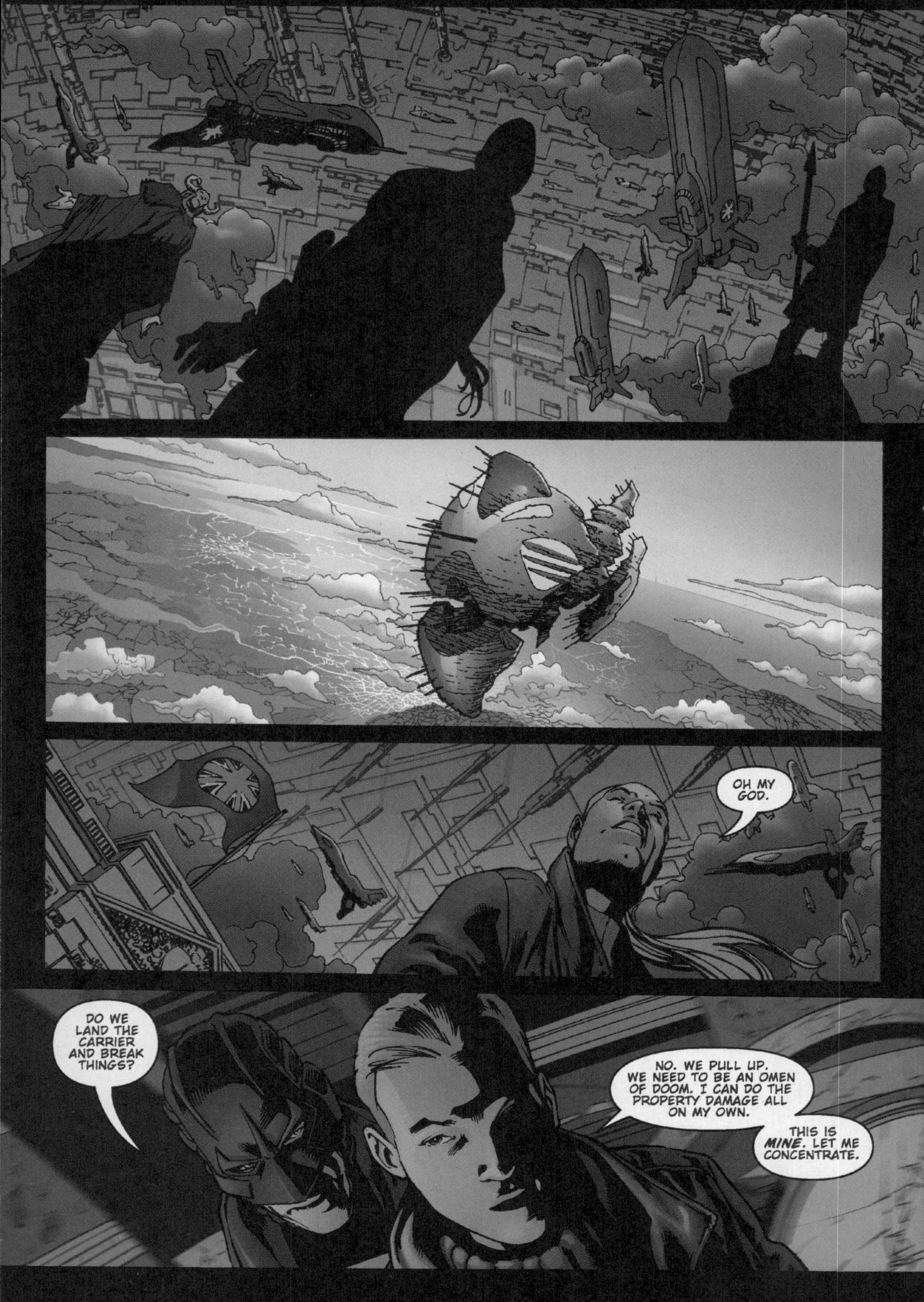
OH MY GOD.
DO WE LAND THE CARRIER AND BREAK THINGS?
NO. WE PULL UP. WE NEED TO BE AN OMEN OF DOOM. I CAN DO THE PROPERTY DAMAGE ALL ON MY OWN.
THIS IS *MINE*. LET ME CONCENTRATE.

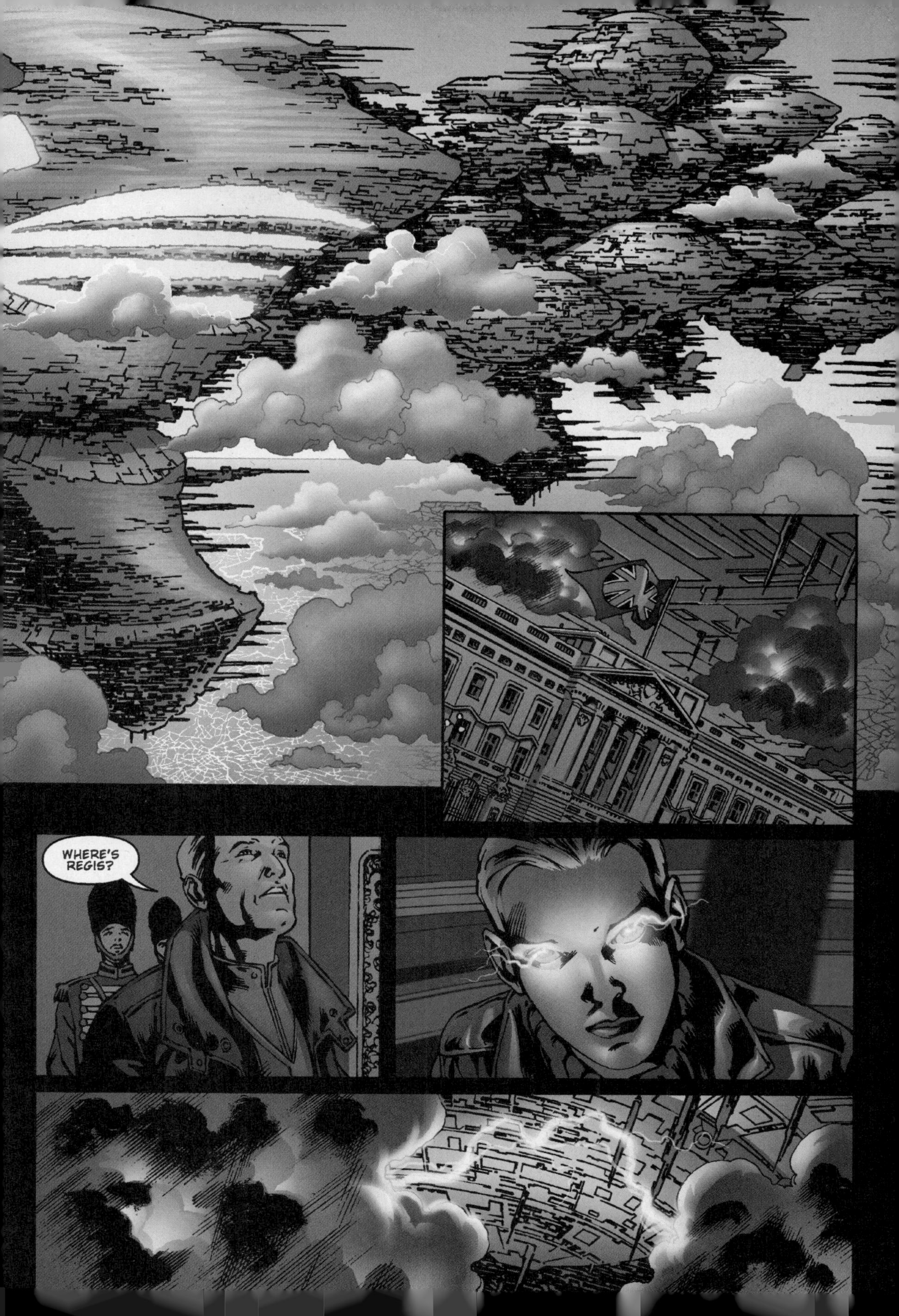
WHERE'S REGIS?

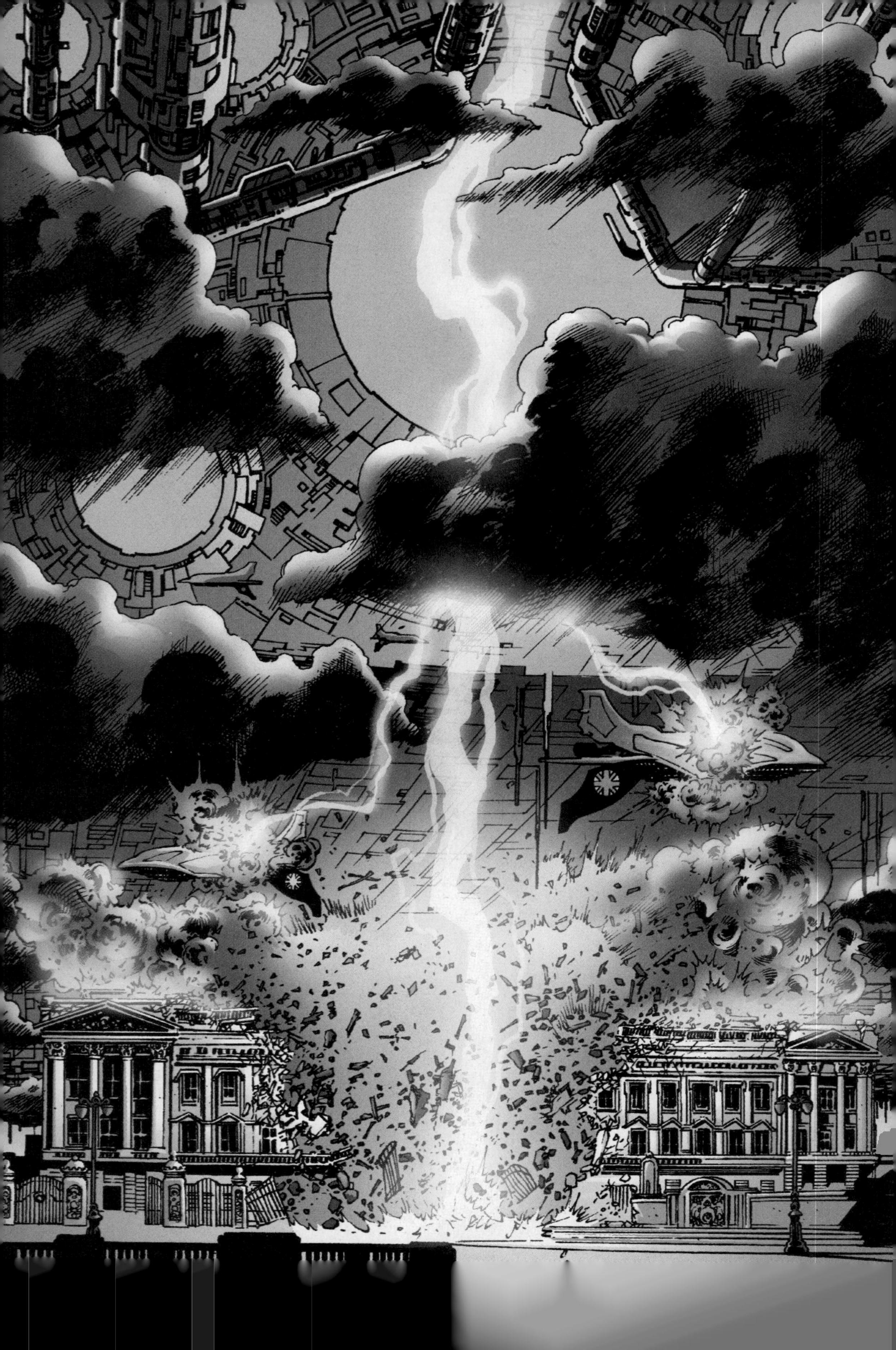

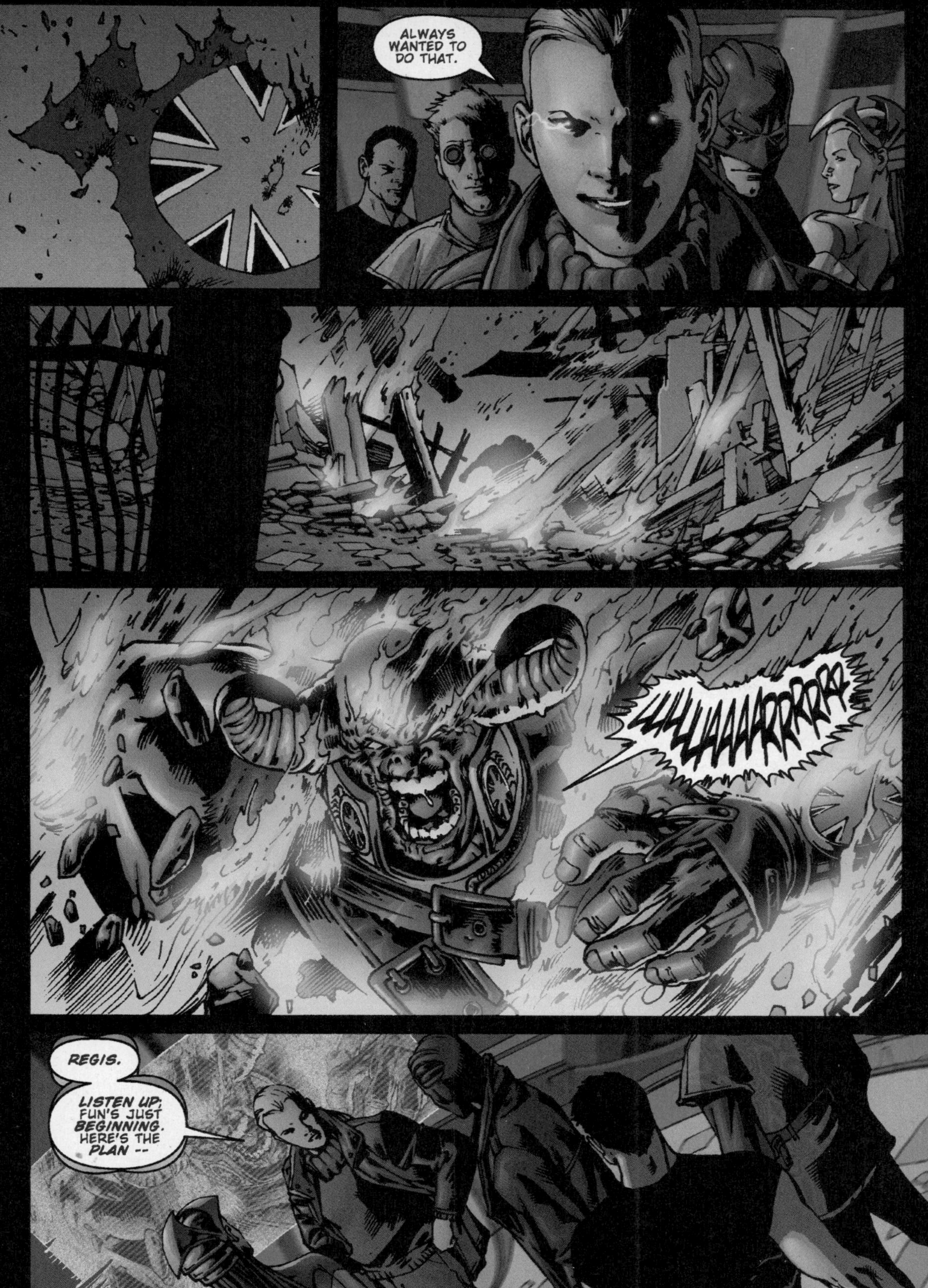
ALWAYS WANTED TO DO THAT.
LLLLLAAAAARRRRRRR
REGIS.
LISTEN UP: FUN'S JUST BEGINNING. HERE'S THE PLAN --

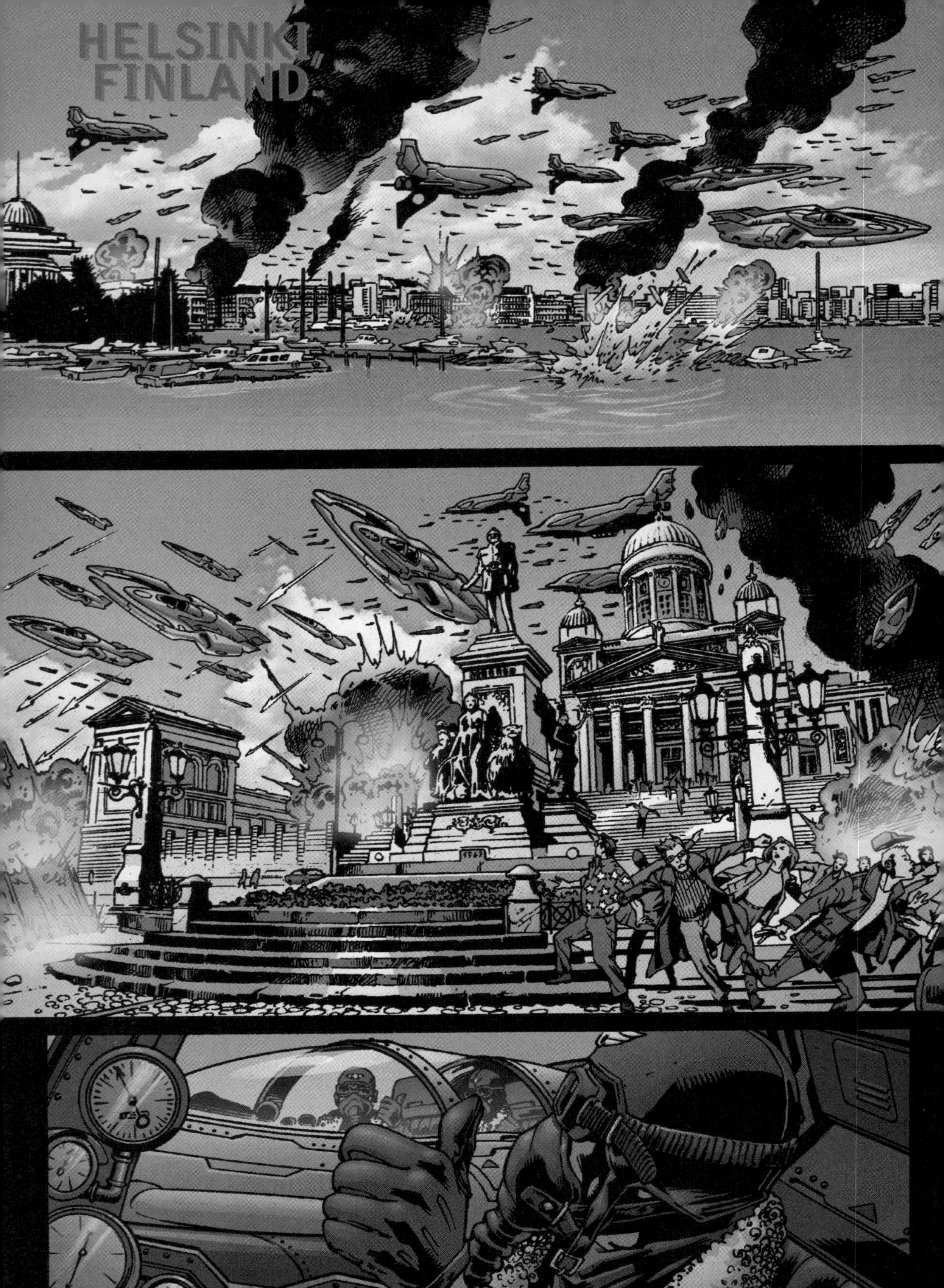
HELSINKI, FINLAND

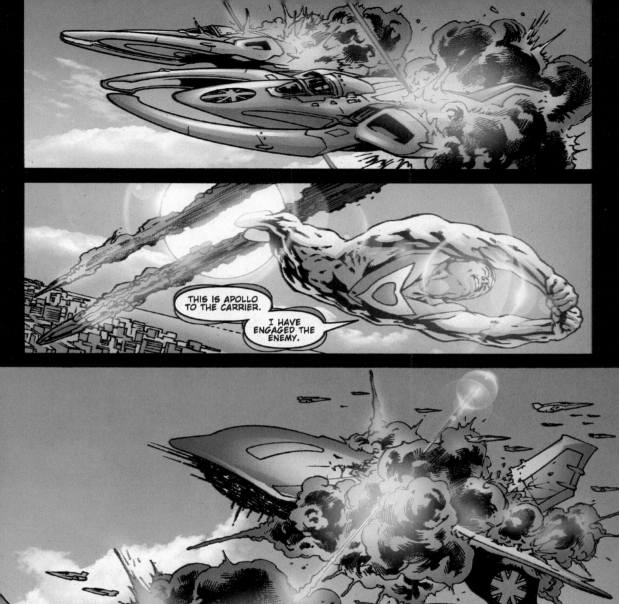

THIS IS APOLLO TO THE CARRIER.

I HAVE ENGAGED THE ENEMY.

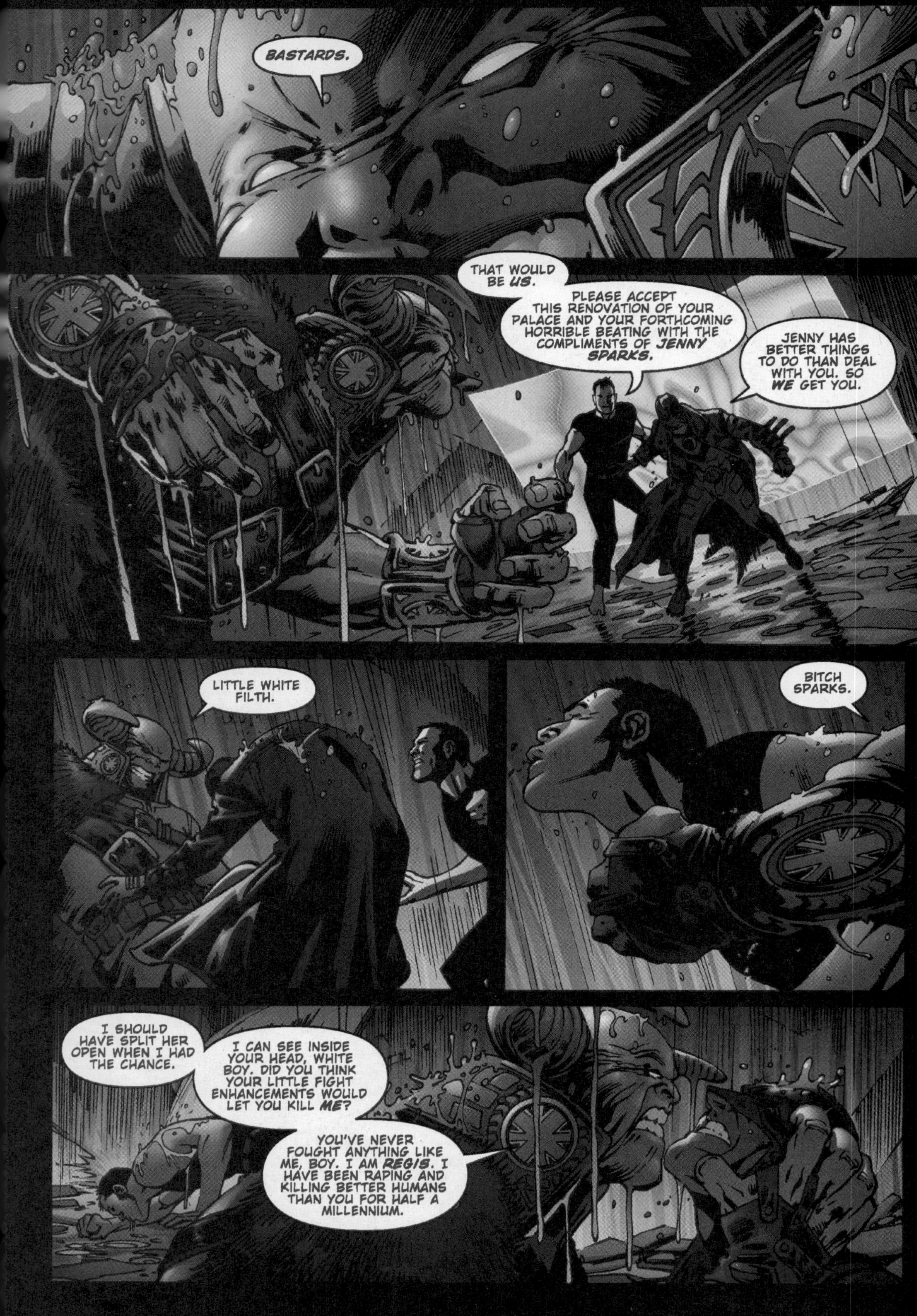
BASTARDS.
THAT WOULD BE US.
PLEASE ACCEPT THIS RENOVATION OF YOUR PALACE AND YOUR FORTHCOMING HORRIBLE BEATING WITH THE COMPLIMENTS OF JENNY SPARKS.
JENNY HAS BETTER THINGS TO DO THAN DEAL WITH YOU. SO WE GET YOU.
LITTLE WHITE FILTH.
BITCH SPARKS.
I SHOULD HAVE SPLIT HER OPEN WHEN I HAD THE CHANCE.
I CAN SEE INSIDE YOUR HEAD, WHITE BOY. DID YOU THINK YOUR LITTLE FIGHT ENHANCEMENTS WOULD LET YOU KILL ME?
YOU'VE NEVER FOUGHT ANYTHING LIKE ME, BOY. I AM REGIS. I HAVE BEEN RAPING AND KILLING BETTER HUMANS THAN YOU FOR HALF A MILLENNIUM.

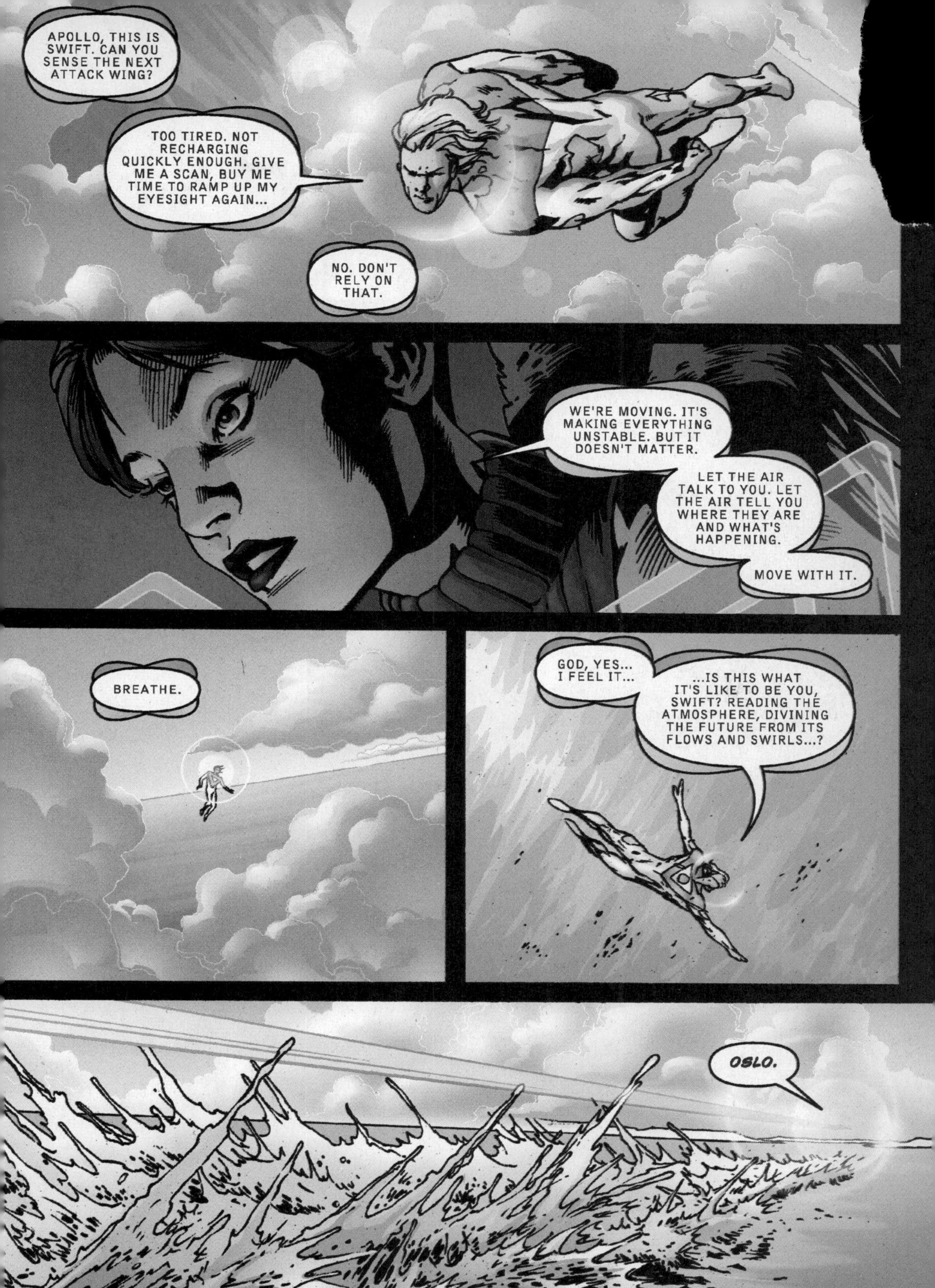
APOLLO, THIS IS SWIFT. CAN YOU SENSE THE NEXT ATTACK WING?
TOO TIRED. NOT RECHARGING QUICKLY ENOUGH. GIVE ME A SCAN, BUY ME TIME TO RAMP UP MY EYESIGHT AGAIN...
NO. DON'T RELY ON THAT.
WE'RE MOVING. IT'S MAKING EVERYTHING UNSTABLE. BUT IT DOESN'T MATTER.
LET THE AIR TALK TO YOU. LET THE AIR TELL YOU WHERE THEY ARE AND WHAT'S HAPPENING.
MOVE WITH IT.
BREATHE.
GOD, YES... I FEEL IT...
...IS THIS WHAT IT'S LIKE TO BE YOU, SWIFT? READING THE ATMOSPHERE, DIVINING THE FUTURE FROM ITS FLOWS AND SWIRLS...?
OSLO.

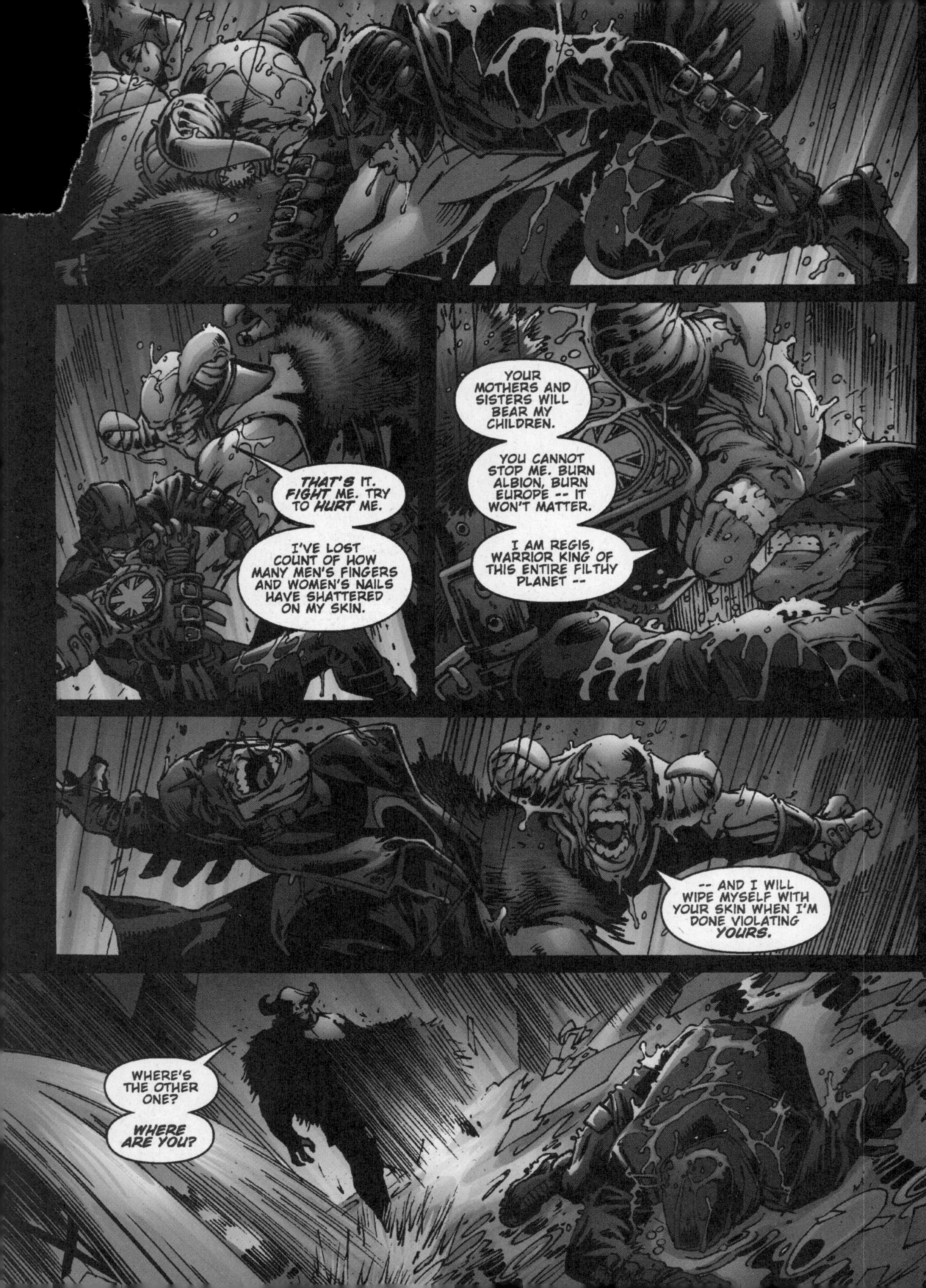
THAT'S IT. FIGHT ME. TRY TO HURT ME.
I'VE LOST COUNT OF HOW MANY MEN'S FINGERS AND WOMEN'S NAILS HAVE SHATTERED ON MY SKIN.
YOUR MOTHERS AND SISTERS WILL BEAR MY CHILDREN.
YOU CANNOT STOP ME. BURN ALBION, BURN EUROPE -- IT WON'T MATTER.
I AM REGIS, WARRIOR KING OF THIS ENTIRE FILTHY PLANET --
-- AND I WILL WIPE MYSELF WITH YOUR SKIN WHEN I'M DONE VIOLATING YOURS.
WHERE'S THE OTHER ONE?
WHERE ARE YOU?

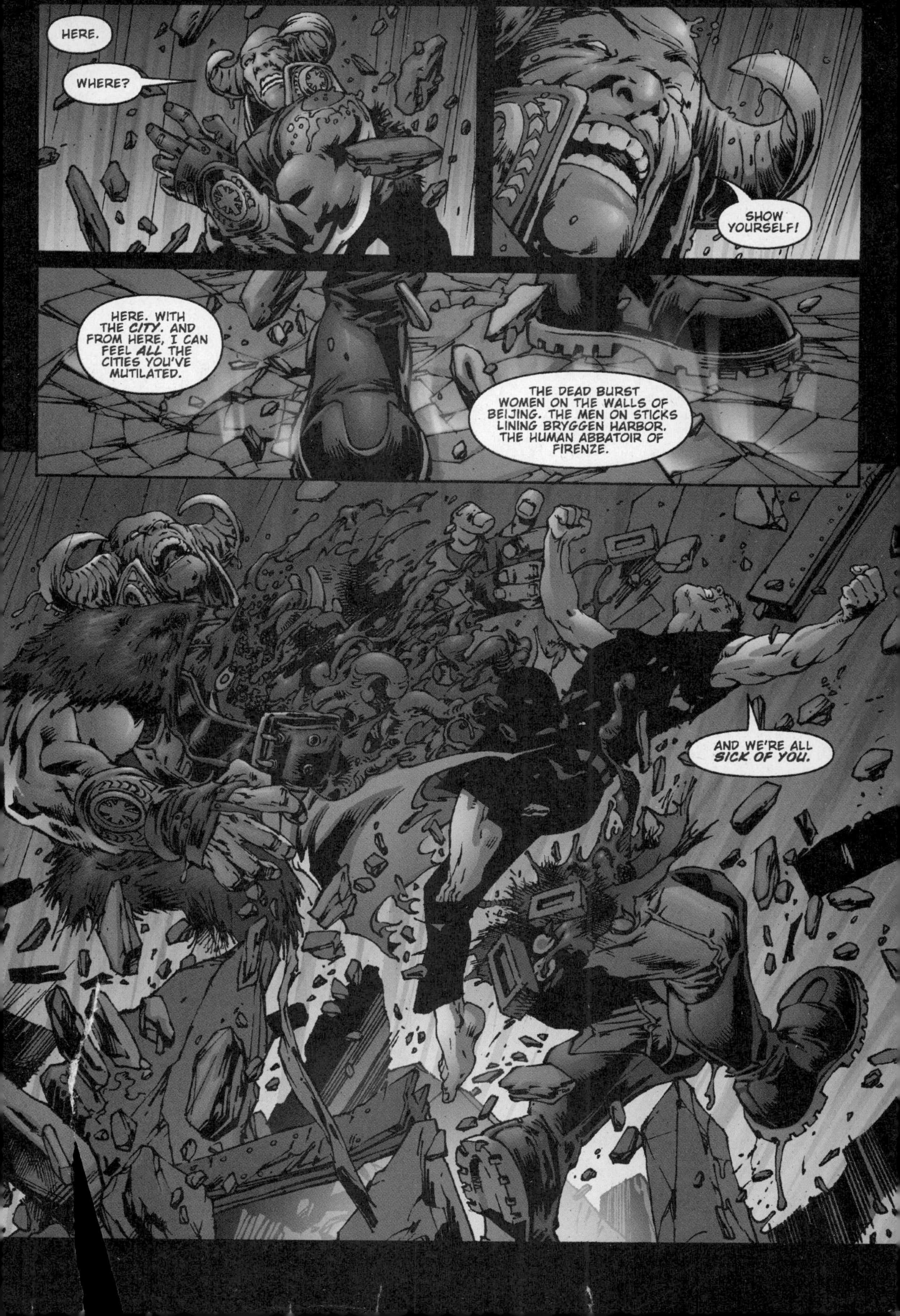

HERE.
WHERE?
SHOW YOURSELF!
HERE. WITH THE CITY. AND FROM HERE, I CAN FEEL ALL THE CITIES YOU'VE MUTILATED.
THE DEAD BURST WOMEN ON THE WALLS OF BEIJING. THE MEN ON STICKS LINING BRYGGEN HARBOR. THE HUMAN ABBATOIR OF FIRENZE.
AND WE'RE ALL SICK OF YOU.

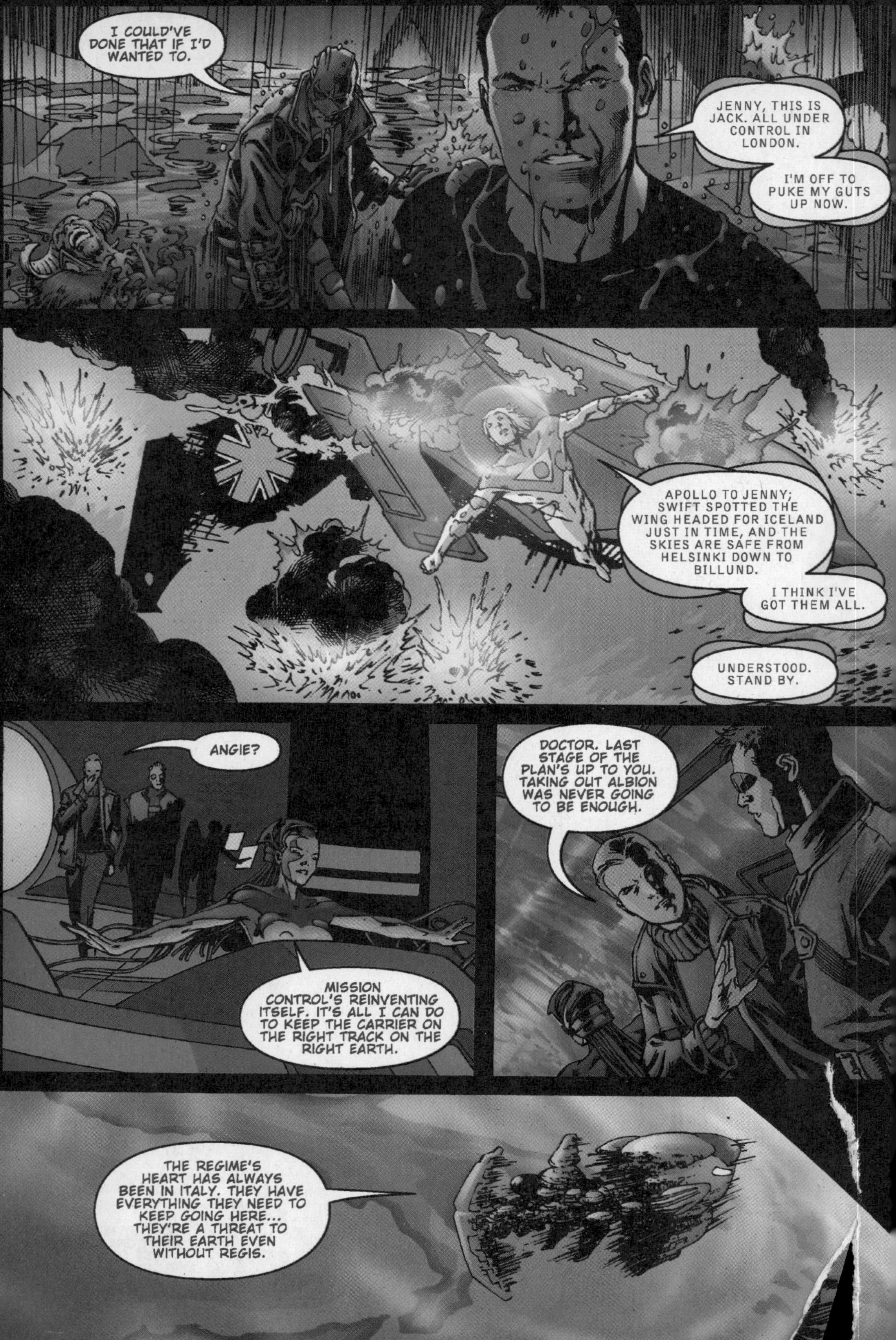
I COULD'VE DONE THAT IF I'D WANTED TO.
JENNY, THIS IS JACK. ALL UNDER CONTROL IN LONDON.
I'M OFF TO PUKE MY GUTS UP NOW.
APOLLO TO JENNY; SWIFT SPOTTED THE WING HEADED FOR ICELAND JUST IN TIME, AND THE SKIES ARE SAFE FROM HELSINKI DOWN TO BILLUND.
I THINK I'VE GOT THEM ALL.
UNDERSTOOD. STAND BY.
ANGIE?
MISSION CONTROL'S REINVENTING ITSELF. IT'S ALL I CAN DO TO KEEP THE CARRIER ON THE RIGHT TRACK ON THE RIGHT EARTH.
DOCTOR. LAST STAGE OF THE PLAN'S UP TO YOU. TAKING OUT ALBION WAS NEVER GOING TO BE ENOUGH.
THE REGIME'S HEART HAS ALWAYS BEEN IN ITALY. THEY HAVE EVERYTHING THEY NEED TO KEEP GOING HERE... THEY'RE A THREAT TO THEIR EARTH EVEN WITHOUT REGIS.

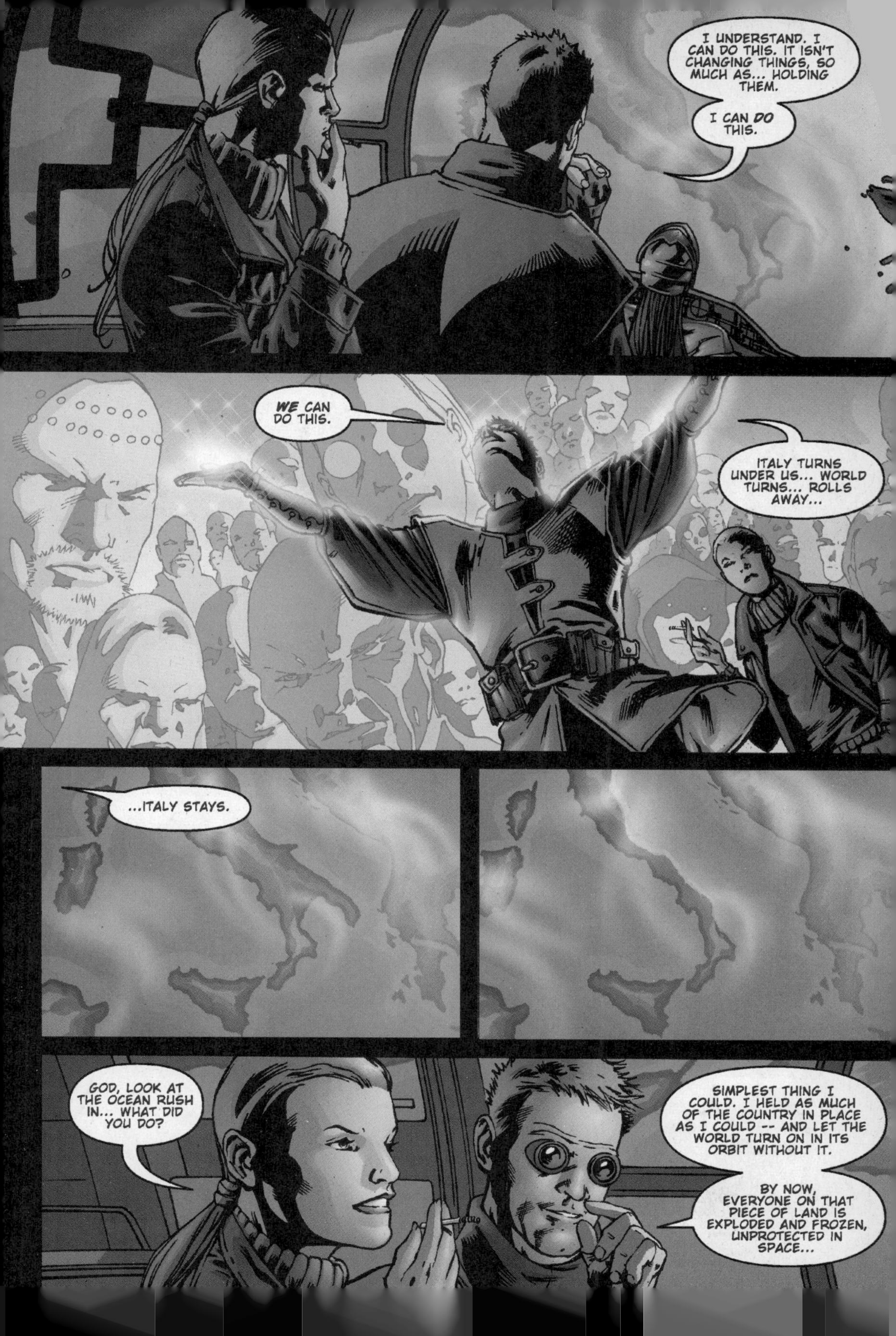
I UNDERSTAND. I CAN DO THIS. IT ISN'T CHANGING THINGS, SO MUCH AS... HOLDING THEM.
I CAN DO THIS.
WE CAN DO THIS.
ITALY TURNS UNDER US... WORLD TURNS... ROLLS AWAY...
...ITALY STAYS.
GOD, LOOK AT THE OCEAN RUSH IN... WHAT DID YOU DO?
SIMPLEST THING I COULD. I HELD AS MUCH OF THE COUNTRY IN PLACE AS I COULD -- AND LET THE WORLD TURN ON IN ITS ORBIT WITHOUT IT.
BY NOW, EVERYONE ON THAT PIECE OF LAND IS EXPLODED AND FROZEN, UNPROTECTED IN SPACE...

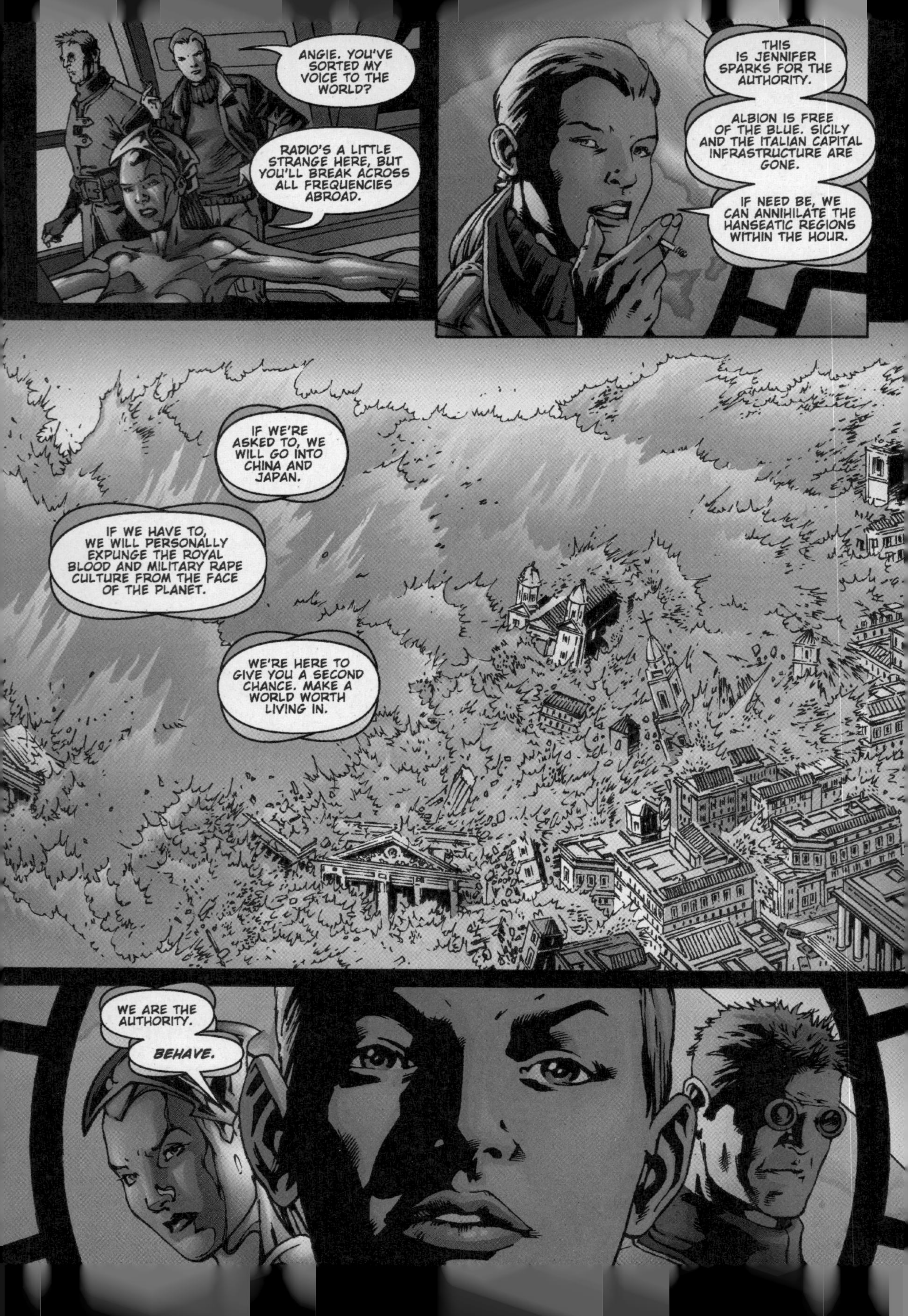

ANGIE. YOU'VE SORTED MY VOICE TO THE WORLD?
RADIO'S A LITTLE STRANGE HERE, BUT YOU'LL BREAK ACROSS ALL FREQUENCIES ABROAD.
THIS IS JENNIFER SPARKS FOR THE AUTHORITY.
ALBION IS FREE OF THE BLUE. SICILY AND THE ITALIAN CAPITAL INFRASTRUCTURE ARE GONE.
IF NEED BE, WE CAN ANNIHILATE THE HANSEATIC REGIONS WITHIN THE HOUR.
IF WE'RE ASKED TO, WE WILL GO INTO CHINA AND JAPAN.
IF WE HAVE TO, WE WILL PERSONALLY EXPUNGE THE ROYAL BLOOD AND MILITARY RAPE CULTURE FROM THE FACE OF THE PLANET.
WE'RE HERE TO GIVE YOU A SECOND CHANCE. MAKE A WORLD WORTH LIVING IN.
WE ARE THE AUTHORITY.
BEHAVE.

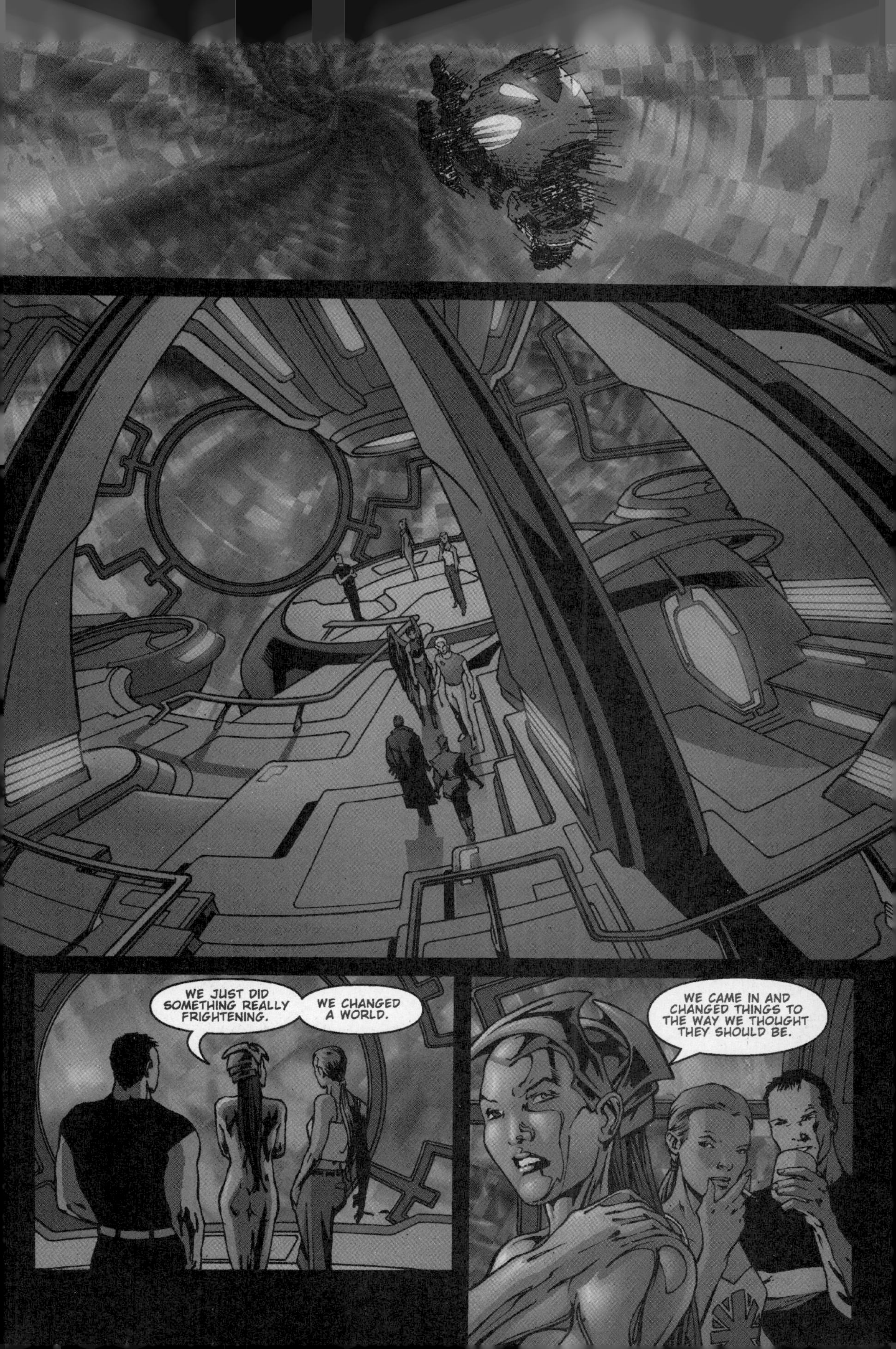
WE JUST DID SOMETHING REALLY FRIGHTENING.
WE CHANGED A WORLD.
WE CAME IN AND CHANGED THINGS TO THE WAY WE THOUGHT THEY SHOULD BE.

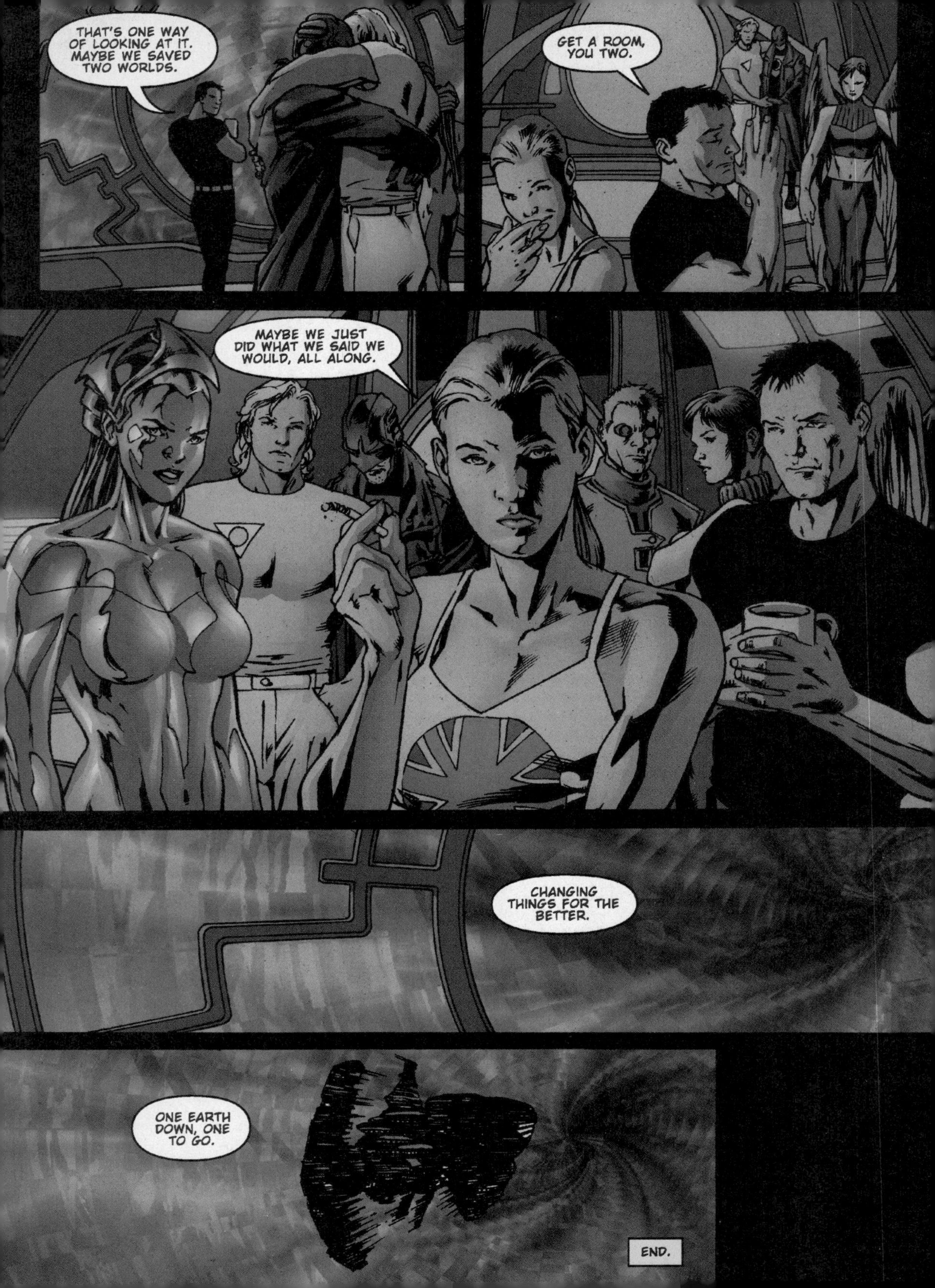
THAT'S ONE WAY OF LOOKING AT IT. MAYBE WE SAVED TWO WORLDS.
GET A ROOM, YOU TWO.
MAYBE WE JUST DID WHAT WE SAID WE WOULD, ALL ALONG.
CHANGING THINGS FOR THE BETTER.
ONE EARTH DOWN, ONE TO GO.
END.

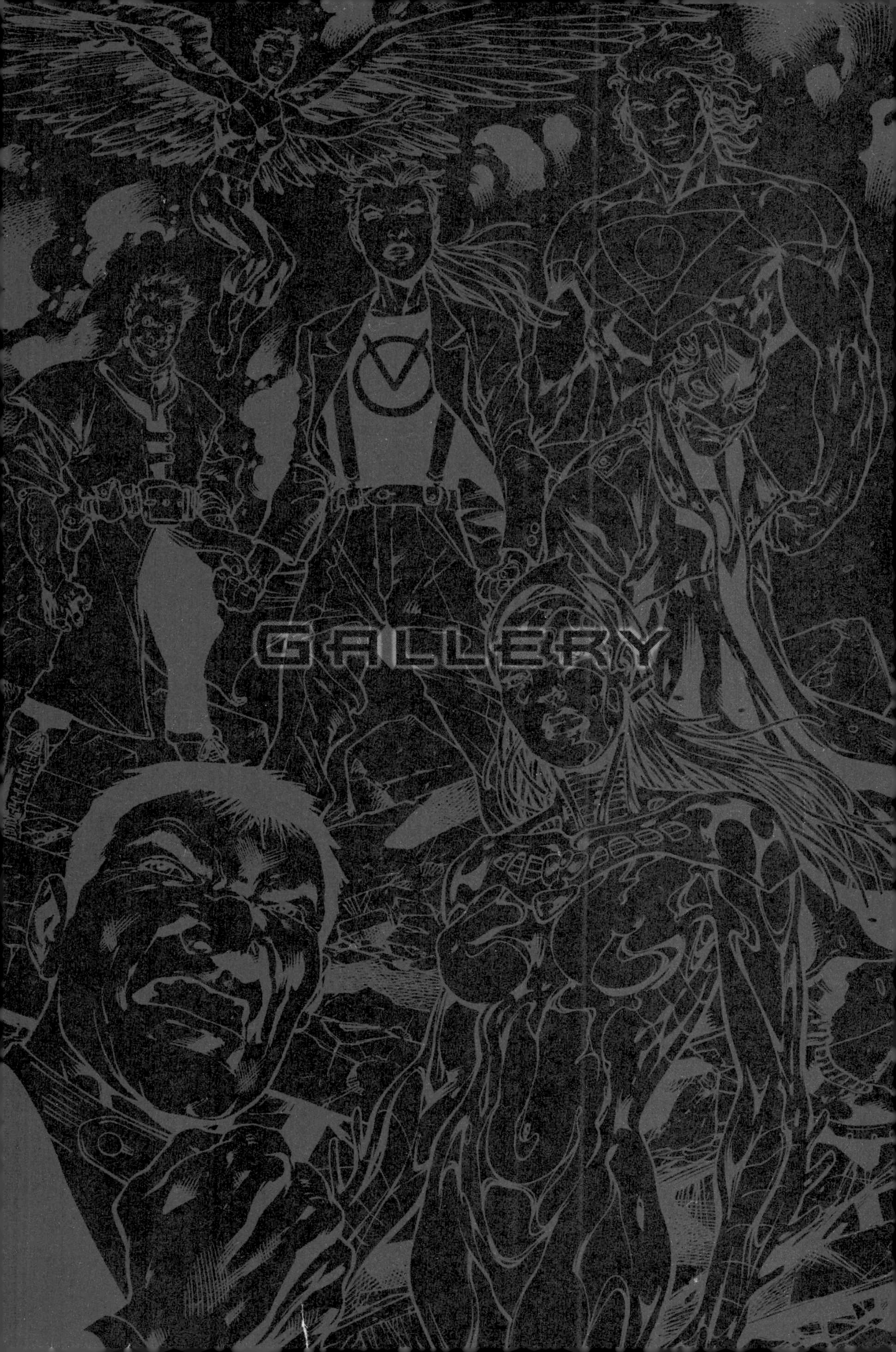
GALLERY

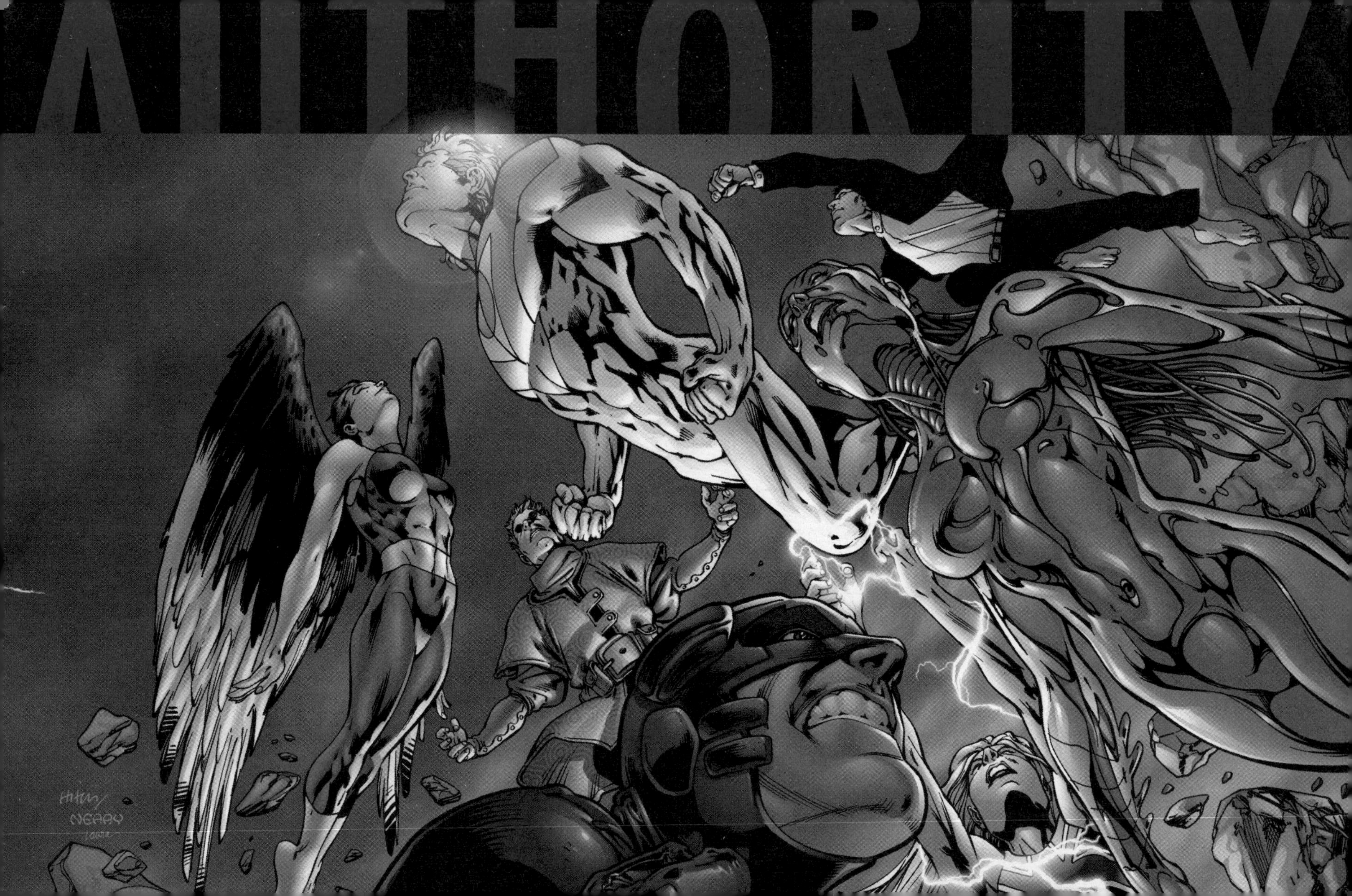
AUTHORITY

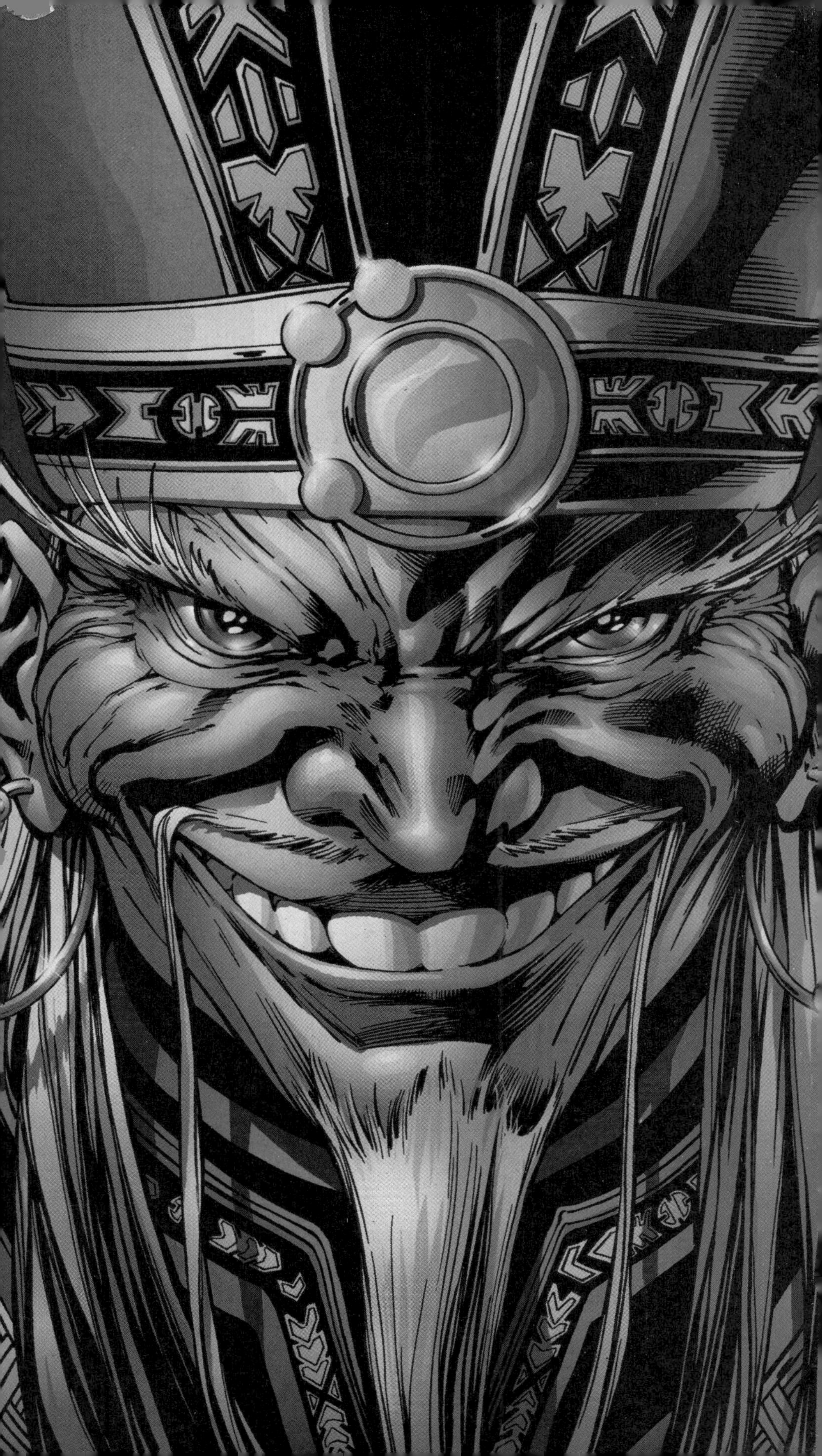

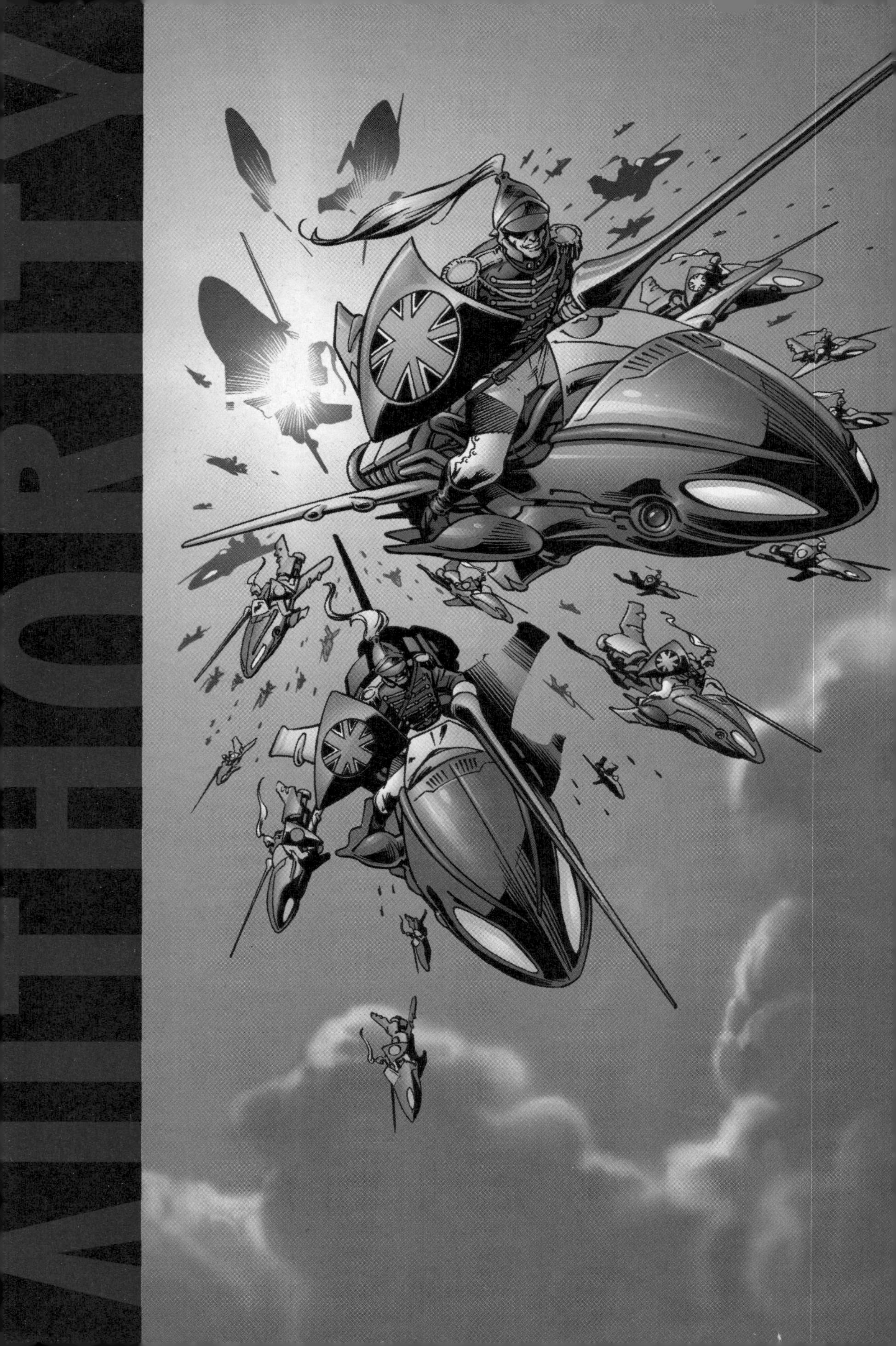
AUTHORITY

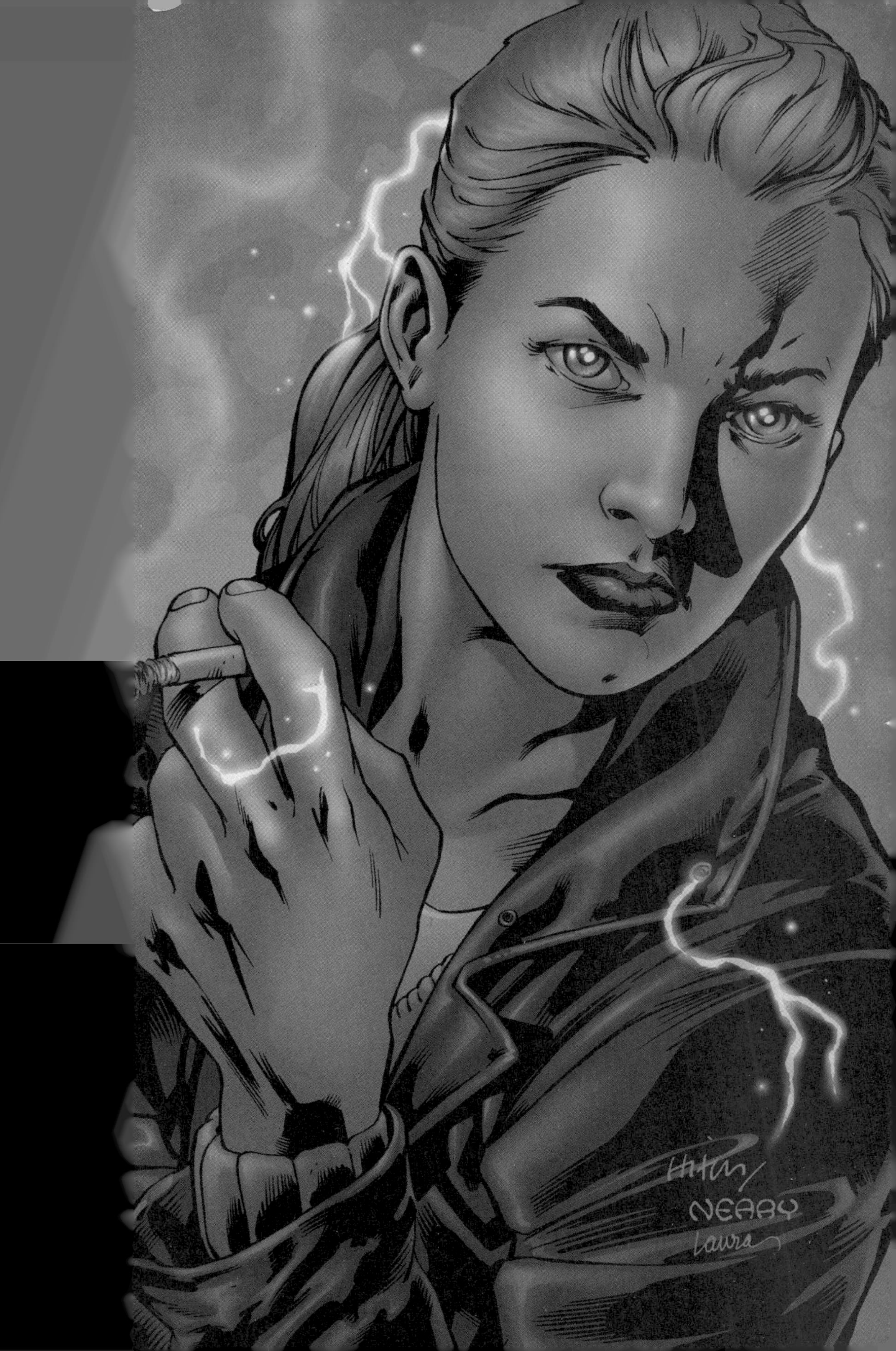
NEARY
Laura

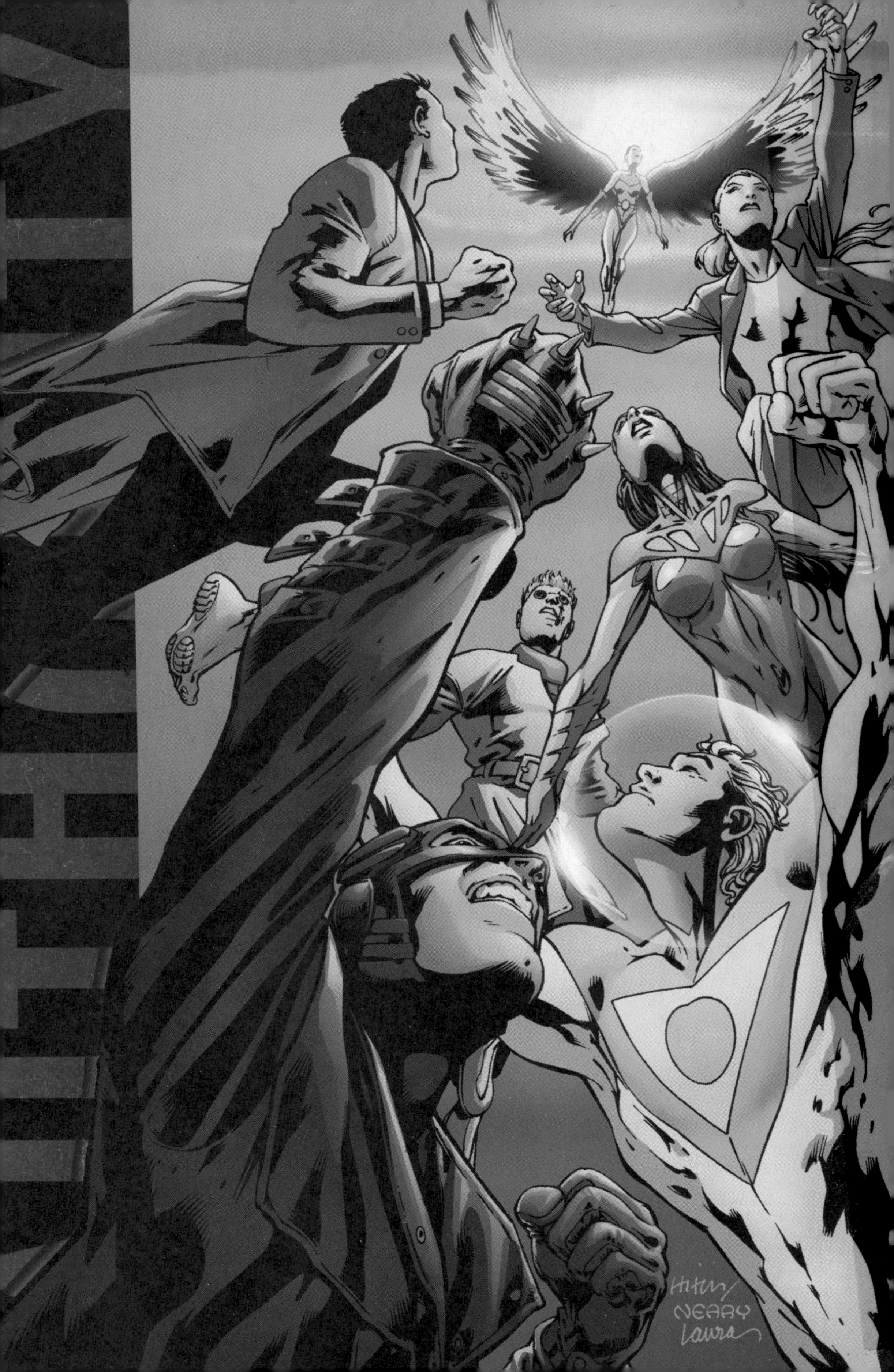
AUTHORITY
Hitch/
NEARY
Laura

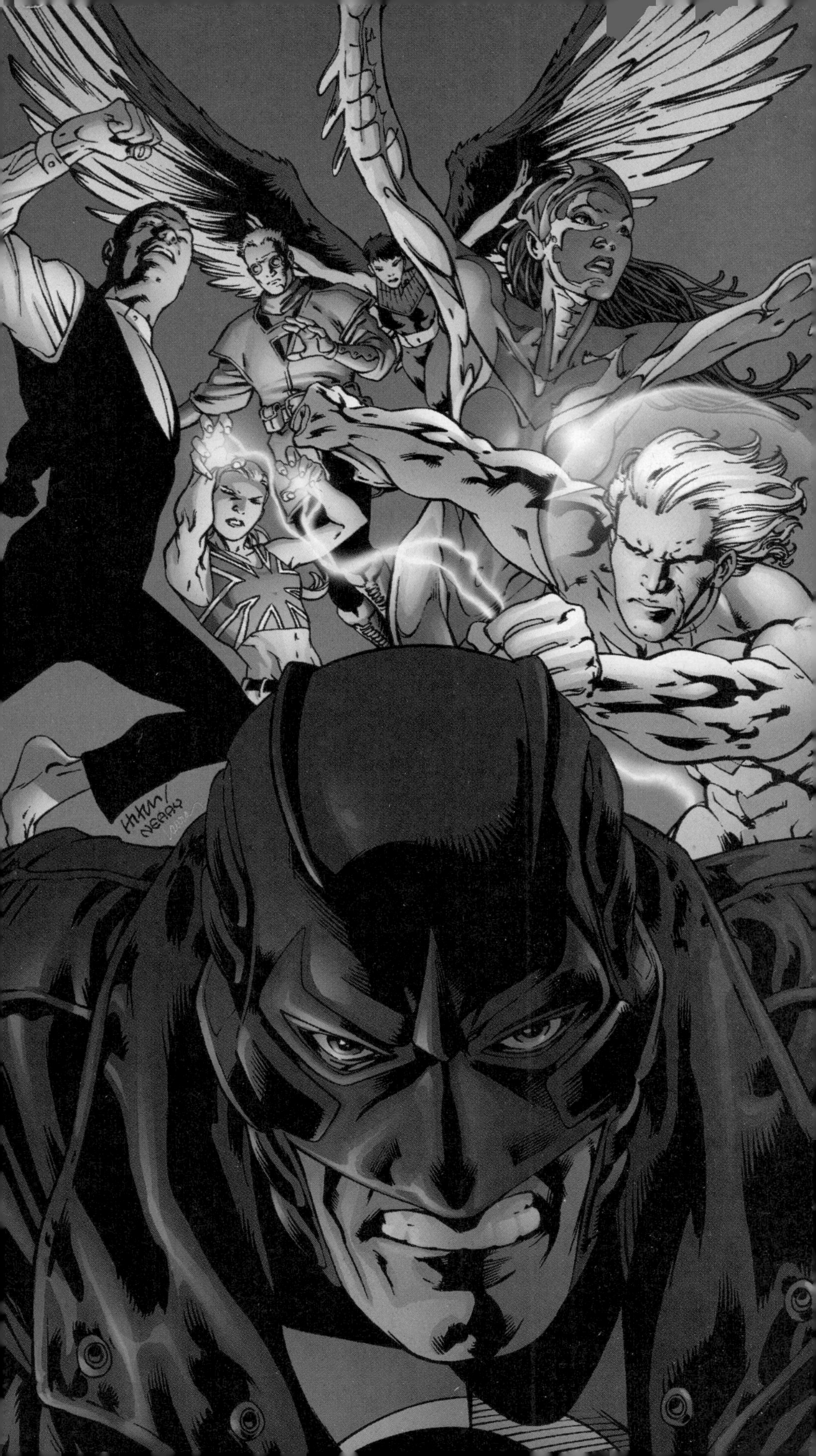

JENETTE KAHN President & Editor-in-Chief   PAUL LEVITZ Executive Vice President & Publisher   JIM LEE Editorial Director - WildStorm
JOHN NEE VP & General Manager - WildStorm   SCOTT DUNBIER Group Editor - WildStorm
RACHELLE BRISSENDEN and ERIC DeSANTIS Collected Edition Editors - WildStorm
RICHARD BRUNING VP - Creative Director   PATRICK CALDON VP - Finance & Operations   DOROTHY CROUCH VP - Licensed Publishing
TERRI CUNNINGHAM VP - Managing Editor   JOEL EHRLICH Senior VP - Advertising & Promotions
ALISON GILL Executive Director - Manufacturing   LILLIAN LASERSON VP & General Counsel   BOB WAYNE VP - Direct Sales